T0272824

AS SERIOUS AS YOUR LIFE

VAL WILMER is an internationally acclaimed journalist, author and black music historian who has been documenting African-American music since 1959. In that time, she has interviewed and photographed almost every significant figure in post-war jazz, blues and R&B, from Louis Armstrong and Thelonious Monk to Sun Ra and Albert Ayler via Muddy Waters and Aretha Franklin. As a photographer, her work features in the permanent collections of the British Library, the V&A Museum and the National Portrait Gallery; as a writer and historian, she has contributed to the *Oxford Dictionary of National Biography* and the *New Grove Dictionary of Jazz*. She lives in London.

VAL WILMER

AS SERIOUS AS YOUR LIFE

BLACK MUSIC AND THE FREE JAZZ REVOLUTION, 1957–1977

WITH A NEW FOREWORD BY RICHARD WILLIAMS

Photographs by the author

A complete catalogue record for this book can be
obtained from the British Library on request

The right of Val Wilmer to be identified as the author of this work has been
asserted by her in accordance with the Copyright, Designs and Patents Act 1988

First published in 1977 by Allison & Busby Limited
First published in this edition in 2018 by Serpent's Tail
an imprint of Profile Books Ltd
3 Holford Yard
Bevin Way
London
WC1X 9HD
www.serpentstail.com

ISBN 978 1 78816 071 1
eISBN 978 1 78283 458 8

Typeset in Garamond by MacGuru Ltd.
Printed and bound in Great Britain by CPI Group (UK) Ltd, Croydon CR0 4YY

Dedicated to Ed Blackwell, Dollar Brand, Don Cherry and Jimmy Garrison, for a memorable night at Ornette's when the music healed my New York blues

Everybody is a potential drum in as much as they have their own heartbeat; of course once their hearts stop beating, they stop swinging. Some people can't stand any rhythm or beats other than their own; these are people whose tuning is off in some kind of way. It seems that anybody with their own heartbeat should be compatible to rhythm, period.

Pat Patrick

If a man does not keep pace with his companions, perhaps it is because he hears a *different drummer*. Let him step to the music which he hears, however measured or far away.

Henry David Thoreau

Contents

Foreword

At the time Val Wilmer sat down to write *As Serious As Your Life*, jazz was about as unfashionable as it was possible for a once-favoured music to be. What remained of the popularity it had enjoyed in the central decades of the century, when it illuminated the lives of generations of nighthawks, flappers, beatniks and hipsters, relied on a willingness to make an often humbling accommodation with the crushing force of the all-conquering rock machine. To the outsider, jazz probably appeared to be on life support. What Wilmer knew, however, was that even as it seemed to be vanishing from the public consciousness in the middle of the 1970s, as the great totemic figures – the Armstrongs and Ellingtons, the Holidays and Monks – were slipping off the stage, life still teemed within the world of the music and those who made it. And what she captured in this classic volume was the combination of unstoppable creativity, faith and stoicism that impelled a new generation of musicians to pursue a calling that held out little promise of the material rewards on offer to the more fortunate of their predecessors.

The 'new jazz', as the author called it in the book's original subtitle, was inspired by a sense of mission that had evolved from the innovations of a group of radical thinkers whose core members included the pianists Cecil Taylor and Sun Ra and the saxophonists John Coltrane, Ornette Coleman and Albert Ayler. Each of these men questioned, from his own viewpoint, the rules of melody, harmony and rhythm and the conventions of vertical and linear structure previously applied throughout the evolution of jazz.

Free jazz, the new wave, the avant-garde, the new thing: those were the names it went by, and its early manifestations were widely disparaged by those who saw the new freedoms as a threat to their cherished beliefs and assumptions. For this was not comfortable music, in any sense. When Coltrane turned Richard Rodgers' 'My Favorite Things' – a song from *The Sound of Music*, for heaven's sake – into a 30-minute ululation that tore obsessively at the seams of conventional musical structure, or when Ayler turned George Gershwin's 'Summertime' inside out in the search for some deeper and darker emotional resonance, the loudest response was outrage.

Unlike the many critics who expressed their distaste, Wilmer recognised that these musicians and those who followed them were far from apostates or heretics. Rather than rejecting the essence of jazz, they had done the opposite by embracing some of the music's neglected core values, in particular a directness of emotional expression that went right back to the raw collective polyphony of the earliest jazz. It was to be rediscovered by musicians whose virtuosity enabled them to extend not just the grammar and syntax of the music but, crucially, the language of their individual instruments.

Through the realisation that self-reliance was the best armour against the indifference of the commercial music business, this group of mostly African-American musicians developed an urgent and empowering sense of community. *As Serious As Your Life* examines events such as the founding of New York's Jazz Composers Guild in 1964 and the creation of Chicago's Association for the Advancement of Creative Musicians three years later, which may have varied in long-term impact (the former flaring briefly, the latter still flourishing as it celebrated its 50th anniversary) but offered equally vital signposts to a future in which musicians could no longer rely on an established infrastructure of club-owners, concert promoters and record companies.

Val Wilmer, born in 1941 in Harrogate, Yorkshire and raised in South London, formed an immediate emotional rapport with American jazz at the age of 12, when she encountered recordings by Fats Waller, Bessie Smith and others. She began attending jazz concerts in London and soon started to write about what she heard, making efforts to contact visiting American musicians to get their direct testimony. She was 17 when her first article, a profile of the American blues and folk singer Jesse Fuller, was accepted by *Jazz Journal*. Over the next few years, often in the face of unhelpful reactions from male colleagues who scarcely bothered to disguise their scorn at the idea of a woman trespassing on their turf, she wrote regularly for *Down Beat*, the *Melody Maker* and other major publications, gradually shifting her area of interest from the mainstream to the musicians operating on the music's leading edge. She was also honing her skills as a professional photographer, illustrating her texts with images that began to show a less frequently examined side of the musicians' existence: not on stage in the glow of the spotlight (although she was good at that, too) but at home in their kitchens, or holding their small children, or getting a haircut, or playing pool together, or catching a nap on the band bus between gigs.

Unlike many who write or have written about this music, Wilmer sees the musicians as human beings first, and their music as the product of that humanity. Her sensitivity to their creative and economic struggle, and her understanding of the challenges facing an outsider, enlarged her access to their community as she became a trusted and valued chronicler of their lives.

Her first book, *Jazz People* (1970), consisted of profiles of 14 American musicians, each accompanied by a photograph. Her second, *The Face of Black Music* (1976), concentrated on the images, its title proclaiming her belief in the essentially African-American core of the music, from the country blues of Baby Tate and Guitar Shorty – whom she encountered on trips to the Deep South – to the high sophistication of Archie Shepp and Miles Davis. Its publication followed a solo exhibition at the V&A Museum in London, where her work forms part of the permanent photographic collection. (Her photographs are also in the collections of the National Portrait Gallery, the Arts Council, the Smithsonian Institution, the New York Public Library and the Musée d'Art Moderne in Paris.)

With *As Serious As Your Life*, however, she produced something different. Here was a book that thoroughly documented, investigated and celebrated the new music, underpinned by a radical political consciousness embracing socialism, feminism, anti-racism and gay rights, and by the fruits of her encounters with African-American poets, playwrights and essayists such as Langston Hughes, Jayne Cortez and Amiri Baraka. It records the complex interlocking creative relationships that developed as the music underwent its rapid development, the invention of platforms on which the music could present itself in the battle to fight exclusion from the mainstream, and the struggle to reconcile the professional and personal demands of life as a player of a music existing in the margins. All these are examined in fascinating and often moving detail.

As a teenager, Val Wilmer's earliest encounters with jazz musicians taught her that those who had received scant public attention were often as interesting and as artistically significant as the ones who regularly appeared on magazine covers. So in addition to shining fresh light on the major figures, this book introduces others – the saxophonist Frank Lowe, the trumpeter Earl Cross and the drummer Milford Graves, for instance – who may not have been as well known outside the community but who were playing important roles in the music's evolution.

Even more striking is the book's pioneering insistence on the significance of the place of women in the music. In a pair of chapters, the author goes beyond the stereotypes to discover the reality of women not just in supportive roles (as partners, fans and organisers) but as committed practitioners. In the field of gender studies, these chapters have been acknowledged as, in the words of Farah Jasmine Griffin, a professor of English and comparative literature and African-American studies at Columbia University in New York, 'an important precursor to contemporary scholarship on the music.' Through her references to such players as the trumpeter Barbara Donald, the pianist Alice Coltrane and the guitarist

Monnette Sudler, Wilmer helped pave the way for a current generation represented by the saxophonist Matana Roberts, the guitarist Mary Halvorson and the cellist Tomeka Reid – women who are accepted without question as the equals of the men with whom they collaborate in musical explorations whose origins can be traced to the big bang of free jazz.

The vindication of this music's dream may have been long deferred, but its explosion continues to resonate. John Coltrane and Sun Ra are acknowledged as giants; the music of Alice Coltrane is being discovered by new listeners a decade after her death; a then-obscure figure such as the trumpeter/composer Wadada Leo Smith is now a revered elder of the twenty-first century, helping to raise the new generations. Val Wilmer's great work, the fruit of a lifetime's immersion in the music and the lives of those who make it, enlightens any reader seeking to know the origins of that explosion and to understand how it opened the doorway to a future whose promise is still being realised.

Richard Williams
December 2017

Author's Prefatory Note

Living through this music from the start of the 1960s was an experience without equal. To stay in New York, to know the musicians and interview them for *Melody Maker* and other journals was exhilarating and exhausting and a lifetime's lesson about dedication. Writing this book was to acknowledge certain responsibilities placed on my shoulders; completing it was a labour of love. Since it first appeared in 1977, corrections and a few revisions have been made, but it is a social history of a particular period and I feel that any attempt to further update the text would be pointless. Times change and so do opinions, nevertheless I stand by most of what I wrote originally and truly believe that the time is approaching when these artists will be as revered for their collective and individual innovations as are the giants of previous eras.

Introduction
A State of Mind

You know, Black music is how *our* lives are, and how we are looking
at, and relating to, the outside world. It's just a state of mind.

Jerome Cooper

In the summer of 1972 I sat in a clapboard house beside a North
Carolina tobacco field and listened to a man called Guitar Shorty
singing and playing the blues. Some of his words were made up
on the spot, others were as old as the music itself. Whatever their
immediate source, however, each phrase derived from the rich
musical legacy of Black America. Shorty's instrumental work,
likewise, was a combination of things remembered and things
invented, but his dynamics were good and the music was full
of surprises. For the earnest student of the blues, though, there
was one thing distressingly wrong: the guitarist seemed blissfully
unaware of the classic eight-bar, twelve-bar and sixteen-bar structures of the most common kinds of blues. He fragmented the
time and switched from one pattern or chord sequence to another
whenever the change sounded right to him, a cavalier attitude to
form that caused one of my companions, a local white guitarist, to
exclaim – albeit with enthusiasm – 'Shorty's a real free-form guitar
player; he don't play *nothing* right!'

On my way back to New York that night I started thinking
about freedom in music and how it is just that refusal to conform
to any preconceived (i.e. European) patterns or rules that is one of
the chief virtues of Black or African-American music. No matter

1

who the performer – a housemaid bearing witness in church on a Sunday or a guitarist playing the Saturday night blues in some downhome bar –the music is never predictable. Polished or basic – Duke Ellington whipping his sidemen through the majestic surge of sound that was uniquely his (and their) creation, Eddie Kendricks singing in his exquisite falsetto high above the Temptations, Albert Ayler wrenching meanings from 'Summertime' that Gershwin never dreamed of – the sound of surprise is what counts. Black music is, with the cinema, the most important art form of this century. In terms of influence, there is scarcely anyone untouched by it.

The music of Black Americans has always been free. It is the white critics and the media, it seems to me, who want to chain it.

Leo Smith, a young trumpeter who grew up in the Mississippi Delta, summed up the musician's attitude: 'I never considered the blues to be twelve-bars, I never considered the blues to be a closed form. The blues is exactly, in my understanding of it, a free music.' To Smith, a strong believer in total improvisation, the blues lay behind all his musical activities, the opinion of critics notwithstanding. 'They say that what we were playing wasn't really anything. That was all right, that was fine, because I have a strong background in the blues in the sense of knowing that whatever course you take, you should not be concerned with the outcome of it because you've decided to take that course.' Smith and Guitar Shorty had more than a little in common; it was the critics who begged to differ.

It was at the turn of the 'sixties with the appearance of a series of recordings made by Ornette Coleman, an alto saxophonist from Texas, that the music hitherto known as 'jazz' began first to be described as 'free' music. Coleman, along with the pianist Cecil Taylor and the tenor saxophonist John Coltrane and, eventually, the drummer Sunny Murray, gave other musicians who were tired of the restrictions placed on their playing by earlier forms the opportunity for greater freedom. The three innovators had different approaches, but basically their message was the same: the player no longer needed to confine himself to a single key, or to use a set pattern of chords as a base for his improvisation, nor did he have to stick to a given time-signature or even, with the absence of a regular pulse, to bar-lines. The New Music, as it began to be known among musicians, opened up new vistas for everyone.

Through improvisation, the jazz musician had been able to present a changing perspective on a given piece each time he played it. The performer in this music is, in effect, the composer who spontaneously creates new compositions, something that the player of Western symphonic music is unable to do because he must stick to what is written down. To the Afro-American, the freedom inherent in improvisation is his or her birthright, and so the possibilities indicated by a lessened need for the musician to relate to a pre-ordained form should, one would imagine, have been cause for celebration.

Instead, it was the signal for an unprecedented attack from the critical establishment. With a few notable exceptions, the critics attacked the unfamiliar directions the music had taken. There is nothing new about that: in the avant-garde of every art the innovators are often dismissed as 'anarchists' or 'charlatans'; the difference here is that this music has been around for twenty years and people who should have known better have not yet caught up with it. The so-called New Music has been treated irresponsibly by many critics, something that could not, I suggest, have gone on for so long had the music in question been created by whites.

The trumpet player Lester Bowie pinpointed the situation by citing the case of a virtuoso instrumentalist, one of the most important musicians of today who is, ironically, equally regarded as a composer in the 'legitimate' sense of writing notes down on paper. 'Look at Anthony Braxton!' he said. 'Because he is a "Black jazz musician", he has difficulty in having his compositions played. If he was called "Leonard Bernstein", he would not have such a problem. But he does "jazz" and it's not *serious* music.'[1]

3

Although it would be hard to imagine someone more serious about the music than Braxton, the comparison with Bernstein is not so apt as it might seem at first, for more than a couple of decades separate them in age. The point is that it is a question of birth rather than longevity that dictates how a musician's career will be allowed to progress. Duke Ellington was turned down for a Pulitzer Prize at the age of sixty-seven, after all. ('Fate's being kind to me,' he said sardonically. 'Fate doesn't want me to be too famous too soon.') In Braxton's case, when his British sponsors attempted to have him classified as a 'concert artist' in order to avoid fulfilling the stringent 'exchange' system imposed on 'non-classical' artists by the local Musicians' Union, the saxophonist was rejected in spite of his singular reputation. The implication was clear. Anyone unfortunate enough to be born Black could never be considered as anything other than a 'jazz musician' – in other words, an 'entertainer' – no matter how many instruments he had mastered or from whatever quarter his artistry had drawn praise. On this occasion, even the endorsement of white critics and composers was insufficient.*

The lack of respect accorded the musical creations of Blacks knows no bounds. Ornette Coleman, who was himself accorded fulsome praise by Bernstein when he first came to New York, went to London to record his symphonic work *Skies of America*. During the early part of the session, two 'cellists with the London Philharmonic Orchestra were discussing the score. 'It almost looks like music when you see it written down', said one of them. Several of the musicians engaged to play Coleman's music sniggered as the conductor ran through individual sections of the piece. Eventually, even the normally imperturbable Coleman had had enough of it. He picked up his saxophone and played the entire passage under

---

* This would, of course, have happened to a white instrumentalist, too, under a system that treats musicians as exchangeable units of labour, but the basis is essentially racist.

scrutiny from start to finish. The smiles slipped rapidly from the dubious faces when they realised how neatly the various sections fitted together. There was an embarrassed silence.

A similar situation occurred when Anthony Braxton hired five tuba players for a recording session. The musicians refused to take his ideas seriously. On another occasion, at a run-through for a television programme in which a group led by the drummer Beaver Harris was taking part, two sound engineers were talking. 'You'd better get them off the stage so we can set up the mikes and take a level.' 'Well,' came the reply, 'all you need for this bunch is a noise reading.' And this took place in the studios of New York *educational* television.

A contemporary white American composer, talking with some British musicians, felt sufficiently relaxed to describe an instrumentalist whose talents he had utilised as 'one of the few Blacks I can talk to'. For the elucidation of the assembled 'foreigners', he added, 'Blacks are getting ridiculous in the States now.' The inference was clear: Afro-American demands for respect for themselves and their creations disturbed his equilibrium. Yet the composer, using the system where recurring patterns are played in phase with each other until they almost overlap, had just been recording a percussion work, the overall sound of which bore a striking resemblance to the *balafon* music of the people of Lawra in northwestern Ghana, a country which had recently had the pleasure of his company.

In addition, the use of phase patterns and tape loops in this context could be said to be only a mechanical approximation of the barely imperceptible shifts in improvisation that occur within a West African drum-choir playing continually over a long period.

At times it seems as though there is a definite conspiracy afoot to inhibit the progress of the new Black music. If that sounds doubtful, examine the facts. Jazz, we are told, is undergoing a renaissance in popularity, and the flood of new records on the market and the opening of new nightclubs confirms this. Yet apart from a few 'token' new musicians (i.e. affiliated to the avant-garde) whose faces fit, little or no employment is available in those clubs for the many fine musicians who, until they started to take matters into their own hands, had no place to play apart from their own homes. The recording business is slightly better but the advances paid to musicians remain pitifully inadequate. At one time there was talk about Underground music, but the new music, the *new jazz,* is the real Underground music.

It is unfortunate that as far as Black music is concerned, its evolution has occurred so rapidly that the champion of yesterday's new sounds has become the opponent of today's in many cases. Despite those politically aware writers involved with bringing Black achievements to a wider public, many 'critics' are oblivious to the social situation responsible for African-American music and unconcerned with its true significance. Such individuals are responsible for propagating the widely held belief that no progress has occurred in the music since the innovations of John Coltrane.

Ignorance about the New Music is appalling even in some sections of the music press. Were one to believe many writers, the exciting and innovative artist Rahsaan Roland Kirk, a man whose expression is not limited to a single instrument, achieved his fame as a result of 'gimmickry' (playing three horns at once) and 'freak' effects. Long ago Kirk developed a way of 'growling' the melody line he was simultaneously playing on the flute, a concept that has been copied extensively. This became acceptable, however, for Kirk was considered a player who belonged to the mainstream of the music. When Dewey Redman, a musician of the same age whose roots went equally deep, discovered how to sing through his saxophone while playing it, his innovation was churlishly dismissed. By aligning himself with the so-called 'avant-garde' through his association with Ornette Coleman, Redman was a radical, i.e. a 'freak', and worthy only of passing interest. He developed the ability to sing either a related line or one that was unrelated to what he was playing on the saxophone and the effect was stunning. It called to mind the voicing of two horns locked head-on in a battling blues band, but what did the critics say? 'Most of the reviews I've read, I've been hollering and screeching into the horn. I never read a review where the guy seemed to know what I was trying to do. It's always that I use some kind of funny effect or a growl or a holler. But it's not a fluke, it's something that I studied, and I have never heard anybody else do that.'

Another example occurred in dealings with a magazine devoted solely to the art of percussion. Month by month, it featured interviews with drummers who are active in jazz, rock and session work. I called up the editor and offered him what I considered to be a 'scoop' interview with three of the leading contemporary percussionists. He expressed a tentative interest in the idea, but when I mentioned the names of the participants, admitted that their names were unknown to him. It was as if the editor of a film magazine had never heard of Godard, Truffaut and Chabrol. Together with another man, two of the drummers concerned were responsible for structuring an entire era of percussion.

It is difficult to imagine an artist like Anthony Braxton being invited to play in the average American jazz club, in spite of the fact that he is generally regarded as one of the most important among the young saxophone players. This is not to say that he was not at one time accustomed to nightclubs – they are the traditional environment for players of so-called jazz, after all, as well as the proving ground – but Braxton does not compromise, something that others are often forced to do.

Overall it is the dedication of the musicians that is the reason for this book. It endeavours to introduce the new musicians, to describe who they are and where they come from. It also explains why some of them are forced to compromise and why, in spite of the fact that it is hard to earn any kind of living from the new music, so many of them refuse to do so.

Above all, I hope it will show that the musicians are flesh-and-blood people, not just names on a piece of plastic playing their hearts out for the benefit of anyone with the price of a record album. 'When people go to hear the music they expect to hear the guy sock it to 'em, *do* it to 'em. And right – I don't blame them, they've paid their money,' said Noah Howard, another of the younger saxophonists. 'But you never know what a guy is going through. I've seen guys go on the stage and play and they've just got a telephone call that one of their parents has died. Musicians are human beings and sometimes, I think people tend to be a little unfair and not recognise them as such. They treat them as a jukebox – put your money in, turn on, and turn it off.'

The cultural effects of the politics and economics of the situation cover the entire span of the musicians' lives and their music, from their chances of work and acclaim to their personal relationships. The music itself describes the political position of Blacks in America just as their position dictates their day-to-day life, the instruments they play and the places where their music can be heard. In the case of African-American music, the fact that the creators are the colonised in a colonialist society has a vital bearing on the way the music has evolved, how it is regarded by the world at large, and the way in which the artists are treated. To ignore the realities and continue to listen to the music is, to my mind, not only insulting but ignorant.

As Noah Howard has also pointed out: 'Let's go back to Al Jolson – he made money painting his face black. Elvis Presley made the money from Little Richard. The Rolling Stones came to America and made five million dollars in thirty days, *playing the blues.* The history of this country has enlightened me.'

In most histories of jazz to date – 'America's only art form', it is generally called, conveniently ignoring its *Afro*-American origins – political interpretations of events have been omitted because these histories were written at a time when Black achievements were seldom documented scrupulously. But how the music evolved and developed can be examined in two distinct ways. Traditionally, histories begin in New Orleans or thereabouts with emancipated slaves picking up the instruments left behind when the Army bands broke up after the Civil War. The other, the political interpretation, concentrates on explaining *why* the only drums to be found among a people who had come from a drum-oriented culture were those played in those military bands. Not one African percussion device survived slavery, in fact.

In contrast to those islands under French and Spanish rule, and with the exception of the special case of Congo Square in New Orleans, the drum was actually banned by the British in America and the West Indies because it was thought that it could be used to incite revolt. It was also an emotive link with Africa. 'You pick up the drum and you think of the Black man,' said Milford Graves, one of the innovators on the instrument. 'You generally think of Africa and you think well, this is really his culture. And just as anything else by the Black people has been suppressed, so the drum has been along with it. It was a great factor in Black Africa and I think this is why it was suppressed – because it played a major part in their whole lifestyle.'

I feel that the long section on drums makes up for some of the omissions of the past. I have documented the career of Ed Blackwell in detail because he is a prime example of a major artist to suffer neglect as a result of this lack of understanding of the role played by his instrument. The drums, after all, echo the heartbeat, and as Milford Graves has also noted: If you study the anatomy of the ear, you'll see that the so-called *eardrum* is nothing but a membrane, and the so-called *hammer* is nothing but a drumstick.' The drums, said Beaver Harris, 'are the spirit behind the musicians'.

Another, seldom acknowledged, spirit behind the male musicians is that of the women who share their lives. The freelance musician has always been forced to lead a precarious existence and his economic plight is increased if he refuses to compromise his art or subsidise his income with a day-job. As a result he generally relies on a woman for support. The majority of the musicians deny this, but wives or 'old ladies' are often responsible for maintaining them spiritually as well as economically, and yet the man who puts his wife and family before the music tends to be rejected by the subculture. In an attempt to redress the balance, I have talked with a number of musicians about the role played by women in their lives, and to the women themselves.

This book does not pretend to be a comprehensive history of the 'New Music'; it has been impossible to mention all the people who have contributed to its progress or to examine European contributions. It will, however, serve as an introduction. I have concentrated on lesser-known musicians as a source of information in many cases because I feel their experience is more typical and so more helpful in contributing to an understanding of the world of Black music. The careers of the major innovators and their contributions have been exhaustively examined elsewhere, and the length of the chapters on Coltrane, Taylor and Coleman bears no relation to their monolithic contribution.

Except where indicated, all quoted remarks arise from conversations with the author. My political attitudes have to a large extent been influenced by the analyses offered by musicians such as Andrew Cyrille, Milford Graves, Billy Harper, Archie Shepp, Clifford Thornton and Charles Tolliver in much the same way that all my listening has been conditioned by almost twenty-five years of exposure to Black Music in all its forms.

In the revised edition, I have corrected factual errors and, in the concluding chapter, contextualised events and briefly analysed contemporary attitudes. For these tasks, I am indebted to Mike Hames and his unlimited discographical knowledge. Several new biographies have been added but space had prevented the inclusion of many other individuals that I would have liked to mention.

'In some countries one is allowed to be what one wants to be, but in others one can go so far and not further. In some parts of the world we are recognised and get credit for what we are. However, here in the USA they take away from us what is originally ours. They get a substitute in our place – not as good as we are but superficially close enough to fool the public. In one sentence: they claim the rights to our God-given talents. This has happened to the Negro in many fields and in jazz music it has been done constantly for the past fifty years. Expressing myself bluntly: many white imitators of Negro jazz – I do not speak of the dedicated and talented white musicians – are called great jazz musicians while the true creators of real jazz have to work for peanuts – if they can get any work at all! It's a shame.'[2]

The preceding remarks could have been made by any of the younger, more politicised Black musicians, and the sentiments are hardly new. That they were, in fact, made by a man born at the turn of the century seems to me ample reason for the continuing need to stress the truth about the music and to expose the injustices that have been and continue to be inflicted on its creators by the music industry and the media.

Notes

1   Interview with Philippe Carles and Daniel Soutif, in *Jazz Magazine,* March 1974.
2   Drummer Herbie 'Kat' Cowans in a letter to Johnny Simmen, published in *Coda,* June 1971.

PART ONE

INNOVATORS AND INNOVATIONS

1

Great Black Music – From a Love Supreme to the Sex Machine

Music is the most powerful force I know; it's the only force that can make you cry, laugh, be happy, dance, fuck, fight. It can do strange things to people. Music is the only pure thing that's left because everything else is so corrupted, and being a Black jazz musician in America is hardly a lucrative thing. I'm happier when I'm playing than when I'm walking to the bank, and I'm happy doing that, too. But the two don't hardly go hand in hand.

Dewey Redman

'Aaah – you knocked me out! You knocked me out! You really got *to* me!' A plump Black woman approaching middle age, her style as commonplace as the cut of her knee-length green dress, grabbed hold of the sweating saxophone player and shouted her enthusiasm in his face. Frank Lowe grinned back his thanks and continued putting away his instruments.

In the background, other versions of this little scenario were being enacted. Children bounded around the multi-coloured set of drums and rapped with the flamboyantly attired conga drummer. Hugh Glover, another saxophonist, sat exhausted at the side of the stage while members of the local community, both young and old, crowded around the instigator of the event to pump his hand and say how much they had enjoyed the show. Milford Graves, sweat-soaked and tired but happy, took it all in his stride.

The Storefront Museum, a converted warehouse, is a community project in Jamaica, the predominantly Black section of the New York borough of Queens. Milford Graves, a drummer who at the time was also engaged as a medical technologist running a veterinary laboratory during the day, is one of the most important musicians playing the New Black Music. He is important as an innovator and also because he has been bringing his uncompromising music into the Black community since the middle 'sixties. It has been said by those who dislike the new music that it has been created in a rarefied vacuum, unlike previous forms of jazz which grew spontaneously within the Black community. To prove their point, they detect an almost exclusively white intellectual following for it and claim that ordinary Blacks are unable to appreciate or identify with it. The response Graves and the other musicians received at the Storefront Museum that Sunday afternoon gave the lie to that.

The concert featured a vibraphone player named Bob Davis, and Raleigh Sahumba, a childhood friend of Graves's who played five different conga drums tuned to tastefully different pitches. In addition to their saxophones, Lowe and Glover handled a variety of other wind and percussion instruments. In his preamble to the fiery proceedings, Graves pointed out how the critics have tried to undermine the importance of the New Music. 'Don't listen for the kind of rhythms you're used to hearing,' he said, and urged the listeners to discover for themselves rhythms and feelings to which to relate. And they had no trouble doing so. Music that might be difficult for a jazz audience accustomed to something more conventional was enthusiastically received at every level by this very ordinary cross-section of the local people.

To understand the importance of Milford Graves and the influence he exerts both musically and personally in the musicians' community is not easy without making reference to a parallel in white society. His counterpart in contemporary music would be someone like Terry Riley; in the art world, possibly David

Hockney, but that gives no indication of his personal influence. The comparison with the latter is rather inappropriate, but there is absolutely no comparison between their bank balances. Milford Graves plays the New Black Music and at this moment in time, that is not a particularly commercial proposition. His records show what he has done as an innovator in percussion, but they don't do him justice. As he himself put it: 'The equipment just can't capture the energy of the music.' Energy is one of the most startling factors in the drummer's music, a quality that is lost when its complexity is transferred to tape. Alone he puts enough concentrated energy into his drumming to take on an army single-handed.

Graves's music is supposed to be esoteric, yet he has taken it into the streets of Harlem as well as the hallowed halls of Yale University and achieved an equally enthusiastic response. In recent years few of his concerts have taken place outside the Black community, yet he feels that were he to confine himself to that audience exclusively, it would limit the creative forces within him. But because he is playing the New Black Music, he receives none of the concert offers that an artist of comparative stature in the world of 'straight' or contemporary European music would expect as a matter of course. In 1973 he made two appearances at the Newport in New York Jazz Festival. One was in the musicians' own section of the Festival, a token series of concerts held in one of the smaller halls at Lincoln Center, offered to pacify the demands of a 400-strong group of dissident New York musicians but poorly attended because they ran concurrently with performances elsewhere by better-known artists; the other was at Radio City Music Hall in a midnight jam session with 'name' musicians from different eras of jazz. In addition to being a compelling percussionist with a staggering technique and inexhaustible fund of ideas, Graves is quite a spectacular showman. He was the undoubted hit on both these occasions, yet whenever he had appeared in concert in the city previously, he had hired the hall himself or in conjunction with other musicians. He refuses to work in bars or nightclubs, the traditional workplaces for the jazz musician.

'People just disrespect you in clubs, the owners and the hip set. There are certain places downtown where everybody goes because everybody's got to be hip and it's the place to hang out. I don't really like that. I find that one thing I can say in the Black community is that there is an awareness of somebody that's trying to be creative. I get a better feeling, there's more response, and I don't run up against people that are just straight alcoholics. Now I've got nothing against playing for maybe an institution that's trying to cure alcoholics, I'm talking about people that get filthy drunk in clubs, laying all over the place, grabbing on you when you come by and using all kind of slang words. I'm just tired of dealing with that right now. I'm trying to be in a place where I can give something to people on a positive level. If I get to a place where there are so many negative things happening, I found it just ruins me.'

In 1975, Graves found himself spending more time teaching than actually playing concerts. While the opportunity for disseminating knowledge pleased him, the lack of opportunity to play his music did not. 'You have to work enough to keep yourself in good shape. There's nothing like an audience in front of you and all the musicians coming in – not coming in from an ego level, you know, but it's a thing of, like, inspiration. You see other musicians coming in, they smile and if you walk off the stage they say, "You sound nice," and it's an inspiration to go up on the next set and play. It keeps your mind really functioning good.'

Energy and emotionalism, the twin demons surging within the music of Milford Graves, are the virtues that fire the music of Cecil Taylor, of Ornette Coleman, of John Coltrane, Duke Ellington, Louis Armstrong and Charlie Parker. It is because of that fire that recordings by long-departed creative spirits like Sidney Bechet, Johnny Dodds or Lester Young sound as fresh now as the day they were made. 'Basically, I think that one of the highlights of Black music is the emotionalism that it projects,' said Ted Daniel, one of the younger trumpet players. 'The New Music has that, and when it's played correctly, it's very exciting. With European music, we already have something where people can sit very still and listen to it executed very perfectly, but our music is very physical and emotional. I think that's one of its main attributes, that it is alive, it is sensual, it is physical.'

Sunny Murray, the most important innovator in contemporary percussion, has suggested that the new musician now has the freedom to discover how his instrument sounds before actually studying it. To some this statement would confirm the belief that the 'avant-garde' is the last refuge of the untalented. Unlike many of his peers, however, Milford Graves is the first to admit that the new music provided an outlet for musicians unskilled in traditional music. At the same time he is aware of the resentment felt of necessity by schooled players on realising that the free structure of the new music can actually help a relatively inexperienced musician to communicate with an audience. 'But I'd ask them this: how do you explain it when a musician that's only been playing five or six months comes out and plays something on his horn and someone can dig it? Or someone who don't know *nothing* about music, getting up there and banging on the drums and five million people start moving and yelling? And then someone who's been in music for ten years and can take every note in the book and play it upside down, but when he gets up there, nothing happens? You can't put that [criticising lack of technique] on a musician who moves the people. You have to ask yourself, "What am *I* doing?" and "Is it really no good?" And I think that's why a lot of musicians were against the new music at first – they saw a lot of people responding to it, and they knew those people weren't crazy.'

The New Music, the new jazz, free jazz or the New Black Music – no one name satisfies all the musicians who play it. The idea of categories limits the music where the size of its audience is concerned, although they are often necessary from the point of view of indicating its approximate period and style. 'It is whites who have put on these labels,'[1] say the Art Ensemble of Chicago. The musicians themselves usually call it 'the music'.

It is generally accepted among etymologists that the word 'jazz' is African although its exact tribal origin is unknown. It may well have come from Wolof – the language spoken by some coastal people of Senegal, Gambia and Guinea who were among those who acted as slave dealers – which is also the source of the word *hipicat,* meaning 'an aware person'. It has, furthermore, been suggested by J. L. Dillard, the noted authority on the history and usage of Black English, that Wolof may also have had some *lingua franca* use by certain interior tribes as a result of this nefarious trading activity.[2] Thus, it becomes increasingly harder to pinpoint an exact origin. What is clear is that it was not a word used by the musicians themselves to describe what they played. As far as most comparatively recent sources are concerned, the word is indelibly associated with its usage in turn-of-the-century New Orleans – or Louisiana – as a colloquialism for sexual intercourse. It is, therefore, apparent that it was used by whites to identify a music of the Black subculture which was a world to which they could only relate in sensual terms. The social restrictions inherent in the implications of the word and the knowledge of *whose* music it identified were obvious thirty years ago to the musicians who first sought to take it out of the nightclubs and give it the respectability of the concert platform, but the majority of today's musicians reject the word for the same reason they refuse to be known as 'Negroes'. 'It's not a word that *we* made up, it's a word where we were told what it was,' said Lee Morgan, the gifted trumpeter who was killed in 1972 at the age of thirty-three.

In a symposium held during the 1973 Newport Festival, saxophonist Archie Shepp said: 'If we continue to call our music jazz, we must continue to be called niggers. There, at least, we know where we stand.'[3] The Art Ensemble of Chicago prefer to call it Great Black Music – 'It's Great, it's Black, and it's Music,'[4] they say, but make the point that in using the term they are not only referring to that music previously designated as jazz, but to the church music of singers like Mahalia Jackson and the drum-choirs of Africa as well. 'Jazz itself is only a mixture of all the music before your time,' said Beaver Harris, a drummer who has worked with Sonny Rollins, Albert Ayler and Archie Shepp. 'This is the reason why I prefer calling it Black Music because this way you have all of your history to draw from.'

To someone like drummer Rashied Ali, whose whole aim in life was to be a 'jazz musician', the situation is confusing and it seems ironic to change the name. 'At one time it was a very proud thing to be called a jazz musician, but it's just like how at one time to call somebody "black" in this country was a terrible insult. When you called somebody "black", you'd better be ready to fight. They were just so fucked-up behind that word, but now, if you call them anything else but Black, then you're ready to fight! So like the name, it really doesn't matter to me. As far as I'm concerned, "jazz" is cool. It was named "jazz", now everybody talking about "I don't like that word". I really don't think it matters what you call that music because it exists and it's here. I'm not trying to rename it anything, but we do know without a doubt that it is a Black art form discovered in this country. So if there's anything to be written about jazz, it should be stipulated that it's a *Black* art form.'

At one time, the trumpeter who was most popular with the Black community in New Orleans earned the nickname 'King' – e.g., King Bolden, King Oliver – but many contemporary musicians hold the white media responsible for establishing the kind of hierarchy in the music that is familiar to most devotees. The anomalies of and the injustices resulting from this situation were explained by Hakim Jami, a bass player from Detroit. 'Jazz is *theirs*, anyway. That term, they really wore that out. Everybody uses this as a great reference to the music, but it ain't no great reference. I look at the older Black musicians and I see them holding on to it and glorifying it, but I really can't dig it because the media never put those cats down as being the greatest. I mean, Duke Ellington wasn't the "King of Jazz", Paul Whiteman was. And if that's the case, then I don't consider Duke Ellington a *jazz* musician.

Whatever he's playing, he's the best I've heard, so I've got to call him the King of that.'

Attempts to define the music as 'Black Music' were defeated by the media who started to use the term to describe music played by Blacks alone. By doing so they altered the original intention, which was to provide a generic description for all music of African-American origin, the race of the exponent being immaterial. As a result, by the mid-1970s the musicians themselves began to question the validity of the description. Milford Graves pointed out how the decision taken by the Nation of Islam to admit whites had shaken the Black community, and related this and similar events to the political changes taking place within the musicians' circle. 'I don't think we should be calling it "Black" music,' he said. 'If you look all around the world you don't find any music designated by colour. What we *do* call it is the problem.' To him, 'African-American' is as good a name as any.

The New Music is, of course, a term of convenience that embraces many approaches, some of which would appear to have little in common. Basically, it is used to distinguish a free-thinking contemporary approach from one that is rooted in bebop, the music that grew in the 'forties through the innovations of Charlie Parker, Dizzy Gillespie and Thelonious Monk. As opposed to the so-called Third Stream, an attempt to blend European music with bebop of which the chief exponents were people like John Lewis and Gunther Schuller, the emphasis is on freedom from the restrictions of harmony and time. This is one of the reasons why the music has been dubbed 'free form' on occasion. Where, in the past, the improvisation was based on the form and length of a given statement – the theme – the new musicians improvise more on a reminiscence of that statement. 'I try to keep this in my mind – what does that melody or that statement remind me of?' said one musician. 'In a way it's in my mind, but it's not played as such.' (This is not to suggest that the 'freest' improvisation could not exist inside highly structured forms.)

But the new music not only was different in terms of how it was done and the solutions it offered to common musical problems, it sounded different. Whereas, fast as it was, you could listen to every note in an Art Tatum piano solo, it is virtually impossible to do the same with Cecil Taylor's playing. Taylor's intense keyboard dissertations hit the ear as great wedges of sound rather than single lines. It is the overall *effect* of his music to which the listener responds.

For the player, the new music has been concerned with ways of increasing his freedom to improvise, but to the listener, its most obvious characteristic was that the musicians constantly explored, and exploited, new sound systems. No sound, in fact, is considered unmusical in the New Music. When John Coltrane incorporated another saxophonist into his quartet, an American critic was astonished at the sounds that he and Eric Dolphy produced: 'Melodically and harmonically, their improvisations struck my ear as gobbledegook.'[5] A couple of years later, ESP-Disk launched their catalogue of recordings by artists in the avant-garde, each album proudly headlined with the message, 'You Never Heard Such Sounds In Your Life!'

Sound as a quality for its own sake became an idea to be pursued. Trumpeter Donald Ayler explained to Nat Hentoff how it could be used as a handhold into the music: 'One way not to [listen to it] is to focus on the notes and stuff like that. Instead, try to move your imagination toward the sound. It's a matter of following the sound … Follow the sound, the pitches, the colours. You have to watch them move.'[6]

Coltrane popularised the playing of chords on the saxophone, a technique learned from Philadelphian John Glenn. Other players of the instrument like Pharoah Sanders, Dewey Redman, Frank Wright and the late Albert Ayler subsequently developed the use of overtones and 'harmonics'. To many ears these revolutionary sounds are shrill and rasping – Ayler's saxophone was once derisively likened to the buzzing of an electric saw – to others they are exciting and stimulating. As the writer Bob Palmer has noted,

23

there is nothing new about the technique. '"One-voice chording" is fairly widespread in West Africa; flute players, vocalists and performers on the double-reed *alghaita* all employ it. When Wilson Pickett and James Brown "scream" they are chording with one voice. Robert Johnson used the same technique, and so do some of the early New Orleans jazzmen.'[7]

Jazz, or the New Music, means many things to many people. It always has done, although it could be suggested that the musicians of the past were possibly more single-minded in their decision to be specifically *jazz* musicians. Everything from waltzes to rhythm-and-blues are part of the musician's vocabulary at some time or another, and many have been forced to continue playing 'commercial' music in order to survive. But now the stress in the musicians' community is more on continuously changing, shifting, 'creativity'. The idea of using improvisation always provided ample freedom for playing variations on a melody or chord pattern, but those among the new musicians who define themselves by preference as 'creative artists' are constantly striving to reach the point where they repeat themselves as seldom as possible.

Trumpeter Leo Smith, for example, is concerned with improvisation in its purest sense. He always attempts to be completely spontaneous and tries never to base his improvisations on pre-ordained patterns. To him, the concept of referring to such a process as 'creative music' is dedicated to developing a heightened awareness of improvisation itself as an art form. 'Improvisation means that the music is created at the moment it is performed, whether it is developing a given theme or is improvisation on a given rhythm or sound (structures) or, in the purest form, when the improviser creates without any of these conditions, but creates at that moment, through his or her wit and imagination, an arrangement of silence and sound and rhythm that has never before been heard and will never again be heard.'[8]

Jerome Cooper, drummer with a group called the Revolutionary Ensemble, defines an artist as *someone who creates.* 'When you create, there's so much stuff involved. The influences that you had that day have something to do with the music and how it will come out, so every time you create, it's supposed to be different. You can't help it, it's the natural law of an artist. In Rock they play the same thing over and over again because they're entertainers, not artists. To me, a person who always plays the same thing, they're like computers or something.'

Some listeners who were accustomed to jazz in its usual mould found this idea perplexing. They were used to the music following a set formula, but with the New Music, no such comfortable reassurance awaited them. The new players deliberately strove to exclude any familiar phrases from their improvisations. To them, something familiar could be construed as 'entertainment' and they didn't want that. 'Take B.B. King,' said Cooper. 'I've worked with him; he's an entertainer, he's supposed to do that. When you go and see him, he has a show. He's an artist, too, but he's a *craftsman*. He's an artist *and* an entertainer. I don't consider myself an entertainer. I consider myself an artist and I do not entertain.'

'Most people,' said Milford Graves, 'will play for the average person's senses. I try to go above the average person's senses.'

In the 'fifties, the musicians delved into their blues and gospel background in a deliberate plan to inject new life into the music which was suffering from a lack of innovation after the bebop revolution of the previous decade. This 'back to the roots' movement reflected the growing political awareness among Blacks that heralded the Civil Rights era, and its implications run parallel with the effects of and the events surrounding the influence exerted by Coltrane, Coleman, Taylor and their followers. As far back as 1967 the saxophonist Jimmy Heath was saying, 'The music business needed a shot in the arm from the avant-garde to give it a lift and the flavour of excitement that it had lost.' Now, with the rejection of many previously held musical standards, the music itself began to take on a political significance for some.

Much has been made of the way its uncompromising and

aggressive nature reflected the fury and anger rumbling in the ghetto, although it is not true to say that every musician involved in the new music was especially politicised. 'Undoubtedly, living in America, I am influenced by what goes on there,' said Noah Howard, a young saxophonist. 'But I don't stand up on stage, put my saxophone in my mouth and think about bullets and destroying the government.'

The style of 'jazz' that continued to attract a large popular following in the 1970s was based on a fusion of the ideas forged by the John Coltrane Quartet and others with rhythms that had hitherto been used only in so-called rock. Miles Davis, Weather Report, Herbie Hancock and the British guitarist John McLaughlin (Mahavishnu), are the most successful exponents of this cosily reassuring style; by 1975, Hancock's album *Head Hunters* had sold more copies than any other jazz album in history. However well it is played, though, jazz/rock or 'crossover', as it is now known, is entertainment music, not an exploration that threatens the listener's comfort or stretches the imagination in any way. And the ease with which people like Miles Davis and Chick Corea have reached their considerable public is not viewed kindly by those artists who have taken a thornier path. 'It seems that the best way to make it these days is to play as *little* as possible,' was the caustic comment from one musician understandably disgruntled by the success of the relatively simple fare purveyed by the contemporary Miles Davis band. 'Seems like you play four notes and then let the rhythm section carry on for a couple of dozen choruses. If you spend time working out a carefully constructed thirty-five-minute solo, the people don't want to know.'

There are plenty of musicians who continue to play so-called free music while earning a living from the jazz/rock formula, but there is a certain political position involved in the choice of those who seldom refer to the more readily assimilated rock rhythms. Even if the individual is not personally politicised, the fact that he plays the new music places him outside the norm, whether that norm be playing the extensions of bebop or so-called jazz/rock. Joseph Jarman, saxophonist and percussionist with the Art Ensemble of Chicago, is a highly politicised individual. He feels that musicians who share his way of thinking constitute a threat to the structure built by those powers who would like to see the music stay – figuratively speaking – in the whorehouses where it was allegedly born. In that way, he reasons, they can continue to exercise control over the musicians. 'You can go hear so-called modern jazz based on the principles of Charlie Parker, Diz and all that – you can hear that any time, anywhere, in the whole world – but anybody that deviates from that a little bit is going to have a hard time. Anybody who says, "Well, that's interesting but I would prefer doing something else", they're going to be discriminated against.'

* * *

As black nationalism developed following the Civil Rights struggle, becoming visible in the adoption of African and Islamic customs, names and dress, so the music broadened to contain obvious references to the strands that had been woven into the fabric of contemporary jazz. On an album called *Message to Our Folks,* the Art Ensemble of Chicago included the traditional 'Old Time Religion' side by side with Charlie Parker's 'Dexterity'. Guitarist Sonny Sharrock recorded a blues called 'Blind Willy', inspired by the work of a religious guitarist and singer called Blind Willie Johnson who was active in the 'twenties. The Revolutionary Ensemble's *Manhattan Cycles* featured violinist Leroy Jenkins improvising against the sound of Billie Holiday's voice relayed from a tape-recorder. Anthony Braxton played material by Parker and Charles Mingus. And the references to Africa, though preceded by works from Randy Weston, Max Roach, Duke Ellington, Sonny Rollins, Art Blakey and Coltrane himself with his 1961 recordings of *Africa/Brass* and 'Dahomey Dance', began to be commonplace. The drummer Sunny Murray, recording in Paris in 1969, paid *Homage to Africa*; the following year trumpeter/trombonist Clifford Thornton offered his free interpretation of melodies derived from rituals connected with two Yoruba deities, Shango and Ogun. And the St Louis saxophonist Julius Hemphill not only gave his record label a Swahili name, Mbari, his composition *Dogon A.D.* was named after the cliff-dwelling people of Mali.

A number of artists even took to employing African and quasi-African techniques. Leon Thomas introduced the yodel, taking Congolese pygmies as his model. The string player Alan Silva took up the violin in 1969 inspired by Ornette Coleman's experiments on the instrument, but he played it held between his legs in the manner of the 'cello, as a result of seeing a group of Sudanese musicians on film, one of whom bowed a violin in this, the original Asian way. When Archie Shepp gave a lengthy musical recitation concerning *The Magic of Juju*, he gathered five men to spin a meaningful web of percussion behind him. For the most part, his saxophone proclamation was accompanied by three of them – Dennis Charles who played the triangle, taking the role traditionally associated with the gong in West African drum-choirs, his younger brother Frank, who performed on the *gan-gan* (pidgin name for the Yoruba talking-drum), and Edward Blackwell who played 'rhythm logs', American-constructed but designed to approximate the sound of certain African drums. In 1974, a *Dialogue of the Drums* recorded by Milford Graves and Andrew Cyrille contained a 'Message to the Ancestors' and 'Blessing From the Rain Forest'.

Where Black musicians of earlier eras had often been forced to reject their roots and the environment that had nurtured them in the cause of acceptance by white middle-class society, today's artists proclaim them with pride. Not only did Archie Shepp record material by Duke Ellington, he dedicated his own compositions to Black culture heroes as diverse as Malcolm X and the pimp ('The Mac Man'). He wrote music in memory of Black artists who died prematurely, among them the painter Robert Thompson and the saxophonist Ernie Henry, and was sufficiently impressed by a chance meeting in a European nightclub with an older harmonica player from Mississippi to try depicting the life and hard times of such an itinerant musician. (Rice Miller, who had long ago assumed the name of one of the hottest Chicago bluesmen, always insisted that he was 'The Original Mr Sonny Boy Williamson', and Shepp's musical portrait of him was named accordingly.) In 1977 the wheel came full circle when trumpeter Floyd LeFlore and saxophonist J. D. Parran of St Louis's Black Artists Group appeared in concert with the veteran barrelhouse pianist Henry Townshend.

Shepp has always been particularly reverential in the matter of his musical antecedents, never failing to dignify them with the prefix 'Mr'. Wilbur Ware's wife reported how Shepp would often visit the legendary bassist, one of the finest musicians Chicago has produced, to learn the bridges of several standard tunes: 'He was very interested in getting an older man to show him.' The new musicians, in common with Blacks in other spheres, are concerned to see that respect be accorded their predecessors, both as individuals and as a people.

Frank Lowe had his saxophone sand-blasted to remove the lacquer and its characteristically shiny surface. 'Ruined a good instrument,' said an older player disparagingly, but he missed the point. Lowe wanted his horn to resemble those he had seen held by people like Coleman Hawkins in photographs of the early big bands. He wanted to feel more securely a part of the line of saxophonists that began with Hawkins, and the physical appearance of his instrument helped him to relate more closely to his musical ancestors in the same way that the *dansiki* increases the wearer's feeling of identification with Africa. On another occasion, his enthusiasm was torn between a new flute he had acquired and a picture he had just seen of Eric Dolphy. He picked up the flute, and tried to imitate Dolphy's pose and embouchure. His actions recalled the often-told story of the young Rex Stewart arriving in New York in the 'twenties and filled with such admiration for Louis

Armstrong that he copied his mannerisms right down to his style of dressing, walking and talking. The esteem in which the younger musicians hold their predecessors is often misunderstood by devotees who expect them to actually sound like their heroes. Imitation may be the sincerest form of flattery in the eyes of some, but in the world of contemporary Black music the concept of Respect goes much deeper.

Byard Lancaster, a saxophonist away from home in a strange European city, called for Aretha Franklin records on a Sunday morning. 'I like to listen to Aretha on Sundays because she's the nearest I can get to the church.' Lancaster, whose music clearly embodies the blues ('A Love Supreme to the Sex Machine and All in Between' reads the slogan on his stationery, the references being to Coltrane and the popular singer James Brown), differs interestingly from a musician like Anthony Braxton whose music is apparently so far removed from the roots that he is able to tackle an entire solo concert performance on alto saxophone and make only one fleeting reference to the blues. Not surprisingly, one of his younger brothers reported to a rather startled friend, 'My brother Tony don't like one doo-wop' (the onomatopoeic name given to 'fifties harmonising vocal groups, now in common Black usage to describe any popular vocal record). Growing up on the South Side of Chicago, however, records by the Flamingoes and Frankie Lymon and the Teenagers were no strangers to Braxton's turntable. In Frank Lowe's record collection, Coltrane and Lester Young share pride of place with 'Shotgun' by Junior Walker and the All-Stars.

'The important thing in music is to always be proud of your heritage,' said Beaver Harris. 'In the past whites would say that Blacks were not proud of their heritage but they lied. In the case of the Black man when he is being himself, the blues roots would definitely show.'

When the musicians get so caught up in asserting their egos that they forget about what has gone before, someone will always come along to remind them. In the case of Frank Lowe, rehearsing furiously with the Revolutionary Ensemble and very pleased with himself, it was Lester Bowie, the St Louis-born trumpeter. 'Lester said, "Don't you-all ever play the blues no more?" And he sat down and played with me and Jerome (Cooper) and Sirone (Norris Jones) and we just played the blues until it made me *cry*.'

* * *

Black music has never stood still. One theory to explain the need for this constant change maintains that it occurs from necessity, that the protagonists are forced to invent new techniques and systems in order to stay one step ahead of white imitators and codifiers. Possibly the musicians of the past were not blessed with an acute political consciousness (hardly surprising in view of their position in society – 'entertainers' playing in brothels and bar-rooms); perhaps it is true to say that until Charlie Parker came along none of them referred to their music as art, but in the 'sixties and 'seventies, the 'different drummer' that Black musicians heard was as often motivated by nationalist considerations as by the aesthetic desire to play something new. As LeRoi Jones (Amiri Baraka) has written, choosing to play the New Music had strong political significance: 'The Black musicians who know about the European tempered scale (Mind) no longer want it – if only just to be contemporary.'[9]

Notes

1   Interview with Marc Bernard, Daniel Caux and Philippe Gras, in *Jazz Hot*, no. 254.
2   Correspondence with the author.
3   Reported by Philippe Carles and Francis Marmande, 'Les Contradictions de Festival', *Jazz Magazine*, September 1973.
4   Interview by Philippe Carles and Daniel Soutif, 'L'Art Ensemble de Chicago au-delà du Jazz', *Jazz Magazine*, March 1974.

5   John A. Tynan, in *Down Beat,* 23 November 1961.
6   Interview by Nat Hentoff, 'The Truth is Marching In', *Down Beat,* 17 November 1966.
7   Bob Palmer, 'Respect', *Down Beat,* 31 January 1974.
8   Leo Smith, *Notes (8 pieces) Source a new world music: creative music,* Connecticut, 1973.
9   LeRoi Jones, *Black Music,* New York, 1963.

2

John Coltrane – A Love Supreme

John was like a visitor to this planet. He came in peace and
he left in peace; but during his time here, he kept trying
to reach new levels of awareness, of peace, of spirituality.
That's why I regard the music he played as spiritual music –
John's way of getting closer and closer to the Creator.[1]

Albert Ayler

In 1972 ABC-Impulse released two previously unissued recordings by the late John Coltrane. *Transition* and *Sun Ship* had been
put on tape seven years earlier, but as trumpeter Charles Tolliver
remarked on their appearance: 'That music is not only as fresh as
today, it is as if it hadn't been played yet.'

Musicians, critics and other listeners may disagree on many
points, but where the music of John Coltrane is concerned there is
never any argument. He was, simply, a giant. The material released
after his death merely serves to confirm this. Sirone, formerly
known as Norris Jones, played bass with Coltrane towards the end
of his career. Although disputing the right of any individual to be
considered 'the greatest' on their instrument in a world so filled
with individual talent, he made one notable exception. 'There was
only one time that I could say that, and that was with John. But
that was the last place he wanted to be. What John did musically,
you could go on for ever talking about it.'

The Coltrane Quartet that included pianist McCoy Tyner,

bassist Jimmy Garrison and drummer Elvin Jones was the most influential band of the post-war period. It was the one group that amalgamated all the threads that had gone into the creation of Black music up to that point and did so in a musicianly way, based in the traditions of the great jazz musical heritage. Even to Frank Butler, a drummer who grew up in Kansas City schooled in the standards of the Swing era, eventually becoming the leading bebop drummer on the West Coast, the Coltrane Quartet epitomised his every musical desire. He listened to the group on record and reacted: 'I said, "Oh, when will the day come when I can just have that group for *me? I* want to play with them by myself. I want that group under *me,* around *me!*"'

'They came up with some helluva music which will take years for people to sit down and analyse,' said Charles Tolliver. 'It will take years to be properly understood.'

From the minute he stamped his personality on the saxophone, every other saxophone player, no matter his field of endeavour, adopted the sound Coltrane invented. After that there was, quite simply, no other way to play the instrument. Coltrane rewrote the method book for the saxophone, just as Charlie Parker had done twenty years earlier and Coleman Hawkins twenty years before that. Even hidebound traditionalists who swore they would never be influenced by his revolutionary ideas found themselves playing Coltrane licks despite themselves as time went by.

The unique tone and the hypnotic mood that John Coltrane established the minute he started to play have become the norm. Although this mood owed its immediate source to his preoccupation with Indian and Arabic music during the late 'fifties and early 'sixties and was, therefore, more his personal responsibility than that of the quartet as a whole, the near-entrancement that distinguished the later work of the group was deeply rooted in African ritual.

As far as the contribution of the individual members of the quartet is concerned, Elvin Jones shared equal responsibilities with

Jimmy Garrison's bass and McCoy Tyner's piano, thereby bringing the drums into the frontline in a way that had seldom been done before. 'Being sandwiched in between Elvin and John was like being in between two professors or two major scientists,' said Tyner. He himself, through exploring the possibilities of modal improvisation, that is, improvising on a foundation of modally based scales rather than of chords, laid down the groundwork for a method that was to be used throughout the 'seventies. Developed in the various groups led by Miles Davis in the previous decade, modal improvisation was the springboard for the work of keyboard players like Chick Corea and Herbie Hancock whose 'popular' excursions took them into the world of rock.

It was Coltrane himself who actually popularised modal jazz, although this had started when he was a member of the Miles Davis Quintet. The definitive statement concerning this method of improvisation was made on the 1959 recording *Kind of Blue*, which marked, in a way, the end of an era. Like Coltrane's own *meisterwerk*, *Ascension*, or his earlier masterpiece 'Chasin' the 'Trane', recorded 'live' at the Village Vanguard in 1961, it was the culmination of all the developments that had taken place up to that point. As far as scalar improvisation is concerned, Coltrane has acknowledged the influence of John Gilmore, the brilliant tenor saxophonist from Mississippi who has been a standby of the Sun Ra Arkestra for over twenty years. During his stay with Davis, Coltrane reached the ultimate in harmonic invention, deliberately stacking new chords on top of those normally employed, thereby giving himself an almost unlimited number of scales and patterns on which to base his headlong flights. The effect was devastating. In effect, he created blocks of sound on his one instrument, rather than single-note lines – 'sheets of sound' was the way Ira Gitler described them.

The saxophonist has said that he used to listen to Miles Davis on record and fantasise about playing tenor the way he played trumpet. Later, when they worked together, the trumpeter influenced him considerably. 'It was Miles who made me want to be a better musician. He gave me some of the most listenable moments I've had in music, and he also gave me an appreciation for simplicity.'

When Coltrane formed his own group on leaving Davis, it was the trumpeter who advised him to continue his chordal exploration but release the rhythm section from such restrictions. It was Davis, in fact, who was one of the first people to improvise on pieces whose harmonic structure was limited to a simple chord. Then Coltrane heard Ornette Coleman, who had abandoned chords completely, and the direction his own music was to take immediately became clearer.

Eventually, the saxophonist was to achieve an almost trance-like state through his music, employing techniques that owed as much to his own spiritual resources as technical ones, the music itself gradually becoming simpler. Following in his footsteps, men like Archie Shepp and Pharoah Sanders took the hypnotic process even further, establishing a rapport with the land whence their ancestors had been transported. 'In all ritual song there is that slow beat, trying to call the gods. There's no rush; it's a slow process as though one is praying,' was the way a Nigerian composer once described it to me. Pharoah Sanders was to achieve precisely this mood on his later pieces such as 'Upper and Lower Egypt' and 'Let Us Go Into the House of the Lord', but it was John Coltrane who influenced him to take this direction. The techniques and strategy used in Africa may be different to those that Coltrane and his adherents employed, but the effect and motivation are the same. Archie Shepp captured the ritual mood in an expansive piece entitled *Yasmina, A Black Woman*, recorded after a visit to the Pan-African Festival in Algiers. The theme consists of two alternating modes and is reminiscent of the kind of vamp McCoy Tyner would play on introducing a Coltrane tune. This lasts for the entire twenty minutes of the piece and the effect is compelling to some, monotonous to others. Repetition is a solid virtue in African music, although at this point it is rarely appreciated by

Western ears accustomed to more involved harmonic invention. A singer from Panama vividly expressed the non-Western view in an interview with John Storm Roberts: 'The more you hear it the more harmony it has,'[2] she said. On 'Yasmina', a variety of drums and other percussion instruments are employed to flesh out the bare harmonic bones and add to the density of the music. Coltrane was the man who started this, adding more instrumentalists to his group, frequently percussionists, in order to weave a denser cloth from which to cut his poignant statements.

As far as new instruments were concerned, Coltrane started to enlarge his arsenal at the beginning of the 1960s. Photographs of early bands such as Fletcher Henderson's show men generally thought of as practitioners on a single saxophone peering out from behind a battery of a dozen or more assorted reed instruments. In the early days of the music such adaptability was common-place among schooled musicians; later, players tended to specialise more. In fact, a musician attempting to take up session work would frequently find himself forced to learn another instrument as a mandatory 'double'. Coltrane and Eric Dolphy, the multi-reedman who joined him for a while in the early 'sixties and had a considerable influence on him, popularised the playing of several horns as a virtue. Coltrane reintroduced the soprano saxophone, Dolphy the bass-clarinet. Where some musicians even felt embarrassed at the idea of carrying an extra horn, almost as if by doing so they were making some kind of admission that they were rejecting the so-called 'hip' jazz existence for the comparative security of the studio, after the example set by Coltrane it became a matter of pride for a musician to add to his or her armoury.

In addition to his musical importance, Coltrane exerted a profound spiritual influence on the musicians who followed in his footsteps. He was, according to all accounts, a modest man involved in a continual search for new areas of self-expression, and he projected a personal quality that younger musicians have drawn on and used as a model for their own behaviour. He was not the first musician to speak of spiritual matters, but his example was one of the most compelling and persuasive. As Frank Lowe put it: 'In the beginning, I wanted to be a "hip jazz musician". But Coltrane changed all that. Of course, the musicians have always been a part of the community, from Buddy Bolden on down. But Coltrane re-emphasised this. He took it out of being a "hip" musician and into being a musician of value or worth to the community. A musician to inform, a musician to relate to, a musician to raise kids by.'[3]

Another young player had similar thoughts on the subject. Noah Howard, living in San Francisco, was so impressed by the Coltrane Quartet when he heard them for the first time that he felt compelled to meet the perpetrator of such musical passion. He found him back-stage, reading a newspaper. 'I was really shocked. As powerful as the sound that was coming out, this was the most gentle and easygoing person I had ever met in my life. He didn't get up and run around and drink liquor, scream and make noise and pull on women's tits or anything like that, he just calmly walked off the stage. It just wigged me out, I couldn't understand it. I hadn't thought about musicians being like that.'

Archie Shepp summed it up: 'I think a lot of horn players try to be like what they think Miles Davis is or what they think Bird was, and like that, when they should really try to get closer to the things that John Coltrane actually taught, which were the qualities of endurance, of strength – a positive stoicness.'

Whatever instrument they may play in actuality, each one of today's musicians carries a figurative picture of John Coltrane on their wall. His influence has had a profound effect on rock music, too. To Elvin Jones, the music of the John Coltrane Quartet appealed to people outside the realm of so-called jazz because of its freshness: 'It was not so new as to do away with what was basic in jazz music, but to get involved in this thing offered a release to a great many minds. It was not that it was so much removed from the blues, but it was like another way of playing the blues – and a better way. It was a way that you could identify with in your own time.'

Frank Lowe missed hearing the Quartet in person because he was in the Army. By the time he was discharged, Coltrane had moved to a higher plane. He made up for this by taking the opportunity to play with every musician who had ever worked with him. He was fortunate enough to be hired by the saxophonist's widow Alice, who continued to lead a band in the tradition Coltrane had established. This, to Lowe, was the next best thing. He said, 'Sometimes I would listen to the records that he did and I would just feel part of the group.' In this, he is far from alone. Although John Coltrane has moved on into another dimension, he remains the most influential musician of recent years.

* * *

John William Coltrane was born in Hamlet, North Carolina, on 23 September 1926 and raised with his cousin Mary. His father was a tailor and amateur musician, his grandfather a Baptist preacher. Soon after his father died, the family moved to Philadelphia where Coltrane continued his musical studies. He worked with rhythm-and-blues bands including those led by Earl Bostic and Eddie Vinson, and played alto saxophone in the Dizzy Gillespie big band. There he sat next to a native-born Philadelphian, Jimmy Heath, whose influence he has acknowledged. (Another colleague in the band, trombonist Charles Majeed Greenlee, later went on to marry Coltrane's cousin.)

After a short spell with a small group led by Johnny Hodges, he joined Miles Davis in 1955. Two years later he worked with Thelonious Monk for an extended stay at the Five Spot in New York, then rejoined Davis in January 1958. He stayed there until he formed his own quartet in April 1960.

By 1961 the lineup of Tyner, Jones and Garrison had come into existence. Jones replaced Billy Higgins in the fall of 1960, and Garrison, who like Tyner and Coltrane had also grown up in Philadelphia, followed Steve Davis and Reggie Workman on New Year's Eve, 1961. Tyner met the saxophonist at the age of seventeen when he was working at Philadelphia's Red Rooster with a band led by Coltrane's longtime friend, the trumpeter, pianist and composer Calvin Massey. The two musicians established a close relationship which continued to flourish as a result of a friendship between Coltrane's first wife, Naima, and Tyner's family. Whenever the saxophonist visited Philadelphia, he would give the young pianist the benefit of some of his knowledge. At the age of twenty, Tyner joined Steve Davis and drummer Pete La Roca in the John Coltrane Quartet just two weeks after its formation. He stayed there until 1965. 'John felt that music was like the universe, which influenced me,' he said. 'You look up and see the stars but beyond them are many other stars. He was looking for the stars you can't see.'[4]

Coltrane had been exposed to Indian music long before such an interest became fashionable. He met Ravi Shankar in the 'fifties, and actually studied with the master sitar player for a short period. On tenor saxophone Coltrane's mood was often 'eastern', but it was on the soprano model that he emphasised his involvement with eastern tonalities. This is especially evident on his most notable tour-de-force, 'My Favorite Things'. Listening to this spectacular display of virtuosity and passion soon after it was recorded, there were, apparently, some young musicians who refused to believe they were not hearing an authentic Indian raga.

It was Coltrane's fascination with the Indian water-drum, essentially a drone instrument used like the *tamboura*, that led him to introduce a second bass player into the group. One bassist would improvise freely while the other played time, and this innovation came about initially through a Chicago friend, Donald Garrett, who played Coltrane a tape of himself and another bassist. In New York, Coltrane started playing extensively in private with Art Davis, a young bassist from Harrisburg, Pennsylvania, a relationship that has seldom been acknowledged, partly because Davis was unable to accept Coltrane's offer to work as a regular member of his group as a result of his previous commitments. He had, however, assisted the saxophonist with some of the chord progressions he used on *Giant Steps*, the epochal album from his so-called 'middle period', and the two men experimented frequently with various modes, sounds and rhythms.

For a two-week engagement at the Village Gate in New York, Davis and Reggie Workman played in tandem with Coltrane, Jones and Tyner. Eric Dolphy was another guest on this occasion, and it was according to him that Davis eclipsed even the indefatigable Wilbur Ware who sat in for one night. 'John and I got off the stand and listened,' Dolphy recalled. 'Art Davis was really playing some kind of bass!' Coltrane's offer stayed open, but Joe Goldberg reported the bassist's reaction: 'I don't think 'Trane thinks of anything but music. He'll come back off the road and call me up to say, "We're opening at the Vanguard tonight." I say, "We are?" and then I have to tell him that I'm working somewhere else. He never seems to think to let me know in advance, so that I can stay free.'[5]

Altogether Davis made six of Coltrane's albums including *Ole*, the original version of *A Love Supreme* which includes Archie Shepp in the personnel,* and *Africa/Brass* for which Dolphy did the orchestrations. The high esteem in which he was held was shown by the saxophonist's insistence that his name be listed with the horns rather than in the rhythm section on the sleeve of *Ascension*. Since Coltrane's death in 1967 from cancer of the liver, Art Davis has played no jazz dates. 'He was my hero and idol,' he says. 'After he died I thought there was nothing going on.'

Eric Dolphy was another of the great instrumentalists who died before he achieved his full potential. He played alto saxophone,

---

*Despite the fact that this was recorded the day following the released version by the regular quartet, it was Coltrane's original intention to play with Shepp and Davis added.

bass-clarinet and flute, and influenced an entire generation of reed players, Coltrane among them. A dynamic artist who brought human sounds into the music as Albert Ayler and Pharoah Sanders were to do later, Dolphy was also occupied with eastern tonalities and had listened to Ravi Shankar. His bass clarinet work on Coltrane's record *India* fits the title like a glove. Initially, he came to sit in with the group for three nights and ended up staying for a European tour. Coltrane liked him for the 'fire' he added to the group. 'Eric is really gifted and I feel he's going to produce something inspired,' said Coltrane in 1961. 'We've been talking about music for years but I don't know where he's going, and *I* don't know where *I'm* going. He's interested in progress, however, and so am I, so we have quite a bit in common.'

Dolphy continued to play intermittently with Coltrane during the following year, then went on to lead his own groups and work with the innovative bassist Charles Mingus. In 1964 during an extended visit to Europe, he died from a heart attack in West Berlin, the cause being apparently related to diabetes. Coltrane was deeply moved by the news of his death. 'Whatever I'd say would be an understatement. I can only say my life was made much better by knowing him. He was one of the greatest people I've ever known, as a man, a friend, and as a musician.'[6]

In 1965 another tenor saxophonist, Pharoah Sanders, joined the band. He came from Little Rock, Arkansas, and won his spurs on the West Coast playing with people like the alto saxophonist Sonny Simmons and drummer Jimmy Lovelace. In New York he earned a living playing rock-and-roll while he made sessions with Don Cherry, Sun Ra and Billy Higgins. He had met Coltrane briefly in San Francisco where they spent a day together trying out mouthpieces in various pawnshops.

It was at this point that a remarkable kind of cross-fertilisation took place. One generally thinks of younger artists drawing on the wisdom of their elders, but in the case of Coltrane and Sanders, the exchange appears to have been completely mutual.

Their simultaneous improvising and weaving of lines, born out of an obvious understanding for each other, was responsible for Frank Lowe thinking of them as a single instrument when he heard them on record. 'Sometimes I didn't know whether Pharoah was doing the growling or John,' he said ('growling' refers to doing exactly that while blowing into the horn, an old technique revived in the music by Sanders, Albert Ayler and others around this time). 'John always seemed to have the lyrical, beautiful sweep, and Pharoah at that time, all he could do was – you know, you don't stand next to a man and copy him – so Pharoah was pushed to other areas.'

Born in 1940, Sanders is young enough to name Coltrane, Dolphy and Ornette Coleman as his earliest musical idols. He had an atonal approach to music and was involved in the search for 'human' sounds on his instrument and in extending the range of the saxophone through the use of harmonics. 'John has influenced me in my playing much longer than I've been playing with him,' he told Elisabeth van der Mei in 1967. 'See, John is the kind of person who is trying to create something different all the time … The way John and I play – it's different, we're both natural players and we have our own way of doing things. Somebody like John is playing things on his horn that make you think a lot of things and he makes me think about doing something in my own way.'[7]

Coltrane himself called Sanders an innovator: 'Pharoah is a man of huge spiritual reservoir. He's always trying to reach out to truth. He's trying to allow his spiritual self to be his guide. He's dealing, among other things, in energy, in integrity, in essences. I so much like the *strength* of his playing … it's been my pleasure and privilege that he's been willing to help me, that he is part of the group.'[8]

Another young player whose approach had a substantial influence on Coltrane was Albert Ayler. As the older man told Frank Kofsky: 'He filled an area that it seems I hadn't got to. I think what he's doing, it seems to be moving music into even higher frequencies. Maybe where I left off, maybe where he started, or something.'[9]

Sanders and Ayler, however, were just two of the many musicians who would sit in with the group during this period. Elvin Jones has recalled how he would hear someone playing, look around and see a musician he had never seen before. 'After a point I was almost immune from surprise.' Whenever Coltrane played, it was almost always open house. Archie Shepp, Marion Brown, John Tchicai, Frank Wright and Carlos Ward were just some of the other saxophonists who availed themselves of this privilege, some of them staying on for a while as members of the group. There were also trumpet players, bassists and drummers, all vying for the opportunity to claim they had stayed the course. Fortunately, their eagerness to play fitted in with the leader's own desires. Elvin Jones said: 'His whole concept of music was *something he wanted to hear,* and these people were readily available.'

Unlike certain leaders, jealous of their position, John Coltrane made it his business to see that talented young players received exposure. He offered personal guidance and counsel and, when he came across someone especially deserving, would call up his record producer, Bob Thiele, and ask him to consider their work. I think that if we had signed everyone that John recommended we'd have four hundred musicians on the label,'[10] Thiele once commented.

Rashied Ali, later to join the group as its regular drummer, started sitting in with Coltrane at the Half Note in the early 'sixties. His ego was inflated by the realisation that whenever he turned up, he was always allowed to play. 'So I'm starting to think now, "Goddamn, I must really be a bitch with the drums, because Elvin Jones is the Number One drummer on the scene!" And this is my feeling, my ego shit, and here I am, upsetting this cat every night – in a sense. Actually I wasn't upsetting nobody! It was just gracious of 'Trane to let me play because he heard a different something.'

One night the saxophonist mentioned to Ali that he was preparing to record and would like him to participate. The drummer agreed, but enquired whether he would be the sole percussionist. 'No,' was the reply, 'Elvin's going to be there. He's in the band, man.' Ali: 'I said, "Oh, man, I don't want to make those tapes!" You dig? I'm saying: "Man, I want to play *by myself*" – dig *that!*'

'He looked at me like "all right", then walked up on to the bandstand and started playing. I asked him, "Let me play?" and he said, "Come on."' Despite the young drummer's arrogance, Coltrane paid him after the session as he habitually did whenever impoverished musicians sat in with him. Some time after this, the record *Ascension* appeared. It was a forty-minute-long collective improvisation, the culmination of Coltrane's work at the time, and featured all the musicians who had been regularly sitting in with him. There were two trumpeters (Freddie Hubbard, Dewey Johnson), two altos (Marion Brown, John Tchicai), two tenors (Shepp, Sanders), two bassists (Garrison, Davis), but only one drummer – Elvin Jones.

Five months later, Coltrane recorded with two drummers for the first time. The record was *Kulu Se Mama*. The saxophonist had frequently said that one of the reasons he liked going out to the West Coast was that it gave him the chance to play with Frank Butler, and when Elvin Jones was unable to make the first week of a Los Angeles engagement, Butler was the obvious substitute. To the Kansas City percussionist it was like a dream come true. Despite the reputation for unreliability he had earned himself by this point, the prodigal abruptly reformed. 'I got my wish, I had it all to myself – beautiful McCoy and Jimmy Garrison, and "Little Rock" (that's Pharoah, now). This was the only job where I was *ready.* I was getting dressed two or three hours before it was time to go to work. It was just that fulfilling to work with 'Trane and that group.'

During the week Butler asked Coltrane whether he would consider the possibility of recording with him and Jones as a trio. At the end of the week he put his drums in the dressing-room and went home. He was relaxing, watching television, when the phone rang requesting his presence at the club. He was surprised because he knew Jones was in town by this time, but on his arrival he found their drums set up alongside each other. In the meantime, Coltrane had sent for his old associate from his Chicago days, Donald Garrett, which meant that two bassists and two drummers were on hand to deal.

The impact of such a heavy lineup on the relatively conventional Los Angeles patrons of the It Club was devastating. Ten years later Frank Butler could still recall their reaction: 'Have you ever looked off the stage and seen people's faces like they're just mesmerised? The club was very small, and there's Elvin and I, *bashing*. Elvin's very hard, anyway, and it seemed like that club was going to explode. It was written all over their faces like, "Hey, what *is* this?"'

After the almost mandatory 'drummers' vendetta', Jones and Butler built up a good musical and personal relationship, even playing at a few afterhours sessions together. Coltrane remembered Butler's suggestion, and impressed with their interaction, started planning to cut *Kulu Se Mama* before the quintet left Los Angeles. In October 1965, they went into the studio with Garrett and Butler, Coltrane also adding the vocals and conga drums of Juno Lewis.

When the saxophonist returned from his stay on the West Coast he was set to appear at the Village Gate. Rashied Ali read the announcement, swallowed his pride and called up to ask for a job.* Coltrane pointed out, tactfully, that Jones was still playing. 'That's all right, man, I don't care who's playing. I'd just like to play,' Ali told him. 'He said, "Come on" and he ain't never said nothing about that shit I was into.'

The tension between the two drummers continued, the idea being to see 'who could outbash whom', although eventually this subsided to a degree. Years later, Ali was to put on record how much he had learnt from playing beside Jones, but the older man remained adamant that Ali was more concerned with competing

---

* Ali and Jones actually appeared side by side on Impulse A9110, *Meditations*, recorded in New York on 23 November 1965, shortly after *Kulu Se Mama*.

than complementing the music. Although he allowed that Ali had developed into a 'very efficient, very good percussionist' through working with Coltrane, it was his presence that eventually led to Jones's decision to leave the group.

The feud between the two drummers is related at length to illustrate Coltrane's extraordinary strength and patience and his ability to deal with his fellow musicians in an egalitarian way. Few leaders would have tolerated the kind of arrogance Rashied Ali displayed, but the saxophonist derived a special benefit from his approach to rhythm. Pharoah Sanders said something that echoed his feelings about Ali: 'He makes the rhythm flow around what I'm doing.'[11]

Ascension is generally regarded as a milestone in free music and in Coltrane's constantly developing journey. It had its precedents in Sun Ra's use of collective improvisation, to which Coltrane had been exposed in Chicago through his relationship with saxophonist John Gilmore, and in Ornette Coleman's *Free Jazz* recorded five years previously. The difference was that the rhythm laid down by Jones was freer, and according to one of the participants less restricting, than what Billy Higgins and Edward Blackwell played in Coleman's double quartet. Interestingly, two versions of the piece were recorded. On the first which was released for a while, Jones played in the style he had employed on Coltrane's other recorded work up to this point, but on the second version, released subsequently, his approach to rhythm was much looser, a foretaste of things to come.

To emphasise his own essentially non-competitive nature in contrast to the prevailing 'go-for-self', Coltrane took no more solo time than any of the other musicians. According to Archie Shepp, this was because he did not want 'stars' on the record. It was intended as a group effort, 'Like a New Orleans concept, but with 1965 people.'[12] The musicians were given sketchy thematic material as guidelines on which to superimpose melodies, little time being spent in rehearsal. This was Coltrane's usual pattern. According to Elvin Jones, most of their recordings were made spontaneously or after only the briefest of conferences. Jimmy Garrison remembered a date when Coltrane announced a number he had never even heard. He pointed this out and Coltrane replied, 'Well, you'll be hearing it now,' and proceeded to play it. To Garrison, by giving the musicians responsibility, he increased their confidence. It was this approach that lay behind the creation of *Ascension*, a work that left many a listener baffled while the participants themselves emerged totally fulfilled. By the time the collective improvisation had reached its climax, wrote annotator A. B. Spellman, 'Your nervous system has been dissected, overhauled and reassembled.'[13] It was, said alto saxophonist Marion Brown with justification, the kind of record you could use to heat up the apartment on a cold winter day.

Critics were divided about what was taking place in the Coltrane camp and so were musicians. To Leroy Jenkins, a seasoned musician in Chicago, the situation was confusing. Coltrane and Shepp played at a Festival in Chicago organised by *Down Beat* magazine and his reaction was that they had 'gone crazy' on the stand. 'They were playing this music, screaming and ranting and raving, and, Lord – I was so *drug*. I said, "*What?*"' 'Is that jazz?' his wife demanded. Jenkins faltered for a reply. 'I *dug* Coltrane but I didn't know what was happening. I thought maybe he had lost his cool or something up there or he was just drunk or outraged at the music industry or something.'

Jenkins waited in vain for the next issue of *Down Beat* to appear and confirm his beliefs. Instead, he read that Coltrane and Shepp were the bearers of the flame. 'I was still with Charlie Parker and Sonny Rollins, man. I was saying, "Coltrane can't play!"'

Elvin Jones was in a position to be more decisive. He left the group, closely followed by Tyner, who was replaced by Coltrane's wife Alice. 'I didn't see myself making any kind of contribution to that music. At times I couldn't hear what I was doing – matter of fact, I couldn't hear what anybody was doing! All I could hear was a lot of noise. I didn't have any feeling for the music, and when I don't have any feelings, I don't like to play.'

Alice Coltrane and Rashied Ali stayed with Coltrane up to the time of his death, various other players being added to the nucleus of the group from time to time. Coltrane continued to move forward at his own pace, and was fortunate to have such an exceptional relationship with Bob Thiele, his record producer, that he was able to go into the studio whenever the mood took him. As a result, the steps he made in his career have been documented in a clearer fashion than has been the case with any other musician before or since. There is no telling where he would have ended up had he lived. His music continues to influence young players all over the world on every instrument, not merely the saxophone.

Although the relationship between the members of the original quartet may have seemed to outside observers to have become a stormy one as the time approached for the disintegration of that lineup, in reality they interacted like brothers. Tyner summed up his feelings on the matter shortly after his mentor's death. 'John was sort of like a big brother in a way, someone who would do anything to help me if he could. And I felt that anything I could do to contribute to his concepts, I would do it for him because I had that much respect for him. Let me sum up in this way: if anyone wanted to know how the three of us felt about John, listen to the music and you can hear the love and respect we had for each other. The music really speaks more than any of us can say.'

* * *

John Coltrane was, by all accounts a tremendously dedicated man who lived for the music alone. Despite the fact that his art has been clearly documented, the force within him that was responsible for his monolithic contribution cannot be measured. Often the quartet would travel by road from New York to California, a distance of three thousand miles. Coltrane himself would do most of the driving, then walk straight onto the bandstand without a rest. 'He had so much energy, it was incredible,' said McCoy

Tyner. 'The length of time he played didn't matter. It was of minor concern because of what he had going on musically.'

The saxophonist had a tremendous effect on those who knew him only through his music as well as those who knew him personally. Books have been written about him, poems dedicated to his memory. What he did through his own example, was to give not only the musicians but the Black community as a whole, an example by which they could live. He respected his wife's contribution to the music and started many players thinking about including women in their music. He wanted the best for his musicians and was always trying to get a better deal for them. Jimmy Garrison was the last member of the original quartet to leave. Shortly before Coltrane's death, he spoke to him on the telephone. Despite the feud that had developed between them over the direction the music had taken, the saxophonist told him, 'James, if you ever need anything, call me, man, because I think I could have done better when you guys were in the band.' Garrison reported his reply. 'I said, "Well, John, that's beautiful of you, man, but I don't think anyone could have been fairer than you." He said, "Yeah, thank you, James, but I could have done much better."'

Shortly before his death, Coltrane was planning to open a loft in the Village where the general public could be exposed to the day-to-day developments that were taking place in his music and the work of other players. Ornette Coleman had attempted to do this before, unsuccessfully, and was to do so for a brief period later, but Coltrane's plan was to allow people to walk in off the street and attend rehearsals for the price of a soft drink. His idea was the forerunner of a reality, admission charges aside.

Posthumously, Coltrane has had to live down the idea that he was some kind of saint during his lifetime. He was a serious man, quiet and reserved, but in no way was he a humourless person. 'Everybody's got their image of what people are like,' said Frank Lowe. 'I mean who knows whether Coltrane used to sit down on a Saturday and drink beer and watch the football game? He didn't always be playing the saxophone!' Rumours of Coltrane's unbending nature have been lent credence by the fact that few photographs showing him smiling have been seen, but the reason for this is that his teeth were so bad he was self-conscious about them. In the Jimmy Garrison household, a small snapshot of a smiling Coltrane was tacked to the kitchen wall. 'People really have no idea of what John was like,' said Roberta Garrison. 'But that was him.'

McCoy Tyner, a devout Moslem, saw John Coltrane as a messenger of God. 'There will always be individuals who will make major contributions to music,' he said. 'Nothing is new – it's all been done before in some way, but individuals like John and Bird seem to have been like very strong freers of the music method. John and Bird were really like messengers, but I'm pretty sure there will be other messengers. In other words, God still speaks to man.' Aside from Coltrane's phenomenal contribution to the music, the principles he stood for, and his dedication, gave not only the musicians but every young Black who questioned the status quo something to think about. He was not just a musician to raise kids by, he became a person by which to raise oneself.

Archie Shepp summed up the general feeling in an interview with Phyl Garland of *Ebony* magazine on the occasion of Coltrane's death. 'He was a bridge, the most accomplished of the so-called post-bebop musicians to make an extension into what is called the avant-garde. I met him when I was still a student at Goddard College and he took the time to talk to me. It was time for that sort of thing, for the younger men to begin to have that sort of exchange with their elders. He was one of the few of the older men to demonstrate a sense of responsibility toward those coming behind him. He provided a positive image that was greatly needed and stood against the destructive forces that might have claimed so many. Having suffered and seen so much himself, he tried to see that others coming along wouldn't have to go through all that.

'Perhaps many didn't understand his music – the sort of thing he was doing in his last two years, not the earlier things for which he was known best – and they might not understand the music we are creating now, but it is truly a reflection of our times, as much as the spirituals were of their time, or Leadbelly. 'Trane's music exemplified his feeling for what *is* and he accomplished a great deal for the short time he was left with us – much more than most do in a lifetime. He left the scene a little different and I believe John's death has drawn us, as musicians, closer together, has brought us closer to a kind of unity. This is the way we must assess a great man.'[14]

Notes

1 Quoted in Nat Hentoff's notes to *Albert Ayler Live in Greenwich Village* (Impulse A-9155).
2 John Storm Roberts, *Black Music of Two Worlds,* London, 1973, p. 28.
3 Interview with Bob Palmer, 'Chasin' the 'Trane Out of Memphis', *Down Beat,* 10 October 1974.
4 Interview by Tony Cummings, 'Tyner Sells In', *Black Music,* March 1975.
5 Joe Goldberg, *Jazz Masters of the Fifties,* New York, 1965, p. 206.
6 Vladimir Simosko and Barry Tepperman, *Eric Dolphy: A Musical Biography and Discography,* Washington, D.C., 1974, p. 87.
7 Elisabeth van der Mei, 'Pharoah Sanders: A Philosophical Conversation', *Coda,* July 1967.
8 Quoted in Nat Hentoff's notes to *Live at the Village Vanguard Again* (ABC-Impulse A-9124).
9 Frank Kofsky, *Black Nationalism and the Revolution in Music,* New York, 1970.
10 'The New Wave. Bob Thiele Talks to Frank Kofsky About John Coltrane', in *Coda,* May 1968.
11 Elisabeth van der Mei, op. cit.
12 Liner-notes to *Ascension* (ABC-Impulse A-95).
13 ibid.
14 Phyl Garland, *The Sound of Soul,* Chicago, 1969, pp. 229–30.

3

Cecil Taylor – Eighty-Eight Tuned Drums

Anybody's music is made up of a lot of things that are not musical.
Music is an attitude, a group of symbols of a way of life, whether
you're conscious of it or not … And of course, it naturally
reflects the social and economic and educational attitudes of
the players. And that's why the fools don't think I play jazz.[1]

Cecil Taylor

If you wanted to hear Cecil Taylor in the 1960s, it was necessary to
know that at 11 p.m. in a certain loft on a dingy, unlit street somewhere in lower Manhattan, the man would be giving a concert.
Cecil Taylor has been playing his intense, uncompromising music
and going his own way for more than twenty years now, but until
very recently the fact of his genius was one of the best-kept secrets
in town.

Chris White, a bass player who rose to prominence with Dizzy
Gillespie in the 1960s and is now involved in education, played
gigs with Taylor intermittently from 1954 to 1960.* He made a
cogent summing-up of the pianist's situation during that period,
a situation that was, incidentally, to continue well into the next
decade.

'Cecil was forced to work in places where he shouldn't have had

---

* He also appears on the United Artists album *Love for Sale,* re-released in 1975
as half of the double-album *In Transition* (Blue Note BN-LA458-H2).

to work. And it wasn't because nobody recognised his genius, it was because *Black genius* isn't recognised – period, in this country. I hate to break it down that simple, but I played a lot of gigs with Cecil where *then* I knew Cecil didn't belong. I knew that then and Cecil knew it, and that's what got Cecil. And he wasn't making any money, either. So when he stopped playing those places, he was forced to take other jobs to survive.'

In 1975, though, Cecil Taylor appeared with his trio for three weeks at the revamped Five Spot on St Mark's Place, and the line stretched around the corner. When they played a return engagement, the curiosity seekers had dwindled slightly in number, but still a substantial audience continued to show up each night for another three weeks.

For years Taylor has been considered the underground genius of the keyboard, the first musician of any importance to introduce atonality into so-called jazz. This means music in which a key-centre, or note in the scale to which everything gravitates when it comes to rest, is absent. It is important because it represents the further development of harmony in jazz. By employing extreme chromaticism, that is, using notes outside the music's key, the artist gains a richer harmonic vocabulary, rather like a language that has more words. Eventually the composer introduces so many notes into the key that a point is reached where the piece appears to be in no particular key.

At every stage in his development, Taylor has played with total sureness and the tremendous drive that is his hallmark. Sometimes he will have several melodies going on at once, all of them in different keys, and even the musicians who play with him are only able to keep up with him and complement what he is doing as a result of the hours they have put in working together in private. A major revolutionary in the musical revolution, yet his fate, until recently, was to be tucked away in the farthest corner of a music that is still considered by many to be obscure.

Cecil Taylor struggled for years, supporting himself with a

succession of menial jobs because his music aroused animosity from club-owners who were unable to sell drinks to an audience engrossed in his all-consuming fire and passion. He always had an audience, but as several musicians have noted, the music of Cecil Taylor is not a particularly encouraging backdrop for sexual overtures, the opportunity for which is one of the factors for successfully operating a nightclub. I know of one woman, temporarily left alone by her husband, who was propositioned by the man beside her while Taylor was playing. Her only reaction was amazement. Where his followers are concerned, there is nowhere else to be other than with him when Taylor is in action.

The Cecil Taylor musical experience is still so demanding, however, that it tends to exhaust those listeners accustomed to more simple fare. Even his own players realise this. 'I think the music is to a point now where the nightclub can't handle it,' says saxophonist Jimmy Lyons. 'It has to be pushed culturally because it is an advanced music; I don't think it can be approached right in.'

Furthermore, the appeal of the pianist has remained sufficiently esoteric for one of his erstwhile drummers to actually regret their association. 'Working with Cecil Taylor was the worst thing that ever happened to me,' declared Sunny Murray, standing outside the packed Five Spot. Murray's free approach to percussion blossomed in the Taylor trio of the early 'sixties when they shared the Five Spot bandstand on several occasions, but now, unable to find work with his own group, he could hardly conceal his bitterness. The coupling of his name with someone as 'far-out' as Taylor was somehow, he reasoned, responsible for his own unjust neglect. 'I became stereotyped in that role and no one wanted to hear me play. I was a good bebop drummer before Cecil. Really – I should have stayed with that.'

It was at the Five Spot in 1956 that the audience for Cecil Taylor's music first became established. It is said, in fact, that it was he who was responsible for changing the bar's clientele, transforming it from a 15-cents-a-beer joint, into a meeting place for celebrated writers and painters. His trio was originally hired to accompany a multi-instrumentalist named Dick Wetmore. Buell Neidlinger was the bassist on the occasion. He later went on to play with the Boston Symphony Orchestra as well as Frank Zappa, but regards his experience with Cecil Taylor as the most important musical event of his life. 'Cecil ran (Wetmore) off the gig the first night. It was a Friday and Cecil started to play some shit behind this guy that was really *out*, you know, and the cat left all his violins and stuff on the piano – came back to get them later.'[2]

In 1975 during a brief period of reopening, the Five Spot was proud to be known as 'the home of jazz on the Lower East Side', but originally it was an old Bowery bar, with the bandstand cramped into the corner beside a strong-smelling toilet. A not unusual reflection of what Chris White would call the way Black genius is treated in America. Much was made in the press of the fact that the pianist was making a 'triumphant return' to the club, little attention being paid to the fact that for a long time the owners had steadfastly refused to rehire him due to the inordinate (to them) length of his sets. Nevertheless, on this latest occasion, Taylor was allowed to play uninterrupted for as long as two hours. The audience listened intently, wrapped up in his every move, and, presumably, spending enough money on drinking to make the owners happy. Black genius, it seemed, was at last coming into its own. This time, too there were several musicians who turned up to sit in with Taylor, among them, for one unforgettable night, the flamboyant trumpeter from St Louis, Lester Bowie. (His contribution, and the response it sparked from Taylor, should have been mandatory listening for the dissenters who put the pianist outside the Afro-American tradition.)

Other young players waited in the wings, saxophone cases tenderly clasped beneath their arms, eager to jump in at the deep end and stay the course with one of the founding fathers of the new music. Taylor allowed some of them to join him, others he chided gently, the suggestion being that they were not quite ready to make the concessions his music demanded. Superficially, it might appear that energy is all the hopeful young player needs in order to add his voice to the trio, but as anyone who has listened carefully will realise, Jimmy Lyons and drummer Andrew Cyrille have actually been studying the pianist for years and are well equipped to respond to his every move. Cyrille, who first played with Taylor in 1958, worked regularly with him from 1964 to 1975. In Lyons's case, he has been echoing and complementing Taylor since 1961, effectively his first and only professional job of any importance. 'Playing with Cecil made me think differently about what music's about,' said Lyons. 'It's not about any cycle of fifths, it's about *sound*.'

Everything the group plays has been organised and carefully planned. Cyrille, the perfectionist, even uses a metronome in rehearsal. The first hour is spent warming up, then Taylor gives the musicians a few notes from a piece he has been working on. 'We'll play – or attempt to play it – and eventually we'll start getting together certain sections of the tune,' said Jimmy Lyons. 'Except for the solo sections – they're all your own.'

'Writing music down seems to me another way of transmitting ideas,' says Taylor, 'and to me, it doesn't seem to be of the utmost importance how the ideas are transmitted as long as they are transmitted. I use different ways, but one thing I feel is that music is a head game, and the idea is that all things that prevent complete absorption of the sound should be cut away as much as possible. So of course we've devised different ways of organising the music, to get to musicians very quickly so that they can absorb the ideas and get it playing around in their heads and operating.'

The fact remains that enthusiasm among musicians other than an enlightened handful is only a relatively recent occurrence. Steve Lacy played soprano saxophone with him for six years, Archie Shepp was there for two, Sam Rivers stayed for five. The bass players have included Buell Neidlinger, Henry Grimes and Alan Silva, but in twenty years of travelling his own road, Taylor has only found three drummers sufficiently broad-minded to accommodate his refusal to play the obvious. And that is very important. The fact that Taylor plays the piano like a percussion instrument himself is irrelevant. He has stated that among the first people to impress him were the Duke Ellington drummer Sonny Greer (a family friend) and another great drummer, the bandleader Chick Webb. Like most children, he fantasised about becoming a drummer, collecting pots and pans from the kitchen and beating on them in imitation of Webb, and for a while he studied with a neighbour who played percussion with the NBC Symphony Orchestra. Critics who saw Taylor mainly as a product of the conservatory – and he has studied extensively – overlooked the extent of his drum-orientation. The great pianists of the past, people like the 'stride' master Willie 'The Lion' Smith, and Fats Waller and Art Tatum, were highly regarded for their ability to produce a full keyboard sound and sustain momentum without the benefit of bass and drums, but Cecil Taylor is different. He has often performed in a solo context but he *needs* drums, he *likes* drums. His collaboration with the percussionist is an Afro-American collaboration, an interweaving of polyrhythms. Those who analyse Taylor's music to compare it with parallel developments in European forms might have been rather taken aback to witness Cecil Taylor, circa 1975, cupping his hands around his mouth and exchanging neo-African hollers and chants with his percussionist, Andrew Cyrille. 'The more I play, the more I become aware of the non-European aspects of the music,' says Taylor.[3]

Rashied Ali never worked in public with Taylor, but he relates an anecdote that illustrates the sheer physical power of his playing: 'I bought this piano and it was second-hand, but a good one. Cecil was in the building at the time the piano came and as I wanted somebody to play it to find out what it was like, he came up. I was practising at the time so he walked around the room for a few minutes, and then he sat at the piano and we played from about 12 at night close to about five in the morning, straight through without any letup. Every now and then I would look over at the piano and Cecil would make like a run down the piano, man, and the keys would be shooting out of the piano like bullets! They were just flying past me! I would look and I'd drop my head because my piano was being really messed around. Cecil is a very strong pianist. It's not that he's the kind of pianist that just wrecks pianos, it's just that the piano was old and it couldn't stand the way he'd strike those keys. I had to get a whole new set of keys but he really broke that piano in for me, man!'

'In white music the most admired touch among pianists is light. The same is true among white percussionists,' says Taylor. 'We in Black music think of the piano as a percussive instrument: we beat the keyboard, we get inside the instrument. Europeans admire Bill Evans for his touch. But the physical force going into the making of Black music – if that is misunderstood, it leads to screaming …'[4]

Rudy Collins, a drummer who was later to form a teaching partnership with Chris White, played concerts with Taylor in 1959 and took part in the United Artists date. A few others, including Milford Graves and Tony Williams, have put in brief appearances, but the first percussionist to stay for any length of time was Dennis Charles, a self-taught drummer from the Virgin Islands, well-grounded in West Indian rhythms but otherwise inexperienced. The second was Sunny Murray, in whom Taylor recognised a potential overlooked by others, and who developed as the leading innovator in free drumming during their association. Andrew Cyrille was the third, a well-schooled percussionist, respected by his peers for his grasp of the rudiments, and essentially a 'clean', that is, technically accomplished, player as opposed to his predecessors. Interestingly, where Murray and Charles came to Taylor from 'out of the streets', Cyrille's background included the church and a thorough professional grounding working with musicians as diverse as Mary Lou Williams, Ahmed Abdul-Malik, Coleman Hawkins and Freddie Hubbard.

In discussions centring on the pianist's music and lifestyle, his involvement with the dance has frequently been mentioned. Taylor has often said that if he did not play the piano he would be a dancer – I try to imitate on the piano the leaps in space a dancer makes,'[5] he has said. When Andrew Cyrille first started rehearsing with him, Taylor asked him to define his conception of rhythm. 'I think the thing that rang the bell was when I said that I think of rhythm in terms of dance. At that time I was very much into learning and playing for dancers. I was playing dance classes for modern dancers, and that's where my head was. So to some degree, that was one of the first things that came out of my mouth. And it was the truth, too, because at that time I was making a lot of shapes in terms of what I felt – or what I had seen the body able to do – and with the vocabulary that some of these dancers had. So I was able to make music for them to move their bodies by, and sometimes the shapes would be very different.'

On one wall of the relatively spacious loft that Cecil Taylor occupies today hangs a framed photograph of the great Black dancer Baby Lawrence, his legs flung sideways in a stylish leap. Alongside it are studies of more formal dance companies, for Taylor's preoccupation with the dance embraces both popular and 'legitimate' forms. (He is, in fact, just as likely to be discovered dancing at a Manhattan disco as at the ballet.) He himself has involved dancers in his performances from time to time and has also written for the ballet.

This combination of instrumental music with the dance is, of course, in the African tradition, a tradition of which Taylor is acutely aware. The naked man who danced down the aisles during a concert he gave at New York's Hunter College, executing his own 'leaps in space' as he interpreted the music, may well have owed more to Alvin Ailey than he did to, say, Yoruba ritual, but not necessarily so. Time was when writers expressed amusement when Thelonious Monk got up from the piano and proceeded to dance around it, yet all he was doing was reasserting his feeling for a culture where the two arts are inseparable. After all, we read that Charley Patton, the so-called 'founder' of Mississippi delta blues, would dance around his guitar as part of his stock-in-trade in the early part of this century.[6] Years later, Milford Graves can be seen doing the same thing. His predilection for dancing around his drumset has influenced some young players to do likewise. In Taylor's case, he not only likes his drummers to play like dancers, he encourages the musicians to shape the music, too, 'to make it more of a living organism', as Andrew Cyrille put it.

Cecil Taylor was the first innovator to come to the music without the benefit of an immediate grounding in the blues. John Coltrane and Ornette Coleman had both played in blues bands, certainly all their predecessors had done so, but Taylor, with a background of conservatory training, was often rejected because of it. First of all, he employed a staggering technique. His use of extreme chromaticism – that is, playing every note on the keyboard so that he could be in any key – made it obvious that here was someone who was very knowledgeable. Furthermore, he rushed all over the keyboard, hitting each note with an intense, percussive touch, as if they were eighty-eight tuned drums. But technique and talent, as Taylor himself is quick to point out, are not necessarily one and the same.

'Anybody having the desire and the economic means to subsidise that desire, can master technique,' he said, 'and the techniques of classical music are all standardised. They change every twenty years or so. The thing that makes jazz so interesting is that each man is his own academy. If he's really going to be persuasive, he learns about other academies, but the idea is that he must have that special thing.'

Taylor graduated from the New England Conservatory of Music, where he had to contend with teachers – he calls them 'clerks' – who, with the arrogance familiar to every Black musician who has ever studied formally, belittled his interest in traditions other than European. His deliberate decision to get out into the New York streets and make up for lost time when he arrived back from Boston has often been mentioned. 'You need everything you can get,' Duke Ellington has been quoted as saying. 'You need the conservatory with an ear to what's happening in the streets.' Taylor is said to have been impressed with that statement. 'The reality was, you come back and you work in Harlem,' he told Joe Goldberg. 'You go there and try to get gigs, you come to grips with Miles Davis, come to grips with the evolution of language, where contemporary jazz is going, as well as being aware of other musics.'[7] The problem is, he said, 'To utilise the energies of the European composers, their technique, so to speak, *consciously*, and blend this with the traditional music of the American Negro, and to create a new energy. And was it unique? No. Historically not. This is what has always happened. Ellington did it.'[8] Eventually he worked with a small group led by the Ellington saxophonist Johnny Hodges, and also with the trumpeter Hot Lips Page, one of the finest blues exponents of his era.

Although Taylor's move was carefully considered, the fact was that the blues was there already. He grew up listening to his father singing shouts and hollers that went back farther than the blues, and although his family attended a middle-class church, he was well aware of the Sanctified one around the corner, The densely layered textures of Taylor's music often make it hard for people to hear his roots; but they are all there. 'Cecil once explained his playing by saying he's like Horace Silver,' said Ted Curson, a trumpeter who worked with him briefly. 'You can hear that Horace is not so much of a pianist as a cat who plays soulful and has drive in what he is doing. The few notes that he plays have a definitiveness about them. Cecil Taylor is like that only he plays all over the keyboard.'

Taylor said: 'There are two cats, two pianists, that they never talk about in relation to myself which I think is unfortunate, the two being Bud Powell and Horace Silver. I listened to them a lot because, in a way, Monk was the most difficult to get to, to *hear* and to listen to what he was doing.' On the early recordings the Powell influence is noticeable; and today you can hear Ellington, you can hear Erroll Garner, a particular favourite of his, you can hear Africa and you can hear the blues. But above all, you can hear Cecil Taylor.

In 1954, the Miles Davis Blue Note recording of *The Leap* with Horace Silver on piano had just been released, and all the musicians were studying it in order to play in a comparable style. ('Cecil was playing it, too,' said Chris White, 'But he wasn't playing it *that* way.') White himself was just out of high school and had only been playing bass for a year and a half. He received a phone-call from a tenor player named Floyd Benny to make a gig at Connie's Five Star Inn, the Harlem bar just across the street from Small's Paradise at 134th Street and Lenox Avenue. When he arrived, he discovered that the other member of the ill-matched team was Cecil Taylor.

'Floyd Benny was a rock-and-roll show tenor player, he played sort of mealy-mouthed. He worked on USO shows and camp tours in Alaska and so on, and it was very strange, him and Cecil. It was Floyd's gig and Cecil was barely in. I mean he was playing strange harmonies. He really played fabulous, but we were only playing standards because that was the kind of music that was happening at the time – you got to the club and you played a tune. Cecil was playing harmonies where you barely could hear any relationship with the harmonies that were part of that particular tune. But I didn't know what the right harmonies were, anyway, so I just followed him. The music sounded very *out* and the people Uptown were very upset!'

In those days, every other Harlem bar boasted a trio or quartet and it was common practice for musicians to sit in. Connie's Inn, where Fletcher Henderson's Orchestra once held sway, was a favourite place for jam sessions. Dennis Charles had come to New York to join his mother at the age of eleven, but a brush with the law in his late teens took him out of circulation for two years. He played trombone while he was in prison, and on his release devoted himself to the drums. He played in a calypso band each Friday, and listened to Art Blakey records, and he practised so much that his mother got the landlord to put him out of the basement. When he felt he had taught himself enough to venture onto the elitist jazz scene, he made his way to the local bars. One night he walked into Connie's Inn, where he discovered a handful of drummers sitting around, pouring scorn on the slightly-built man sitting at the piano.

'Everybody was laughing and telling each other how crazy Cecil was. They really put him down; they didn't dig Cecil *at all*,' he recalled. 'And I was shocked because you never had a chance to play there, all the drummers would be fighting to get up on the bandstand.'

When Taylor took a break, Charles asked if he could sit in. 'He was shocked – here was somebody who wanted to play with him. So he said, "Yeah, come on," and the next set we got up and played. And he was *gassed*. You know, we had a ball. He took my address, phone number and everything, and invited me down to his house.'

Eventually, Benny lost his five-dollars-a-night gig to a more adventurous, bar-walking tenor player known as Frank 'Floor-Show' Culley, whose specialities included taking his horn out in the street, and strolling into the ladies' bathroom where he thought nothing of blowing up the women's skirts. It was all good training for Taylor. By the end of the six weeks the combination endured, Dennis Charles was playing on a regular basis and 'Taylor was playing the D flat blues.'

White and Taylor continued to gig together despite the fact that, as the bassist admitted, he was still learning to play and was not yet ready for Taylor's music. Their relationship dissolved as a result of increasing disagreements which had nothing to do with music, and Buell Neidlinger, who had come across the pianist in Boston during their student days, became more important in Taylor's life. Where Dennis Charles was concerned, his musical development was at the stage where he was eager to play with anyone. He was catapulted into the world of Cecil Taylor with no idea of what he was letting himself in for, but he stayed there for several years.

He grew from the straightforward boppish drummer to be heard on Taylor's first date for Transition into the self-assured weaver of polyrhythms heard to his best advantage on tracks taped with Steve Lacy's group in 1963 and released eight years later.*

'What turned me on to Cecil at first was that he had so much energy. After playing with him for a while I was sort of in a fog. It was so much, it was *too* much. I never heard anything like that before, and after a while I didn't like it no more. I wouldn't know what to do, it was just over my head. The first couple of weeks, I thought Cecil was really crazy. After I started going to his house, we played a few places and I'd listen to what he was doing or some tunes he would write, and I would say to myself, "This cat's got to be crazy." I mean, it was *so much*.'

Charles finally came to terms with Taylor one night when the pianist played a particularly demanding piece and left him totally confused as to what to play on the drums. 'I kept saying to myself, "Well, he can't repeat that." (We were rehearsing the tune and he had his music in front of him on the piano.) I kept saying, "He's making it up," but it dawned on me as we kept playing it over and over that Cecil knew what he was doing. It was a helluva tune. He kept repeating passages till it dawned on me and he really opened my head up. It's the same for listeners, I know, and I went through the same phase. He was too powerful, man. A lot of the times I didn't know what to do.'

Now that Taylor had found a drummer who could follow him, albeit clumsily at first, the two men started working frequently together. They teamed up for West Indian dances, and they played for cocktail sips in Harlem with a trumpeter called Johnny Capers, a man Taylor has credited with helping to develop his strength and confidence. Dennis Charles described him: 'He dug Satchmo [Louis Armstrong], the handkerchief and everything. Can you

* *School Days* (Emanem 3316) by the Steve Lacy Quartet: Lacy (soprano sax), Roswell Rudd (trombone), Henry Grimes (bass), Dennis Charles (drums).

imagine him and Cecil on piano and no bass – just the drums? Johnny had these gigs on Sunday afternoons, and he would sing like Satchmo, and play the trumpet like him, and Cecil would play the bass line with his left hand. Cecil was good at that; he loves that.'

Soprano saxophonist Steve Lacy, who had entered the picture around the same time as Charles, confirmed this. 'Sometimes we'd play for dancers and there'd be no bass, so he'd play the bass on the piano – he was a great bass player, too.'[9] The power of Taylor's left hand has always been in evidence, pushing, stabbing, often repetitive as he plays the piano like a drum. He frequently continues playing the theme with his left hand while dashing all over the keyboard with his right in a flurry of arpeggios. His vocabulary may be a little different, but in terms of what he is actually saying, he talks the same language as the rent-party piano players and 'stride' masters of an earlier era.

Taylor plucked Steve Lacy from out of a group led by the traditional pianist Dick Wellstood. His first question: 'How come a young fellow like you is playing Dixieland?'[10] Lacy was somewhat taken aback; he did not think of himself as that young, and secondly, he had never considered playing anything else. Yet he was to become one of the most important exponents of his instrument and was, apparently, the inspiration behind Coltrane taking up the soprano saxophone. Their first job together was with Calo Scott, the brilliant 'cellist whose career was abruptly terminated by a stroke a few years back. As in Taylor's relationships with his other protégés, 'working' meant playing a variety of dances and bar-room jobs as well as spending extensive time in rehearsal. Lacy was involved in Taylor's first recording, 'Jazz Advance', which, made for Transition in 1955, was the earliest example of the new music to find its way on to record. In 1966, Lacy said: 'Taylor seemed to be right in the tradition, and he still does to me. As for harmony, he showed me that harmony was colour, and I found I understood his colour right away.'[11] Since then, Lacy has gone on to develop his own increasingly ascetic music. He often appears in a solo context, appropriate for a player who has pared away the inessentials. There is no reason to suppose that he has changed his mind in his conclusions about his mentor.

To some ears, Dennis Charles seemed to be at odds with Taylor's more sophisticated approach. True, he had none of Murray's intuitive flair for making rhythm appear to lose its meaning, but he played *time* drums in a style that few have equalled. On records like *Looking Ahead!* made for Contemporary in 1958 with Lacy's replacement, the late Earl Griffiths on vibes, Charles's brilliantly tuned drums and eager attack are a joy to hear, and stand in vivid contrast to the rather stodgy and conventional bass of Buell Neidlinger. 'He does beautiful things with a cymbal,' said Taylor in the liner-notes to that album. 'Like all the great drummers, he can touch the top of a table with his finger and make music.'[12] 'I try to play like a horn with my left hand while the right keeps time,'[13] Charles explained.

The actual *sound* that Dennis Charles produced was a foretaste of things to come. His rimshots, for example, are a glorious mixture of the prevailing Blakey influence and the kind of rat-a-tat fills used by many a Caribbean percussionist which have become a part of the universal repertoire through the popularity of reggae. On *Air*, which was made for Candid in 1961 and originally issued as *The World of Cecil Taylor*, there is such a delicious urgency about the way Charles trades fours with the pianist, that he is propelled from his seat in the rhythm-section right into the frontline (that is, if we regard the piano as a horn).

Archie Shepp, who plays saxophone on two of the tracks, was making his recording debut, although it was not until he ran into the pianist on the street the day before the session took place that he realised his presence was required. Steve Lacy had told him of the pianist's interest but he did not really take him seriously. When they did eventually play together, however, Shepp felt 'peculiarly sensitive' to Taylor's direction. Before that point he had never attempted to play without using chords. Suddenly he realised just how limiting his experience had been.

When he started playing with Taylor, Dennis Charles owned only a snare drum. He relied on using his brother's drums until the group opened at the Five Spot in 1957. Buell Neidlinger bought him a set for the occasion. Archie Shepp had become a regular member of Taylor's group by the time they appeared onstage together in Jack Gelber's play *The Connection*, and it was through playing together nightly for a considerable period that Charles and Neidlinger finally got under the skin of Taylor's music.

Ironically, the group started to disintegrate at the same time. 'I regret the way it broke up with Cecil, man, after all the years of playing with him,' said Charles. 'He'll tell you, Buell'll tell you, too. After all the years it really started happening. I really started feeling exceptionally comfortable. And it's funny, as soon as I got inside of it, everybody started hollerin' at each other. I don't know why.'

* * *

Up until the time that *Looking Ahead!* was recorded, Taylor was still working with chord changes, although his dissonance was growing. He used an orthodox musical framework in as much as he played songs with twelve- or thirty-two-bar choruses, but his twelve-bar blues, recorded at the Newport Jazz Festival in 1957, is so dissonant that both the chord changes and bar-lines have disappeared. By the time he and Sunny Murray started playing together in the early 1960s, Taylor himself was completely harmonically free and the beat, as such, was reduced to a feeling rather than a deliberate 1-2-3-4 pulse. A chance meeting in a West Village coffee-house brought the two outcasts together: Murray, who was constantly being accused of turning the beat around, Taylor, the pianist who broke up every session. 'All the dudes immediately started packing up,' Sunny Murray told Robert Levin, 'and when I asked them why, they said, "You don't know Cecil Taylor. The way he plays, can't *nobody* get together with him." Well, you know, I've always admired a cat that stood out in a crowd because it meant he was – very useful! He was a necessity. He wasn't one to shun, he was one to dig. And I thought, if you pack up when a man comes in to play then he must be *something*. Let some more come in that make you pack up and I'll be around some really good musicians.'[14]

Eventually, Murray replaced Dennis Charles, although when Jimmy Lyons first met Taylor in 1961, he and Charles were working as a duo in another Greenwich Village coffee-house. Archie Shepp was still a member of the group during this period, Neidlinger eventually being replaced by Henry Grimes, who was to play intermittently with the pianist until leaving New York in 1966.

In 1962 when Cecil Taylor decided to go to Europe for the first time, only Lyons and Murray accompanied him. They spent six months there altogether, playing in Oslo and Stockholm, then recorded two important albums during an engagement at the Café Montmartre in Copenhagen. The open-ended drumming concept employed by Murray was highly significant and the appearance of the first of these albums was the earliest indication of the existence of such a revolutionary approach to rhythm. While they were in Stockholm, tenor saxophonist Albert Ayler made himself known to Taylor. He followed the trio to Denmark and played with them at the Montmartre. By the time they returned to America, Ayler was involved with the pianist on the basis of mutual exploration, but once again, there was little work. Flushed with their European success, the musicians expected an improvement. It was, in fact, almost a year before they actually worked again. A 1963 concert at Lincoln Center was the last time that either Ayler or Murray played with Taylor. (Murray's vital contribution to the work of both men is discussed later.)

Taylor's recorded output has, in the main, concentrated on trios and quartets, his usual working format, although he sometimes expands his personnel for concerts. In 1964 he worked with two basses for the first time, with the addition of the young Alan Silva who was studying with trumpeter/composer Bill Dixon. Although the two-basses concept had been established for at least four years, it still proved a deterrent for some players. Silva found working with Taylor too demanding at first, but when he decided to concentrate on the bow, he was able to develop certain *arco* techniques that fitted perfectly with Henry Grimes's intricate *pizzicato*. On 'Unit Structures', recorded by a septet, and 'Conquistador', which includes Bill Dixon in the personnel, the two bassists interact almost demonically at times, a relationship they were to continue to expand with Albert Ayler. As far as the prodigious Grimes was concerned, he and the pianist shared an empathy that was, according to Andrew Cyrille, 'like radar'.

Since this period Taylor has continued to explore his own innovations with men like Jimmy Lyons and Andrew Cyrille and the tenor saxophonists Sam Rivers and David Ware and, during the three years he was involved in education, with members of the student body.

* * *

Ten years ago, in 1967, Cecil Taylor sat in his cluttered apartment, sandwiched between noisy, grimy warehouses on West 22nd Street, discussing the possibilities available to the Black artist on reaching the top of a decidedly shaky tree. Paul Chambers, the brilliant bassist from Detroit who came to prominence with Miles Davis, had recently died, hardly into his thirties, and Taylor, being only too aware of the losing battle facing the creative Black artist, was embittered. 'Jazz is certainly one of the strongest art forms at the moment in terms of player potential,' he said. 'It's related to the others in that there are only a certain small percentage of people who are shapers of the form, but in that jazz is really the expression of the Afro-American community, it would seem to me that the toll might even be greater. The death of the people is so great and so shocking and so quick and so soon – and I don't mean the physical death necessarily.

'First, this is a materialistic society and no one ever asked you to be involved in spiritual values. If you are, you have to accept the responsibility of that, and if you're a Black man, this is complicated in many, many different ways. This also means that it is more difficult, finally, for a man like Paul Chambers *to* live, because unless he has like an awareness which doesn't necessarily arrive in a place like Detroit, chances are that the greater the contribution you make, you're not even remembered except by people that are old enough or have happened to be on the scene.

'What's available? I'll tell you what's available – it's despair which results from, like, there's no place to go. When you have a tremendous talent like Paul had and you've played with Miles Davis, I mean what do you do then? You know, there is no foundation, for instance, that will give you a grant to say, well, go off in a room or hire your own band and just practise and develop the idea. There are only clubs and club-owners who couldn't care less.'

It was not possible to foresee at the time Taylor was speaking that the alternative means of survival he proposed would actually become available for some so-called 'jazz' musicians. In the early 1970s, however, the pianist inherited Bill Dixon's post as Visiting Professor at the University of Madison, Wisconsin, where one of his students included a former Motown drummer, and some time later, received a Guggenheim fellowship. When he spent two years at Antioch College in Ohio, he created an unprecedented situation by taking Jimmy Lyons and Andrew Cyrille with him as Artists-in-Residence. At the same time he continued playing his own music. An ideal situation wherein he has found his own way to escape the ghetto, yet despite the many accolades he has received, Taylor has always held a realistic view of the position of the Black artist in American society.

Cecil Taylor's recent career is proof that justice does exist for some, albeit usually long overdue when it comes. In 1976 he returned exhausted from an extended European tour during which he played at just about every festival. There was enough work available for him to stay on for another two months, but his main concern in going back to New York City was to look for a new drummer. It was business as usual in the life of the itinerant musician.

Relaxing from the rigours of three months on the road, he discussed the reverse side of the success coin with particular reference to Gladys Knight, one of his favourite singers who has, in the vernacular, 'gone to Hollywood' (tamed down her music for a wider appeal). 'Success makes people less fiery,' said Taylor. 'Somehow they become more *amiable.*' In his own case, though, such a reaction is doubtful. Maybe he has become more relaxed as an individual, maybe the struggle to survive has become less acute, but his determination remains. At the keyboard itself, Taylor is unrelenting. His music, likewise, continues to surge forth with an almost desperate intensity, a formidable expression of Black genius at its greatest.

Notes

1   Joe Goldberg, *Jazz Masters of the Fifties,* New York, 1965, p. 213.
2   Alan Heineman, 'The Many Sides of Buell Neidlinger', *Down Beat Yearbook 1972.*
3   Gary Giddins, 'An American Master Brings the Voodoo Home', *Village Voice,* 28 April 1975.
4   John Litweiler, 'Needs and Acts: Cecil Taylor in Wisconsin', *Down Beat,* 14 Oct. 1971.
5   Goldberg, op. cit., p. 215.
6   John Fahey, *Charley Patton,* London, 1970, p. 26.
7   Goldberg, op. cit., pp. 214–15.
8   ibid.
9   Interview by Martin Davidson, 'The Great Big Beautiful Sounds of Steve Lacy', *Into Jazz,* May 1974.

10 Interview with Max Harrison, 'Musicians Talking', *Jazz Monthly*, March 1966.

11 ibid.

12 Quoted in Nat Hentoff's liner-notes to *Looking Ahead!* (Contemporary LAC 12216).

13 ibid.

14 Robert Levin and Pauline Rivelli (eds), *The Black Giants*, New York and Cleveland, 1970, p. 59.

4

Ornette Coleman – The Art of the Improviser

The first time we played at Ornette's house, the music startled
me; I'd never heard anything like it before … I learned more
about listening (from) playing with Ornette than I ever
learned in my life from anyone, because to play with him
you have to listen completely to everything he plays.[1]

Charlie Haden

One afternoon back in the early 'fifties, Ornette Coleman and the
New Orleans drummer Edward Blackwell were playing together
in the living-room of Coleman's house in Los Angeles. Blackwell,
already a respected and experienced drummer, was adept at the
conventional style that prevailed at the time: when he played a
piece of music written in the 32-bar song-form, his usual procedure
was to complete a chorus with a pressroll on his snare drum on the
'turn-around', then go back to the beginning and start again. On
this particular occasion Coleman stopped playing and put down
his saxophone. 'Why did you do that?' he asked Blackwell. 'Why
did you end my phrase?' What he meant was that if he played a
line which through its own melodic logic carried over the limit
set by the formal 32-bar structure, the other musicians involved
should *play out the phrase* rather than sticking to the form.

This freedom to play unhampered by the restrictions of four-,
eight- or twelve-bar units was one of the factors that established
Ornette Coleman as the first truly 'free' musician. It also led to a

considerable degree of confusion among musicians who had been educated in the belief that improvisation must be contained within a relatively rigid framework. Coleman abolished pre-ordained harmonic structures from his music (that is, chord changes and keys) and, implicitly, bar-lines. Cecil Taylor had done this, too, but whereas some critics see Taylor's approach as a further sophistication of the European borrowings made by African-American music, Coleman's emphasis on the melodic invention was a rejection of these borrowings. He went off in an entirely new direction that embraced the roots of the music while allowing the participants potentially unlimited freedom.

What he was saying constituted a revolution in the formal world of so-called jazz, although free improvising did have its obvious precedents in rural blues, church music and field hollers. Less obviously, it existed elsewhere. Nothing could be 'freer' than the dramatic upper-register cries the legendary trumpeter Leo 'The Whistler' Sheppard smeared across the stratosphere above the raunchy Lionel Hampton band of the late 'forties or, for that matter, the magnificent version of 'I Got Rhythm' recorded at a Harlem jam session the same decade, where the trumpeter Hot Lips Page solos daringly with a complete disregard for the chord changes.[2] But in terms of an actual *concept*, the freedom proposed by Ornette Coleman was entirely new. Furthermore, because he emerged during a period when the improvising artist had come to rely increasingly on extending the possibilities offered by harmonic exploration, John Coltrane being the leading exponent of this system, his propositions actually presented a dilemma to formally schooled musicians. Coleman made music that was as natural as breathing, but in doing so, he was suggesting something a little too 'natural' for some.

On their early recordings made for the Atlantic label during the period 1959–61 (*The Shape of Jazz to Come, Change of the Century, This is Our Music, Ornette!, Ornette on Tenor, Twins, The Art of the Improvisors,* and *To Whom Who Keeps a Record*), the four members of Coleman's group shared equally in the proceedings. With the quick-thinking Don Cherry playing trumpet, Charlie Haden on bass and either Billy Higgins or Edward Blackwell on drums, the degree of interplay involved was greater than at any other time before, the collective improvisation of New Orleans music notwithstanding. Engaged in a continuous musical conversation and playing *together* in the truest sense of the word, this quartet more or less 'invented' free jazz improvising even if they seldom went out of tempo.

In addition to this, bass and drums took a much more *melodic* role than had previously been the case. The responsibilities of the bassist up to this point had been rhythmic, initially, then mainly harmonic. Jimmy Blanton, working with Duke Ellington in about 1940, first gave the bass a melodic voice, and Charlie Haden continues the development of the instrument in this direction as did, to a lesser extent, the more virtuosic but bebop-rooted Scott La Faro. (Best known for his work with pianist Bill Evans, La Faro played on *Ornette!* as well as interacting with Haden on *Free Jazz*, the iconoclastic double quartet album organised by Coleman in 1960.)

There were precedents for the drummer colouring the melody, too. New Orleans drummers, Baby Dodds outstanding among them, tended to play melodically, as did Max Roach and Art Blakey in a later era, but Blackwell, especially noted for his ability to play 'tunes' on his drumset, was the uniquely sensitive percussionist this music required. His rapid grasp of rhythmic possibilities enabled him to follow Coleman as he swept aside bar-lines and preset patterns. At the same time he made a substantial contribution to Coleman's own understanding of rhythm. Billy Higgins, a younger man who entered the picture after Blackwell despite the fact that he is the drummer on the first Atlantic recordings, developed into a distinctive player and learned equally from both men.

Pianist Ellis Marsalis, a hometown colleague of Blackwell's, spent the summer of 1956 in Los Angeles with him and Coleman. They played in a variety of combinations together and with two other New Orleans musicians, clarinettist Alvin Batiste and the noted arranger Harold Battiste, who was playing piano and saxophone at the time. Marsalis confirmed Blackwell's rhythmic significance: 'It was very interesting to hear Ornette and Edward play, just the two of them, because the things that they would do accentuated a certain kind of rhythmic importance and rhythmic emphasis that was in Ornette's music and in which the lack of a certain conventional kind of harmony – that is, the harmony that comes from piano, bass, guitar or whatever – was not even missing. Ornette's music was sufficient enough, especially with Edward, that he didn't need that.' Harmonic instruments have figured rarely in Coleman's music. For a short period in the 'seventies, he used a guitarist, James 'Blood' Ulmer, but the piano has only cropped up on one record date. This was his first, made for Contemporary in Los Angeles in 1958 under the title *Something Else! The Music of Ornette Coleman*, on which the pianist was Walter Norris. Another session, taped by pianist Paul Bley around this time and later released in France, features Coleman, Cherry, Higgins and Haden, but was made under Bley's leadership.

Coleman's compositions, many of which, like 'Beauty is a Rare Thing' and the memorable dirge 'Lonely Woman', have become standard vehicles for improvisation, consist of basically simple melodies. His method of improvising involves taking these simple lines and other motifs, often repeating and developing a simple phrase and letting the melodic line develop organically according to *its own terms*. Whatever he uses as a theme, whether it be conceived as a 12-bar blues or a 32-bar song, the improvisation itself transcends the form. Often, too, a Coleman theme is written in a way that is actually conducive to development. At a session held in 1976 which reunited several of his former colleagues, Don Cherry played through a piece written by the saxophonist entitled 'Handwoven'. 'It's so *smooth*,' he said warmly, 'The way Ornette writes, it just makes the music flow like water.'

Bobby Bradford is a trumpeter who has known Coleman since they were both teenagers in Texas. He has played with the saxophonist intermittently over the years, and in an interview with the British writer Richard Williams he shed some light on the challenges that Coleman sets: 'Ornette's scores leave some margin for interpretation. He'd say to you, "We're going to play this piece fast," but how fast was up to you, the player. You had to start on the first note, end on the last, and not miss out any in between. What happens in effect is that the piece is different every time, because there are a lot of overlaps and consequently different harmonic implications. Ornette thrives on that.'[3]

The theories that Coleman advanced have had a far-reaching influence, yet for a long time there were those who thought that what he was saying heralded the approach of anarchy in the music. As Edward Blackwell put it: 'A lot of musicians couldn't really dig his type of music because they were so brainwashed to that same formula – the beginning, you know, then the bridge and the end of the tune; then you solo and take it out. But with Ornette it's not like that. You start it and then you're on your own. As long as you're aware of where the music should go, there's no problem at all how it would be. When Ornette starts a tune, there's a certain place he intends to get, but there's no certain way to get there, and a lot of cats are not aware of how that happens.'

Because Coleman improvises without the benefit of a structured form beneath him on which to fall back, he has to make up his improvisation in relation to what the other musicians are playing. In doing so, he has to build his own musical edifice, working harder than a conventional player who can rely on a fixed harmonic structure. The rigorous demands of this method and the degree of commitment required are typical of his dedication and in keeping with his main artistic concern which is spontaneity. Coleman plays just as hard in rehearsal as he does in performance, and he expects those involved with him to do the same. 'My playing is spontaneous, not a style,' he told Whitney Balliett. 'A style happens when your phrasing hardens.'[4] Relying on learned and practised artifices is a survival tactic for musicians as it is in other creative pursuits, yet Coleman falls back on cliché rarely. Although his style has changed since the early Atlantic recordings, becoming more formulated and precise, his desire to produce 'living' music remains equally intense. He writes constantly and plays with young musicians in the privacy of his home when he is not readying himself for a public engagement. When he re-emerged from a two-year retirement, he had added two new instruments to his armoury, trumpet and violin, both of which he had taught himself to play. In his quest for total musical expression, Coleman has written for symphony orchestras and performed with woodwind quintets, and taken his saxophone into the streets of Nigeria.

To watch Coleman working on a new piece of music is to experience a level of creativity and, above all, involvement that is to be found rarely and then only amongst the greatest artists. Music seems to flow from him unhampered by the usual considerations of time and place. He sits at a rickety table covered in sheets of manuscript paper, writing as he plays. Other instruments lie on the table – a broken saxophone, his trumpet, a couple of violins and bows to go with them. Coleman plays a few bars on his alto then scribbles down what he has just played, using his own individual notation. He picks up his horn again, rocking precariously on a little stool as he blows, pencils slipping all over the table and burying themselves beneath the unwieldy sheets of paper. He puts down his horn and scrabbles around for a pencil with which to jot down another idea. Occasionally he picks up the trumpet as another sound strikes him, then he returns to the saxophone. At some points the ideas flow faster than he is able to articulate them on his instrument or put them down on paper. The spontaneity he desires always seems to be there, however, and has a deep influence on the musicians around him.

'As human beings we don't use our whole senses strongly, we're too lazy,' said Don Cherry, the Oklahoma-born trumpeter who for a while was Coleman's musical and personal *alter ego*. Today Cherry lives and works in Europe for most of the year, but whenever he returns to the United States, he plays with Coleman, either in public or in private. 'Certain types of music strengthen the senses to work at their fullest and this, to me, I would say that Ornette Coleman's music has. It really lets you feel something as you experience it, and realise the work you have to do on yourself to experience more within yourself. His music really lives because you can see there is no time period. *Style* is only related to a certain period, Ornette's music goes beyond.'

Coleman developed his theory of 'non-tempered' music – that is, music that does not stick to the twelve tones of the Western 'tempered' scale – when criticised by musicians and writers for, supposedly, 'playing out of tune'. Similar criticism had been levelled at people like Bunk Johnson and George Lewis, exponents of an earlier form of the music, when they travelled north from Louisiana at the peak of the New Orleans Revival that took place in the 1940s. The truth is that these artists play on more levels than the Western listener is used to hearing, although the degree of melodic imagination contained in their music is common in other, non-Western cultures.

At first, Coleman told Richard Williams, he was worried at the suggestion that by basing his playing on the 'natural' pitch of the instrument, he was playing 'out of tune'. Then he realised, 'My emotions were raising my tone to another level ... I could still hear the centre of what I was reading.'[5] The saxophonist believes that every human being has a 'non-tempered' psyche. As a result, he says, written music impedes natural expression. His theories were borne out when he made his first visit to a non-Western culture. In 1972 the writer and clarinettist Bob Palmer took him to Morocco, where he played with the famous Master Musicians of Joujouka in the Rif Mountains. It was there during the Festival of Boujeloud, an ancient ritual which is believed to have its roots in the worship of Pan, that he encountered a mass of people playing in what he calls their own individual 'octave'. The problem of playing 'in tune' simply does not arise in a situation where the individual *is his own intonation*, he told Williams.

'I saw thirty of them [the Master Musicians], playing non-tempered instruments in their own intonation, *in unison*. They would change tempos, intensities and rhythm. They changed together, as if they all had the same idea, yet they hadn't played what they were playing before they played it!' This dalliance with the unknown is the aspect of improvising that has always intrigued the saxophonist. 'To me, that's known as a jazz concept ... Originally, jazz must have been about that: individuals don't have to worry about the written note in order to blend with it.'[6]

It was not only in terms of spontaneity that Coleman went back to what jazz had 'originally been about'. His innovations took place during a period when his contemporaries were trying to recapture some of the spirit of immediacy the music had lost after the innovations of bebop had started to stagnate. This desire to go 'back to the roots' was, in some cases, politically motivated, too, but it was soon seized on by the record companies as yet another commercial possibility. Coleman, however, went back even further. He delved into the music's history for inspiration, drawing on all the resources he had assembled during his career which, at one point, had included travelling through the South with an oldtime minstrel show. As a teenager in Fort Worth, Texas, he played traditional gutbucket tenor, doubled over backwards with the bell of his horn pointed over his shoulder, bending his knees and walking across the tabletops. It was a past that many Blacks wanted to forget; Coleman could not and would not. 'When you hear me you probably hear everything I've heard since from when I was a kid. In fact, it's a glorified folk music.'

With his highly vocalised 'cry', the most expressive tone to be used in jazz since the days of Bubber Miley and Johnny Dodds, Coleman brought back a quality to the music that had vanished as the artistic aesthetic developed. This essentially 'human' sound was, of course, still to be heard in rhythm-and-blues music as epitomised by such boisterous players as saxophonist Arnett Cobb, but it had gradually been eliminated from the elitist art music that so-called jazz had become. There were exceptions – saxophonist Eddie 'Lockjaw' Davis was a very 'human' player, while bassist Charles Mingus inspired men like Jackie McLean to produce decidedly wild and 'blue' voices for ensemble playing – notably 'Pithecanthropus Erectus' from 1956 – but Coleman consistently went back to the core, the heart of the music, playing the blues with the verve and poignancy of a Big Jay McNeely or Louis Jordan, men who had been his models in the Texas honkytonks. He used a plastic saxophone to relay his message, finding that it absorbed the sound less than its metal counterpart.

That he framed his heartcry in a rejection of form that was progressive enough in its implications and promise to influence every young musician who followed him while at the same time attracting the attention and praise of establishment figures such as Leonard Bernstein and Gunther Schuller is further proof of his stature. Schuller, in fact, was later to feature Coleman alongside Eric Dolphy in an extended piece of 'third stream' music entitled 'Jazz Abstractions'.

Today, Alvin Batiste heads the Jazz Institute of the Black Studies department at Southern University in Baton Rouge, Louisiana. He believes that Ornette Coleman was actually responsible for creating a background for the current climate of receptivity that exists for 'roots' music. Furthermore, he maintains that much of this was due to the essentially warm and *human* sound the saxophonist employed.

Shortly after the summer he spent with Coleman in Los Angeles, Batiste joined the Ray Charles Orchestra. As they toured the country, one of the main subjects of conversation among musicians centred on this 'country boy' from Texas who 'thought he could play alto'. Batiste found himself defending Coleman strenuously. He had played his music, after all, and although he found it 'controversial' he always enjoyed it. 'Right now, everybody is into that. Ornette's music was the music that put jazz musicians in the frame of mind to go back to the roots.'

* * *

James Clay is a saxophonist from Dallas, Texas. He has been with Ray Charles since his Army service ended in the early 'sixties, but prior to that he lived in California. One night he walked into a Los Angeles nightclub where the individualistic pianist Sonny Clark was playing with Frank Butler, the most respected drummer on the Coast, and a bassist. He recalled how a Black saxophonist with long hair and a beard stood up to play, and the trio walked off the stand. 'I said to myself, "Evidently that's Ornette Coleman." I'd never heard anything like it before.'

Clay's reaction was typical at the time although, oddly enough, he was later to play with Coleman for a while. Coleman was making his second visit to Los Angeles on this occasion, and undergoing the humiliation of being thrown off the bandstand by musicians of the calibre of Dexter Gordon for going 'outside', the musicians' term for playing without reference to a fixed harmonic structure. It seems safe to assume that Coleman was often criticised for the rawness of his actual sound as much as for his rejection of form. Players like Gordon had honed their music down to a fine, polished art in which 'funkiness' was allowed to creep through in a controlled manner. Now here came this untutored 'primitive' from out of nowhere, a denial of all they had learned.

Ornette Coleman's career began in Fort Worth, Texas, where he was raised in a family that was 'poorer than poor'. His initial encouragement came from his cousin James Jordan, who also played saxophone and was later to become his manager, and Thomas 'Red' Connors, the town's leading player. At school his fellow students included several musicians who later became known through playing with him in New York or, like the late King Curtis, in their own right. They included the drummer Charles Moffett, and saxophonists Dewey Redman and Prince Lasha. All of them agree that Connors, who died at an early age, was playing then what John Coltrane was to play in his later years. Prince Lasha called him 'The greatest inspiration in the South-West'.

By the time he was in his early teens, Coleman was playing in the Forth Worth nightclubs with a band that included Lasha and Charles Moffett, at that time playing trumpet. His family's financial circumstances were dire, and as a result he spent half his day in school and half his night working in disreputable joints for employers who were not too particular about hiring underage musicians. The competitive spirit was strong in Texas, though, especially among saxophonists, and standards were high. King Curtis, who was to become one of the best-known instrumentalists in popular music, is generally acknowledged to have been an outstanding technician, yet even he suffered at the hands of the 'local power'. According to Leroy Cooper, another Texas reedman, Red Connors used to tell Curtis, 'Get off the stand, man, the heavy guys are coming on now!'

Playing in such a heavily charged atmosphere was an invaluable experience for a developing artist like Ornette Coleman. Eventually, Connors took him under his wing and taught him the elements of bebop. He made him aware of the distinction between the popular music of the day, which was rhythm-and-blues, and the serious music, which was what people like Charlie Parker played.

For a while Coleman played in Connors's band, mostly for dances where the blues accounted for eighty per cent of their repertoire, and, occasionally, in white nightclubs. Then he formed his own group, backing blues singers like Big Joe Turner. He had begun to realise that Texas was not the place for him and started to look for a way out. He was already starting to experience some difficulties because of the unconventional way he played. Leroy Cooper remembers hearing him playing alone in the city's baseball stadium in the middle of the night, 'playing his heart out'. Few of the touring bands that came through Fort Worth wanted a 'freak' on the road, and Coleman was left with few alternatives. In 1949 he got a job playing tenor with a minstrel show and ended up stranded in New Orleans. A local cornet player, Melvin Lastie, gave him a place to stay and lent him his brother's alto saxophone, but few of the New Orleans musicians would play with him. Even Edward Blackwell paid him little attention. As Plas Johnson, now a leading Hollywood session saxophonist put it: 'He was out of time.'

Eventually Coleman decided to move on. When guitarist Pee Wee Crayton, who had scored a nationwide hit with 'Blues After Hours' two years before, came through town, the saxophonist discovered Red Connors in charge of the band. He also learned that Crayton was on his way to Los Angeles, and talked his way into a job in the reed section. They had worked together before in Fort Worth, uneventfully, but the Ornette Coleman of 1949 was a different proposition. Although Coleman has said that by the time they reached Los Angeles Crayton was paying him *not* to play, the guitarist says otherwise. Crayton remembers him as a 'dark, brownskin boy, with hair long, play alto' who didn't eat meat. 'He could play the blues but he didn't want to. I *made* him play the blues and I paid him *to* play.' The message was clear; Crayton enlisted Connors and the trumpet player to put it across: 'If you want to stay in this band, you got to play the blues. If you don't then I have to get another saxophone player.' Coleman capitulated. As Crayton said, 'If you're not working, you're going to do your best to do it!'

Coleman stuck out the gig until they reached Los Angeles, then he left. He moved into the Morris Hotel, a place which was home for some of the less successful musicians, and started to make his presence felt. Soon after this, Ed Blackwell moved to the Coast and the two men found mutual ground for making music together. Apart from a brief period when he returned to Fort Worth, California became Coleman's home until 1959.

In 1953 he ran into trumpeter Bobby Bradford, who had known him in his hometown, Dallas, when Coleman would come there at weekends, playing tenor with Red Connors's band. Bradford, who had moved to Los Angeles to live with his mother, had already recognised Coleman's unique quality. 'Bird and Sonny [Rollins] would use the device of playing half a step above the key for one phrase, just to add that little taste of piquancy, but Ornette would go out and stay there – he wouldn't come back after one phrase, and this would test your capacity for dissonance. I was very impressed by the fact that he had the courage and the audacity to test Charlie Parker's law, partly because I was at the stage of worshipping Bird. That's when I began to think of him as a genius.'[7]

There were very few places where Coleman was able to play his own music, although he did work with Bradford and Blackwell and, occasionally, a pianist named Floyd Howard. In the main, however, he supported himself and his family – he had married in Los Angeles – with a variety of menial jobs. In 1954 Bradford went into the airforce, to be replaced by Don Cherry, and Blackwell went back to New Orleans soon after.

Don Cherry was working around Los Angeles with a group called the Jazz Messiahs which he co-led with James Clay, a former schoolmate of Bobby Bradford's. One morning, Clay was woken by the group's drummer, Billy Higgins, coming by his house to cook breakfast. With him was Ornette Coleman, whom Higgins, still in his teens, had met on the saxophonist's first visit to Los Angeles. Clay invited Coleman to join them for their daily workout at Cherry's house. At first Coleman refused. He was depressed at the treatment he was receiving from local musicians, as well he might be – Clay was sceptical of his ability and had invited him only because, he reasoned, there was nothing better to do – but eventually he was persuaded.

The musicians began holding regular sessions in the garage of saxophonist George Newman, the Jazz Messiahs' pianist at the time. Blackwell was still on hand and he and Higgins sometimes played together in this group. Coleman brought in a book of his own tunes, all of which, according to Clay, were 'written wrong'. He could play Coleman's music with him, but found difficulty in reading the odd combinations of notes that Coleman wrote in each bar. Clay says that all the musicians protested about the lack of form initially, but Coleman was quietly insistent that his music could be played by them. The two saxophonists have a mutual respect for each other and remain on friendly terms, but eventually Clay went his own way. Cherry and Higgins stayed, impressed with the freedom Coleman offered, but their response to his music was unusually positive.

In the main, Ornette Coleman could find no one else to play his music. They would go from place to place, auditioning for jobs, unable to get a bass player unless they had work. At one jam-session, Blackwell recalled a bassist who was so frustrated by Coleman's concept that he stopped playing in the middle of a tune. 'He started screaming, "Man, listen! Why don't you-all play something everybody can play?" He got so hung-up, and boy, he created a scene! Everybody cracked up.'

Don Cherry had an explanation for the mixed reaction the music received. 'There was this thing when we played where there were those who really loved it, the growth of it and the spirit of it. And then there were those who didn't like it because they felt it was jeopardising their position in life.'

Eventually Coleman was to find the bass player his music needed. His name was Charlie Haden, he came from a singing family in Shenandoah, Iowa, and like two of the four bassists that Coleman has used for any length of time, he was white. (The others were Scott La Faro and David Izenzon. Jimmy Garrison, who left Coleman to work with John Coltrane, was Black.)

Haden was working in a group led by pianist Paul Bley at the Hillcrest, a club in the Black section of Los Angeles, when he met Coleman. The group's drummer, Lenny McBrowne, brought him in one day, and almost immediately they started playing together.

Haden's recollection of the first time he went to Coleman's house is typical of experiences others have related. 'I walked into his room and he had music everywhere. It was on the floors, the chairs – even on the bath. You could hardly move in case you stepped on it. He'd just pick up a piece and say, "Hey, play this."'

Haden was filled with enthusiasm. His whole life at this point was devoted to music, his ambition to play everything within his reach. He was a natural for Coleman's 'woodshed' and pretty soon he was playing with him every day, together with Billy Higgins and Don Cherry, both of whom he had met while still at school. Years later, his attitude to Ornette Coleman remained the same. In 1971, Coleman restricted much of his playing to rehearsals. Haden's expressive bass work was in demand from several 'name' groups but whenever possible, he would make the rehearsals. 'I play Ornette's music because it's the only *living* music,' he said.

* * *

Ornette Coleman is probably the most influential single figure to emerge in African-American art music since Charlie Parker. In 1959 he made his New York debut at the Five Spot Café and aroused interest and controversy in equal amounts. He had Don Cherry and Charlie Haden playing with him, and Billy Higgins was at the drums. Later, Blackwell came up from New Orleans and took Higgins's place. The two men have been in and out of Coleman's groups ever since, sharing the drumseat with Coleman's old school friend Charles Moffett, who played with him consistently in the three years prior to 1967.

Although his innovations were treated with scepticism by many, it was not long before Coleman began to exercise a considerable influence on all those who heard him. He even caused the two major saxophonists of the day, Sonny Rollins and John Coltrane, to rethink their entire approach. In Rollins's case he actually went into self-imposed retirement for two years, and when he re-emerged, it was to open at the Village Gate with two of Coleman's former colleagues in tow. With Don Cherry and Billy Higgins on hand, the music his quartet offered was grounded in the suggestions proposed by Coleman.

John Coltrane came to the Five Spot nightly. 'He would grab Ornette by the arm as soon as we got off and they would go off into the night talking about music,'[8] recalled Charlie Haden. The two men became close personal friends and spent a considerable amount of time playing together, many of these sessions being, in fact, taped by Coleman. Coltrane himself said that this exposure enabled him to improvise with greater abandon. Another revolutionary, Albert Ayler, also frequented Coleman's home during a period when the latter was not playing in public. These exchanges were merely part of a pattern of personal interaction that has long existed in the musicians' community, but in New York, spending time with Ornette Coleman is, in fact, one of the prerequisites for entry into the toughest community of all.

Coleman continues to work infrequently, a state of affairs which is based on economic considerations yet which exists partly through his own choice, but his immediate personal world is always full of music. His home is always open to musicians and other creative people, for such is his love for art – and 'love' is a term he uses frequently to describe his relationship to music as well as humanity itself – that he is generous with his time and experience. There are some who gain from his wisdom but others merely drain him with their demands on his energy and the material success they suppose him to have had. Coleman has never been a success in financial terms, and in that statement lies the anomaly of the situation in which the Black creative artist finds him or herself constantly. He can be praised by the critics and media alike, yet by virtue of the financial reward that is offered to him, continue to be forced to live like a bar-room entertainer. The fact is, that in the eyes of many an entrepreneur, that is just what he is.

'I really haven't had the facilities and opportunities to do what I do as good as I can do it,' Coleman told Richard Williams. 'Being born in America means that I'd need three million dollars, just to be able to do it on the level of being natural. But I don't have that kind of image to other people. I still have that "Black jazz" image, I'm an entertainer who's supposed to exist on a certain level, and that's it.'[9]

Just as he has always had to suffer the criticism of those who said he could not play his instrument, so Coleman's attempts at extended composition have been treated churlishly. The saxophonist was indeed a self-taught instrumentalist, but he later acquired enough knowledge of harmony and composition to enable him to cope with the mechanics of writing music down. As far back as 1950 he had started to write big-band scores, and many other works have followed: a string quartet performed at New York's Town Hall in 1962, a woodwind quintet played in England three years later. There was a piece entitled 'Forms and Sounds' for which Coleman himself played interludes on trumpet with the Philadelphia Woodwind Quintet, and several movie scores. In 1969 he started on an ambitious project entitled *The Skies of America* which he planned would be played by his quartet and an eighty-piece orchestra. Coleman was perhaps being a little over-ambitious for a so-called 'jazz' musician. Despite the fact that he was under contract to a major American record company, he was forced to cross the Atlantic to save money on the orchestra and not allowed to take his sidemen with him.

Coleman feels that an important distinction exists between those he calls the '9 to 5' people, that is, the working class, and the '10 to 3' people, the executives. A great many Black artists interpret the use of the word 'classical' in describing an art form as meaning something designed for a certain 'class'. Coleman, however, feels that this was a situation peculiar to Europe, and it is the gulf separating the various racial groups in America that is responsible for the problems with which he has to deal. There, he said, 'A person could listen to someone strumming a bathtub bass and a washboard and say, "Oh, the forty-nine states would just love that," but be so far removed from what that *actually* is that he could appreciate what someone could create from those instruments. America has never been a class-conscious art world as far as music is concerned, but as far as other images of social class and minorities, wealth and race, it is conscious of that.' And as a member of a minority group himself, Coleman feels that his image lies outside the '10 to 3' life and thus creates a barrier between him and the people who make decisions. As he put it: 'It's hard for me to call up Boulez or somebody and say, "Hey, man, I just wrote a piece – would you be interested in it because it's music?"' He is all too aware that acceptance of his works often stems from tokenism, too.

He recalled an incident when an orchestral executive telephoned him to determine where a piece he had written might 'fit in' to a particular programme. His reaction was that he had not written a piece of music to be an item on a menu, 'some whipped cream to go with the sweet potatoes. I said either you want to perform a piece because it's music, or not. I'm not interested in making a good meal for the people when they might not even want to eat it! I wasn't put off by the words "fit it in", I was put off by what they thought they were doing. So many people are not interested in how well you want to do something; they're mostly interested in finding something to make you insecure about.'

By 1965 Ornette Coleman had reached the point where he was tired of being touted as a significant artist while at the same time being kept in ignorance of the mechanics surrounding his fate. He had employed a succession of managers but felt that each one was holding something back from him. He decided to take matters into his own hands. He travelled to Europe to try his chances there, taking with him the two musicians who had been working with him in New York, Charles Moffett and David Izenzon. The trio played in several countries, making two notable 'live' recordings in the process. The first, released in two volumes by Blue Note, was taped at the Golden Circle in Stockholm, Sweden. The second, made at Fairfield Hall in Croydon, England, also featured some of Coleman's written work performed by a chamber group.

When they returned to New York, Charlie Haden returned to the fold to participate in a rewarding two-basses partnership with the virtuosic Izenzon, then in the way of most groups, the personnel fluctuated. On a trip to San Francisco, Coleman renewed his childhood acquaintance with Dewey Redman, and when the tenor saxophonist decided to come to New York in 1968 he joined Coleman's group. Edward Blackwell spent much of this period living in Morocco and Billy Higgins frequently filled the drumseat, sometimes alternating with Coleman's son Denardo, but when Blackwell returned to the United States, he started to work with the saxophonist again.

The late 'sixties and early 'seventies were a period of relatively frequent recording activity for Ornette Coleman. The album *Science Fiction* marked Bobby Bradford's first appearance on record with him, playing alongside Don Cherry, Redman, Higgins and Blackwell. Despite this, Coleman performed rarely in public. Almost single-handedly, the saxophonist had been waging a campaign against the entrepreneurs who, he felt, had withheld from him the financial reward commensurate with his talent. This he sees as another manifestation of their need to exercise a hold over the artist in order to control him.

To Edward Blackwell, the club-owners and promoters actually thrive off the need musicians have to play their music. 'They exploit the fact that simply because you love it you have to play it. The fact is that they know that you want to play and you're *gonna* play, and they offer you what they want to give you. We'd go in a club and we'd want to jam and the cat would give us a proposition about working a weekend and then offer us pennies – you know? And since we were going there to jam, anyway, we'd just accept it for somewhere to play.'

When he first came to New York, Ornette Coleman was adopted by some of the leading artistic figures as one of their own, a situation he neither invited nor encouraged, yet which he did not reject. Leonard Bernstein even gatecrashed a rehearsal and sat in, though, according to the musicians, the noted conductor remained in ignorance of what the music was actually about. This kind of situation is all too familiar to an artist of Coleman's stature. No longer forced to serve white society directly, he must nonetheless continue in the role of minstrel, making himself available to all kinds of humiliation in the process, in order to be allowed to work. In Coleman's case, his gentle manner and humble nature endear him to the entrepreneurs, who see the mantle of militancy hanging uneasily on his shoulders. Nevertheless, he has kept to his standards and refused to be sidetracked by personal considerations.

The saxophonist has continually had to struggle with the realisation that the West does not allow creative people to survive, unplagued or unhampered by the value judgements of others. As he put it: 'The public is not worried about whether I'm rich or poor; all they're worried about is if they like you or not. It's the person that's in the position to allow me to function that I have the problem with. Some people call it the middleman, some people call it the white man, some people call it the art world – they've got many titles for it but basically you have to adjust to what this person *wants you to do.* And usually the first thing he does is to try to make you insecure – *not* because he thinks he's going to get you to do more of what it is that you do, but because he wants to convince himself that what you're about is no more than the fact that you just want some money, that you're not really an artist, you just want to be where he is.'

Whatever happens to Ornette Coleman in terms of his own economic success, he remains convinced in his first priority which is to play creative music. 'I'm always trying to bring the listener something that he doesn't have to know but that does him good,' he said. 'I try to do that and I know when I'm doing it. I think this is the closest opportunity to try to get to instant art – if there is such a thing as "instant art".'

Notes

1 Bob Palmer, 'Charlie Haden's Creed', *Down Beat,* 20 July 1972.
2 *Hot Lips Page After Hours in Harlem* (Onyx 207).
3 Interview by Richard Williams, 'Memories of Ornette', *Melody Maker,* 17 July 1971.
4 Quoted in Joe Goldberg, *Jazz Masters of the Fifties,* New York, 1965, p. 243.
5 Richard Williams, 'Ornette and the Pipes of Joujouka', *Melody Maker,* 17 March 1973.
6 ibid.
7 'Memories of Ornette', op. cit.
8 Palmer, op. cit.
9 'Ornette and the Pipes of Joujouka', op. cit.

5

Sun Ra – Pictures of Infinity

I'm actually painting pictures of infinity with my music, and
that's why a lot of people can't understand it. And when I
say so, a lot of people don't believe me. But if they'd listen
to this and to other types of music, they'll find that this has
something else in it, something from another world.

Sun Ra

Back in the mid-sixties, African and Eastern-style clothing was still
relatively rare in New York, even in the East Village as it was then
known. A light-skinned Black man, carrying a shopping bag and
wearing a glittering tunic under his jacket, was bound to attract
some attention on Second Avenue before noon, especially with
his greased-down hair tied around with a star-spangled bandanna.
He led the way up some stairs and into a room ablaze with light.
The light came from inside a huge rubber ball suspended from the
ceiling, and the room was filled with musicians and instruments of
every description. Marshall Allen had been out to buy food for the
occupants of 48 East Third Street, who included in their number
the legendary pianist, poet and philosopher known as Sun Ra and
several members of his Solar Arkestra. Another day at the Sun
Studio was just beginning.

The night before, the musicians had rehearsed for four or five
hours, something they did every night without much promise of
remuneration in the foreseeable future. Sometimes they would

play in a coffee-shop across the river in Newark, occasionally they might have a gig in the Village. Where they were concerned, however, Sun Ra, a thick-set man in his fifties with a paunchy face and hairline moustache, was the heaviest guru around. For Sun Ra himself, dressed in equally glittering attire and with a ten-pointed star shining out of the turban he wore on his head, their continuing presence was proof of the superiority of his music, despite the limited audience it enjoyed at the time.

Since those days, Sun Ra and the Arkestra have toured Europe and America and even visited Egypt. In Germany, they heard local bands come out playing solos taken almost note for note from some of their earlier recordings. In Cairo, the Minister of Culture arranged for a performance by the Egyptian Ballet to be cancelled so that the Arkestra could play. At one point, the thousand-strong audience leapt spontaneously to its feet to join the Arkestra in their chant; 'Space is the Place'. The musicians took their cassette recorders to the pyramids and into the tombs and played their music there.

For a while, Sun Ra was Artist-in-Residence on the University of California campus at Berkeley. The Arkestra itself has moved to Philadelphia, but some things never change at the Sun Studio. Then, as now, it was not uncommon for Sun Ra's apprentices to sit up half the night waiting patiently for the master to prepare an arrangement. Nearly all his writing is done at rehearsals, like Duke Ellington with the particular capacities of the individual in mind. 'I write according to the day, the minute, and what's going on in the cosmos,' he says. 'And actually each one of my numbers is just like a news item, only it's like a cosmic newspaper.'

Sun Ra's music had already been a driving force for ten years when he and the Arkestra moved to New York in 1961. Even before they left their original base in Chicago, their devotees would ask those who had heard them play on consecutive nights, 'Has the band caught up with Sun Ra yet?' His innovations, not to mention his espousal of the idea of intergalactic travel and its implications

for the human race, have always been in advance of the contemporary attitude, yet it has been suggested by one writer that he 'tied
in' with New York's growing free-form movement on his arrival.
The truth of it was that he and his musical spacemen were already
there. 'If you're going to talk about "avant-garde",' said drummer
Clifford Jarvis, 'Sun Ra is the first in that particular music.'

'Musically, Sun Ra is one of the unacknowledged legislators
of the world.' Roger Blank, another drummer who played and
recorded with him, paraphrased Shelley in an attempt to describe
his influence. Saxophonist Marion Brown, who has studied and
taught extensively, is convinced that Sun Ra is greater than Stravin-
sky or Bartok, 'And by my standards and by the standards I've
acquired in getting my traditional education, I would say he is
more *creative* than Cage or Stockhausen.'

On a record made before an audience in Cairo, Egypt, in 1971,
Sun Ra was asked to define 'progressive music'. 'It means keeping
ahead of the time,' he said. 'It's supposed to stimulate people to
think of themselves as modern freemen.'[1]

Sun Ra has become conspicuous for his colourful attire, dressing in a style seemingly derived from somewhere midway between
Africa and the realms of science fiction. It has been years, in fact,
since he has allowed anyone to see him in Western dress (although
there is a film in existence made at a party in the 'fifties where
the guests stood around, drinks in hand, asking each other, 'Have
you heard the New Music – this new jazz?' and the answer was
provided by Sun Ra, conducting the Arkestra, all of whom were
dressed in white tuxedos). His musical explorations are invariably
related to journeys into Infinity beyond the Universe itself. 'The
Heliocentric World of Sun Ra', 'Lights on a Satellite', 'The Others
in their World', are the kind of titles he gives his compositions.

But these were idiosyncrasies. Sun Ra, who adopted the name of
the Egyptian sun god and has always been deliberately mysterious
about his origins, was ahead of the times in other ways. In Egypt,
the Inspector of Antiquities told one of the musicians that he had

never met anyone who could support the tremendous wisdom the name traditionally implied. Sun Ra has gone a long way towards doing so. He was the first artist to speak of spiritual matters and the need for personal discipline amongst musicians. Anyone who wanted to play with him had to accept a severe personal regimen – at least while they were in his company. Some of his shorter pieces even carry the titles of various numbered 'Disciplines'.

'Sun Ra runs his band like an army,' a young saxophonist related from painful first-hand experience. 'When he says, "Stand up!" they stand up. When he says, "Sit down!" they sit down.' He even has one of their number stand guard at the door all night.

'It's like anything else,' says Sun Ra. 'When the Army wants to build men they isolate them. It's just the case that these are musicians, but you might say they're marines. They have to know everything. In their case, knowing everything means touching on all places of music. Of course they won't get as much chance to play as other musicians, but on the other hand, they're getting *more* chance to play.'

There is a certain anonymity about the players he chooses, however interesting or exciting their actual solos can be. At times it seems that Sun Ra's influence is so strong that the musicians express *him* rather than themselves. In their kind of cold detachment, the musicians, though mature, appear in a student role. Implicit in Sun Ra's statement, though, was the need he feels for the suppression of ego in those young players who flock to him full of hope, some of whom he sees having only ulterior motives. 'They are selfish. They want to play to satisfy their ego and so that someone can applaud them. They refuse to throw their energy into a pool with someone who could be the link to do something with it.'

At the same time, Sun Ra, the visionary and catalyst, knows that his school provides an opportunity for really *playing* – no shucking, no jiving – that is without equal. Clifford Jarvis saw many young men crumble in the face of Sun Ra's wisdom and demands.

'He can build your hopes up and tear you down at the same time,' he said. 'A lot of guys wig out, you know. Some of them can't stand to be that sincere. They don't have any foundation to be that staid and stable with what Sun Ra has to offer.'

Sun Ra believes that discipline is the foundation of all freedom. He sees this reflected in nature and the universe itself, but just as no two organisms created by nature are alike, no two people are alike. He thrives off the notion of the individual's 'duality'. He says: 'You can't have harmony and you can't even have real music unless you have two or more sounds. And you have to have two or more people to have harmony.'² Each individual, he believes, is music himself, and if he is unable to express this feeling, he must have his 'spirit companion' – i.e., the musician – to do it for him. To him, 'the people are the instrument.'

'I want to do some things in music but I don't have too many musicians to work with because they're weak and they're also powerless. Everything I do, I do because of the necessity of doing it. I wouldn't be out playing, really, unless I had to. Doing something that's really evolutionary at this point is way-out, it's an incredible thing, but you've got to pull the musician along and you shouldn't have to do that. If we have a limited mind, we'll play limited music. Most musicians, particularly in America, have limited minds.'

Up to fifteen musicians play with the Arkestra at any one time, a number of whom live with their leader in something of a commune. Some older men who were married have left their wives in order to move into his protective custody. One wife likened the situation to 'a mother in her house surrounded by all her children'. Not all those who play with him agree with his philosophy, but for those who have a spiritual need Sun Ra provides guidance and fulfilment. He is, in fact, a substitute for the family. In turn, he is protected by the constant presence of his men. He seldom appears in public without a bodyguard, occasionally, though by no means always, drawn from the ranks of the Arkestra.

He develops involved philosophies and explanations for

everything. For example, at one time he frequently lectured the band on the nutritional value of the humble turtle-bean – according to one follower's lady, this was because it was the cheapest protein source available and times were lean. The musicians, however, spoke almost in awe of the bean's untold properties. Sun Ra succeeded in keeping their stomachs full and the Arkestra intact.

'Sometimes I meet musicians who are emotionally out of it,' said Sun Ra. 'Maybe their wife left them or something. I took in a lot of musicians that were nothing, and I helped them get themselves together. They went on and they always left. As long as they didn't have any money, as long as they needed my help, my demands were never too heavy. Then after they got on their feet, they would forget about me.'

Sun Ra is bitter about the ingratitude he feels some musicians have shown by leaving him, but the limitations he imposes are too confining for all but the most dedicated to stay the course for long. 'His standards of discipline are on a very high order which most average people don't understand – especially Black people,' said Clifford Jarvis. Another man, a trumpeter, said: 'You have to be in total agreement with him in order to really make it with him. He's got a lot of demands and if you can stick with his demands, then you can be a good player in his band.'

Sun Ra does not allow his musicians to bring women to the house, because he considers their influence distracting. Drugs and alcohol are expressly forbidden, too. There are several players who have lost their position in the Arkestra through their continuing involvement with narcotics.

Sun Ra is a phenomenon even in a world where the unexpected is the norm. He has kept a band together with an unchanging nucleus for over twenty years, only recently reaping any financial benefits from the dedication of his disciples. His repertoire, the tone colours he achieves, and the breadth of his musical vision have no parallel in the big band field with the exception of Duke

Ellington. His music has been well documented because he has seen to that himself, constantly recording rehearsals as well as live performances and releasing material on his own label, Saturn. In all probability the earliest records appeared in a limited edition of fifty copies; nevertheless, this is the first time any band has been so exhaustively chronicled – at one stage, a new album was appearing every three or four months. As a result it is possible to follow the progress of the Arkestra from the mid-fifties and notice the strong influence Ellington has had on his writing up to the present day. Sun Ra's ideas are a little drier, his orchestrations less flamboyant, but when it comes to being a latterday equivalent, the cap fits. Sometimes the Arkestra echoed the precision and swing of the Count Basie band, occasionally his writing was melodramatic with an almost Hollywood quality. On the earlier tracks, there was a Tadd Dameron feel to his ensembles. His investment, incidentally, paid off, for he was finally able to lease selected tapes to major companies.

On the records made in the 'fifties, Sun Ra's piano playing was fairly conventional, even cold. Later, at fast tempos, he would play harmonically free, superficially coming from the Cecil Taylor school; unsentimental, tough and percussive. He has increasingly turned to the use of electronic keyboards, thereby bringing a more ethereal quality to the music. He started with an amplified celeste played simultaneously with the piano, and has gone through a whole succession of organs, claviolines and electric pianos. The Moog synthesiser, with its ability to echo the sounds of the elements as well as those we have come to associate with interplanetary travel, seemed almost to have been invented with him in mind; Sun Ra's use of it is inspired and original. His work epitomises Marshall McLuhan's thesis that electronic media herald a rebirth of tribal conditions. McLuhan has pointed out the Afro-American talent for making audible the new possibilities of electronics, and Sun Ra, along with Stevie Wonder, it should be said, has done for the synthesiser what Jimmy Smith did for the organ and Charlie

Christian did for the electric guitar. His ideas have had considerable effect on Rock groups and others involved with the possibilities of electronic music. Although some white keyboard players operating in the rock area are better known than Sun Ra, it is impossible to imagine them arriving at their direction without him having first laid down the guidelines, in the same way that no white player could have produced the freer forms of blues guitar without the precedents established by Jimi Hendrix.

The bass is at the heart of Sun Ra's music but it is its rhythmic rather than harmonic qualities that he utilises. He is the major pioneer in the extensive use of percussion and treats the bass as if it were another kind of drum. At times, it even provides the only source of rhythm, with a feeling like that of a more resilient tuned tom-tom. The Arkestra was the first to feature two or three drummers playing polyrhythms together and in the company of hand-drummers. Sun Ra encouraged his instrumentalists to play miscellaneous percussion, although only those who were 'career' drummers were allowed to play the actual drum-set. John Gilmore, who doubles on drums and saxophone, has always been the exception to this. This emphasis on percussion, combined with chants set up by the musicians, was the first sign of *conscious* Africanisms to appear in the music since Dizzy Gillespie's Afro-Cuban period. Culturally speaking, this went back to the vocalised 'growling' of Bubber Miley's trumpet in Ellington's 'jungle music' and beyond.

Clifford Jarvis pointed to Sun Ra's involvement with rhythm as another similarity shared with Ellington. 'Drums are important enough for one of the fathers of jazz to write around them, and Duke Ellington is the answer to a drummer's dream. The drummer has always played a major part in his band; at one time he used to star the drummer. Always he built his music off the rhythms. Sunny's like to the extreme with it, but it's the same thing. His band is set up around the drums. He loves the drums to dynamically guide you all the way through.'

There are few musicians associated with the new music who have not played in Sun Ra's academy, as well as many who are thought of as being more conventional. Marshall Allen, John Gilmore and Pat Patrick, the three anchormen who have been members since the early 'fifties, play virtually every reed instrument between them, and in 1958, bassist Ronnie Boykins joined the band and became an important factor in the way the music developed. Among the other notables have been trombonist Julian Priester, saxophonists Marion Brown, Charles Davis, James Spaulding and Pharoah Sanders, and bassists Richard Davis, Richard Evans and Wilbur Ware. On a visit to Indianapolis at the end of the 'fifties, the late Wes Montgomery jammed alongside the Arkestra's guitarist, Sam 'Bebop' Thomas, and Billy Higgins, everyone's favourite drummerman-for-all-seasons, sat in frequently when the band came to New York. So also did bassists John Ore and Bob Cunningham. For a reunion in Central Park, New York, Sun Ra was able to assemble a hundred-strong Arkestra of ex-alumni. And there are no young players who have not directly, or indirectly, experienced his influence. John Coltrane, who knew Sun Ra in Chicago in the late 'fifties, has said that he listened to John Gilmore before recording his iconoclastic masterpiece 'Chasin' the Trane', and in fact, Gilmore often relies entirely on harmonics for his solos, building an impenetrable edifice with devastating assurance and a degree of vigour equally, or even more astonishing than that displayed by the late Albert Ayler. There are, furthermore, many indications that Sun Ra was one of the first musicians to explore the possibilities of modal music.

His influence has not been confined to musical matters. From an early age Sun Ra developed the philosophy from which his associates have drawn. At home, in the South, he rejected the Gospel music enjoyed by most Southern Blacks of his generation, and listened to jazz instead. He evoked parental wrath when he turned his back on the church, but he detested the palliative effects of religion and the way it led to the resigned acceptance of the status quo by the people around him. Later, in Chicago, he attempted to show the Black urban proletariat ways of improving their situation. 'I felt that the Black people of America needed an awakening,' he said. He became involved in a nationalist organisation as its leader and started distributing pamphlets in which he pointed to the technological developments taking place in the world and the practicality of pursuing studies in the fields of electronics or engineering. His exhortations to 'stay in school' pre-dated James Brown's by more than a decade. It was during this period that John Coltrane was playing with Miles Davis. Pat Patrick introduced the saxophonist to him. According to John Gilmore, Coltrane had not yet formulated the style he was searching for. He was exposed to Sun Ra's poetry and philosophy as well as his music, and things started falling into place for him. As a result of reading Sun Ra's literature, he managed to break a heavy drug habit, and three months after taking the Arkestra's records to study, he left Davis and started to take a new direction in both his musical and personal life. Coltrane was not alone; several notable players have been helped straighten their tangled lives and kick their addiction through the pianist's wisdom.

* * *

Sun Ra was born Herman Sonny Blount in Birmingham, Alabama, somewhere between 1910 and 1916. In high school his band director was Professor John Tuggle Whatley, who was a pioneer in the field of securing grants to purchase instruments for his young students; as band leader 'Fess' Whatley, he was also responsible for helping several musicians on the road to fame, among them 'Old Man' Jo Jones (the drummer) and Erskine Hawkins and Teddy Hill, who were later to become leaders in their own right. The young Sun Ra formed a group of his own while the band director was out of town, and attracted such a following that Whatley bought a bus for them and arranged for them to tour the South.

He made his way North in the 'thirties by way of Gary, Indiana, and a spell in college in Washington, D.C., where he studied with a private tutor, Lula Randolph. Like thousands of Black Southerners before him, he eventually settled on the South Side of Chicago.

There were plenty of jazz records in the Blount household back in Birmingham, but the only ones that Sun Ra remembered were those by Fletcher Henderson. Through the years, he grew to appreciate the man who had led one of the greatest big bands of the 'twenties while laying the basis for the 'swing' style that catapulted Benny Goodman to fame. 'I always liked what Fletcher was doing. Nobody else had seemed to notice him too much, but he had this particular swing or rhythm that other people don't have.'

Whenever he had the chance, Sun Ra would buy records by Henderson as well as Ellington, and in 1946 he took over the piano chair in Henderson's band at the Club DeLisa. He spent a year there, sometimes playing for visiting blues singers, with Henderson directing and taking the occasional piano solo himself. 'I've always played the same type of thing chordwise and thoughtwise, but playing those chords with Fletcher, I had trouble out of the band. They didn't understand it, so finally I quit. But Fletcher wouldn't hire another piano player and I thought, well, since he plays piano himself, he knows what I'm doing. And so I came back.

'But a lot of musicians are backward, you'd be surprised. The band said they could play anything because they'd played music by the best arrangers in the land, but when I came back with arrangements on "I Should Care" and "Dear Old Southland", they tried for two hours and they couldn't play it. It was subtle.

'"Dear Old Southland" had three notes in each measure but they weren't used to that kind of syncopation. Yet I told them teenagers had played it because I'd taught them. Finally, though, they had to get used to it because the bandleader was perfectly satisfied.'

In November 1948, Sun Ra made his recording debut with Eugene Wright's Dukes of Swing, a group led by the former Brubeck bassist that included saxophonist Yusef Lateef. Coleman Hawkins and violinist Stuff Smith were living in Chicago then and Sun Ra played a month with them on the North Side.* The job was nominally Smith's, but with a virtuoso like Hawkins on hand, the leadership was effectively shared. Smith hired Sun Ra because he liked his playing, but Hawkins's interest went deeper. Whenever he was not playing, he would watch the pianist's hands. Eventually he asked him to write out his arrangement of 'I'll Remember April'. Years later, Sun Ra told the story to Baroness Nica de Koenigswarter, Rothschild heiress and long a patron of innumerable musicians, as well as a close friend of Hawkins. She took the pianist to meet Hawkins in order to gauge his reaction. At first the great saxophonist could not remember him, but when Sun Ra reminded him of the occasion, he replied: 'Yes, you wrote a number out for me that I couldn't play. It was the only music I've ever seen that I couldn't play, and I couldn't play it now. I can't understand why.'

Saxophonist Leroy Cooper remembers being handed an entire book of arrangements Sun Ra had written for the singer Lorez Alexandria. 'They were really weird combinations of notes. Some of the guys said, "How can you play this?" But when you played it, it sounded just right.'

'The only way anybody could play my music,' said Sun Ra, 'I'd have to teach them. I suppose it's the rhythmic feeling. It has a sort of two-way thing going. Most jazz will lay out over one rhythm but my music has two, maybe three or four things going, and you have to feel all of them. You can't count it.'

During the 'fifties, Sun Ra worked sporadically at Chicago's Birdland and Roberts Lounge, and played piano with Red Saunders, who had the houseband at the Club DeLisa. He was also responsible for the arrangements. On Saunders's off-nights, he would provide the band himself and, depending on the artist, would find himself playing the blues, ballads, jazz or gospel. Red

---

*One track, 'Deep Purple', on *Dreams Come True* (Saturn 485), features Stuff Smith with Sun Ra on piano and electric organ.

Holloway, a seasoned musician who has worked with Roosevelt Sykes and the Spaniels as well as Sonny Stitt, met Sun Ra in 1953 when they worked the Argyle Room together. They were also hired for a series of gigs by the late Al Smith, sometime bassist who once managed Jimmy Reed and T-Bone Walker. Today, Holloway leads the houseband at Los Angeles' Parisian Room and plays tenor saxophone with British rock/blues star John Mayall. He remembers Sun Ra as a quiet person who would seldom speak unless spoken to and who, despite his own abstemious habits, never frowned on those who indulged. In 1957 Holloway also led the band at the Club DeLisa and concluded that Sun Ra was 'fantastic' both as an arranger and musician, a pianist who could play in any style. 'And he was playing then, like in the 'fifties, the same way he is doing now. He's learned more, but he has always been a very *mystifying* pianist. He had his own type of playing and everyone used to listen and try to figure out what he was doing, because at that time it was strictly a straight-ahead type of jazz playing. You didn't have a lot of the chords that you would have today, you see, and so normally when you had a gig, it was just a straight gig. But when Sun Ra was on it, it became a *mysterious* gig – trying to figure out what the chords were!'

Although Sun Ra was politically active by this time, Holloway could not recall him speaking of any particular creed or religion. On one occasion, though, the pianist told him of his plans to visit New York in order to obtain some books. Later he reported that the trip had become unnecessary because he had found a way of going without actually boarding a bus or airplane. 'He said he just sent his body, his – oh, I've forgotten the words that he used – astral projection? Yeah, that's it. And he said he got the information he wanted.' When other people laughed at him, saying, 'Man, you hear that stuff that Sonny Blount is talking about?' Holloway would reply, 'Well, can you prove he's wrong?'

Sun Ra frequently accompanied blues artists of the stature of B.B. King, and a particular favourite of his was the little known Dr

JoJo Adams, a man he describes as 'a real blues singer on another type of level' whose penchant for wearing red, pink or shocking blue tuxedos and full tails in various colours – he had seven different sets – must have appealed strongly to Sun Ra's sense of the visually spectacular.

In 1953 Sun Ra was leading a trio with Richard Evans on bass and Robert Barry on drums when John Gilmore walked into the club and asked to sit in. The next night he was hired. 'It took me six months to actually hear how deep the things Sun Ra was doing were,' said Gilmore. 'He was so much advanced harmonically that although I could play his tunes since I could read music, it took me that long to see how different and how beautifully constructed his music was.'[3] As Red Holloway put it: 'He was always correct in his playing, it was just the way he would voice his chords.'

It was while playing 'Saturn', later to become one of the theme songs of the Arkestra, that Gilmore finally discovered what made the music tick. 'The intervals and harmony of his music required that you move in different parts of your horn you normally wouldn't get across, not even in classical music or jazz.'[4]

Gilmore, who came originally from Mississippi and had previously spent four months with the Earl Hines big band, became one of the Arkestra's mainstays. He has worked with other bandleaders from time to time, among them Art Blakey and Freddie Hubbard, and in the 'fifties, he rehearsed regularly with Miles Davis before Coltrane joined his group. The need to eat is always a pressing factor in the music business, yet Gilmore has always returned to the fold.

At this point Sun Ra was busy assembling the astonishing three-man reed team that was to remain intact over twenty years later. The interaction of the players and the multi-coloured sound textures they produced provided a blueprint for ensemble playing and collective improvisation between saxophonists and other instrumentalists in larger units.

In the tenor battles of bebop days, two saxophonists challenging each other were a frequent event. Sun Ra developed this idea, but exploited the actual voicings possible from pitting two protagonists together, their ferocious horns interlocked like duelling stags. When Marshall Allen played a duet with another alto saxophonist, it became impossible to work out who was playing what. These duets were the precursor of the furious forays into collective improvisation by as many as four alto players at a time that became a trademark of Sun Ra's constantly changing Arkestra by whatever name it was known. At various times he called it his Solar Arkestra or his Band From Outer Space; later it was Solar-Nature, Space, Myth-Science – eventually, Astro-Intergalactic-Infinity Arkestra. The names were as broad as the palette Sun Ra used in painting his 'pictures of infinity', building layer on layer of textural densities on top of a constantly shifting base of polyrhythms.

The baritone saxophonist Charles Davis was one of Sun Ra's earliest disciples, and by 1954, Marshall Allen and Pat Patrick had joined the band. When Sun Ra secured a residency at the Grand Terrace, the lineup was completed by trumpeter Art Hoyle, trombonist Julian Priester, and alto saxophonist James Scales. Patrick first heard Sun Ra while he was in high school. Later, they would run into each other on gigs and in rehearsal bands. On one of these jobs, he recalled, 'He was playing so much piano and getting sounds from the piano that didn't sound like a piano. I looked around and was utterly amazed.'[5]

Laurdine 'Pat' Patrick has an impressive background. He studied piano and drums as a child and took trumpet lessons from his father and Clark Terry. He played with James Moody and Quincy Jones, and worked with numerous Latin and Afro-Cuban bands, among them Mongo Santamaria's. He was, in fact, the band's musical director during the days when 'Watermelon Man' was riding high in the charts. He co-composed 'Yeh-Yeh' (a song recorded with varying degrees of success by Lambert, Hendricks and Bavan and Britain's Georgie Fame), and he has also written for the theatre. In 1970, he replaced Charlie Rouse in the Thelonious

Monk Quartet. On another occasion he took Russell Procope's place in the Ellington band and had the opportunity of sitting in the reed section between Johnny Hodges and Harry Carney, the two men who *were* the Ellington sound.

Sun Ra's music struck a familiar chord in Patrick and aroused his curiosity. The pianist, he says, 'is the type of musician that inspires you towards improvement and a better output on your horn. There is always something to be learned from him, and by becoming aware of so many things it also made me realise that I *wasn't* playing, too. Sun Ra can be a pretty strict teacher in that he has very high standards. With Sun Ra as a foundation and with my early musical exposure I have been able to function in many areas of music.'[6]

Marshall Allen, who comes from Louisville, Kentucky, played clarinet and C-melody saxophone in school. He studied the alto saxophone at the National Conservatory of Music in Paris and played there with the American pianist Art Simmons. He also toured Europe with James Moody before returning to Chicago at the turn of the 'fifties. His influences at the time were Johnny Hodges, Willie Smith, Benny Carter and Charlie Parker, and his ambition was to play lead in the saxophone section like two men he admired, Smith with Lunceford and Earle Warren with Basie. The sound quality he wanted was summed up in Hodges's ability to play pretty but retain a big sound. 'I felt I wanted to play on a broader sound basis rather than on chords,' he said. 'I couldn't play this way until I started playing with Sun Ra.'[7]

In 1956, Sun Ra made his first recording for Transition, and it was through hearing this that Allen decided he wanted to play with the pianist. He ran into King Kolax, the trumpet player whose r & b band was one of the leading units in Chicago at the time, and learnt Sun Ra was recruiting musicians. It was not long before Allen started attending rehearsals regularly.

Marshall Allen became one of the most reliable forces in the Arkestra. He added many instruments to his alto saxophone, among them flute, oboe, cor anglais, clarinet and the *morrow*, an instrument he designed himself. To begin with, Sun Ra confined the musicians to conventional instruments and taught them to explore their sound possibilities. Later, he allowed them to add the instruments he had collected from all over the world, including Africa (*kora*), Japan (*koto*) and China ('single-stringed violin').

Ronnie Boykins was the first bassist with sufficient strength to follow people like Wilbur Ware and Richard Davis. He became the pivot around which much of Sun Ra's music revolved for eight years, as well as one of the most determining elements in the sound of the Arkestra. His *arco* solo on the 1959 'Rocket No. 9 Take Off For the Planet Venus' is probably the first recorded example of the bass being played as a horn in a relatively 'free' context. Boykins's airy lines, described by Victor Schonfield as 'a characteristic New Black Music noise', run parallel with Ron Carter's 'cello developments, to be heard on Eric Dolphy's 'Out There', recorded a year later, and pre-date the kind of bowed work that the symphonically trained David Izenzon was to produce with Ornette Coleman, not to mention Alan Silva's high-register contributions to the music of Cecil Taylor and Albert Ayler.

Like Gilmore and Patrick, Ronnie Boykins had studied at DuSable High School under the famous 'Captain' Walter Dyett, who has turned out such notable musicians as Richard Davis and the violinist Leroy Jenkins as well as saxophonists Johnny Griffin and Clifford Jordan. He also studied with Ernie Shepard, a powerful player who later went on to work with Duke Ellington.

Together with a trombonist friend, Boykins had once opened a private club, The House of Culture. 'We were thinking that people – especially the Black community – should become aware of the existence of a Black culture.'[8] Sun Ra's statement to the effect that it was time Black musicians worked for themselves found an echo in the bassist's own philosophy. The discovery of 'a big band, a new music, a new philosophy' was exciting, but equally important in pledging his allegiance was the realisation that Sun Ra lived his philosophy: 'The reverse of so many people who said you mustn't smoke or drink and who never stopped smoking or drinking !'[9]

By the time Boykins joined, the Arkestra was already rehearsing for long and often arduous periods. Julian Priester, a native Chicagoan who later went on to play with Max Roach, Ray Charles, Art Blakey and Herbie Hancock, joined the band soon after he left High School. He gives some idea of what it was like to be in Sun Ra's 'woodshed'. For someone going straight from the blues bands of Muddy Waters and Bo Diddley, where a relatively stylised contribution was all that was required, it was a unique experience. Sun Ra would set up the slightest musical idea amongst the musicians, then Priester would look up and find a finger pointing at him to solo. 'I'd get up but I wouldn't know what was going on! I wouldn't know where I was in terms of a harmonic framework, I'd just have to listen to what was going on in back of me with the band – which was liable to be just about anything – and I'd have to work from that. I'd have to measure things instantly and start playing.'[10]

At the time, the trombonist did not quite grasp the importance of what was taking place; later he realised that Sun Ra was providing his first lessons in musical and personal freedom. 'I began to realise what sounds were. All notes are sounds and all sounds are notes – in a way, and I learned a lot about structure, how even the most limited structure can start you out improvising and how things can change immediately from there depending on what you play. It was a lot of knowledge.'[11]

The rehearsals began gradually to attract many of the younger musicians in town. If Sun Ra liked a musician, he would find a way for him to participate. Leroy Cooper, who played baritone saxophone with Ray Charles for almost twenty years, attended several rehearsals at the Sun Studio in 1957, the same year he joined the singer. When Sun Ra noticed his instrument, he told Cooper he had no baritone parts but would write some. 'He went away and came back the next day with a whole book – all of them written in pencil!'

Not all the visitors became converts. Sun Ra's music has always attracted as much abuse as it has praise, and more often than not it has been the musicians who failed to understand what he was doing. 'The music up till recent years was always about "Sweet Sue" and "Mary Jo", it was always about love,' he said. 'Jazz, too, all the songs were always about love. Very seldom did they branch over into anything else unless maybe it was about the blues. It was always about human emotions that everyone could feel, but it was just a repeat thing. It wasn't bringing people any new emotions, you see, although they got a wide range of emotions that they never used, a lot of feelings they never felt.

'Unfortunately the Black musician over here has been diverted into playing that sentimental music instead of playing the natural things we're supposed to play as Black men. Instead of holding their units together to play for their people in an organised way with the big bands, they moved down to trios and combos. They moved down to duos and the ego, they moved down to all of that. And then, you look at what the Black race did in America and it's not what I can be proud of.'

To Sun Ra, who grew up in an era when everyone could name at least a dozen big bands, each with a style of its own, the big band and the hard work that lies behind its precision epitomised all that is fine and heroic in Black music. Where he was concerned, the sheer professionalism of an organisation like Ellington's, Lucky Millinder's or Jimmy Lunceford's gave the Black community an ideal to admire. When these larger ensembles were forced to cut down through economic necessity, 'Black people lost their determining factor as to what was really natural or really sort of the master type of music for them.' He alone, with virtually no money at all, continued to develop in the tradition he approved.

Several musicians who later went on to join Chicago's other famous musical institution, the more pragmatic AACM (Association for the Advancement of Creative Musicians), were associated with Sun Ra at one time. Among them were trumpeter Phillip

Cohran, one of its founder members, saxophonist Virgil Pumphrey (now Absholom Ben Shlomo), and drummer Alvin Fielder. The AACM had always been dedicated to progress, yet at one time some of its members felt that Sun Ra had gone too far. One of them, according to drummer Alvin Fielder, was pianist Richard Abrams, the guild's *éminence grise*. Later, in New York, said Fielder, he sought out Sun Ra to tell him he had made a mistake. 'In Chicago I was saying "No", but I just came up this day to tell you "Yes".'

Alvin Fielder came to Chicago from Mississippi after studying pharmacy in New Orleans and Houston, Texas, and playing musical jobs in his spare time. He was introduced to Sun Ra by a saxophone player who took him on a West Side dance gig they were playing. He was invited to go along to the next rehearsal and as a result, mainly, he thinks, of coming from the South, was asked to join the band.

'Sunny really exposed me to a new way of playing, but I didn't really understand it at the time. I had been playing then for, I guess, a total of ten years, and *really* playing for five. Sunny would always say, though, "Just play", "Play loose", "Play anything" – "Play free". I didn't know what "free" was because at that time I was playing more like Max Roach – trying to, at least. Max was my idol.'

During the two years Fielder spent with the group, they worked quite frequently but for very little money. When they played in Indianapolis, the musicians came out with ten dollars apiece. Robert Barry, who is on most of Sun Ra's early albums, was the main drummer, but there was often another, usually William 'Bugs' Cochrane, and sometimes a timpanist, James Herndon. Fielder would play in tandem with one or the other, sometimes both. 'I had to stop trying to be the best drummer because I couldn't outplay them. This was like a learning thing. I was learning from Bugs, I was learning from Robert Barry, I was learning from Sun Ra, John Gilmore, Pat Patrick. They were like teachers and they were like big brothers. It was a family type thing and I was like the little boy.'

One of the places where the Arkestra worked nightly was the Queen's Mansion, a homosexual bar which boasted a large stage and dance-floor. It was located at 64th and Parkway in the heart of the South Side's musicland. New material was rehearsed each day, the band going over a tune once and playing it the same night. Subsequently it might be played another four or five times, then they went on to something else. The band book was about ten inches thick. Sun Ra carried a big tape machine with him and recorded the performance most nights.

By 1960, the work situation had deteriorated in Chicago and the Arkestra left for Canada, where an agent had found them work in Montreal. Ronnie Boykins, the only member of the band with a driving permit, borrowed his father's car and drove non-stop to Montreal. He arrived exhausted and collapsed in front of the hotel and was taken to hospital. On being asked his religion, he replied, 'Cosmic philosophy.'

The agent, however, had never heard the Arkestra play and, seeing their costumes and lighting effects, assumed they were a rock-and-roll band. The engagement only lasted a few days but they were rescued by the owner of a bistro situated in the University area. There they soon found an audience. Sun Ra was interviewed on television and the Arkestra played several dates elsewhere before the authorities told them they were refusing to renew the musicians' work-permits. The reason? They were 'disturbing public order'.

After four months in Canada, they made their way to New York instead of returning home. For about a year, they worked at the Playhouse, a room in Greenwich Village owned by Gene Harris, formerly the pianist with a group called The Three Sounds. Pharoah Sanders, newly arrived in New York, heard them there and took a non-musical job in the club in order to follow their nightly activity. When John Gilmore took a leave of absence to make a European and Japanese tour with Art Blakey, Sanders took his place. He was, of course, recorded by the leader who is planning the eventual release of the tapes. 'It should be very interesting to show the world what pre-Coltrane Pharoah Sanders was like,' was his comment.

Slug's, the home of jazz on the Lower East Side, was the place where most of the people playing the new music were heard for the first time. A brick-walled bar with sawdust on the floor, it was as important to the new music as Birdland had been to bebop. There was one main difference in that drugs were not as prevalent as they had been at Birdland. The musicians who frequented Slug's were – initially – more likely to be preoccupied with the idea of health food.

The bar was situated on East Fourth Street, a few blocks from Sun Ra's home-base, and from 1966 until its closure in 1972, the Arkestra was a more or less regular fixture on Monday nights. The stage was so small at Slug's that it was difficult to make out where the band stopped and the audience began. Conga drums and African drums of all shapes and sizes lined up behind as many as three regular drum-sets, sometimes played by Clifford Jarvis with Roger Blank or Jimhmi Johnson, later by John Gilmore and Lex Humphries. Often the Arkestra would play in total darkness, the only source of illumination being lights that flashed from Sun Ra's or Marshall Allen's headgear. As they grew in popularity and their financial situation improved somewhat, a light show would accompany the proceedings. From time to time films would be projected on the wall behind the players. The audience was always well-padded with instrumentalists from all generations; people like trumpeter Art Farmer and drummer Art Blakey were frequent listeners. For several numbers, it was customary for the musicians to parade around the club, blowing their horns, and trumpeter Earl Cross who played for a while with the Arkestra, recalled one night when there were only musicians on hand and saxophonists Jimmy Heath and Cannonball Adderley followed them around the room, listening to each individual player.

The ritualistic aspect of Sun Ra's performance was especially in evidence during the concerts at Slug's. Brightly garbed dancers would often appear with the band, some of them carrying various sceptres and other totems such as the sun-harp, a metal instrument shaped like the golden rays of the sun that Sun Ra had played at one time. In Chicago, the Arkestra had always attracted dancers even when not actually playing for them. It was considered a mark of some achievement to be allowed to dance with the band. Although he had listened to African music, Sun Ra described this preoccupation with ceremonial as stemming from 'my natural Blackness'. He was once asked how he had managed to retain this ethnic virtue. His reply: 'By isolating myself from Black folks in America and by isolating myself from white folks in America. I'm ME and that's more than either one of them can say. So therefore what I'm playing is just natural.'

Sun Ra puts his men through endurance tests more suited to athletes than musicians, often playing sets that last non-stop for five or six hours. His own energy is little short of amazing. The sessions at Slug's would finish at 4 a.m., but Sun Ra would always wait until all the instruments had been packed away before leaving for his home-base in Philadelphia, a distance of some ninety miles. He would be awake and on the case two and a half hours later. As Ronnie Boykins had discovered, he practises what he preaches.

In order to really hear the Arkestra, the listener would have to catch them every night for a month; the possibilities are that varied. The music can range from swing to neo-bop to free collective improvisation, all in a single night. An updated version of Duke Ellington's 1932 recording 'Lightnin'' is rapidly followed by a searing rendition of 'Yeah Man!' from the repertoire of the Jimmy Lunceford Orchestra of the same period. Sun Ra even plays a surrealistic version of Jelly Roll Morton's 'King Porter Stomp'. His treatment of such material, preserving the feeling of the original while investing it with a contemporary flair, serves the memory of the composers and their work far better than does the anachronistic NYJRO (New York Jazz Repertory Orchestra), brainchild of promoter George Wein, which not only preserves the original arrangements but repeats the solos more or less note for note.

One night, the hugely underrated Gilmore will be the featured soloist; another night, the percussion is predominant. The recording 'My Brother The Wind' features Gilmore's percussion work exclusively. 'Sometimes I don't consider that the world had really heard John,' said Sun Ra, who will only feature Gilmore if he has a strong bass player in the band. He himself likes the bassist to be near him. 'John's from Chicago and he has to have this strong rhythm behind him in order to play what he really wants to. He gets disturbed if the bass player isn't playing what he's used to hearing in Chicago. The bass players from Chicago play strong and other bass players don't seem to play like that.'

Ronnie Boykins became involved in more lucrative commercial pursuits in 1966 and felt obliged to leave the Arkestra as a result. Seven years later, Sun Ra called him to say he was having such problems finding a suitable bassist that he was being forced to use two bass players in order to get the sound he wanted. He became so disgusted with Boykins's successors, in fact, that he started playing the bass-line himself on one of his keyboards. He even lost one sideman because of this. 'I'm not going to play with that thing,' he told Sun Ra. The leader suggested they play together. 'No,' was the reply. 'You don't need me, man.'

Despite the rigorous principles that they must adhere to, the musicians have nothing but respect for Sun Ra and what he represents in the community. Earl Cross called him an 'institution'. Clifford Jarvis said their respect was 'frightening'. He, in turn, has nothing but respect for the musicians that helped him in his youth and taught him their own fine principles. I never met any people as unselfish as the jazz musicians I met when I was growing up, who I played with. They wasn't playing for no dollars, they was playing because they wanted to play. And you can hear it in the music.

There isn't anything else like it in the world. The early jazz records, the spontaneity. They were playing because they *liked* jazz.'

In an interview with the Nigerian journalist Tam Fiofori, who was a member of his entourage for a while, Sun Ra paid the kind of tribute to his musical antecedents that is relatively unusual: 'While in High School, I never missed a band, whether a known or unknown unit. I loved music beyond the stage of liking it. Some of the bands I heard never got popular and never made hit records, but they were truly natural Black beauty. I want to thank them and I want to give honour to all the sincere musicians who ever were or ever will be. It's wonderful to even think about such people. The music they played was a natural happiness of love, so rare I cannot explain it. It was fresh and courageous; daring, sincere, unfettered. It was unmanufactured avant-garde, and still is, because there was no place for it in the world; so the world neglected something of value and did not understand. And all along I could not understand why the world could not understand. It was all there. Was it because the world considers music as only a commercial commodity? I am glad that that is not my code.'[12]

Notes

1   *Sun Ra in Egypt* (Thoth Intergalactic).
2   Interview with Tam Fiofori, 'Sun Ra's African Roots', *Melody Maker*, 12 February 1972.
3   Interview with Tam Fiofori, 'Gilmore: a Tenor Spearhead', *Melody Maker*, 3 April 1971.
4   ibid.
5   Interview with Tam Fiofori, 'Pat's Rhythm Thing', *Melody Maker*, 10 April 1971.
6   ibid.
7   Interview with Tam Fiofori, 'Right Sound at the Right Time', *Melody Maker*, 27 March 1971.
8   Interview with Jacqueline and Daniel Caux, in *Jazz Magazine*, June 1974.
9   ibid.

10 Interview with Eugene Chadbourne, 'Wandering Spirit Song', *Coda*, December 1974.
11 ibid.
12 Interview with Tam Fiofori, 'Sun Ra's Space Odyssey', *Down Beat*, 14 May 1970.

6

Albert Ayler – Spiritual Unity

My music is the thing that keeps me alive now. I must
play music that is beyond this world. That's all I'm asking
for in life and I don't think you can ask for more than
just to be alone to create from what God gives you.

Albert Ayler

When the body of Albert Ayler was fished out of the East River
at the foot of Brooklyn's Congress Street Pier on the morning of
25 November 1970, the music world lost an iconoclast, and Black
culture gained another martyr. The New York Medical Examiner's
office ruling was 'asphyxia by submersion – death by drowning',
and as there was apparently no suggestion of foul play, a post-mor-
tem was not ordered. The Brooklyn police force may have been
satisfied but the musicians' community was not. Ayler's death,
less than five months after his thirty-fourth birthday, came too
soon after the passing of his friend and mentor John Coltrane.
The musicians were stunned. Six months later, rumours that the
saxophonist had been shot, that a bullet wound in the back of his
head had been put there by the police, still persisted.

The police had, in fact, been called to his Brooklyn home shortly
after his disappearance, and that was how the rumour began. Call
Cobbs Jr, the pianist who had been involved in his music since
their first meeting in 1964, identified the body in the company of
Ayler's father. He stressed that no bullet wound was evident and

the death certificate certainly makes no reference to one. According to friends, however, the saxophonist had not been seen for twenty days before his body was found. If he had been in the river for some time, it is not difficult to deduce that any wound or abrasion would be hard for the layman to recognise.

It was Mary Maria, the singer and songwriter who was his constant companion for the last two years of his life, who called in the police. She did this because, she said, she feared for his safety. She is reluctant to elaborate further and until she does, the theory of police involvement will continue to be speculated on and to fuel discussion in the musicians' community.

The mysterious circumstances of the saxophonist's disappearance reinforced a belief held by some Black musicians concerning the equally sudden deaths of Coltrane and the guitarist Jimi Hendrix. They see more than coincidence in the fact that these artists died at the point when their music had reached a level of persuasiveness sufficient to enable them to control their creative product. In Coltrane's case, he built a studio at his Long Island home and formed his own record company. Hendrix was similarly involved. Ayler was nowhere near the financial bracket of either artist, but his record label *appeared* to be grooming him for a place in the popular music mainstream.

Albert Ayler was the latest innovator in a line that reached back beyond Buddy Bolden, yet he was one of the most maligned. He toured Europe in 1966 at the height of his notoriety and made a tele-recording for British television. The BBC were horrified. They locked the tapes away like an Inquisition dealing with the works of witchcraft. Later, along with other 'unusable' and 'unimportant' material, they were quietly destroyed. An illicit copy of the tape is believed to exist.

Ayler's brief career was a catalogue of misunderstandings. When he spoke of playing a 'silent scream' it seemed incomprehensible and faintly ludicrous at the time to those outside the musicians' circle, but on some of his later recordings where his exceptional technique enabled him to virtually 'invent' a new range for his saxophone, he consorted with violin and 'cello and double-basses bowed in the high register – even managing to sound like a stringed instrument himself – and created an effect of almost painful singing – or screaming – with a kind of peaceful silence at its core. Whereas when Coltrane was running full tilt through his modal cascades it sometimes seemed that the climax would never arrive, Ayler resolved his improvisations with the definitive stroke of a Coleman Hawkins.

Be that as it may, his *Down Beat* obituary claimed that his playing 'bore little resemblance to any other jazz, past or present'[1] – which only goes to show the futility of categories. Ayler was Great Black Music personified; his music encompassed every thread woven into the fabric of so-called jazz. He took as his source material the spirituals, funeral dirges, bugle calls and marches of the past, and, though he seldom did so, he could *really* play the blues.

He used a tough plastic reed, a Fibrecane No 4 – the hardest – and had a sound that scared the shit out of everyone who heard him. Rollins, Coleman and Coltrane had explored the use of the saxophone's harmonics or 'overtones', but Ayler was the first person to actually base his style on them. The saxophone's series of natural harmonics can be played by using a combination of fingering and embouchure; Steve Lacy is one of the players using this conventional method. Coltrane occasionally used this combination but generally found his harmonics through 'lipping', that is, tightening or loosening the embouchure to either raise or lower the pitch. Ayler appears to have used embouchure alone. He growled through the saxophone from the back of his throat to produce coarse, guttural effects, a technique that went back to Earl Bostic and Illinois Jacquet and beyond. Where jazz players of the preceding era had used the 'scream' only as a kind of exclamation mark, even consciously avoiding it to distinguish them from the 'cruder' exponents of rhythm-and-blues, Ayler 'screamed' unashamedly with a disregard for the niceties and conventions of bebop. On top of this, few *jazz* musicians had employed as wide a vibrato since the New Orleans days.

Ayler's music combined all the forces that set the consummate artist apart. He had the fire and passion of Charlie Parker and Ornette Coleman and the sheer 'damn-you' audacity of Jacquet or Big Jay McNeely or any honking saxophone player that ever walked the bartop in a thousand funky joints from one end of America to the other. At the same time, even in his most jubilant moments, he projected an aching sadness reminiscent of Billie Holiday or Miles Davis at their most poignant. There was an essential feeling of celebration in Ayler's playing which was thrown into relief by the marches and gospel tunes he chose as a framework for his improvisations. Above all, he had an inner calm, a religiousness of purpose and a gentle nature that expressed itself in some of his slower themes and the titles he gave to his compositions.

Ted Joans, the Illinois-born poet and sometime trumpet player, described the experience of hearing the saxophonist for the first time. He was sitting at the bar in a Copenhagen jazz club, waiting for Ayler and his group – trumpeter Don Cherry, bassist Gary Peacock, drummer Sunny Murray – to start playing. Beside him, the New Orleans clarinettist Albert Nicholas was discussing the merits of various reeds with two young local musicians: 'I turned to say something to Albert Nicholas, and then like an unheard of explosion of sound, they started. Their sound was so different, so rare and raw, like screaming the word "FUCK" in Saint Patrick's Cathedral on crowded Easter Sunday. Albert Nicholas's hands trembled, causing his beer to spill. The two grey boys turned white as clean sheets on a wedding bed. Then all of a sudden their faces were fire-engine red and wet. The entire house was shook up. The loud sound didn't let up. It went on and on, growing more powerful as it built up. It was like a giant tidal wave of frightening music. It completely overwhelmed everybody. Some of the Danes responded with their rude whistling, others shouted at the musicians to shut up. I sat shocked, stoned and amazed by what I was witnessing. Their music was unlike anything that I had heard before.'[2]

Joans maintained that it was as a result of Ayler's impact that Nicholas, who had played with King Oliver's reed section back in the 'twenties, started to reassess the work of the young musicians. Later that year, he was to be seen every night listening intently to Archie Shepp's group who were playing in a Paris club. He was not alone in his generation. Don Byas, fractionally younger than Nicholas and like him a longterm expatriate, told Sunny Murray that he had wanted to play like Ayler since he was a boy. Byas, whose lifetime obsession was with strength, intensity and fullness of tone, was filled with admiration for the sheer honesty and freedom he detected in the approach of his fellow tenor saxophonist.

Of all the 'second wave' of new music players to emerge in the wake of Coleman, Coltrane, Dolphy, Rollins and Taylor, Albert Ayler was the most revolutionary. He improvised in a deceptively simple way. He tended to place considerable stress on the melody itself and frequently return to it. This is especially noticeable on his early recordings where he was hampered by rigid and unsympathetic musicians – 'startled' is probably a more appropriate description for them – and may well have needed to refer to the theme for reassurance, although he later said he liked to play something people could hum. He was a melodist by nature, though, and enjoyed wringing every possible nuance from the lines of his compositions rather than using them just as a springboard for getting down to the main business of improvisation. For the most part, any steady beat was absent from his work prior to 1968, but wherever there was a recognisable pulse, Ayler would play *around* it in the manner of a New Orleans player.

His music contained many elements that went back to the earliest forms of jazz, in fact; his 'Truth is Marching In' would not have sounded out of place en route to the cemetery. Together with Sunny Murray, he was the main populariser of small-group collective improvisation – 'rejoicing collectively to the spirits,' he called it – in the modern context. Apart from Ornette Coleman's *Free Jazz,* this was the first time it had been attempted consistently outside of New Orleans-style ensembles. Not surprisingly, Ayler claimed that New Orleans marches would suggest themselves to him while he was playing.

It was by the use of such methods that Ayler, possibly more than any other player, epitomised Archie Shepp's oft-quoted view of the music: that it reached back to what jazz was originally, a rebellion against the ultra-sophisticated art form it had become.

'I think one thing he proved was that he could *traditionally* blow his horn,' said Milford Graves, who played with Ayler for a short period. 'He could *really* play honky-tonk, he knew all the gut things, and, not taking away from any other horn players, he was the kind of horn player with whom I could really play my axe. You could see Albert knew exactly what was happening.'

* * *

Albert Ayler was born 13 July 1936, in Cleveland, Ohio, the elder of two sons. Donald Ayler, who was later to play trumpet with his brother, was six years his junior, and a third child, a daughter, died at birth. His father Edward played saxophone in the style of Dexter Gordon and was known on a local level; he also sang and played violin.

The family lived in Shaker Heights, a pleasant residential district with a racially mixed population, and the Ayler boys grew up surrounded by religion and indoctrinated with all the middle-class Black values. In 1966 the Pittsburg-born drummer Beaver Harris stayed at their home after playing a concert with the brothers at the WEWS Radio Station auditorium. 'It was just like all the comfort in the world,' he recalled. 'His mother is highly spiritual, solid, active in the church, and they believe in a lot of very important spiritual things.'

From the age of three, according to his mother Myrtle, 'Albert would blow on anything he could find.' He would position himself by the radio when the big bands came on; then he would pick up a foot-stool, put the leg to his lips and 'play' along with Lionel Hampton and Benny Goodman. Edward Ayler, frustrated by his own inability to make a career out of music, recognised the youngster's potential and some time later started teaching him to play. At the age when most youngsters were out and about, playing baseball and so on, Albert was forced to stay home and practise daily.

His first instrument was the alto saxophone, and his father's teaching continued for four years, by which time they were playing duets together in church each Sunday. Lloyd Pearson, a saxophonist who leads a popular jazz/rock group in Cleveland, knew Ayler from kindergarten days. A couple of years his senior, he was able to remember him giving solo recitals while still in the second grade, playing on an instrument that almost dwarfed him.

Ayler himself recalled being taken by his father to hear the crowd-stirring saxophonists Illinois Jacquet and Red Prysock. At home, recorded listening concentrated on Lester Young, Wardell Gray and Charlie Parker, as well as Freddie Webster, the noted Cleveland trumpeter whose sparse recorded work was later to influence the younger son.

At ten, Albert Ayler began studying at the Academy of Music with Benny Miller, a musician who had once played with Charlie Parker and Dizzy Gillespie. He spent seven years there altogether, and his prodigious technique blossomed. At John Adams High School he always played first chair in the school orchestra and doubled on oboe. He became impatient with sheet music in the school's marching band, and when reprimanded, insisted that he could do as well without. The band director allowed him his way, but told him, 'You play one note wrong and you're out of the band!' And of course, Edward Ayler remarked proudly, 'He didn't play one note wrong.'

During this time, Albert also became interested in golf. He captained his school team at a time when golf was still an exclusively white game, and when the only Blacks permitted on most courses were caddies or groundskeepers. The numerous trophies he won still stand on the mantelpiece in his parents' home, and his success at this Jim-Crow sport gave him considerable status in Cleveland.

Lloyd Pearson started playing saxophone in Junior High School, inspired by the example of the younger boy, and the two started 'buddying around' together until Ayler went in the Army. Their interest in music was strong, and they defied the law in the classic tradition, sneaking into bars while still under-age in order to listen to the music. 'We'd see all the horn players, all the good ones, the bar-walkers and everything. We had a good basis because that's all we did – music, music, music'

By the age of fifteen, Ayler's reputation had spread beyond church and school. Pearson formed a band known as Lloyd Pearson and his Counts of Rhythm with himself on tenor and Ayler playing alto, and the two teenagers started to flex their muscles in competitive local jam-sessions. Gleason's Musical Bar was the place where visiting musical acts would go to pick up sidemen, and sitting in with the houseband, led by guitarist Jimmy Landers, was an important step. It was there that Ayler met Little Walter Jacobs, the harmonica player from Alexandria, Louisiana, whose unique chromatic work gained expression accompanying Muddy Waters. He played several small local clubs with him, then Walter took him on the road. Pearson was also in the band.

'When he got the job he was so excited he could hardly believe it,' recalled Edward Ayler. 'He came running home shouting about, "They're gonna take me with 'em, they're taking *me!*"' Nevertheless, it was a gruelling experience for a young man from a middle-class background, for the rest of the musicians were hard-drinking, barely literate 'country' bluesmen from the Deep South. He carried his food with him because the pay was poor. 'The manner of living was quite different for me – drinking real heavy and playing real hard. We'd travel all day and finally arrive, take out our horns and play.'

Ayler spent two summers on the road with Little Walter and his Jukes, but at the beginning, the harmonica player criticised him for his inability to hold a note in the time-honoured way pleasing to their kind of audience. The young saxophonist worked on this and was soon on their wavelength. In spite of the hardships, he considered that 'being out there amongst those really deep-rooted people' played an important part in his development. To Ayler, the past was an obvious part of the present: 'Blues and Rhythm – how could you miss that? You had to have that to have what we have now.'

Lloyd Price, the New Orleans singer, also took the young saxophonist on the road briefly; then for a while, he and Pearson started hanging out at the barbershop on 55th Street frequented by the local 'Macs', or pimps (the word has ambiguous connotations in the Black community). Ayler, always a sharp dresser and already noted for his success with women, revelled in the swagger and the braggadocio that is an integral part of Black masculinity and which went hand in hand with the music and the nightlife. They had their hair processed as was the fashion and imitated the 'Mac' style. 'But the music, man, that was another thing,' recalls Pearson.

Ayler formed his own rhythm-and-blues band on leaving school, but its future was limited. He spent one year in college, but due to a lack of money, he finally capitulated and joined the Army. Before he left Cleveland, his playing bore no apparent trace of the style that was to establish him as an innovator in the music while astonishing the people with whom he grew up. 'Conventional' was how Lloyd Pearson described it.

Ayler earned himself the nickname of 'Little Bird' at a time when other Cleveland saxophonists were more concerned with 'honking' and walking the bar – hardly surprising tactics in the birthplace of Bull Moose Jackson. Both he and Pearson devoted their attention to learning the changes (chords) and enlarging their repertoire of tunes.

'Al played like Charlie Parker and all them cats because he could play a lot of tunes, ballads and so on. Later on, some people would say that he couldn't play, but I remember him from when he first started, and he could play all of them standard tunes like they weren't nothing. Before he went away, he was more advanced than anyone. He had went through a lot of things that horn players play after they've been playing for fifteen years.'

Ayler was twenty-two when he joined the Army. He stayed three years and was put into one of the Special Services bands. For six or seven hours a day, he played concert music, and the rest of the time would be free to concentrate on developing his own ideas, 'trying to get a new way to play the music that would be my own'.

Beaver Harris, who was later to record and tour Europe with Ayler, first met him when they were both stationed at Fort Knox, Kentucky. He was also attached to Special Services, though not as a musician; his major preoccupation at the time was baseball. Having the freedom of the post, he was able to mix with the musicians who included saxophonist Stanley Turrentine and Chuck Lampkin, a drummer who played with Gillespie in the early 'sixties.

Ayler still wore his hair in a process, but his unusual beard (half of it grew out white as the result of an unpigmented patch of skin on his chin), his personal style of dress and the bright colours that he favoured set him apart. Harris was struck by Ayler's spiritual qualities and warmth as much as his actual music which, for a musician like himself reared in the Max Roach tradition, tended too much towards the 'honky-tonk' vein. He was impressed by the saxophonist's 'very, very powerful chops', and the obvious fact that, whenever he tackled a straightforward bebop tune, he was intent on forging a new direction. 'We would always get along, whereas certain other musicians he really didn't get along with. He and Stanley Turrentine didn't really communicate. Stanley was what you would call the heavier type of musician who had been exposed to Charlie Parker, Dexter Gordon, Gene Ammons and Lockjaw Davis and everyone, and so he had more of an experience than Albert and more of a so-called "soulful" quality. You can't really weigh a soulful quality in a Black man, though, because all Black musicians tend to have this quality, but some musicians will play in a way that the technique will dominate the soulfulness. Albert had the technical ability that dominated his soulfulness at times, whereas Stanley was strictly a "soul" player.'

For a while, Ayler and Harris played together, taking a few jobs in Louisville, the nearest town, before the saxophonist finally shipped out to Europe. He was based in Orleans but frequently found his way to Paris, where he would sit in at various clubs. His natural appetite for martial music – 'he knew just about every march you could think of,' said Beaver Harris – was whetted by the French military bands. He became especially attached to the national anthem – 'La Mayonnaise', as he called it. Later, he was to recall the period that had shaped much of his musical thinking by recording 'Spirits Rejoice!', a theme which bore certain similarities to that anthem.

It was during this time that Ayler switched to the tenor saxophone. Like Ornette Coleman, who felt that 'the best statements Negroes have made of what their soul is'[3] had been made on this instrument, Ayler dug deeply into its ethnic and sociological implications. 'It seemed that on the tenor you could get out all the feelings of the ghetto. On that horn you can really shout and tell the truth,' he told Nat Hentoff. 'After all, this music comes from the heart of America, the soul of the ghetto.'[4] He visited Denmark, and Sweden, a country that has always shown its hospitality to Black musicians; not surprisingly, it was there that his experiments were first treated with respect, and he planned to return there on quitting the Army. His discharge came in 1961 in California, where he made the acquaintance of the comedian Redd Foxx. The local musicians gave him short shrift, as they had done Ornette Coleman a dozen years earlier, but like Erroll Garner, who had heard him play in Amsterdam on the night of Don Byas's conversion, the comedian told him: 'Play what you believe in.'[5]

Back home in Cleveland, his attempts to introduce his

revolutionary ideas were greeted with disbelief by most of the musicians. Lloyd Pearson's first reaction was that the Army had affected his mind in some way and that he had not touched his horn throughout his Service sojourn. 'I just said, *"Damn,* the cat sure done got *weird!"* At that time everybody was into the changes. If you didn't play the changes, cats said you couldn't play. He was rejected by the audience, the musicians, and all of them for a minute. Everybody was laughing at that style because they hadn't heard it.'

Pearson hid his amazement from his old friend, even allowing him to take over his band for a couple of nights, but coming from a culture where the sacred and secular occupy distinct positions, he was rather disturbed by the fact that Ayler now included spirituals in his repertoire. To him, they were out of place in a nightclub. The late Joe Alexander, then the city's most prominent saxophonist, found something even more out of place when Ayler sat in with him on soprano and refused to play the chord changes. Later on, apparently, Alexander took the matter up with Coltrane. He maintained that the soprano just could not be played that way. Coltrane's response was to the point: 'Well,' he said, 'he's playing.'

'He used to come to me and tell me he had found the real music and the real religion, and it had a lot to do with God – which sounded strange to me at the time,' said Pearson. 'But then he sounded like a lot of noise, like someone just beginning. When he played a ballad, he didn't play the melody line. People would say, *"Goddamn!* Play the melody line!" But he wouldn't give in. In other words, he would say, "To hell with them." He used to walk in with his horn and they'd say, "Uh-uuuuh, here he comes!" But he had a helluva – technically – big tone. It takes a long time to get a tone of that quality. He played the lows and the highs, he did everything, but I didn't look at him like that. He used to play so pretty on all the ballads, then to come back and he didn't touch none of that ...'

Ayler decided he had finished with the 'stupid mentality' of his fellow Americans. He told his mother he had to go where the people understood his music, although he could hardly understand himself at the time. 'The music was not quite formulated in my head. I played it, but it came slowly, not immediately like it does now.'[6]

He saved enough money to return to Sweden, and during the eight months he spent there toured with a commercial band. Whenever he could, however, the saxophonist made his way to the 'Old City' or the subway to play for the children: 'They heard my cry.'[7]

Fortuitously, the owner of a small private record label also heard his cry. On 25 October 1962, Bengt Nordstrom persuaded Ayler to record for the first time. His Bird Notes album was made in front of an audience of twenty-five people at the Stockholm Academy of Music. The unfortunate bassist and drummer picked to accompany him were oblivious to his conception from start to finish. Ayler sounded a little like Sonny Rollins, but already the unmistakable stamp of his personality was showing through.

Three months later he was invited to Copenhagen to tape a transmission for Danish Radio. The results, subsequently issued on Debut as *My Name is Albert Ayler,* include his only released recorded performance on soprano, 'Bye Bye, Blackbird', and 'Summertime', one of the classics of the new music. It is a passionate expression of almost unbelievable pathos. His dramatic swoops and masterly shading recall the sweeping *glissandi* of Johnny Hodges, while the completeness of his statement gives the lie to the notion that he was going through an 'experimental' period.

It was during this time that Don Cherry made a European tour with Sonny Rollins. The lineup was completed by Henry Grimes and Billy Higgins, and Ayler came backstage after their concert. He and Cherry visited the Jazzhus Montmartre together where Don Byas and Dexter Gordon were appearing. The trumpeter was invited to join the veteran saxophonists for a ballad medley, then Ayler offered a rendition of 'Moon River' which startled all those present. Cherry likened the impact to the first time he heard

Ornette Coleman. 'It's a thing where even though it's the first time you're experiencing it, it feels familiar.' Later, Ayler and Rollins played together on many occasions and, according to the latter, influenced each other.

Back in Sweden, Ayler had been playing with Candy Green, a professional gambler and pianist from Houston, Texas, who had recorded with the blues singer Gatemouth Brown. Twice daily in a small restaurant, the saxophonist dug back into his blues roots to earn enough to pay the rent. On his return from Denmark, he told Green he could no longer 'hear' that kind of music because he had just played with Cecil Taylor. Sunny Murray, who had made the journey to Europe with Taylor, recalled their first meeting at the Montmartre. 'No one would give him a job and he was getting depressed. When he came to hear Cecil's band, he started scream-ing, "I finally found somebody I could play with! Please let me play!" So we said, "Who's this cat?" I'd never seen him before, but later Cecil hired him in the band.'

Ayler's association with Taylor was comparatively short-lived because little work was available. They worked together at the Take Three in Greenwich Village with Jimmy Lyons playing alto, Henry Grimes on bass and Murray on drums. Coltrane and Eric Dolphy, appearing nightly at the nearby Village Gate, would regu-larly come to listen. Ayler began to be heard all over New York, sitting-in and proving himself.

By this time, there were a few young bloods in Cleveland who had become interested in what he was doing. Frank Wright, origi-nally a bass player, started playing the tenor in a similar style, as did Mustafa Abdul Rahim, who had been at school with Donald Ayler. One of the first stops Ayler made when he came back from his stay in Europe was at the home of trumpeter Norman Howard. They had grown up on the same block and played together before Ayler went into the Army. It was there that he also met and played with Earle Henderson, at the time a struggling self-taught pianist.

Now known as 'Errol' Henderson, he was impressed by Ayler's

modesty as he recounted his European successes. 'Though he spoke as though things were going well for him, he was never pretentious or aloof.'[8] The saxophonist's main concern, apparently, was to discover whether any new players had come on the scene in his absence so that he could challenge them 'in a place not unlike the O.K. Corral'.

The leather suits that Ayler had worn since his Army days were still considered unique attire for a Black man during this period, and the highly personal style of dress he favoured had always been a subject of admiration amongst his peers. Henderson's recollection of every detail is typical:

'Albert was wearing an evergreen tailored leather suit that was *murder*, perfect for Northern or European winters. The shoes were unique also. They were leather, too, like slippers, but with an extended tongue that bent back towards the toe and which made them appear like something a man from Sherwood Forest might wear on his feet. I have never seen such an individual taste in Winterwear before or since. A Russian-type fur hat topped this ensemble fit to fight blizzards in.'[9]

He went on to describe his initiation to Ayler's music. 'We talked, laughed, reminisced and projected over many things for a while when Albert get the taste for his tenor. He began unpacking it casually, all the while talking about this composition he had just written. Well, he assembled the instrument, took a bite of the mouthpiece and began to play this melody.

'Smooth, oh so smooth and easy did the music ease from the tenor's bell, with such tone, with such feeling. The melody was a haunting little ditty, not remarkable technically but moving. But when he began to improvise, this is when I became startled by his music's style. It was like the wind sometimes, moving fast. At other moments it hovered, and at others it oscillated back and forth with sounds that would strike the earth to its centre, or soar until the penetration of the sound would clear the sky of clouds.

'The sound was so pure, the disposition of the feeling so obvious, that I was entranced. He, the music, went directly to the feeling. He was speaking from or with his very soul, for himself and for me and for all the other people who wanted to discard certain values and judgements that had been deemed unalterable. As he played, Albert was a pilot of an exploration, but the landscape was familiar at least through experience, consciously having travelled it countless times. But for the initiate, it was a journey of sheer spectacular beauty. I had never heard anything like the music of Albert Ayler before except in pieces out of my conscious musical and non-musical past, then only in pieces here and there.

'After the trip, after Albert brought us back to Cleveland and to the present, there was nothing to say about the music we had just heard. The music was the feeling, the feeling was the music and the music of feeling was Albert Ayler. Norman and I looked at each other and said nothing aloud, but the expression on Norman's face and the expression of my heart said, "Yeah, man, yeah, Albert; you got it." Of course, upon recovery we told him how pleased we were with his exhibition.'[10]

A few days later the three men played together, but by and large, Ayler had little opportunity to play in Cleveland. He would walk into nightclubs on his own, his saxophone under his arm, a loner in his hometown. He had brought fifty copies of the Bird Notes album *Something Different!!!!!!* from Sweden, and sold them on the street corner. His personal reputation was still considerable, though by and large, his dress drew more favourable comment than his music.

Mustafa Abdul Rahim described the peculiar status Ayler enjoyed, earned through his gentle manner, his generosity and spiritual nature as well as his earlier achievements on the golf course. 'He was always treated with a certain degree of respect. So you see, even though from time to time a club owner because of his materialistic nature might ask Al to vacate the premises (after an "outside" solo), the patrons had to give Al respect just on his personal accomplishments.

'Al's playing always possessed and radiated an uplifting and heal-ing-type feeling. Whether he was sitting in with r & b or "fat-back" music, the healing and uplifting force persisted.'[11]

Nevertheless, it was obvious to Ayler that his future lay outside this mid-West town. Despite the fact that he had a wife and child in Cleveland, he moved to New York in 1963 and took an apartment in a house owned by his aunt on St Nicholas Avenue. Saxophon-ist Charles Tyler and Errol Henderson, playing bass by this time, were living in another building on 130th Street at Lenox Avenue with several other young musicians from Cleveland, and several times a week Ayler walked across Harlem to play with them. The new music, still in its infancy, was being created within the Black community – contrary to the beliefs of some of its detractors. As Henderson put it: 'We young bloods, we bearers of the torch of certain tribal traditions, raised the skies over Harlem every night with the steam of our music.'[12]

Ole Vestergaard Jensen, the man responsible for Ayler's Debut album, arranged for him to go into the Atlantic studios to tape some more music. *Spirits*, later issued on Freedom as *Witches and Devils*, contains some of Ayler's most majestic playing and marks his first appearance on record with musicians of his own stature. He used Norman Howard and Earle (Errol) Henderson, as well as the ubiquitous Sunny Murray and a second bassist, Henry Grimes. Murray, who is a leading innovator in the new music, has been described as one of those crucial figures in jazz who appear just at the time they are needed. His unchained approach to percussion gave Ayler the freedom to travel his own road that had hitherto been lacking.

It was around this time that Ayler and the other Cleveland musicians started to make regular visits to the basement apart-ment where Ornette Coleman was living, just off Washington Square. A considerable exchange of ideas took place and on one occasion some of the music was taped by a 'Rich White Friend' of Coleman's in his loft. Coleman played trumpet on this session,

Ayler tenor, Charles Tyler played C-melody saxophone, Norman Butler played alto and 'cello and Henderson was the bassist. The 'RWF' added his own contribution on guitar, and was eventually responsible for making the tapes available to a limited number of *cognoscenti*. Although these bootlegs are circulated amongst a narrow group of collectors, enriching their appreciation and understanding of the music, their existence does pose a problem. As Henderson put it: 'The music we made that afternoon is now a product floating around Europe making money for some and being enjoyed aesthetically by others, no doubt. However, as regrettable as that situation may be in terms of distribution of the financial gain of this undercover, uncommitted-to-the-artists-involved operation, it is the only recorded occasion featuring the legendary Albert Ayler and the consciousness-raising Ornette Coleman on trumpet.'[13]

But it was not only with younger musicians that Albert Ayler associated in New York. One older man was Call Cobbs Jr, who also rented a room in the house on St Nicholas Avenue. Cobbs (who had once worked as Billie Holiday's accompanist and had also played with Lucky Millinder and Wardell Gray) is the pianist on another set of tapes cut in New York at the *Witches and Devils* debut session. The tunes, all spirituals, are played by Ayler on soprano saxophone, accompanied by Cobbs, Grimes and Murray. Later that year, Ayler played the tapes to Bernard Stollman, who was just readying himself to launch his catalogue of avant-garde music in ESP-Disk and had already agreed to record him. Stollman was upset to hear spirituals played in that way, just as Lloyd Pearson had been. Ayler's reaction was to smile gently. 'In retrospect,' said Stollman, 'I imagine that he realised that one day I might understand it.' To date, however, the tapes remain unreleased.

In July 1964, against the advice of Cecil Taylor and other musicians who thought that artists should hold out for a price commensurate with their talent, Ayler made his first recordings for ESP.* 'I felt my art was so important that I had to get it out. At that time I was musically out of this world. I knew I had to play this music for the people.' *Spiritual Unity*, a trio date with Gary Peacock on bass and Sunny Murray on drums, revolutionised the direction for anyone playing those three instruments. The music was shockingly different – Ayler disquietingly harsh and brutal but at the same time deeply tinged with pathos, Peacock listening as he played monumental bass figures, Murray behaving, as LeRoi Jones once put it, as though 'he might just want to disappear'[14] – but its conclusions seemed so simple when you listened to it. Ayler, Murray and Peacock had created the perfect *group* music. With it, Ayler felt that the ultimate stage in interaction had been reached. 'Most people would have thought this impossible but it actually happened. The most important thing is to stay in tune with each other but it takes spiritual people to do this.' On *Spiritual Unity*, he said, 'We weren't *playing,* we were listening to each other.'

Such is the position of the Black artist, however, that the next time Denmark called, Ayler was offered only a one-way ticket. He reluctantly agreed to the terms because 'American-minded people' were still rejecting his vision and he felt he had to leave. It provided a better opportunity to expose the music than at home where opportunities were, frankly, non-existent. The fortunes of the white artist were not any better; Peacock had been without food for fifteen days when Ayler dragged him from his bed to make the trip. The lineup was completed by Murray and Don Cherry and they played in Holland and Sweden as well as Denmark. The more lyrical extrovert Cherry, with his quick-thinking and open mind, was the ideal partner for Ayler's loosely assembled melodies and darker moods.

It was during this period that the younger Ayler started to

---

*In 1964 writer Paul Haines taped Ayler's performances at the Cellar Café, 14 June 1964. ESP-Disk issued some of this material as *Prophecy* (ESP 3030) in 1976, but enough material for a second album is said to exist.

play the trumpet. Like Albert, Donald had started out on alto saxophone, but became frustrated when he could not achieve the mobility and sound that had come so easily to his brother. At one point he even put a tenor reed into his alto in an attempt to 'sound like Coltrane'. He decided the trumpet was better suited to his personality, and started playing with saxophonist Charles Tyler. Although raised in Indianapolis, Tyler was distantly related to the Aylers and had occasionally played with the older brother during his summers in Cleveland. When Albert left for Europe this time, he gave instructions for Tyler to bring Donald's playing up to a professional level because he intended to form a new group which would include him. Tyler worked hard at the basics, and Donald spent up to nine hours a day practising.

On his return to the States, Ayler formed a new group which included Tyler and his brother. The bassist was Lewis Worrell, whom he had met in the Army, and Sunny Murray was still playing drums. When his plane was fog-bound in Cleveland, Charles Tyler missed the 1965 date at the Village Gate which was recorded by Impulse for the album *New Wave in Jazz*, but he was to take part in the classic concert at Town Hall, recorded as *Bells* by ESP. Every aspect of this performance was to prove influential – Don Ayler's skittery, up-tempo streaking, Ayler nagging at an idea like a dog worrying a bone, Murray's shivering cymbal-work and the banshee wail he kept up throughout the performance. The intense, braying ensembles and raggedy bugle-calls and marches – the younger Ayler's idea on this occasion – preceded Archie Shepp's use of march themes and became standard practice for any ensemble of the period that considered itself hip. To Ayler, whose religious roots ran deep, the musicians were playing in a 'spiritual dimension'. He said: 'We can get a divine harmony or a divine rhythm that would be beyond what they used to call harmony.'

The saxophonist's association with Call Cobbs was important to him because it provided the opportunity to discuss his ideas with an older man. The pianist would write out some of his themes for him and make suggestions, frequently, in spite of himself, tempered by his conventional approach and schooling. Cobbs was a journeyman musician and his associates failed to see what fascination Ayler's music held for him. His reply: 'I'm intrigued by it and I like it. He's doing something and I don't fully understand it, but I'm learning things.' Shortly before his death, Ayler took Cobbs to the south of France for concerts. He also planned to take him on his tour of Japan. He expressed his respect for the older musicians who had never received their due by intimating that if he enjoyed his European visit, he would arrange for him to stay on there.

In September 1965, *Spirits Rejoice!* was recorded at Judson Hall on West 57th Street. Albert had wanted Cobbs to play vibes on the date but eventually settled for harpsichord, the instrument that provides the luxuriant waves of tinkling sound on 'Angels', and the later Impulse recording *Love Cry.* The musicians dined at an Indian restaurant after the session and later, Cobbs and Ayler went back to his aunt's house and talked way into the night. 'That was a beautiful thing,' the pianist recalled. 'Somebody else was there and they were talking about the free music. I was very quiet because I wanted to listen. Everything was new to me, I didn't really have the connection then, but I could hear. From then on we were inseparable.'

Cobbs had known John Coltrane when they worked together in the 1954 Johnny Hodges band, and when the saxophonist came to the Apollo one week, he went backstage to see him. 'He had grown so big I never will forget. He remembered my face and he said, "Call Cobbs?" and he grabbed me in that bearlike hug. He laid out on the bed and said, "Just talk. I don't want to be indifferent, but I'm very tired." I told him about Albert and he said, "Oh, that's beautiful, he's a wonderful person." Albert at that time was in Cleveland and he said, "When Albert comes back, tell him to call me and tell him that we have met."'

Apart from the fact that Coltrane helped Ayler financially, the relationship between the two men was a very special one. They talked to each other constantly by telephone and by telegram and Coltrane was heavily influenced by the younger man. One of his last wishes was that Ayler and Ornette Coleman, the other important influence on his later career, should play at his funeral. The Ayler brothers played 'Truth is Marching In' accompanied by Richard Davis's bass and Milford Graves on drums.

Coltrane was instrumental in securing Ayler a contract with Impulse Records, but this took place after Ayler had sent him copies of *Ghosts* and *Spiritual Unity*. Soon after this, Coltrane recorded *Ascension*. He called Ayler and told him, 'I recorded an album and found that I was playing just like you.' Albert's reply: 'No man, don't you see, you were playing like yourself. You were just feeling what I feel and were just crying out for spiritual unity.'[15]

It was near the time of Coltrane's death that Ayler met Mary Parks, known professionally as Mary Maria. She began to handle his affairs and take part in his music, although from a critical point of view their relationship led to some of his least stimulating music. Many musicians have suggested that she exercised an undue hold over him, yet their relationship seems to have been a mutually satisfying one. Maria played piano and harp and wrote song lyrics and Ayler suggested she add the soprano saxophone. They started playing together daily, any time and anywhere the mood took them. Once the police chased them out of Brooklyn's Prospect Park for playing too loudly. From time to time, Call Cobbs would also join them, but rehearsals for actual performances took place elsewhere, Maria being added for the date like the cherry on top of a trifle.

In September 1968, Ayler recorded *New Grass*, an unconvincing excursion into rhythm-and-blues territory. A gospel group provided responses while he himself sang a batch of mystical, quasi-religious lyrics. When he played the horn, though, Ayler sounded oddly ill-at-ease for one steeped in the idiom. Despite the presence of a Black drummer, Bernard Purdie, the beat owed more to rock music than the blues, too. The laidback quality on which the James Browns and Juniors Walkers thrive was missing. The feeling among Black intellectuals was that Ayler was treating an important tradition with disrespect. Writing about *New Grass* the album, Larry Neal isolated the essential difference: 'Like it's not too cool to get to the Rolling Stones or the Grateful Dead to learn things that your old man can teach you … I mean the direct confrontation with experience as *lived* by the artist himself is not there.'[16]

Ayler told Jacqueline and Daniel Caux that his record producer, Bob Thiele, wanted him to play with a group of young rock musicians. Reluctantly he gave his agreement, though he stipulated that if he had to play pop music, he would find his own group. As a result, the Canned Heat guitarist Henry Vestine, who made it known that he wanted to record with Ayler, went into the studio with the saxophonist's regular group – bassists Bill Folwell and Stafford James, pianist Bobby Few and Muhammad Ali. Whatever Ayler's reasons for recording this music, his – and Maria's – tortuous singing was light years removed from the sheer majesty of *Witches and Devils*.

It has been suggested that Ayler's contract stipulated that he must sing, but in actual fact, he and Mary Maria had been playing – and singing – her compositions at home long before Bob Thiele knew of their existence, from the time Ayler picked up one of her notebooks and discovered that he liked her work. He decided to help her gain exposure as a songwriter by recording some of her compositions. It was, says Maria, his own idea to sing because he felt it unlikely that the record company would agree to him using an unknown vocalist.

The saxophonist was hurt by the negative reaction to his new work. He believed that the artist changed continually. 'You have to make changes in life just like dying and being born again, artistically speaking. You become very young again through this process, then you grow up, and listen and grow young again.'

As Ayler's career progressed, however, his accompanying

musicians became more lightweight. Beaver Harris, who replaced Ronald Shannon Jackson in August 1966, toured Europe with Ayler and recorded with him until 1967, was a relatively straight-forward drummer. Milford Graves, who replaced him, was more demanding in some ways than Murray and, although he recorded with the saxophonist in February 1968, did not stay long with his group. Allen Blairman, who played on his last visit to France, was unadventurous compared to Murray or even Muhammad Ali.

From time to time, Ayler used two academically trained musicians, violinist Michel Sampson, who toured Europe with him in 1966, and the 'cellist Joel Freedman, who had also worked with Sunny Murray. Where bassists were concerned, Alan Silva's *arco* upper-register work on the album *Live in Greenwich Village* was stunning, but the men who followed him were unremarkable. Ayler always regretted that he was unable to find a replacement for the brilliant Peacock, who quit music for a while to study Zen in Japan. Henry Grimes, who was, with Charlie Haden, the other great bass player of this era, went to California and became involved in acting before he, too, disappeared.

Cobbs, although a close friend of the saxophonist was, one felt, along for that reason and the undemanding nature of his accompaniment. But like Sidney Bechet, an artist he greatly admired, Ayler dominated any ensemble whether the others were his peers or inferiors. Because of the rejection he experienced, it was of considerable importance to him when he met a person with whom he could communicate spiritually and musically. Charles Tyler suggested that unlike so many of the musicians who gravitated to him, Cobbs was never a drain. 'He was always there when Al needed him.'

In July 1970, Ayler played two historic concerts in the south of France. These Nuits de la Fondation Maeght took place at Saint-Paul de Vence (the town where James Baldwin makes his home). They were recorded by the French company Shandar and released shortly after his death, spectacularly emblazoned with a wrapper giving the details of the tragedy, presumably as an added selling-point in the tradition of the Memorial Album. The music is not quite as passionate as the early New York recordings but it is a far cry from the saxophonist's last ones for Impulse. *In Heart Only* sums everything up. Gentler than the rawest offerings – *Spiritual Unity, Bells* – and less majestic than the stark themes of *Love Cry*, it is the declaration of an artist who has considered all the possibilities, and now offers this as a refined statement of his musical self. Ayler had expressed a desire to play for the tourists. 'Let's play something I don't normally do,' he told Cobbs: 'Let's play the blues.' The rocking 'Holy Family' was, apparently, the result. Ayler stretches out in a pure reminiscence of what Little Walter wanted from him eighteen years earlier. 'The people went wild about it,' Cobbs recalled. You can hear them on the record.

There is no escaping the religious nature of Ayler's music. It was not just that what he played could only have been created by a man of his spirituality. Many of the figures, themes and the *feeling* itself sprang directly, unadorned, from the Black church. His saxophone punctuates Mary Maria's phrases on 'Music is the Healing Force of the Universe' – 'Let it come in, the music of the Universe, the music of Love' – as though they were side by side on the moaners' bench. It often seemed as if the church were the very place for which this music was intended. Call Cobbs played every Sunday for a small congregation in a second-floor church on 125th Street; behind Ayler's horn on 'Universal Message', the notes are the same ones he fed to the witnessing Harlemites. 'The music was like a Bible to Albert,' said the pianist, who was himself to die tragically, less than a year after Ayler, hit by a speeding car.

* * *

There were indications that Ayler was emotionally disturbed at the time of his death. Donald Ayler was one of New York's casualties, and apparently Albert blamed himself for the breakdown he suffered in 1968 when their musical association ended. Back at home in Cleveland, Donald gradually recovered his health and put on weight. His trumpet, though, lay on the table out of its case, gathering dust and totally ignored. Six years later, he started playing again, sometimes with Mustafa Abdul Rahim and occasionally with Al Rollins, a tenor saxophonist who owns a Cleveland barbershop, yet wherever possible, he would avoid referring to his brother by name.

Albert Ayler's state of mind can be judged from an article he wrote in 1969 for *The Cricket*,[17] a Black music review founded by Imamu Baraka, A. B. Spellman and Larry Neal. The piece is in the form of a sermon. It is confused, but the overall tone is spiritual, in keeping with his own gentle, essentially private nature, and religious upbringing. At one point he refers to Elijah Muhammad, although according to Mary Maria he was neither a member of the Nation of Islam nor a follower of the creed. The rumour persists that Ayler took his own life, and is given some credence by descriptions of his personal behaviour. Noah Howard remembers seeing him that summer, wearing a full-length fur coat and gloves, his face covered in Vaseline – 'Got to protect myself' – despite the sweltering heat. But Mustafa Abdul Rahim's story is contradictory. He last saw the saxophonist as he was leaving a restaurant on Times Square. Ayler was alighting from a car driven by two beautiful Black women who were singing with his group at the time, and was dressed sharply as ever in a leather suit. He spoke of the successful visit to France and mentioned a forthcoming record date to which he wanted Rahim to contribute. He also talked excitedly about an imminent tour of Japan he never fulfilled.

Charles Tyler spoke of Ayler's innate melancholy. 'Al was really a sad person despite his charisma and everything. That "old-time religion" was what caused his sadness; it was in his music. Al was a heavy guy, and there won't be nobody like him. And it seems that in his death he's going to be more so. When he was living, everybody thought he was a faker, but now there's a lot of interest in him. Didn't nobody know that he had studied being a musician all his life, that he knew the basics as well as he did. When Al and I played together, we could suppress the natural shit we had learned and make ourselves sound like two crazy people who didn't know nothing about music! But still, someone said Al got depressed and jumped off the bridge. I wouldn't be surprised his religious background followed him through to the end.'

Ayler spoke constantly as if he had a premonition of death. Before he had even signed with ABC-Impulse or been widely acclaimed for his innovations, he hinted at the delay in his recognition, saying, 'It's getting rather late now, I've been feeling the spirit for a number of years.'

There are critics who would agree with him, for he made that statement in 1966 and his most complex work had already been put on record. He had moved rapidly from complexity to simplicity, honing out the inessentials faster than any artist of previous times. It was as though he knew how limited his lifespan was to be.

Notes

1. *Down Beat,* 7 January 1971.
2. Ted Joans, 'Spiritual Unity – Albert Ayler – Mister AA of Grade Double A Sounds', in *Coda,* August 1971.
3. A. B. Spellman, *Four Lives in the Bebop Business,* New York, 1966, p. 102.
4. Interview with Nat Hentoff, 'The Truth is Marching In', *Down Beat,* 17 November 1966.
5. Interview with Jacqueline and Daniel Caux, 'My Name is Albert Ayler', *L'Art Vivant* (Paris), February 1971.
6. ibid.
7. Hentoff, op. cit.
8. Henderson, correspondence with the author.
9. ibid.
10. ibid.
11. Rahim, correspondence with the author.
12. Henderson, op. cit.

13 ibid.

14 LeRoi Jones, 'Apple Cores No 3', *Down Beat*, 1966; reprinted in Jones, *Black Music,* New York, 1968.

15 Mary Maria/Mary Parks, notes to *The Last Album* (Impulse AS-9208).

16 Larry Neal, 'New Grass/Albert Ayler', *The Cricket*, Newark, 1969.

17 Albert Ayler, 'To Mr Jones – I Had a Vision', *The Cricket,* Newark, N.J., 1969.

7

The AACM – Chicago's Alternative Society

A piece of improvisation is done, and after it's done, there's nothing to be said about it because it affects your life whether you like it or not.

Leo Smith

Leo Smith is a young trumpeter from Leland, Mississippi, in the heart of Delta blues country. His stepfather, Alex 'Little Bill' Wallace, is a contemporary and friend of B.B. King and although musically inactive today was, apparently, a fine guitarist in the same tradition. He said: 'Leo had a real talent for our music; I can't understand what's happened to him. His mother begged him with tears in her eyes, but seems he wants to bring this music from overseas and make something out of it.' In Mississippi, Smith's experiments, begun in Chicago with kindred spirits in the Association for the Advancement of Creative Musicians (AACM), sounded European. His mother's reaction was hardly surprising; her preference was for the smooth, relaxed singing of Al Green. Yet while Smith was away in Europe, playing at concert halls in France and Germany and recording, James 'Son' Thomas, a guitarist less than fifteen years his senior, could still be heard performing 'Dust My Broom' and other blues in the Elmore James style in juke-joints less than a mile from the Wallace home.

Jazz players had always striven for a big, bold sound, but basing a judgement on six solo improvisations Smith recorded,[1] here was someone apparently denying the characteristics of the horn. He did not want to be limited by the normal range and nature of the instrument, but to explore all its possibilities. This he has done by playing it without a mouthpiece, using the sound produced by the manipulation of the valves alone, and blowing into the trumpet's bell.

Neither does Smith confine himself to the trumpet and flugelhorn. His percussion set-up includes drums, cymbals, gongs, metal plates, bells, aluminium saucepans. He also plays sealhorn, zither, autoharp, harmonica, recorder, wooden and metal flutes and whistles, and one of those old-fashioned rubber 'squeeze' car-horns. He is carrying on a Southern tradition that started with children banging on washboards and tin-cans, blowing down pieces of rubber-hose and strumming wires stretched between nails on a wall, a tradition deeply rooted in Africa. Some members of the AACM, in fact, have gone out of their way to include simple household instruments and utensils in their music, not just for the purpose of utilising their particular sound qualities but to draw attention to the music's origins.

The music Leo Smith plays bears little resemblance to anything Louis Armstrong played – or Don Cherry, for that matter. The AACM musicians have been seen by some observers to have more in common with the aspect of 'chance' in music proposed by John Cage. Leo Smith rejects this comparison. 'We have,' he says, 'developed out of the areas of our ancient, and immediate, past.'

The AACM musicians have always been disturbed by this comparison, which they view as stemming from the continuing white need to point to white precedents for all Black musical activity. Smith referred to Cage's earlier period during which he built up a repertoire for percussion bands and developed the idea of writing for non-pitched instruments. He mentioned a concert that took place in the mid-forties: 'It was supposed to be one of the most innovative things to take place in music, and all they did was add different rhythm instruments and things that he had compiled, supposed to be his "sound-making" tools. We'd been doing that for years – as people in this country – not just in Africa.'

An artist like Leo Smith who appears to reject his immediate background must have firm intentions in mind. He grew up with all the right credentials, after all. It was in the church that he first 'received' music – 'quite early, like all dark people do' – and he actually started playing the blues before he knew all the notes on his trumpet. Today he no longer relates to the restrictions of scales and chords. To him, music is about two things only: sound and rhythm.

He has explored this idea on his own and in a trio with saxophonist Anthony Braxton and violinist Leroy Jenkins, later expanded by the addition of drummer Steve McCall and known as the Creative Construction Company. He also developed it in two duo situations, first with the alto saxophonist/percussionist Marion Brown, a young veteran of the new music, then with bassist/percussionist Leonard Jones, a former colleague in the AACM. It is an idea he shares with other members of the Association and one they have all examined in their individual ways. The Chicago musicians have used just about every instrument imaginable to explore all possible textures of sound rather than relationships of pitch or tonality. They have created new techniques for playing instruments not used before in the music, as well as applying this new knowledge to conventional ones.

Anthony Braxton, who introduced such unusual horns as the contra-bass clarinet, feels that the real contemporary instruments have yet to be made. 'In the next period of the music, the musicians will make their own instruments,' he said. 'Those instruments developed for today relate to the system of music they were designed for, and the music that will happen in the future has nothing to do with that outside of acknowledging the systems that are happening now. We don't need *notes* any more. I'm looking for instruments that are not concerned with actual fixed pitches, instruments with *whirls of sound in them.*'

Braxton's first three years in the AACM were spent learning about the advances made in the music by Coleman and Coltrane, then the research into 'sound-tools' began. Eventually Braxton rejected the use of different sound materials and became more concerned with structures and sounds as such. He was interested in the potential provided by natural environments. For example, he developed a composition intended to be played in a steel-yard. He went on to compose for a tuba ensemble, to play solo concerts on alto saxophone, and perform duets with the brilliant British guitarist Derek Bailey – a multiplicity of mediums of expressions few older musicians would have considered. 'There are so many possibilities of creativity in the new music and I see myself as a scientist in some respects,' he said.

Working with people like Braxton and Leroy Jenkins, Smith dug deeper into the idea of *total creativity.* 'We have no part in saying, "Now we're *in* space, now we're out of space." We apply these things *on* space,' he says. In other words, by avoiding the 'trap' of a constant rhythm – the player is completely free to be at his or her most creative. 'Tempo is a limited use of time,' says Braxton. 'I think of time as *all* the time.'[2]

If what they say appears to be the antithesis of what the music has generally been considered to be about, that may depend on who is writing the history books. Leo Smith sees the critics making rules for the music in order to limit it. 'No one can tell you what anything that has a sound or makes a rhythm *means*, but they come out with the ingredients like, for instance, "swing". Like, "It must swing" or, "People must play solos" – or what-have-you.

'I take it upon myself to try to be completely free of any reference to anything because that's the onliest way that I can create music. I don't want to have the opportunity of being spoken of as a person who plays in this style or that style, because to me there's no marked-out line between styles. As an attitude and as a reference point, I don't even want to relate to any music at all. I want nothing to do with the past or the future.'

Smith's attitude was typical of a new way of thinking fostered by the AACM through its spiritual leader, pianist/clarinettist Muhal

Richard Abrams. Despite the fact that Smith himself went to work in a solo context, he was originally involved, as were all his colleagues, with the concept of group music in which each individual contributed equally. 'They were able to accept each other's ideas and exchange ideas – which is unheard of in music,' he said.

Politically and artistically, the AACM was the forerunner of the musicians' collectives that sprang up during the last decade, among them the Black Artists Group of St Louis, Boston's Society for the Creatively Concerned, and Strata-East in Detroit. Behind its practical role as grassroots academy and training ground for young creative spirits lies Abrams's proposition that the era of the individual is a thing of the past. The AACM engendered the idea of musical socialism.

Leroy Jenkins, who worked with several combinations within the AACM, was away teaching stringed instruments in Mobile, Alabama, when the Association was formed. He came back to Chicago and took a similar job in the public school system there, and played whenever he could and whatever was needed, solely in order to make money. 'Everything was for money, I had no philosophies or anything. I just wanted to be a good player which is like mostly all of the guys. Everybody was like that in those days, that was the thing. What happened (to change me) was that I was introduced to the AACM.'

Like every musician who came up against Abrams and saxophonist Roscoe Mitchell, generally considered to be an equivalent force in Chicago circles, Jenkins began to have second thoughts about music and the reasons for playing it. In his case, his chosen instrument had been rarely used in jazz – Eddie South, Stuff Smith, Ray Nance and Joe Venuti were the only notable precedents – but the AACM, through its exploration of unconventional instrumentation, helped him to see the violin in a more positive light. Jenkins had discovered most violinists reluctant to play improvised music because they imagined this necessitated a certain sacrifice of technique. The AACM taught him the beauty of employing a technique derived from oneself. In other words, he explained, inventing your own technique *per se*.

'We only use technique to get out of an instrument what we want to get out of it, regardless of what kind of music it is,' he said. 'The violin has always been based on European ideas, too, so now that we're talking about change, we're talking about revolution and all that kind of stuff, so, well, we're doing it in the music.'

* * *

The AACM was established in May 1965 by four people: pianists Muhal Richard Abrams and Jodie Christian, drummer Steve McCall and trumpeter Phil Cohran. Membership was built around four or five groups playing in Chicago at the time, their primary aims being self-reliance and control of the music. Later, players came from other parts of the country – Leo Smith from Mississippi, drummers Leonard Smith and Phillip Wilson and trumpeter Lester Bowie from St Louis – and joined or became associated with the AACM. Newcomers had to be nominated, and on acceptance a meeting was held at which they were told what was expected of them. The rules were strict but the way they were administered was lenient. When one of the men used Association money to buy drugs, he was asked to return it, not given a lecture on personal morality. The dues they paid were minimal, just enough to cover the costs of administration, most of which was handled by trumpeter John Jackson.

The Association presented regular concerts and held open rehearsals twice a week where musicians could come down and listen to what was taking place. On Saturdays, a big band was formed that included all the members. Said Jenkins: 'The rules were that if you wanted the band to play your music, you had to write for everybody – I don't care if they were playing a kazoo.'

Jenkins was taken to his first AACM concert by his teacher, Bruce Hayden. Roscoe Mitchell's group was playing and for the first time, teacher and pupil roles were reversed. Jenkins found himself being asked to explain what was happening. 'I didn't know either but it really shook us up! What made it so bad was it was good but we didn't understand it. And we thought we was so hip! Roscoe just knocked us out. It was new, fresh, it really did something to me. I said, Oh, this must be the direction that the thinking people are going in.'

There was something *about* this music and the seriousness of the participants that drew other players to the AACM. Jenkins experienced this when he attended a rehearsal held in Abrams's basement. He found the musicians sitting in a circle, playing from directions that Abrams gave them. He had known the pianist from his school days – 'When I knew Muhal he was a thug. He was one of them kind of cats that would take money from you at school' – but when he approached him to play, he was told he had to come back and listen three times. On the next occasion, Jenkins was overwhelmed by the music. He rushed to the car and got his violin. 'I said, "I don't care, man, you've got to let me play!"' Abrams relented and started including him in his directions. 'He started giving me notes like, "I want you to play this note, man, over the rest of the cats." And then I started rehearsing with them.'

Abrams and the AACM were responsible between them for creating a new kind of dedication and instilling the idea of self-respect in musicians who had previously had other priorities. Joseph Jarman is an imaginative saxophonist who was introduced to the Experimental Band, the forerunner of the AACM, by Roscoe Mitchell. He said: 'Until I had the first meeting with Richard Abrams, I was "like all the rest" of the "hip" ghetto niggers; I was cool, I took dope, I smoked pot, etc. I did not *care* for the life that I had been given. In having the chance to work in the Experimental Band with Richard and the other musicians there, I found the first something with meaning/reason for doing. That band and the people there was the *most* important thing that ever happened to me.'[3]

Malachi Favors, one of the strongest, most inventive bass players in contemporary music, plays with the Art Ensemble of Chicago, a group which grew out of several AACM combinations. His experience is considerable. He has worked with Freddie Hubbard, Dizzy Gillespie and so on, and can even claim an appearance on some 78 rpm records with Andrew Hill on piano. His spiritual apprenticeship in the AACM has kept him from pursuing the lucrative work that a man with his credentials could expect. 'If the cosmics didn't lead me, I would be in some lounge making two or three hundred dollars a week, playing tunes,' he said. 'Many times I'd like to go back because this is a difficult road. It has taken me away from many people that I used to know. I come home now and I see people and they ask me, "Where you playing at?" not knowing that I'm into another thing. Cats call me for gigs and so forth; this really has taken me into something else.'

Not all those who joined have stuck with the Association, its aims and ideals, but it has left an eradicable mark on many lives. Deep in Mississippi, away from the acknowledged centres of musical activity, it continued to be a driving force in the life of one of its founder members. 'It was like a church – it *was* my church,' said drummer Alvin Fielder. 'Music is my church and, of course, the AACM was my denomination.'

* * *

The AACM grew out of the Experimental Band, which was formed by Abrams in 1961. Abrams was a schooled musician who was frequently called on to back up visiting firemen. For some time he had been developing new ideas with Donald Rafael Garrett, a bassist and multi-instrumentalist whose influence has been extensive. By 1963, the Experimental Band included Fred Berry (trumpet), Lester Lashley (trombone and 'cello), Roscoe Mitchell, Joseph Jarman (alto saxophones), Gene Dinwiddie, Maurice McIntyre, a.k.a. Kalaparusha Ahra Difda, Henry Threadgill (tenor saxophones), Charles Clark, Donald Garrett (basses), Jack DeJohnette, Steve McCall (drums), the latter a seasoned professional like Abrams, Favors and Jodie Christian. For a while alto saxophonist Troy Robinson shared much of the writing with Abrams; later Mitchell and Jarman made contributions. Jarman has loosely classified the areas of their individual interest: Abrams, 'chromatic', Mitchell, 'polytonal', Jarman, 'serialised' music.

Several of these players attended the first meeting of the AACM. Also on hand was Jimmy Ellis, an alto saxophonist in whose brother's big band Abrams has played from time to time. Eddie Harris, a saxophonist with a sizeable following who plays the tenor in what sounds like almost an alto register, criticised the 'free' players. He said: 'All you fellows want to do is play free; you can't play in clubs for *people*. You want to play concerts because you can't play anything else.' It was a common admonition during the early days of the new music, and such was the enthusiasm among the young musicians that it was like water off a duck's back. Alvin Fielder, then the drummer with Mitchell's group, was present at the meeting. He said: 'It got stronger and stronger and it left a mark on me. It was just the most beautiful thing going as far as the musicians were concerned, the first of its kind. Along with Sun Ra, it actually shaped my lifestyle in music.'

Abrams, the *éminence grise* and leader, became President of the AACM, but Mitchell is the catalyst most musicians cite as responsible for taking them to that leader. Leroy Jenkins calls Mitchell 'the freest musician I ever heard'. Alvin Fielder's first meeting with the saxophonist took place on a typical bebop gig of the period: 'A romping, stomping thing – like, "Everybody play hard *all* the time!"' Mitchell walked in, unshipped his alto and started playing. 'Everything just loosened up so. It was a beautiful thing. After he played, he packed his horn up and left. And I said, "Goddamn! I wonder who the saxophone player was?" Because he was playing so strange then – like up, down, around.'

Fielder, possibly the most schooled and precise drummer to

play in the Association, was practising in Abrams's basement three months later with Kalaparusha and Malachi Favors when Mitchell walked in. 'Roscoe stood around a while and listened, and after we finished he asked me could I play "free" music. I had been on the fringes of free music with blues groups for maybe a year and a half. The cats would say, "Hey, man, just give me some time," and I would get bugged. But Roscoe – I said, yeah, I could play free music, so he invited me to a rehearsal at Freddie Berry's house. Mai [Favors] was there, too, and as soon as we started playing, there was this beautiful thing that just popped up.'

While the revolts that took place in the streets of Watts, Detroit and Newark were yet to erupt, another kind of revolution was taking place in Chicago. When Sun Ra left the city in 1960, taking his entire Arkestra with him, the AACM continued to foster the unity amongst musicians that had always existed there. The growth of the Arkestra and the formation of the AACM would not have been possible without this spirit. Soon after Sun Ra left, the AACM started promoting concerts and offering free instruction in theory and Black music history as well as individual instrumental training and spiritual guidance to youngsters in the community.

Because of the hard work the AACM put into cultivating the Black community – playing free concerts on the beach, and so on – Chicago has a larger Black following for its new music than exists elsewhere. Their desire to build a more positive image for the musician is apparent from their manifesto:

> Our curriculum is so designed as to elicit maximum development of potential within the context of a training programme that exposes youngsters to constructive relationships with artistic adults. Superimposed over our training framework is our keen desire to develop within our students the ability to value *self*, the ability to value *others* and the ability to utilise the opportunities they find in society. It is felt that such values should be based on the cultural and spiritual heritage of the people involved.

From the beginning it became obvious that the AACM musicians had a new approach to improvisation. Although their direction as individuals was influenced by the giant steps made by Coltrane, Dolphy, Coleman and Taylor, they applied themselves to their new-found knowledge with less urgency than some of their New York counterparts in the Second Wave of the new music. 'The AACM's originality is an earmark of *Chicago*,' said Richard Abrams. 'Understand, it's this environment. You can't find two musicians in Chicago who play alike. Because we were never drawn to copying another cat's style in order to get a certain gig or whatnot.'[4]

There was a feeling amongst musicians that things were somehow done differently in the two cities, especially in terms of personal relationships. The AACM musicians had the advantage over their New York counterparts of rehearsing and playing together more consistently. The benefits of such mutually shared experience are obvious when compared to the results of pick-up sessions where the participants are unfamiliar with each other's direction. Leo Smith gave the example of the understanding that is implicit amongst New Yorkers concerning the return of the favour whenever called for a record date. 'That's completely stupid. He's not using me because I dig playing with him or our music comes comfortably together. I don't particularly dig that; I play with someone that has a need for me to play with them.'

On the whole, the Chicagoans showed greater imagination than the Easterners. They frequently found room for humour, and, in particular, they knew all about the skilful use of silence. New York music of the period may have been dynamite, but there was a desperation about it that reflected the pace of life there. In Chicago, it seemed that the musicians had had time to sit down and do some thinking. The structure of the musics played in the two cities reflected the actual architecture: New York thrown together, higgledy-piggledy and stifling, Chicago with its open spaces giving the buildings room to breathe.

Abrams's own musical plan was to play a series of lengthy improvisations that lasted for an entire concert, the sequence marked by almost imperceptible shifts of coloration and rhythmic impetus, directed with a light, almost magical, touch. He had written out parts for the early versions of the Experimental Band, but Donald Garrett told him that he foresaw a time when musicians would no longer need these guidelines. 'I had to write quite a bit until I had musicians who could *create* a part,' he told John Litweiler, untiring documenter of the AACM's activities. 'Now I can take eight measures and play a concert.'[5]

Inevitably the first groups drew heavily on Ornette Coleman's concept. Early tapes in Fielder's possession of a 1965 Mitchell quartet with trumpeter Freddie Berry, then a young music teacher, Favors and himself, reveal this debt, but soon a new pattern emerged. The Mitchell Sextet's *Sound*, recorded in 1966 for Delmark, the Chicago record company run by blues enthusiast Bob Koester, was the first intimation the outside world had of what was happening in the city. Included in the personnel are trombonist/'cellist Lester Lashley, whom Abrams links with Donald Garrett for his inspirational qualities, and trumpeter Lester Bowie.

The ideas behind the recording predicted the path that many musicians were to follow in Chicago and elsewhere. 'That word "Sound" has strong significance,' said Leo Smith. 'It's no accident that Roscoe called that important piece of his "Sound". Sound – not pitch – that's the difference.' Mitchell described what lay behind the music: 'The musicians are free to make any sound they think will do, any sound that they hear at a particular time. That could be like somebody who felt like stomping on the floor … well, he would stomp on the floor. And you notice the approach of the musicians to their instruments is a little different from what one would normally hear. The cymbals are used to amplify this, not the drums. The cymbals are used for their overtone effect.

'I always "felt" a lot of instruments – and I feel myself being drawn to it. I'm getting more interested in music as strictly atmosphere, not so much of just standing up playing for playing's sake, but my mind stretches out to other things, like creating different sounds.'[6]

Lester Bowie is, quite simply, one of the most impressive and persuasive players in the new music, on any instrument. He was born in 1941 in Frederick, Maryland, the son of a trumpet player and music teacher, and grew up in St Louis where he started playing at the age of five. He alternates between the heraldic and the gut-bucket, using effects that span the seven decades of jazz. Squeezed half-valves – a St Louis trademark – nudge at carefully constructed lines, and there are New Orleans echoes in the wide vibrato he often uses. There is hokum aplenty, humour, anger, sorrow. But above all, there is irony. He shares this quality with Mitchell, Favors and Jarman and it is responsible for the feeling of innate *knowingness* communicated through the music they play together as the Art Ensemble of Chicago.

Before settling in Chicago in 1966, Bowie paid his 'road' dues with bands led by singers Jerry Butler, Gene Chandler, Jackie Wilson and Joe Tex. This period prepared him for the days of austerity with the Art Ensemble. Working with Little Milton, for example, he earned 25 dollars per night only to see ten go on expenses.

Like Ornette Coleman, Bowie even toured with a couple of carnivals. In Dallas, Texas, he played afterhours sessions with tenormen James Clay and David 'Fathead' Newman. In St Louis he played bebop with alto saxophonists Julius Hemphill and Oliver Lake, pianist John Chapman and drummer Phillip Wilson. The latter was later to play with the Mitchell Art Ensemble for nine unforgettable months before leaving to earn the money his superlative talents deserved. For a while he earned a living with the Paul Butterfield Blues Band. Now he is working in New York.

In St Louis, Bowie worked with Albert King and with Oliver Sain, like himself a Little Milton sideman who had been elected band-leader when he left the singer and found the rest of the personnel following suit. Singer and pianist with the band was Fontella Bass, whom Sain had hired for Milton, later to become Bowie's wife. When her solo records, some written and produced by Sain, started making a mark, Bowie became her musical director. Two of his brothers, the trombonist Joseph and saxophonist Byron, subsequently filled the same role.

Whether they were avant-garde or bebop-oriented, Lake, Wilson and Bowie had 'made a habit of just *smoking* cats' (outplaying them), but in Chicago, the trumpeter was amazed to find so many musicians of his own calibre. He sat in with the Experimental Band the first time he went to a rehearsal and never looked back. For a while he and Mitchell played at the Hungry Eye with the Vanguard Ensemble, founded by AACM drummer Ajaramu (Gerald Donovan) with Amina Claudine Myers on organ; saxophonists Kalaparusha and Gene Dinwiddie occasionally added.

Said Bowie: 'If you get a job playing rock-and-roll, you can maybe be a little hip on it, but you're still basically dealing in that idiom. With bebop and free jazz, the boundaries are defined. But with Mitchell there was no limitation about what you could deal from. It was a combination of any kind of way you could do it, and it was the only group I had seen that I could really do anything I wanted to without feeling self-conscious about it.'[7]

Of the four founder members of the Art Ensemble, bassist Malachi Favors is the eldest. He was born in Lexington, Mississippi, in 1937, the son of a preacher, and grew up in religious surroundings that encouraged the belief that anything other than church music was taboo. At the age of fifteen, though, he found himself drawn towards the bass. Now he plays both the electric and acoustic models, the banjo, zither, *balafon* and many other 'little instruments'. He is one of the strongest bassists in the history of the music, and much valued by his colleagues for his unifying force and evenly balanced thinking.

Chuck Nessa was responsible for getting the AACM musicians on to record when he went to work for Delmark. In 1967 he started recording them for his own label. His first selection was by a group that was the forerunner of the Art Ensemble, Bowie's *Numbers 1 & 2*, with Joseph Jarman added to the trumpeter's group of the period. The following March, *Congliptious* was recorded under Mitchell's name with Robert Crowder guesting on drums.

Jarman, an impish little man who once made history by appearing on stage wearing only a saxophone sling, is poet, philosopher and polemicist as well as musician. He was to become the spokesman for the Art Ensemble and frequently, though not intentionally, the AACM itself. While Mitchell was making his first appearance on wax, Jarman had been involved with his own groups, often with Bill Brimfield, trumpet, and Fred Anderson, tenor saxophone. The nucleus of his music, though, revolved around the impressionistic pianist Christopher Gaddy, and the virtuoso young bassist Charles Clark, a pupil of Wilbur Ware and, according to one observer, 'the busiest, most popular AACM member', and drummer Thurman Barker, who was confined to a kind of decorative role by Jarman, frequently playing *ideas* of rhythm rather than rhythm itself.

Jarman met Mitchell at Wilson Junior College in 1961 and they began playing together. He wrote impressionistic pieces like 'Non-Cognitive Aspects of the City' (*Song For* on Delmark), a rambling picture drawn with words and music of a kind that had not been attempted in Black music before. The attempt to reject many of the prevailing standards was obvious in this programme music. John Litweiler wrote of Abrams that his music was not only unromantic, but 'sometimes deliberately anti-romantic'[8] and of Jarman's work and, later, Anthony Braxton's it could be said it was deliberately anti-rhythmic.

By the time Jarman recorded his second Delmark album, *As If It Were the Seasons*, Gaddy was dead from heart disease. A few months later, Charles Clark was also to die, his brilliant voice stilled at the age of twenty-four when he was stricken by a cerebral haemorrhage on his way home from a rehearsal with the Chicago Civic Orchestra. Naturally, losing two of his main men was almost too much for Jarman to take. He did not feel strong enough to continue with Barker alone, and so when Bowie, Favors and Mitchell asked him to join them for concerts and a record date, he agreed. J. B. Figi, another of the most dedicated chroniclers of the Chicago scene, reported him saying: 'Finally, it was just the thing, you know. We realised that we all had this vital thing in common, which was the spirit of searching.'[9]

In June 1969, the Art Ensemble left Chicago for France and appeared at festivals, concerts and clubs all over the Continent. Don Moye, a drummer born in Rochester, N.Y., in 1946, was added to the group in Paris in 1970. During their initial stay, the Art Ensemble taped over fifteen albums which gradually appeared on labels in France, Britain and Germany, and recorded two film soundtracks, one of which, *Les Stances à Sophie*, was later released by Chuck Nessa. Each album was entirely different from its predecessors. The Art Ensemble never ceased to astonish in their search for areas of expression. And because of their extensive theoretical knowledge, they felt no compulsion to reject established values, either. One minute they would be playing the blues, the next minute, totally 'free'. Like Sun Ra, they would examine swing, bebop and extensions of Ornette Coleman side by side. By the time they arrived in Europe, they played so many instruments between them that it took them two hours to set up on stage. 'It's just impossible to explain the subtlety of the structures and forms that we're interested in,' said Joseph Jarman. 'Also, we create problems for ourselves – musical problems – that I'm sure other people would not be interested in looking at.'

He gave the example of himself, Mitchell and Bowie playing a melodic line: 'You have three horn players standing in line. You've got three different interpretations first, so we have to work together to try to get that phrase so that it's one sound. We're more successful at that particular kind of problem than unsuccessful, therefore that's encouraging. Then we go out and try to work with somebody else to get three horn players to do that, too.'

* * *

Chicago, the final stop for many migrants from the Deep South, has always provided downhome blues to suit their tastes. Most of the AACM members had played the blues at some time. Leo Smith, growing up in Mississippi, his house filled with musicians who are nationally known today; Maurice McIntyre playing with J. B. Hutto and Little Milton, Roscoe Mitchell with Jerry Butler, Phillip Wilson with Otis Rush and Paul Butterfield; Lester Bowie's credentials were enormous. Yet their experience and consciousness saying otherwise, they used only the timbre of the blues at first, seldom, at least on recorded evidence, the form itself. This was one of the factors that led to their comparison with Cage and other white composers, not to mention their rejection by several New York musicians who regarded their creative activity as cerebral rather than soulful. On later records, the Art Ensemble grew increasingly involved with the blues. Earlier on, though, it seemed that they wanted to avoid such basic *forms* at all costs, in contrast to the prevalent attitude of the 'fifties which was to play the blues wherever possible.

Anthony Braxton explained the reasoning behind this. 'What most people accept as being creative for the most part are standard sort of systems either technically or conceptually. At some point these have been embraced to the degree where it's not so much about creativity any more as much as it's about fulfilling other people's ideas about form.'

Shortly after the Art Ensemble left Chicago for France, Braxton, Smith and Leroy Jenkins followed. Prior to working together as a trio, they had played with Charles Clark, Thurman Barker and Kalaparusha, but more than any of the Chicago musicians they could be said to epitomise the rejection of form and the tried and trusted formulae of the past. Indeed, their music had been dismissed by Litweiler as 'academic and arbitrary'. Braxton, he said, 'often seems determined to destroy whatever collective ensemble tendencies appear in the course of the Trio's performance.'[10] Earlier, he had found the saxophonist's music 'awkward and difficult'[11] and Jenkins's 'formless solos' lacking in 'rhythmic variety and melodic substance.'[12] At the time, this may well have been considered fair comment from a listener nurtured on existing ideas, yet both Jenkins and Braxton in subsequent performances clearly revealed their knowledge of the past, not to mention that arbitrary definition, 'swing'. Smith has already acquitted himself in that department and chosen to move on.

Braxton, as it turned out, is now regarded as one of the most important figures in the new music. He feels, though, that genuine creative activity has been so suppressed that the gap between the people and 'the real creative vibrations' grows wider each year. Although he enjoys good stylists, he has always preferred to focus his attention on the real innovators, 'the people who initiate new worlds'.

For this reason, he has spent increasingly more time in Europe, where he has derived much of his inspiration from playing with European musicians, an unfashionable path for a Black artist to take. Such people as guitarist Derek Bailey have, he says, become very important for him. 'They're doing things that are creative to the degree where you have to enter their own universe. They've defined the thing already.'

Despite a personal disillusionment with the idea of 'groups', Braxton, like all those touched by the AACM, finds it impossible to turn his back on the knowledge he gained from his scholarship under Muhal Richard Abrams. He and his compadres share a feeling put into words by Leo Smith: 'I only play when there is an opportunity for you to really explore yourself, when each occasion would bring to those people and myself a complete challenge. And when I say "challenge", I don't mean some reference in the back past, but like challenge *right now*, where we're at right now – because it is the future.'

Smith caught on to the Chicago concept more rapidly than anyone else, according to Leroy Jenkins, and this despite the most traditional of backgrounds. There is nothing traditional about his lifestyle, however. Living in a small Connecticut town, he has adopted a dedicated, though relaxed, personal regimen. He has cut himself off, limited and paced his music to the point where he feels capable of turning in a high-level performance every time. He refuses to take his horn on his rare visits to New York, or socialise with the musicians there. To him the idea of 'sessions' is a thing of the past: 'the music has moved on from there.'

He expressed his single-mindedness: 'I don't want it to be felt that I'm in New York and that I'm *important* in the sense that I'm doing something with a group of New Yorkers. I want to feel important *inside myself* and let that be my secret.' The New York environment, he feels, is damaging because it encourages sameness amongst artists. As a result, their music is 'cut from a material that can be gathered not *any* place, but *everyplace*'. He sees this same- ness in music and lifestyle producing a lack of concentration as far as the individual's direction is concerned. 'It involves detours from your daily drill.' In Smith's case this drill might consist of an instrumental workout, then some other kind of relaxation to balance this, followed by a walk for reflection – activities it would be hard to imagine taking place in New York where the pace is too frantic for such 'indulgences', but easily associated with musicians indoctrinated by the AACM. 'Being cut from sameness, or being in an environment that appreciates and perpetuates it, you can't do these things,' said Smith.

For these reasons, Smith regards New York as being 'almost lost as a place of creativity'. Despite the fact that the majority of the musicians continue to live there? The Atlantic Ocean lapped lazily at the shoreline near his house. Smith looked towards it and smiled. 'You can look over at this part of the ocean and you can say, "Well, that's where all the water's at," but water don't have to be clean.'

In an article in *Black World*,[13] Abrams and John Jackson described the AACM's primary concerns as survival, accountability and achievement. In May 1975, the Association celebrated its tenth anniversary with a four-day festival of music, arts and crafts. After ten years, the 'Black cultural missionaries' had managed to survive against the odds. Through their commitment to the idea that the creative learning process should never cease, the AACM have continued to enlighten the world about African or Afro-American contributions. 'Black people,' wrote Abrams and Jackson, 'have now reached a juncture where, they have assumed and/or rekindled a spirit of pride – an intelligent pride that has become so infectious and inspiring that other ethnic groups have rediscovered their heritage and are beginning to place high premiums on their ethnic backgrounds.'

Through the example of the AACM, musicians all over America have started to organise their own activities. As Abrams and Jackson said, 'It is the contention of the AACM that it is not the potential which Black people have which will determine what they do but, rather, how they feel about themselves.'

Notes

1   *Creative Music* – I (tms-1).
2   Notes to *Three Compositions of the New Jazz* (Delmark DS-415).
3   Notes to *Song For* (Delmark DL-410).
4   Interview with Ray Townley, in *Down Beat,* 15 August 1974.
5   John B. Litweiler, 'Chicago's Richard Abrams: A Man with an Idea', *Down Beat,* 5 October 1967.
6   Interview by Terry Martin, 'Blowing Out in Chicago', *Down Beat,* 6 April 1967.
7   J. B. Figi, 'Art Ensemble of Chicago', *Sun Dance Magazine,* November 1972.
8   Litweiler, op. cit.
9   Figi, op. cit.
10 John B. Litweiler, "Three to Europe', *Jazz Monthly,* November 1969.
11 John B. Litweiler, 'Altoists and Other Chicagoans', *Coda,* March 1967.
12 ibid.
13 Muhal Richard Abrams and John Shenoy Jackson, 'The Association for the Advancement of Creative Musicians', *Black World,* November 1973.

PART TWO

WHO ARE THE NEW MUSICIANS?

8

As Serious As Your Life

That thing about 'jazz is dead' is ridiculous. That really
takes me out when somebody says that because jazz is the
musician himself. When they say 'jazz is on the way out',
isn't that like saying the Black man is on the way out?

Billy Harper

'There's nothing like learning to play, believe me, because I stayed
in the house week after week – and week after year, as a matter of
fact – learning how to play. And what I was learning might have
been old, but it made playing something else in the future much
easier because I knew how to manipulate my instrument – just
some, I mean. I'm not a Master yet, but that's what I'm after – to
be able to play whatever I hear at any time. Then I won't have anything to say at all; all I'll be able to do is play. I would like to get
everything down that small where that is all I do. When I become
my instrument and my instrument becomes me, I'm not a person
any more. I would like to walk around the street looking like a
trumpet if possible, because that's what I am.'

Earl Cross, trumpet player – thirty-nine years old and still
more concerned with self-satisfaction than searching for a heap of
gold. Cross has been playing music for a long time. In California
he made enough money in the clubs and studios to support his
family without leaving town. For a while he worked with Larry
Williams, singer and author of such epics as 'Dizzy Miss Lizzie'.

Rock-and-roll bands, jazz groups and unknown blues singers have all had the benefit of his big, fat sound which makes good use of the slurring and half-valve effects that feature prominently in the work of trumpeters from his home town – Clark Terry, Miles Davis, Lester Bowie and Floyd LeFlore among them. To some ears his music might not be as polished as what is being laid down by one of the more fashionable bands that all the hip young musicians from Tokyo to Toronto are trying to copy, but it has in it some of the spirit and urgency of the early bebop days. Above all, you feel it is being truthful to itself.

For a while, Cross worked with Rashied Ali and Noah Howard, then he decided to devote most of his energy to exploring his own musical concept. It was not an easy decision for a man with no real fame and with the rent to pay, especially a man approaching forty. At that age the musician who has not achieved notoriety generally graduates to safe commercial jobs or gives up playing altogether. It does, however, indicate the kind of dedication that drives an artist to produce something personal even if it means cutting down on some of life's little luxuries like bread and meat.

Nobody looks down on the so-called 'legitimate' musician whose horizons are bounded by the music of others, but for the improvising musician to limit himself to playing what someone else has written is the antithesis of what his art is all about. When a person refuses to play commercial music, though, he is virtually signing his death warrant unless he has an additional source of income. Economic pressures are so strong in a city like New York that any good musician who can find employment in the recording studios tends to stay there even if his original intention was to work just long enough to save some money. Few of them return to the idea of actually creating anything individual once they become accustomed to a regular salary.

Although Cross was not involved in the lucrative New York studio world, he did at one time earn a living playing backgrounds on blues records and could, presumably, always find that kind of work again. 'But you don't get a chance to explore, you just play the same thing over and over and that's just like having a job – that's not music. I'm not any perfect person, I just know how I like to do things, and I've played enough blues and rock-and-roll to know that a blues band can't hire me right now. Maybe next week, but right now they can't do that to me.'

As a child, Cross had wanted to be in the airforce, and that was where he headed on leaving high school. During his teens, he listened avidly to records, and whenever he and his friends wanted a little amusement they would carry a handful of Gillespie, Parker, Kenton and Tristano sides to a weekend party and slip them on the turntable. 'That was one of the things. If you wanted to break up a party, you'd stick a jazz tune on the record player, then sit down and listen to records and smoke reefer.' Where his family was concerned, though, jazz was all right in its place – on record or in the nightclubs – but when he went home to announce his plans to make it his career, 'They nearly put me out of the house! They said, "You can't play no music in here, you'd better get a job," and so I had to cut out.'

The Cross family's reaction was not unusual. The young Black man has frequently been discouraged from entering the music world because of the knowledge that it provides a precarious existence at best, and also because of the unsavoury picture of the lifestyle painted by the stereotype. On top of this there is the suggestion that Blacks can only succeed in white society as entertainers or athletes. 'It's demoralising to think about it, and then you say – hey, what's wrong with that?' said Cross. 'And so you take up something and you defend it with everything you've got. And the only way you can defend it is to produce something good out of the music. You can't fight nobody and tell them you're a good musician, you have to play and show them. And so far I've done pretty good.'

Art 'Shaki' Lewis had a different experience. He was born in New Orleans but his family migrated to the West Coast when he was five years old. His father played trumpet, his grandfather played trombone, and an uncle played drums, so there were no obstacles to him becoming a drummer himself. 'In a Black community, music is part of everyday life,' he said. 'It was in my blood, and as my whole family were musicians, it was easy for me to do that. Some people respected me, some people didn't, but there were others who envied me. It was like a part-time thing, though, like a sideline, a weekend thing, nothing to really get serious about. But I got to the stage where I couldn't do nothing else, nothing else would satisfy me. It was like I was doing the people a service, I was like the witchdoctor. I would go around playing music and turn people on and make them feel good and they'd have a good time.'

The Pattersons of North Philadelphia (an area known as 'the Jungle' and a decidedly unpopular destination with cab-drivers) were another musical family. When Robert Patterson Senior changed his name to Rashied Ali, he changed his sons' names, also. Two of them became drummers of note. Muhammad, formerly Raymond, has worked extensively with saxophonist Frank Wright in New York and Europe. The eldest, also Robert and also renamed Rashied, was the man John Coltrane chose as his drummer for the last two-and-a-half years of his life. He remembers his father as a 'frustrated horn player who had every record that was happening'. Once, when he was sick in bed, his father brought him Billie Holiday's record of 'Gloomy Sunday' as a get-well gift. The record had just come out, but Ali's mother did not consider its suicide theme particularly appropriate. 'What kind of a record is that to buy somebody that's sick?' she said. 'That's not so slick.'

At one time, Ms Patterson had sung with the Jimmy Lunceford Orchestra, one of the top swing bands of the day, and her own mother, an ordained minister, led a little Baptist church where the Sunday congregation was made up mainly of family members. Ali's mother and her five sisters all sang and played piano, and the whole family had to sing in the church choir. 'It was the rule of the house to take piano lessons. My grandmother made us all take them, from them down to us – little cats and everybody. She didn't dig jazz too much because she called that like, "the devil's music", but they played it in the house.'

Ali's youngest aunt was married to a drummer and they would hold rehearsals while his grandmother was at work. Sometimes she would come back early and catch them in action, but eventually she said, 'If you want to play that, just play it. I just don't want nothing to do with it,' and shut the door on them. 'I used to sit and watch them play drums because the drums always fascinated me,' recalled Ali. 'I would watch the drummer; I was watching my aunt – one of the most talented pianists I ever heard in my life – I was watching the bass player and the horn player. I was just sitting there watching, and if they did some stuff that they didn't want me to know about, they would put me out. And then I would go around the front of the building with my brothers, and we would boost ourselves up to the window so we could just watch 'em while they be playing and smoking reefer and all that stuff. And that's when I really first got into playing music, but I was young – must have been around nine.'

Ali's aunt died at an early age and his parents separated around the same time. He moved away from his grandmother's house and his interest in music temporarily ceased. 'I was just being a kid, running around doing all kinds of stuff, but there were still kids in the block that were always practising like Freddie Simmons, the piano player, and McCoy Tyner. I used to say, "Why don't you stop that bullshit and come on out here? We want to play some Dead Man's Gulch" [Dead Box – a checkers game], or "We want to run in the empty house." But them cats would practise, they would never come out. All the time you could hear them running up and down the piano because their families were a little stricter. My mother and my old man had broken up and the only thing she was strict about on me was she made me take voice lessons. I had to do that. I had to sing and try to play the piano, but I wasn't even thinking about messing with drums. I'd get little gigs in church around the corner – I guess I was around twelve or thirteen – I used to have to sing on Sundays and then I used to get in talent shows, singing, too.'

Earl Cross, Art Lewis and Rashied Ali – three experienced musicians in their late thirties who have pushed aside more obstacles in pursuit of their chosen careers than most people have to deal with in a lifetime. They grew up in different parts of the USA yet their stories and attitudes combine to present a composite picture of what it is like to be a Black musician involved with an uncommercial ideal in America today. Until fire gutted the inside of the building, they shared a Brooklyn address with Roger Blank, another drummer. 105–7 Broadway was a legendary musicians' commune where Coltrane once held rehearsals. At one time or another, practically everybody in the new music had lived there – Don Cherry, Marion Brown, Clifford Thornton and so on. The building deserved a plaque on its wall; instead, it acknowledged the combined talents that had graced its portals with a minor case of arson and a 'Keep Out' warning nailed to the door.

Coltrane thought enough of Ali's 'multi-directional rhythms' to describe him as 'definitely one of the great drummers'. He said, 'I can really choose just about any direction at any time in the confidence that it will be compatible with what he's doing,'[1] but it did not help him to make records or secure employment with his own group after the saxophonist died. He had to open up his own home as a studio eventually to be sure his music got a hearing. Cross had to work with unknown rock bands and Lewis with nightclub singers and dance troupes, but there is no doubt about what they would rather be doing. 'I got involved in the new music when it seemed like there was no other alternative,' said Lewis. 'From my standpoint, bebop had been played as much as it's possible to be played, and it just seemed like it was the natural alternative to get into the form of music that was getting clearer and freer.'

For Lewis and Earl Cross, playing music was a matter of choice, but for Rashied Ali, growing up in one of the tougher Black neighbourhoods, it was either that or a hustler's existence. James Baldwin has written that in Harlem, a young man had to be either a preacher or pimp in order to make an impression with his peers; and, somehow, the musician is a kind of preacher, the next best thing. 'A lot of people get into music because they really admire the musicians,' said Art Lewis. 'They want to be in with them but they really don't have any talent. They want to be on the scene because they figure it's very glamorous and you cop a lot of chicks, you're out at night and you can sleep in the day, and you can feel a part of that minority, clannish kind of thing.'

Art Lewis came to New York in 1966 with the singer Jon Hendricks, but before that he had worked with saxophonist Harold Land and most of the musicians who lived on the West Coast. His fascination with the music began when he started to frequent Bop City, the after-hours club in San Francisco where people like Dexter Gordon, Charlie Parker and Bud Powell would sit in whenever they were in town, and most of his early experience was gained from actually playing with the visiting firemen. The quality he found most impressive about their music was the actual sound. 'It gave me a good feeling inside so that I wanted to create that feeling, too. I was kind of bashful to approach the people I really admired until I started playing and met them on another level. I always thought that I could do it, though, because when I was real young, I was a good dancer and I would win dance contests. They would have all these big dances, you know, with B.B. King and all those groups, and I would always dance and a crowd would gather around.'

Don Cherry has pointed out that it is impossible to determine exactly *when* something occurs in the musical life of a Black artist – 'When you're born into a Black family in America, you're born into music. You're around dancing and singing all the time, you shoot craps to music, you shoot marbles to music, then when you go to church it's music all the time' – but despite this, the status of the musician in his own community varies from place to place.

In Ossining, a little town situated thirty miles up-state from New York City, trumpeter Ted Daniel and his cousin Sonny Sharrock were the only people in their age-group who wanted to play in the 'fifties. There were plenty of harmony vocal groups around and Sharrock, who remains an avid collector of 'doo-wops', was involved with them, but if the cousins wanted to hear instrumental music, they had to take a half-hour train ride into Manhattan. Daniel would often stay up all night listening to Symphony Sid's live broadcasts from Birdland, then get up and go to school without having slept. When they did finally organise a band to work in local bars, their efforts were supported by a small, loyal following, but eventually it was necessary for them to move to New York.

In Chicago, a musician would be respected only if they were making money. Unlike New York where there are other means of survival, most Chicago musicians work at a day-job or in some other kind of music. While the members of the AACM might be working on their individual projects, Muhal Richard Abrams, for example, could also be found playing bluesy piano behind a saxophonist in a down-home bar on the South Side while Thurman Barker would be on the road with a musical, playing drums in the pit band. 'It's not a compromise,' said Abrams, 'because that's not a performance. It's a gig. That don't interfere with doing your concerts. If you go on the stage and play compromise music, that's different.'[2]

Jerome Cooper, born 1946, is a drummer who has played at Theresa's, the famous blues bar on Chicago's South Side, as well as with the Art Ensemble of Chicago. He said: 'They got the day-shift and the night-shift and when they see a cat at home all day and all night, they be wondering what shift he's working! A musician might be *the cat* among certain individuals, but I'm talking about the overall picture.'

Leroy Jenkins, another Chicagoan, who plays with Cooper in the Revolutionary Ensemble and is fourteen years his senior, had a slightly different experience because the violin was his chosen instrument. He gave recitals every Sunday in the Ebenezer Baptist

Church alongside Bo Diddley, later an important seminal figure in rhythm-and-blues, then an accomplished violinist. In contrast to the myth of the musician's irresistible appeal to women, he felt that his was a rather effeminate occupation. He was actually so embarrassed by his instrument and the machine-gun-type case in which he carried it that he developed a way of walking that would hide it. 'I wasn't any better or any worse than any other person in the neighbourhood, but because I was a musician, people looked up to me. They always thought I was an extra-nice boy or an extra-smart boy. When I started to give a little trouble to my parents, nobody could believe it.'

Street people have always viewed the musician with respect, a privilege shared with the other ghetto heroes – the pimps, gamblers, hustlers, studs and storefront preachers. It is the hard-working sector where he faces the most discrimination. Saxophonist Jimmy Lyons found acceptance among street-people who thought he must be an addict and offered him narcotics whenever they saw his horn. He had to fake a habit in order to keep their respect. Nevertheless, his mother had first-hand knowledge of famous musicians who lived in impoverished circumstances, and although she bought him his first instrument, she tried to dissuade him from taking up music as a career. 'She'd look at a man like Bud Powell, playing the way he was at that time, and the financial situation he was in then – you know, to have nothing. The clothes he had on were raggedy, been slept in for days, and as beautifully as he played, my mother said it would be a crime if I turned out to be a musician.'

Alvin Fielder was one of the first drummers in the AACM. He was born in Meridian, one of the larger town in Mississippi. The status of musicians there was poor, although the town boasted six or seven bands. They were regarded as 'very lowly' because they worked day-jobs. 'Most of the guys were just regular cats.' Fielder's earliest experience was gained in the school band and, enviously, at the elbow of a friend. 'He wasn't really playing but he was young and everybody thought he was *superbad* – you know. I decided to play drums, too. I didn't get a chance because all the cats looked down on me in comparison to him. He was like a competition thing to me and my thing was to outplay him. I was in Mississippi and that was the Mississippi mentality – you know, outplaying instead of playing *with* and learning *from*.'

In the rural South, it was another story. In Leo Smith's community in the Mississippi Delta, musicians were held in high esteem. 'They considered the musicians to be "above the game". In other words, they said that the musicians didn't have to work out in the cotton fields, the spinach fields and the bean fields and do this and that, break their backs and so on.' In an area where the only work Black men could find was manual, musicians were respected because they were 'dealing with their minds'.

Frank Lowe was born in 1943 in Memphis. Growing up in the city that was the first stop on the road North for poor Mississippi Blacks, he remembers hearing singers and guitarists playing the blues on the infamous Beale Street. He studied vocal music at school until he heard the heavyweight tenor saxophonist Gene Ammons, and was captivated by his playing on records like 'Hittin' the Jug'. He spent some time at the University of Kansas: 'I said I wanted to do sociology, though I knew music was going to take over. I just said that so my parents wouldn't flip out and say, "Wow, there he goes – a big musical trip wasting all the money!"'

He worked for a while in the record shop connected to Stax Records, later to become an important record company, but in 1955 just a small part of a theatre situated on East McLemore Street. Rufus Thomas was the hottest Stax property at the time and Steve Cropper, Booker T and the MGs were just beginning to make an impact. Otis Redding and Sam and Dave were yet to materialise, but Lowe had the opportunity to hear all the records he wanted to hear and to associate with the musicians. Through these meetings, the idea of becoming a professional musician himself began to grow. Like Jimmy Lyons, who blossomed in the company of musicians and found their philosophy ahead of the prevailing climate, Lowe liked the air of freedom projected by the musicians. 'Although we've all got this same mental and physical enslavement, they seemed freer mentally because they could just get up there and *create* something.

'In Memphis, if you were a musician of the Otis Redding or Rufus Thomas type calibre, you were as good or as cool as the mayor or a councilman. But I knew an older fellow then – he was kind of like thirty-five and I was fifteen – and he always used to come in and say like, "Man, listen on Eric Dolphy and listen to Ornette." And I used to say, "OK, man, I'll listen," but he was actually considered strange. His name was Benny Moss; he was just like people are now. Musicians like that would have a hell of a time, they'd always have to do day-jobs and so on.'

Frank Lowe became a saxophone player and moved to San Francisco. From there he went to New York in 1966 and became involved with Sun Ra's Arkestra, and on a second visit, ran into Alice Coltrane just as she was preparing to take a band on the road and lacked a saxophonist. It was inevitable, though, that reactions to the new music should be a little slower in the South, for it has always been necessary for a musician to go to New York in order to become known outside his immediate circle. This procedure not only ensures that those who stay at home to take care of their parents or raise their families – or merely because they are unambitious or apprehensive – will seldom be recognised elsewhere for their contributions, it determines that they will generally not be that conversant with the latest developments in the music. They might hear them, for with greater access to recordings through the radio it is difficult to avoid what is going on, but the majority of musicians who stay at home are unadventurous. They usually continue to respect the wishes of their local public and give them what they are accustomed to hearing. In Memphis today, said Frank Lowe, Coltrane, Dolphy and Ornette are known and respected, but in order to get a response from a local audience, 'You still have to go down there with a boogaloo thing happening.'

This is not to imply that fresh ideas are not hatched outside New York – Ornette Coleman formulated his concept in Texas and California, after all, not to mention the varied achievements of Sun Ra and the AACM. At one time each city, state and rural area had its own distinct style – the St Louis trumpet sound, for example – and these styles would be picked up by travelling musicians and passed on to others elsewhere, but with recordings, new ideas become common property more rapidly and it is harder to determine the origin of any specific ingredient.

Hakim Jami, a bassist born in Detroit who later played with musicians as diverse as Don Byas and Sun Ra, worked and studied all over the East Coast before moving to New York. For him it was a common experience to turn up on a gig and find only one other musician there who could hold his own. 'The rest of them would be *leaning* so heavy, man, that you could never take off. But you come to New York and I'd say nine times out often it's going to be happening. You got to be playing to keep up. I used to hear it when cats used to come through that were living in New York. I said, "Man, that is something else about the music when they go to New York!" Now, when I go out sometimes and play with other cats, I feel like I have to hold back or I'll run over them.'

To Art Lewis, growing up on the West Coast, it was important to try to play everything differently from other musicians. At first he would isolate a figure from a record and try to copy it, but when he realised that this was impossible, he applied himself to achieving the best possible personal interpretation. 'It was always hard for me to just play a certain thing that somebody else had played, but you get more respect if you create your own sort of sound.'

Increasingly, where the new Black musicians are concerned, it has been no longer vital to make it in the Apple (New York City). Some members of the AACM proved this by earning a reputation in Europe. They were followed, in turn, by musicians from St Louis's Black Artists Group. To anyone living and travelling elsewhere in the country, the choice of New York-based musicians to hold centre-stage often seemed arbitrary and, in the face of their listening experience, singularly inappropriate. 'It was always assumed that you had to go to New York to play, and that you weren't playing anything unless you were in New York,' said Lester Bowie. 'But all the time I would read these things I would be travelling, and I would be meeting cats, and I would say, "What d'you mean?" I mean, here's Joe Smith or somebody you never heard of, and he's just *ferocious!* So that's why I never had anything for going to New York. There's so much talent everywhere.'

For a while Byard Lancaster divided his time almost equally between Europe and America in order to survive. In his home town of Philadelphia, his talents are also split two ways. There is the spiritually refined version of free music he plays with the group he co-leads with drummer J. R. Mitchell – they have played together since he was fourteen – and the Sounds of Liberation, a septet led by vibraphonist Khan Jamal which is essentially more commercial and works fairly steadily as a result. Since 1965 he has worked with Sunny Murray. He said: 'You can go to any town and there's always one man there who is the top jazz musician and another who's the leading violinist. There's another category where there's someone who makes a good deal of money playing music in his hometown, and there's another cat who travels to make it. I think it was like Bach or Beethoven or somebody like that – one travelled and one stayed at home, one had kids and one didn't. So when you really read into music history, then you begin to understand that there really are no stars. It's just like Sly Stone said – "everybody is a star". Each man has a job to do and when he realises what it is, he develops a personal technique about himself and it comes out in his music. Some people's job is to stay in the community because of the need for their knowledge to raise the young warriors. If all the warriors left the village, the young boys wouldn't have anybody they could see.'

Donald Garrett, who prefers to be known by his second name, Rafael, is a warrior who stayed in the village for a considerable time.

In San Francisco, he occupied a unique position in the musicians' community. He has appeared on record with Coltrane, Shepp and Dewey Redman, playing bass, clarinet and bass-clarinet, and in a series of duets with his wife Zuzann, on ESP, but to musicians, his wisdom has long been valued as much as his playing. Frank Lowe is indebted to him for his philosophical approach. 'Rafael told me this – you can't devote all your time to music. You've got to paint the house or work a couple of hours a day doing something else. That Utopian thing used to be for the musician to stay in his corner and when he comes out, all he can do is play his horn. But we've got to get out here and deal with the people that's on the streets. You have to stay in touch.'

Garrett, who comes originally from El Dorado, Arkansas, was raised in Chicago, where he attended High School with saxophonists John Gilmore and Clifford Jordan. This was at the time when it was considered hip to mess with heroin and Garrett's experiments led him eventually to the Federal Narcotics Institution at Lexington, Kentucky. Prior to this, he had been known as a clarinettist and saxophone player, but after meeting the indefatigable Wilbur Ware in Lexington, he emerged as a bassist, too. Through his mixed experiences, Garrett developed as a different person. The hip street dude became a creative guru. He spent his time making instruments and talking to the young musicians who constantly flooded into his house seeking knowledge. Among the instruments for which he became famous are thumb-pianos and bamboo flutes, and it is said that there are few bands in San Francisco without one of these.

While Coltrane was still with Miles Davis, he and Garrett were always together when the Quintet played Chicago. It was at Garrett's house that Muhal Richard Abrams first met Coltrane. ''Trane loved him,' said the pianist. 'He always wanted Garrett to turn him on to some new rhythms, so he introduced him to Ravi Shankar.'[3] The two men played together in Chicago, and in 1965 Garrett spent a fruitful three weeks with Coltrane's group. It was during this period that they made *Om, Kulu Se Mama, Selflessness* and later, *Live in Seattle,* but Coltrane had snared Garrett during a temporary emergence from his home in the mountains at Big Sur. 'In a way, I regret it,' said Garrett. 'I would have liked to see what would have happened if I'd stayed there, because in six months, I was *depleted*, man. All that shit was going round in my mind again.'

Garrett places great value on adaptability. To him, all instruments are basically the same, it is just in the fingering that they differ. He considers the truly creative musician is one who can play any instrument. 'It's up to you how deep you want to go with it. If you're scared of losing your technique by changing instruments, you probably haven't got it, anyway. A lot of people have got stagnant by just having a tenor saxophone hung around their neck for years instead of trying to play, say, the drums. You start out to be creative but maybe you get caught up in the mill and it squeezes you dry. It might seem that super virtuoso technique goes hand in hand with creativity and we're supposed to have it, but creativity is the thing.'

* * *

In the heart of Atlanta, the burgeoning commercial centre of the New South, there is a plush nightclub planned and rigged out like an old man-o'-war. Three consummate musicians who have been together since 1963 work there six nights a week using a repertoire that takes in originals as well as material by Stevie Wonder and Roberta Flack. The hours are long but they look contented because the gig is secure and their salaries are frequently increased. Paul Mitchell, Allen Murphy and Laymon Jackson are the perfect example of what Byard Lancaster was talking about, for they grew up with the noted alto saxophonist Marion Brown, who has recorded on Impulse as well as in Europe, and the vigorous bassist Norris Jones, who has played with everyone in the new music from John Coltrane and Archie Shepp to Cecil Taylor and Ornette Coleman. In 1974, though, Brown was teaching in an alien city in order to keep his family in food, and Jones, now known as Sirone, was struggling to keep his music from the rats and roaches in a dingy first-floor apartment in the heart of the Lower East Side. The Paul Mitchell Trio put a record out in 1973 and their followers swept up all available copies. They are far from lightweights when it comes to music, but they knew the kind of life they would prefer at the age of forty.

In common with many people, Marion Brown had left Atlanta disgusted at the reactionary South, but a couple of years later, he had worked with every big name in the new music including John Coltrane. Sirone went to New York in 1966 in response to a call from him. He said: 'The cats were a little afraid of New York, all those stories and so forth, but to have someone call you and ask you to come and make a job in New York, and when he runs down to you who he's playing with, the first name is John Coltrane, you don't know how you're going to do it, but you know that if you have to walk to New York you're going to make that job.'

Sirone had started out playing trombone. He was approaching twenty-eight when Brown called him and creating his own jobs in Atlanta. He considered the band he led there was 'dynamite' and ahead of its time, and it came as a real surprise to him to arrive in New York, the much-touted Mecca for musicians, only to find that so many of the people he admired were scuffling and, in several cases, personally disturbed.

'You really have to adjust to a whole 'nother way of life because there are certain things that you're going to be deprived of, and right away it's money. It's a very sad thing, this attention that is put on money, but if it's not there, you don't have to stop existing. Still, I hope we could get enough money to have a centre for young musicians; you take a kid that is coming from Atlanta to New York – the only thing he knows about New York is that New York is what's happening.'

Not every musician born in the South headed northwards. There were several who went to Los Angeles or San Francisco to escape from the stifling limitations of the South. Sonny Simmons, Prince Lasha, Dewey Redman and Frank Lowe were four saxophonists who moved to the West Coast; Noah Howard was another. In New Orleans, where music can be heard in every front room, bar and alleyway, Howard had found himself constantly turned on by sound. It was not until he moved to San Francisco, though, that he heard his first Coltrane record. 'I was overwhelmed. I thought it was fantastic. I thought it was the greatest thing I ever heard. It made me want to play but I didn't know *what* to play.'

Dewey Johnson, the trumpet player who was later to participate in Coltrane's landmark *Ascension* date, temporarily provided the answer. Howard started taking lessons from him in the house they shared on Haight Street with Byron Allen, one of the first new-wave saxophonists to appear on record. The house was filled from II o'clock in the morning to late at night with a constantly fluctuating musician population, and Howard underwent the total musical experience. 'I just became increasingly more engrossed in music,' he recalled. He was dissatisfied with the trumpet and began taking lessons from Allen, playing on an alto he had acquired instead of his original choice, the soprano model. 'The more I played, the more difficult it became, but the more I dug it. It just became like a cancerous kind of thing. I became possessed by this metal thing; I had to keep getting into it.'

He discovered that the more he pursued the saxophone, the more there was to learn. For Howard, it was the first time he had not been bored with a new toy. 'Although I wanted to play the instrument, I didn't want to play it the way that other saxophonists played it. In order to play the instrument, you become impressed by other saxophonists, but if you do have something deep down inside the core of you, then eventually this thing starts coming out. It's something inside a person that will make him play a series of notes one way rather than five or six ways that other people have played them.'

Howard eventually moved to New York and Europe, but James Black, a drummer from his hometown, remains one of that city's Underground heroes. The New Orleans 'funk' beat is so unique that even Berry Gordy, the Motown president, made reconnaissance trips to secure it for his recordings; James Black is one of its major exponents. He plays with a kind of nonchalant arrogance, and is considered to be a 'musicians' musician' in New Orleans, a label he slightly resents but one that ensures he is seldom out of work. He left New Orleans with a rhythm-and-blues pianist called Joe Jones. During six years in and out of the city, he worked with Cannonball Adderley, Horace Silver, Yusef Lateef and Lionel Hampton. He was one of the musicians who chose to return, although with his talent and credentials, he could have made it anywhere.

His initial experiences in New York illustrate the way the unproven musician must operate on arrival. He was befriended by two men – the late Frank Haynes, the tenor player, who taught him all a musician needed to know in the city, and Brian Perry, 'a drummer of sorts who was really a pimp', who had another speciality. 'Brian showed me all about the other parts of the action, the gangsters and whatever I looked around and I'd say, "Wow – New York!"'

Black's main contact, though, was Wilbert Hogan, the New Orleans drummer who worked with Lionel Hampton and Ray Charles. Walking down Broadway together one day, Hogan pointed out Hampton to the younger man and proceeded to collar him. 'Gates, this is James Black, a drummer from my hometown. He's a bad motherfucker,' announced Hogan. 'Why don't you let this cat come by and audition for a job? He needs one.' Hampton's reply was, 'OK, Wilbert, if you say he's good, he's good.' Black made the audition and got the job.

'Wilbert Hogan was sort of like my passport, otherwise I probably wouldn't have gotten into anything. He was in with all the local cats and they all knew and respected him. By me being from

New Orleans we had a mutual admiration thing going – he'd just pull me on in.' Black remembers the other musicians as being 'sort of friendly', but most were indifferent. At first he thought their attitudes stemmed from dislike, later he realised it was fear of competition. 'I used to ask could I sit in and some would say "No!" But some would say OK, so I'd sit in and *do* it. And them cats'd be looking at me strangely and saying, "Yeah, that was pretty good." They'd growl "thank you" and that'd be that. Nobody wants to lose their job and if there's anything you can do to keep somebody from taking it, you're going to do it. So they look at you like, "Here comes another one, maybe we can discourage him and send him back." But I wasn't very easily discouraged.'

Noah Howard, returning home after two years in the Army, found New Orleans stifling in spite of its charm and had to leave. To James Black it was 'the Big Easy' after the tension and squalor of New York. 'I was ready to go at a moment's notice all the time, but here I can relax, kick my shoes off, and walk down the street in my undershirt if I want to.' He also noticed that the most talented musicians were often the ones who worked the least, while those who could just about scrape by would always be on the bandstand. To stay off the breadline, he formulated an aggressive technique for dealing with club-owners. 'If you just sit there and wait, you'll never get anywhere. You got to be able to go in and grab a cat by the collar and say, "I'm so-and-so – give me a job!" And, "If you don't give me a job, I'll burn your place down" – so to speak.'

* * *

While aggressiveness is a valuable safeguard for the established musician who has paid his dues, it is no substitute for the tact and diplomacy required to enter the uncompromising world of the New York musicians. Every aspect of life in the city is tough but the cliques in the music business are virtually impregnable unless the newcomer is prepared to undergo a new process of learning.

'You don't just come in town and jump in,' said Art Lewis. 'You have to prove that you really want to, that you're really devoted to music, and you have to prove that by your sincerity and involvement and by coming out and meeting the people.' Many a young musician has gone home with his tail between his legs because he did not realise that he had to be seen around, keep quiet and wait to be asked to play before he could be considered as capable of even blowing his nose.

The musicians are thick-skinned and with good cause. They know their worth but are seldom given the chance to show it. Whenever a new player comes in town, he is ripe to be challenged. One such saxophonist, who arrived preceded by a reasonable reputation, had been living in the city for a few weeks when he received a phone call from two of the heavyweights on the instrument. They summoned him to a dingy apartment on the Lower East Side where they were living at the time, empty save for the barest necessities and a single light bulb dangling in a corner, and simply told him 'play'. The telephone suggestion had been for the three to play together, but no such situation materialised. The newcomer put his horn in his mouth and blew for a solid half-hour while the jury in the Kafkaesque setting carefully weighed his credentials. He stopped when he considered he had played enough to prove his worth, but all the arbiters had to say was, 'So you're going to make a record, huh?'

At a loft session on another occasion, it was considered permissible for two members of the tight and proven circle to ask to sit in during the interval, but not for an unknown saxophonist to stand up and blow along with them. A callow youth who did this was roundly condemned from the stage by the musicians who laid down their instruments, laughing mockingly and making audible comments of the 'How 'bout something *hip?*' variety. Eventually the organiser of the festivities put an end to the young man's misery by applauding him ostentatiously right under his nose and compelling the audience to join in, but it was ensured that the novice would never repeat his offence.

'Nobody says a word if you're bold enough to jump up on the bandstand and take your instrument out and play it – if you can play,' said Earl Cross, but to him and those others who have put in time and study on their instrument, there is nothing worse than someone who picks up a horn in a pawnshop and after a week of blowing, considers himself a musician. He cited an instance that occurred in Tompkins Square Park, a popular open-air venue for musicians on the Lower East Side.

'Along comes this cat with his trumpet in a knapsack, can't blow a lick. He jumped on the bandstand and started messing up the whole thing. He really got the cats mad and 'bout ready to hurt him. Eventually they had to put him off the bandstand, but I've seen it happen quite a few times. I didn't do it when I first got to New York and I'd been *playing* before I got here. But now, with that different kind of style, they just bite down on their reeds and blow, they blow through the trumpet just flagging the valves, and don't try to make any music at all! I mean, I *know* about a trumpet. You can't just pick it up and blow it.'

In the past, said Cross, the musicians were too tolerant of the unschooled and untalented musician. Now, those musicians who can play are demanding that other people control their instruments and stop 'scribbling' before being admitted to their circle. They feel that the 'non-playing cats' are responsible for many of the clubs closing down, and for deceiving the audience about the nature of the new music. 'How many times does a person who likes music cut out from his day-job and when he sees it, it's all that confusion and distortion? They don't want to be bothered with it no more. They say, "Oh, the music's changed," and so I can understand that, too. That group of people who can't play are actually messing up the other group of cats who can.'

Jimmy Lyons admitted to being a purist if the term implied a knowledge of one's instrument. 'A lot of cats who play trumpet or saxophone, their approach is that anything is OK for the artist. They can pick up ashes and throw them up in the air and that's supposed to be part of it. Technically, cats like Louis Armstrong and Charlie Parker had something to say. It wasn't just a question of rambling and hoping they'd run across something by accident. I'd rather be a saxophone player first than an artist.'

Experienced musicians who play without reference to chords and time-signatures, do so from choice. They know it is impossible to play the new music without an awareness of what has preceded it, and have scant respect for those newcomers who are hung up on the superficialities of the style. Rashied Ali feels that the musician worth his salt should be able to play with any band: 'If you come out playing honks and squeals, that's all you're going to play. I don't care how long you play, you're not going to get over that. But if you know the fundamentals, if you know what's happening with it, you can study, and as you study, you're there. You change because you know what's happening with it.

'The music is here, now, but you can't just give somebody a horn and let them jump in on what's happening. You say, "Look, man, let's play free, but let's play like in a blues – let's get into some kind of structure with it." And those people, they can't produce, because they don't know anything about that. They may feel they don't need to know, but musically, they're not going anywhere, and they'll find out that if they don't get to it musically, they won't move. They'll just play the same things that they know over and over. Discipline makes musicians grow.'

* * *

The cliques that abound are based on a variety of factors. Those leaders who are frequently in the recording studios generally use the same sidemen who are expected to return the favour whenever they secure a date. Other cliques are formed by musicians who want to project a certain sound, and in this case the sound is more important than the personal relationships between the members of the group. Musicians who come from the same home-town often work together. Some artists who have accepted Islam derive satisfaction from playing with other Moslems, although this is not an exclusive coterie, but as one convert pointed out, a knowledge of Eastern history and the involvement with new tonalities that comes from studying Arabic are useful adjuncts to the Eastern-related tonalities that abound in the music today. Elvin Jones has said that at one point several musicians were studying the same branch of Hinduism as John Coltrane, and this made it easier for them to play together on a variety of horns. 'It wasn't too much of a step for them to utilise some of the sounds found in Indian music.'

(Parenthetically, it should be noted that Islam has been instrumental in helping a number of Blacks, musicians among them, with a dependency on drugs or alcohol, although in some cases, the more orthodox converts have stopped playing. When a Black American changes his name, however, it does not automatically follow that he is a convert to the faith. The cultural nationalist adopts an African name – often taken from the Arabic-based Swahili, *lingua franca* of East Africa – for obvious reasons. In the case of Maurice McIntyre, he felt he had reached a higher state of consciousness with the years and so he became Kalaparusha Ahra Difda. Norris Jones took the components of his 'slave name' and became Sirone. 'I have a lot of respect for Islam like I do for all religions, but I just didn't feel that I could be true to Islam at this particular time. Yet still I felt some way inside of me that there was something else besides Norris Jones.')

On the other hand, just as in the rock world, there is amongst musicians who get high on certain drugs a comradeship similar to that which exists between homosexuals in the theatre. One musician claims that he was actually fired from a band because he was a non-user. 'When you're on the road, you know, the phone-call comes: "We're going to leave for the concert at 8 o'clock, everybody be in so-and-so's room at 7" – except me, that is, because there's no reason for me to go. And this is what happens – everybody gets high and they get it together spiritually for the night.'

There are musicians who use neither drugs nor alcohol and yet are treated with respect – McCoy Tyner, himself a Moslem, is a good example – but in the main, this is one way of cementing the bond of brotherhood. Drugs have always been used in the music world, including (despite what some writers would have us believe) in New Orleans. For many of today's musicians, though, they provide a kind of compensation for lack of recognition. It could be said that some people use in order to be noticed.

The untalented newcomer sometimes sees the provision of such aids to euphoria as a means of getting close to the musicians he admires. But whether he comes up with a bottle of Wild Irish Rose or a bag of heroin, it does not necessarily follow that he will be allowed to do anything other than sit on the sidelines. There have been cases of merely adequate players being tolerated for their good connections but they are rare. The musicians are not playing games. 'Different musicians use different things,' one man explained. 'A lot of 'em like smoke, a lot of 'em like coke – a lot of 'em like nothing. Some of them like wine, some of them like scag [heroin] and if a person wants to get in there and really wants to learn his instrument and has certain people that he wants to learn from, he'll make a point of finding out what this person likes and getting some of it and bringing it with him … When the cat comes in town, the guy he comes to see or the people he wants to hang out with obviously have more knowledge about music than he does. So by bringing them something, in a kind of way he's buying their knowledge.'

(It is a condition of learning that has always prevailed. Red Holloway, a saxophonist from an earlier era, learned what he could from older players. Lester Young was helpful and although he never got to know Charlie Parker well, he responded to requests for different 'licks'. When he eventually had the opportunity to work for six months with Ben Webster, he brought a fifth of scotch to the nightclub schoolroom each night. 'He was giving me all kinds of licks and telling me how to play chords and whatnot. So like it was really a great help.')

The quality of sound, the execution and the young player's spiritual quality are indicators of his potential where Art Lewis is concerned. Technique he considers important but not sufficiently to take precedence over these other virtues. His willingness to share his knowledge with anyone who has possibilities depends on their sincerity. He explained his hesitancy: 'A lot of people, they dig the life and one night they might fancy themselves as a musician. That might last a couple of months or a year, but there's so many horns in the pawnshop it ain't funny. It looks easy, but it's a lot of hard work and boring practice.' Lewis estimates that it takes ten to fifteen years before the player can feel like an artist and the real test of dedication comes after that. 'I feel now like I'm just growing into my own sound.' Do you get the reputation that you're not prepared to compromise? 'Yeah, well that's the sort of reputation you're trying to get …'

Hanging-out rituals are undoubtedly essential before a musician becomes established, but individuals interpret their relevance in different ways. 'You have to put in your hanging-out time,' said Ted Daniel. 'But you have to know when to do it and when not to. I'm not out just to be *out* – especially in New York, because all you can do when you come out is spend money.' Frank Lowe compared the ritual to music school. 'Max Roach can sit down and say a few words and it'll be enough to yield discovery. You follow those cats around for their knowledge because they got it and they're going to pass it on. It's a heritage and it's a music you want to study. That's why I associate with them because they're the professors and I'm the student. It's for them to pass on some of that knowledge that attracted me to them in the first place and made them so great and so appealing. It's secretive but it's not a secret.'

Lowe is as true as his word, for everywhere you go in New York, you'll run into him, working here, sitting-in there, and rehearsing uptown and downtown with anyone who'll have him. When he's not playing, he's listening, and when he's not listening, he's talking – always about music. He is a perpetual student. His lifestyle reflects an attitude of Hakim Jami's: 'When you say now "I play music", that means a course in life.'

Frank Lowe may not be making money from his music, but he is well aware that he might have been in a worse predicament had he not met Alice Coltrane at the right time. As a result, the first time a jazz audience saw him, he was playing in her group alongside Archie Shepp, Jimmy Garrison and the two drummers Clifford Jarvis and Freddie Waits. But in order to prove to the musicians he wanted to play with that he really knew his instrument, he also made a point of being heard everywhere. 'I went to a lot of dingy clubs and played, and I tried to get my Charlie Parker licks together on some gigs. I really didn't have them under my fingers, but I scrambled with them.' Frequently he came home, exhausted and frustrated, at four or five in the morning, and would be up three hours later, trying to play what had escaped him the previous night. He paid his dues sitting in with people like Elvin Jones, who played so strongly at Slug's that the stage vibrated. The first time he tried this, a man jumped on stage and started dancing while he was in full cry. Lowe was nervous because he was trying his hardest to impress everyone within earshot and all he was aware of was the shaking of the stage and Jones's regular saxophonist, Frank Foster, pounding him on the back and yelling, 'Blow! Blow! Blow!' He was confused, but he made up his mind there and then that should a piece of the ceiling drop on his head, he would not be deterred.

* * *

The musicians come to New York preceded by their hometown reputation – if any – and in varying degrees of poverty. Usually they head for the Lower East Side, formerly the Jewish, later the Polish, ghetto, now a decaying collection of streets inhabited by Puerto Ricans, Jews, Italians and Afro-Americans in equal proportions. The area is littered with broken bottles and garbage, and in the summer, the sidewalks are flooded with people. Squalid though the surroundings are, a feeling of vitality throbs and pulses in the air, and this is vividly echoed in the music of the people who live there.

When Pharoah Sanders came to New York he had no money and slept in the subway and under the stairs in tenement hallways. He also had to pawn his horn. Rashied Ali slept in the parks. When he did get an apartment, he had to carry his drums to and fro from a fourth-floor walk-up. There was one outlandish saxophonist from the South who allegedly appeared in the Apple wearing his hair in a 'process' – that is, with the kinks straightened out – and driving a Cadillac, but the majority arrive in less spectacular style. This particular man, showing off some of the 'Black Man's badges of success', represented a lifestyle that the musicians playing the new music had rejected.

Unless they have friends or relatives, the newcomers must move fast to find a job inside, or outside, music or to drum up some other means of support. Musicians have been salesmen, packers and dishwashers, and there is always work in the post office. Archie Shepp sought work as an actor. At the same time, they have to be seen around and make their presence felt in the musicians' circle. The first few months in the city are as hectic and energy-consuming as they are crucial to the newcomer's reputation.

When a musician has established his credentials, he becomes, in effect, a 'New York musician', and can play with anyone whose concept he fits. At the same time, it can take him a while to find those people. 'Before you can find three musicians that you can lay out and play with – and hang out with – you can go through a thousand,' Earl Cross was once told by an older musician. Roger Blank, the drummer, realised this too late. Living outside Manhattan, in Westchester county, he had to move into the city to keep up with the progress of the 'fire' bands. Any ego problem he might have had was checked by living in close proximity to strong musicians – he shared a loft with trumpeter Charles Tolliver and pianist

John Hicks – but his problem was enthusiasm. He was impatient to become part of the circle of older musicians. 'I put my wares right in the ears of people who'd been playing many, many years before, and that's kind of damaging.'

In the 'sixties, Blank was the house drummer at Harlem's famous Hotel Theresa which, prior to Malcolm X's assassination, housed the headquarters of his Organisation of Afro-American Unity. Hank Mobley played regularly at the hotel and Blank's job gave him his first opportunity to meet musicians of the stature of this noted saxophonist. One night, the pianist was Barry Harris, well-respected for his track-record, his teaching and the time he spent with Charlie Parker.

In the face of the older man's experience, Blank felt uncomfortably aware of his shortcomings. 'He was very polite, he didn't put me down too tough, but I guess that's because New York hosts so many musicians from all over the country and older musicians have to be polite and courteous.' When other drummers would come by the Theresa, though, Blank noticed how they would be invited to play in preference to him. He was hurt when he realised that he did not have the strength needed to endure alongside the veteran musicians, a strength that could only be arrived at and built up by continually playing with musicians of his own age group. 'There were times when I'd play and I would enjoy it and the other people I played with would enjoy it, too, but the majority of times I could still feel a great need for that year-in and year-out just *doing* it, *doing* it and *doing* it, that so many musicians that are on the scene now lack.'

In 1972, Roger Blank was back in a familiar situation, playing Monday nights with the late Kenny Dorham at Minton's, the Harlem bar acknowledged to be the birthplace of bebop. He considered that by having to play with immature musicians (himself and bassist Benny Wilson), the trumpeter was in a similar position to Harris and Mobley at the Hotel Theresa: 'You know, with young fellows who've been playing just two or three years and want to come out and dig how they sound – especially in a place like Minton's with the historical precedent that it has.' This time, though, he knew better. He held back and listened for what was required from him.

It is not surprising that young musicians do sometimes overreach themselves in an attempt to impress others, for work is at a premium and, as Hakim Jami has pointed out, the idea of the music is to be heard. There is no fun to be had from playing in solitude. 'You know, I could play up here by myself all the time,' he said, indicating his rugged apartment. 'For years and years when I wasn't getting the work that I'm getting now, that's how I was able to still feel that I was a musician. I knew that I could go behind closed doors and play my butt off whenever I felt like it. But you need that feedback, you need that rapport. Like we played a concert last night and a young lady told me that she had started not to come because she had a headache. But she came and sat down and listened to the music and her headache went. That's a beautiful thing that the music can do, and that's what it's *supposed* to do – to heal.' There was nothing unique in the instance related by Jami; Marion Brown, Milford Graves and Malachi Favors have all experienced this reaction. And Albert Ayler called one of his pieces 'Music is the Healing Force of the Universe'.

The brotherhood bond appears to be stronger between certain musicians than in other comparable Black groups, despite the money factor which is the most dominant weapon in the game of 'divide and conquer'. When Leroy Jenkins arrived in New York, though, he was forced to alter his outlook. He came from a well organised Black community in Chicago where the meaning of Black Power was really felt in everything, but in New York he found himself thrown into an entirely new situation. Like most of the Black musicians with no relatives in the city, he headed straight for Greenwich Village only to discover that most of his neighbours were white. 'I didn't exclude myself from the Black cause – in fact I was very much in it when I got here – but in the process of doing it, I found out so many things about the Black people I looked up to. They actually weren't doing what they'd say they were doing.'

Jenkins's disillusionment was compounded by the realisation that white musicians were often treated as badly as Blacks. 'When it came to paying the musicians, everybody in America – Black and white – seems to think they should work for nothing. In other words, they seem to think in America that it's more of an honour to be famous than financially solvent.' This was further brought home to him one night at Ornette Coleman's loft where the saxophonist was entertaining a well-known white musician who had made substantial sums with his recordings. 'This cat told him he didn't even know how much money he made! And Ornette was shook up – me, too. I guess we had forgotten that white folks get beat, too.'

Faced with the economic realities of New York, Jenkins started to rethink his attitude to his music. 'I'm not so much of an *artist* as I was, because that's a strike against you. Being a musician, white or Black, that's a strike against you, and being a Black man – that's three strikes against you. So I figured that I'd better cut some of these odds down. I couldn't cut off the fact that I was Black, but the artist part – I cut that out. Now I say that I came here primarily to make money. I had wanted to be famous, but after seeing Ornette and what fame had done to him, I cut that out. Fame doesn't help, man. You can be famous and poor as hell. You lose a lot of friendships, too, being famous – and broke. And the landlord'll put you out of the house faster.'

One of the important differences between the new musicians and their predecessors is that they have had the opportunity to stand back and look at the mistakes of the past. Not all of them have been able to learn from the tragic examples of the artists whose priorities were confused, but there are enough people aware of the methods that were used to keep the musicians enslaved to ensure that those who follow them will have a better example to go by. 'For too long you'd get up there on the stand and here's a

Jimmy Garrison, 1971

Elvin Jones and McCoy Tyner, 19

Don Cherry, New York, 1988

Dewey Redman, Ornette Coleman and Charlie Haden, Newport Jazz Festival, 1971

Eric Dolphy, 1961

Cecil Taylor, Five Spot,
New York, 1975

Ed Blackwell and Denis Charles, New York, 1982

Andrew Cyrille, Countee Cullen
Library, New York, 1976

ny Murray, Ladies Fort, New York, 1976

Albert Ayler, Harlem, New York, 1966

Marion Brown, Greenwich Village, New York, 1966

Earl Cross (flugelhorn) and Roy Brooks (standing), New York
Musicians' Festival, Tompkins Square Park, New York, 1975

Khalil and Rashied Ali, Brooklyn, New York, 1971

Jimmy Lyons (right) teaching ex-addict in
Narcotics Rehabilitation Programme, New York, 1971

Ornette Coleman and Anthony Braxton,
Prince Street, New York, 1971

Sun Ra, Village Gate, New York, 1976

Ahmed Abdullah (trumpet, left) and Marshall Allen (kora, right), Village Gate, New York, 1976

Lester Bowie, Chicago, 1971

Revolutionary Ensemble:
Leroy Jenkins (violin) and
Bill Dixon, Vermont, 1972   Sirone (bass), New York, 1971

Rashied Ali and Frank Lowe, New York, 1972

Roger Blank, New York, 1976

Amina Myers, Wimbledon,
London, 1979

Giuseppi Logan, New York, 1972

Milford Graves, Seventh Avenue, Harlem, New York, 1971

Claude Bartee and Billy Higgins jam under a picture
of Malcolm X, Brooklyn, New York, 1971

Sonny and Lynda Sharrock,
New York, 1971

Bea and Sam Rivers, Studio Rivbe
New York, 1972

Cal Massey, Archie Shepp and Beaver Harris discuss album
'Attica Blues' with inmates' attorney William Kunstler, New York, 1972

cat with a 250-dollar suit on, 200-dollar shoes and a diamond ring, playing his horn,' said Frank Lowe. 'He goes home, man, and he's got rats crawling around his pad. I know so many people like that, still. Some of them are my associates, some of them are even my friends, but they got an old-style way of things going. They function off it and it's valid for them; it's just not valid for me. I choose to play with people like Alice [Coltrane] and Milford [Graves], family people who seem like they're responsible and can function in – and out – of the music world. There's just no room any more for ignorant musicians. You can't just play your instrument and say, "All my spirit, my spirit comes from the instrument." OK, you do play from the spirit, but when you go out there you've got to know how much the man's charging you for a bowl of rice. *And* why the cost is up, and what you can do about it – if anything.'

'The ultimate achievement,' said Dewey Redman, 'is not to play in New York, but to *survive* in New York. In a way I make a living but in a way I don't. I never think of it as making a living, really – and you have to face that fact. I spend most of my time thinking about music. I have faith in music, and I believe that if you have faith in music, if you're sincere and honest about what you're doing, you'll be provided for. And so far, it has worked out.'

* * *

While most young Blacks had been glad to get away from the South, conditions there in the 'seventies had improved noticeably. Marion Brown had turned his back on reactionary Atlanta, but in 1970 he returned in order that his son might be born there. During a lengthy stay in Europe he had been made aware of the importance of tradition and the way that people relate to their history. He realised that he had a heritage, too, but it did not lie in New York. 'I knew I had to come back to the South for a while to see things, for this is where the strength of the Black people lies.'

In Atlanta, his family had lived in a dirt street which was

constantly filled with 'all kinds of troubadours passing through. There were jug-bands and washboard bands. There were guitar players, some blind and some of them blind alcoholically. They'd be hollerin' up and down the street just like "Porgy and Bess". A constant opera. But you've got to see it like that, and most of us couldn't see.' On his return, Brown revisited old places and spent many hours talking with his uncle, the Minister of a tiny Baptist church there. From him he learnt where his maternal grandfather had come from and this knowledge has been instrumental in his growing inner strength. 'To be close to nature like I was when I grew up, to be among trees, hear birds singing and dogs barking – all these things are so important now that my interest in ethnic music has become so keen.'

Alvin Fielder went back to Meridian when his father started talking of selling the family drugstore. He was a qualified pharmacist himself and decided to take over the business. 'I thought about it and I figured there should be good players everywhere – even in Mississippi.' By the time he returned, however, the last of the state's 'jazz' players had left. As a result, Fielder has been unable to find any local musicians to work with. The AACM members were puzzled by his decision, but he refuted any accusations of 'sell-out' by immediately applying for various grants. Through the Mississippi Arts Commission he has been able to bring several AACM players down for concerts, and the National Endowment on the Arts has enabled him to hold a series of classes in Meridian. These were especially valuable in this musically backward State because Fielder has literally encyclopaedic knowledge of the music. Continuing to live by the code of the AACM, he is determined to share it.

The jazz player has nearly always been an elitist whose musical preferences set him or her apart from other musicians. Historically, the choice of what kind of music to play has seldom been open to the Black musician. Thus, while generally speaking the word 'elitism' is class-oriented and suggestive of white privilege where most Blacks are concerned, a musician's decision to play anything other than blues or doowop can still be seen as an elitist choice within the Black community. And, while that in itself is indicative of a certain freedom, inasmuch as the jazz player's lifestyle would appear to epitomise 'hipness', it has often been beyond the capacity of an individual to cope with the degree of dedication required to live that life. As far back as the early 1930s, the Andy Kirk band refused to allow their pianist, Mary Lou Williams, to indulge in meaningless conversation when the music was at stake: 'It was "put everything into your music" and "keep your mouth shut", I couldn't even talk to anybody for years. All they wanted was to do music, to think music, sleep music.'⁴ Really the situation has not changed. The difference between a serious musician and one that isn't serious, playing for the thrill of pulling a chick or how somebody might say, "He's such a fine-looking guy," is that they're not playing it for the thrill of the music but for the thrill of somebody thinking they're a big-shot,' said Rashied Ali. 'Most of those cats who were in it for the glamour of it all, they didn't really make any mark in the music, anyway. They didn't do anything for it – if anything, they took something away from it. Now – and yesterday – there's always been serious musicians that cared about the music. That's why the music's here today because if there don't be no serious musicians, there wouldn't be no music.'

Notes

1   Reported in liner-notes by Nat Hentoff, *Coltrane/Live at the Village Vanguard Again* (Impulse A-9124).
2   Steve Lake, 'Number One Man', *Melody Maker*, November 1973.
3   Interview with Ray Townley, in *Down Beat*, 15 August 1974.
4   Interview with Roland Baggenaes, 'Mary Lou Williams', *Coda*, July 1974.

PART THREE

GIVE THE DRUMMER SOME!

9

The Spirit Behind the Musicians

James Brown recorded this tune and I remember him saying,
'Give the drummer some!' That opened a lot of eyes and ears.

Beaver Harris

'Some Africans believe that it was through the sound of the drum
that God gave man the ability to speak or to understand one
another in contrast to the lower animals, to differentiate him from
the lesser creatures. So this is in a way symbolic or figurative, but it
is like how close the drum is to them. And you know, in our music
the drum is like the mother of the music, it's like the heartbeat.
It transmits the pulse, the energy, the basic feeling of the music,
so this is something that is like very, very close. If you take the
drum out of most Black music it would probably almost be life-
less – even down to rock, because the whole thing people relate to
in rock or rhythm-and-blues is the drum and the other things are
just embellishments.'

Andrew Cyrille, who worked with Cecil Taylor from 1964 to
1975 including two years as Artist-in-Residence at Antioch College
in Yellow Springs, Ohio, lectures frequently on the drum and its
historical place in Afro-American music. In 1974, he had a weekly
series on the subject on Radio WKCR-FM in New York. He knows
that when the drummer gives up in Black music, things fall apart;
the centre cannot hold, for the drums, after all, are there to take
care of business.

Baby Dodds, who is generally regarded as the first major influence on jazz drumming, once called the drummer the conductor of the band. Roger Blank, a young drummer who has played with Sun Ra, likened him to a coachman: 'He's got four horses and he's got the whip. He controls the speed of the horses – to an extent. He's not the leader but he has the capacity to change the rhythm up.' White critics, though, coming from a non-percussion-oriented background, found difficulty in relating to the drums. They taught listeners – and sometimes their ideas influenced other drummers* – to conveniently overlook that the drummer is the one component of any group of musicians capable of dictating the feeling of a piece of music regardless of the composer's, i.e. the soloist's intentions. It is for this reason that the importance of a drummer should be assessed in terms not only of what he does himself as a stylist or individual – i.e. playing to a set formula – but also, what he contributes to the band through his playing *with* the other musicians.

Andrew Cyrille feels that originally most critics tended to compare jazz to the type of European music with which they were familiar. 'And that's foolish to begin with because they're two languages. The drum, of course, is one of the first instruments outside of the voice. I think after people began talking, they probably started banging on tree-trunks, and as a result drums began to be formed. The drum as it is used in European music was mainly in a supporting role or in a role for accidentals, to mark places, whereas in African music or music of other peoples like, for example, the [American] Indians, the drum played a very important part in everything they did. It was absolutely necessary and drums were consecrated.'

---

*Connie Kay, an integral part of the Modern Jazz Quartet for nineteen years, actually dislikes drum solos. He told Whitney Balliett in *Ecstasy at the Onion*: 'Drums are a flat instrument, and besides Catlett is gone and there's only one Buddy Rich. I know how I feel when other drummers solo. It seems like you've heard it all before. There just aren't that many original people around.'

To Cyrille, the drummer shapes the music 'like the skeleton in a body'. Although the drums have not exactly dictated the direction of the music of each era as has been suggested, he feels that the drum is implicit in the work of all the innovators. 'By that I mean that their rhythm is very definite and even though [what they are doing] is melodic and harmonic, it's really playing rhythm. Even Louis Armstrong – what made him such a great innovator is the fact that his rhythm is so strong. So literally it may not be so, but figuratively it is the drum.'

Roger Blank realised this when he played with Pharoah Sanders on *Tauhid*, his first recording for Impulse. After two weeks of exacting rehearsal, he began to realise that Sanders's emotional style of playing in the high register of his saxophone sprang directly from the rhythms behind him. 'In each tune there is a particular rhythm that identifies itself to the melody. They get together and there's a marriage, they have children and they branch out. Now if there's no rhythm to bring it together, then the melody's just floating out there by itself.'

Elvin Jones, born Pontiac, Michigan, in 1927, was one of the drummers who extended the idea of time-keeping by playing a *supplementary* time over the *given* time. This had been suggested by other drummers before but culminated in Jones's work with the John Coltrane Quartet. Up until Jones's rise to prominence, the drummer tended towards keeping strict time with his right hand on the open cymbal, while the left hand played a variety of accents on the snare drum. The right foot provided further accents on the bass drum, and the sock-cymbal or hi-hat, which consists of two cymbals, one of them inverted, was operated by the left foot, usually to clash together on the second and fourth beats in the bar. (This is simplifying matters somewhat because every individual has a different approach to playing rhythm.)

The main function of the drummer has always been to act as a metronome behind the soloists, and to fill in wherever necessary or possible according to taste and capability, but Jones, although not the first drummer to keep time and also pick up at a split second on whatever the soloist was doing, took the process a step further than, say, Max Roach who, playing with trumpeter Clifford Brown, had been the supreme master of this until this time.

A regular beat on the cymbal had been mandatory prior to Jones's inception, but to him it was no longer necessary to state every beat in every bar and he would frequently drop the steady cymbal beat in favour of punctuations on the snare drum. With Jones, the drummer ceased to be an accompanist and became an equal participant in a conversation with the other instruments.

Elvin Jones worked with John Coltrane from 1960 to 1965, and during that time he played an equal part with the saxophonist in the creation of the sound, the music, that came to be known as the John Coltrane Quartet. The British drummer John Stevens has even suggested that Jones's contribution may have more bearing on the future of the music than Coltrane's because of the conversational relationship he developed with the soloist and the other instruments in the quartet. Jones did not take the percussionist's usual subservient role, neither did he play anything superfluous to the soloist's direction. The conversation and the sharing of responsibilities were precursors of the way drumming would be regarded in the future. And Jones himself has said that he was very conscious of deliberately changing the time around.

His successor, Rashied Ali, has pointed out: 'Now John Coltrane was, we know, the innovator of the horn, but he had to have a rhythm. Everybody has to have a different kind of rhythm to make that different kind of sound on the horn get over, so consequently, Elvin Jones had to play a very free type of drumming to play with the kind of music that Trane was playing. In other words, when Bird was playing, there had to be a Max Roach around to cope with that style, to make it move. If the rhythm ain't correct, then the group's not happening.'

Jones is a major innovator in the music, but unlike Sunny Murray or Milford Graves, later innovators who play completely free of the need to maintain any kind of time, his conditioning places him in an earlier era. 'The role of the drummer is primarily to keep time,' he says. 'Whether you think you are or not, always in one way or another, either consciously or subconsciously – or unconsciously – the drummer is keeping time, or implied time. Regardless of how abstract it may seem, if it's analysed to its fullest extent, it will be ultimately a very definite repetitious rhythm.'

Edward Blackwell and Billy Higgins are the two most important drummers to play with Ornette Coleman in terms of their contribution to the group's music, although Charles Moffett, a former classmate of Coleman's, worked with the saxophonist from 1961 to 1967, and Elvin Jones has also recorded with him. On Coleman's recording of 'Free' from the album *Change of the Century*, Higgins plays time, but as John Stevens has pointed out, at one point he can be heard 'taking the bottom off' the rhythm in such a way that his playing suggests freedom. Fourteen months later, Higgins and Blackwell both played on the epoch-making Coleman Double Quartet album, *Free Jazz*.

'Billy is a natural,' said Steve Lacy, the soprano saxophonist who once worked with Cecil Taylor. 'He can play on an ashtray, on top of a bar or on the floor, and it'll sound beautiful. He has besides a natural awareness of form, a real musicality, so that you can say of his work – unlike the playing of most drummers – that it's melodious.'

Blackwell constantly plays *rhythms*, as opposed to Higgins who is more concerned with cooking up a happy *swing* feeling. Blackwell uses every part of his drumkit with precision, even utilising the cymbals as additional drums as opposed to dealing with their conventional role. He is very direct, almost playing *on* the beat, and can be said to be a direct descendant of Max Roach, the man he cites as his major influence.

'Drums, even though they're not very melodic, can be very suggestive in that way. They can have some very warm emotions, they can suggest moods. You can tell stories with drums. Some people,

211

though, approach the drums like the average layman would, just as something to beat on, whereas the drums can be something just as melodic as any other instrument except that you don't have the facilities for having a melody come out like the other instruments. But when you use different volume control, different accents and other things – in other words, if you *sing* with the drums, then you really get it to happen. It comes out like you hear it, and that's what I try to do. And in Africa that's the way the drummers play. They have this same thing, especially in Nigeria where they have the talking drum. They really sing with their drum and it's phenomenal.'

Higgins and Blackwell, like Elvin Jones, are 'time' players, although both of them have worked with musicians who require a free, unrestricting background. Another influential drummer in the 'sixties was Tony Williams, who joined Miles Davis in 1963 at the age of seventeen. Williams was very fashionable, though not quite as innovatory as suggested. He took a number of figures and ideas created by his predecessors such as Roy Haynes and assembled them in a way that continues to be influential. For example, his trick of hitting a rimshot between beats came as a surprise and was very appealing. It has been used by countless drummers since. Williams belongs to the tradition of the drummer as showman. He was playing with the hippest band of the day, he was young and looked good and he knew it. Unlike Blackwell, Higgins and Jones, he did not attempt to hold a conversation with the soloist, rather, he played alongside him and complemented his line with an equally hip one of his own. When he left Davis, he formed a rock-oriented group, Lifetime, in company with organist Larry Young and two British musicians, bassist Jack Bruce and guitarist John McLaughlin, and could no longer be thought of as an influential force in the music.

Sunny's Time

During the time that Tony Williams was travelling the world with Miles and moving in and out of the Blue Note recording studios as a house-drummer, the two men who showed just how far the drummer could move from his traditional time-keeping role were being heard around New York. With Sunny Murray and Milford Graves, the drumkit ceased to be a collection of instruments, each with a specific function. Murray's aim was to free the soloist completely from the restrictions of time, and to do this he set up a continual hailstorm of percussion. His concept relied heavily on continuous ringing stick-work on the edge of the cymbals, an irregular staccato barrage on the snare, spasmodic bass drum punctuations, and constant, but not metronomic, use of the sock-cymbal (hi-hat). He played with his mouth open, emitting an incessant wailing which blended into the overall percussion backdrop of shifting pulses rather than specific rhythms. The listener had to imagine the beat in Murray's drumming, and in fact, if listened to in the conventional way, his playing often seems to bear very little relation to what the soloist is doing. What he did do, though, was to lay down a shimmering tapestry behind the soloist, enabling him to move wherever he wanted. With Albert Ayler, he developed a way of playing where he himself could hear everything that was going on. Later, though, he became more dominant in the music.

At first his drumkit was small, limited, possibly by economic considerations or the fact that it was usually borrowed, to snare drum, bass drum, hi-hat and a single cymbal. Later, in order to obtain a wide variety of sounds, he added tom-toms, gongs, Chinese rhythm-blocks and as many as three regular and four sock-cymbals. 'I like to assimilate more natural, human sounds. By giving yourself more to play at the drop of a hat, you can do this. It's important to have a lot of equipment around you so you don't have to look so far. Some people have a lot of stuff around them, but they don't have the energy to play. It's like you become like a nuclear warpile or something!'

In Murray's case, the comparison was fairly accurate. His relatively tempestuous life began in 1937 near the Indian Reservation at Idabel in South-eastern Oklahoma. His mother sang and danced and a sister sang with Red Prysock, but he was raised by an uncle who was to die after being refused treatment at an Oklahoma hospital because he was Black. His stepbrother John, who died prematurely of a heroin overdose, once played drums with Lionel Hampton and was responsible for his introduction to music. At the age of nine, Murray was playing drums. His teens, which included two years in a Pennsylvania reformatory, were spent in the roughest part of Philadelphia. He switched temporarily to the trumpet and trombone, but by the time he moved to New York City in 1956, he was back behind the drums. His musical education until then had been as sparse as his life had been ugly, but he was serious about music and spent two years studying percussion. He earned his living in such diversified occupations as building superintendent and car washer and eventually lost part of two fingers in an industrial accident. By the end of the 'fifties, though, he was playing with people like trumpeter Ted Curson and saxophonists Rocky Boyd and Jackie McLean.

He also worked with such older musicians as the trumpeter Henry 'Red' Allen and Willie 'The Lion' Smith, the pianist, before a chance encounter with Cecil Taylor altered his entire way of thinking about music. The year was 1959 and, he recalled, 'For six years all the other things were wiped from my mind.'

He told Robert Levin: 'Other drummers had played with him, of course, but they had played something conventional like "tanka-ting". But I decided not to play that way. I was playing on one. I thought it was very hip to play on one. Bass players would always say, "Oh, motherfucker, you keep turning the beat around." So a lot of cats didn't like me – though some cats did.'[1]

Murray went back to play with the beboppers after that night and they all started to laugh at him. They kept saying, "Hey, Sunny played with Cecil," and making a big joke out of it. And I was thinking who *is* Cecil? Who the devil *is* this cat I played with?' He started to search for the pianist who had made such an impact on him and obviously, though in a different way, on the other musicians. Eventually he ran him to earth and Taylor found him a loft in the building where he himself was living. It took Murray three weeks before he could summon up the courage to play in front of Taylor again. The pianist would lie in bed all day and watch him set up his drums. One day he got up and joined in, playing on his beat-up old upright. 'I want you to play something like you never played before,' he told Murray. 'What do you mean, like a drum solo?' Murray started to solo but Taylor told him, 'No, stop. Just let yourself play.'[2]

It was not until almost three years later that Murray realised Taylor was leading him into a new system of music. He is one of only three drummers to fit comfortably and work for any length of time with the pianist. The others are Dennis Charles, whom he replaced, and Andrew Cyrille, who succeeded him in 1964. Charles was a strict time-keeper up until joining Taylor, while Cyrille had a reputation for his command of the rudiments. ('Everyone in Brooklyn knew that,' said Milford Graves. 'Andrew had *hands*.') Murray had been a time-keeper, too, although his occasional 'freer' excursions had not endeared him to the more conventional members of the musicians community. His playing changed radically, he says, when he became aware of what Elvin Jones was doing. 'I realised I couldn't play this way any more, and for five years, none of the other drummers could stand me.' It was Taylor, though, who encouraged his unconventional style and worked on it with him. Murray created an entirely new concept of drumming, building impulses rather than identifiable rhythms, giving an entirely new meaning to the word 'swing'. 'Do he swing? Do anything?' asked LeRoi Jones about the feeling generated by another drumming innovator. 'The tap you hear is your own pulse, fellow human being.'[3] With Murray – 'a conductor of energies', Jones called him – his pulse became a shifting metronome, a metronome that kept a new kind of time.

To most other drummers, though, what he was doing was a complete rejection of everything the drummer stood for. It was not until he returned from a 1962 visit to Europe with Taylor that the first established players to fall under his influence started to be heard around New York City, J. C. Moses and Paul Motian among them.

Murray's 'time' playing can be heard on the three tracks by the Taylor Quintet that includes Jimmy Lyons, Archie Shepp and Henry Grimes on one side of *Into the Hot*, an album issued under Gil Evans's name in 1961 as a result of his insistence that the pianist's work become known. Murray actually went to Europe for the first time with Taylor and Lyons in 1962, and the resulting records made in Copenhagen at the Café Montmartre show a much freer approach to the question of rhythm. 'With Cecil, I had to originate a complete new direction on drums because he was playing different then; he wasn't playing so rhythmically.' Less than two years later, though, Murray's simple boppish drumming could still be heard on tracks such as 'Like a Blessed Baby Lamb', recorded by the New York Contemporary Five (Shepp, Ted Curson and bassist Ronnie Boykins, with guest trumpeter Don Cherry).

Murray himself actually considers that his rhythmical role with Taylor accelerated the increasing comprehensibility of the pianist's music, as it also did in the case of Albert Ayler. He and Ayler met and recorded together for Danish television in December 1962 as members of the Cecil Taylor Unit. On their return to America, they started to work together. The following year, they made their first recordings together. Two albums for the Danish Debut label were followed by the revolutionary trio date for ESP-Disk with Gary Peacock on bass. In all, Murray made nine recordings with Ayler, though one of the ESPs, *New York Eye and Ear Control* was a co-operative effort, and *Sonny's Time Now* was issued under his own name on LeRoi Jones's Jihad label. 'Holy Ghost', recorded live at the New York nightclub, the Village Gate, in 1965, appeared as a single track on the Impulse album entitled *The New Wave in Jazz*.

Murray is obsessed with the idea of strength and intensity in music. In 1966 he felt that the new music had reached a certain level of intensity and that he was the one drummer sufficiently equipped to break through this barrier. Because sound for its own sake is one of the distinguishing features of the new music, he considers that the drums as we know them are virtually obsolete. 'They only have a certain pitch, and that's all that can be played. They can't sustain, and with this music becoming more of a sustaining, ringing type of thing, it's even getting beyond rhythms.

'First of all, there is nothing more you can do – all the way down to breaking the bass drum or making the cymbals split. There is no more there, and that is actually reaching the point of unmusical music – it's below the cultural octave or something.' With this in mind, Murray has been trying to develop a different kind of drumset that uses electricity to sustain oscillating pitches. This, in effect, will be 'more in touch with the human voice in terms of humming and screaming and laughing and crying'.

In 1966, Murray recorded with his own group for ESP. Bassist Alan Silva, saxophonists Jack Graham and Byard Lancaster and Jacques Coursil, a trumpeter born in Paris to parents from Martinique, were the nucleus of the session and, with tenor saxophonist Frank Wright, of the groups the drummer assembled for the infrequent jobs he found during that period. Later he started to travel to Europe under his own steam, frequently joining forces there with Lancaster and Silva and occasionally with Wright. In 1968, he recorded for Columbia with an eleven-piece orchestra but the album was never released. According to one report, the official word from the company was that 'the music was so chaotic we couldn't release it'. (At the same time they did issue a recording by the white pianist Burton Greene, although, it was pointed out, 'that wasn't selling either'.) Included in the perpetration of the alleged chaos were the stalwarts Wright and Silva, along with Dewey Redman, the saxophonist who had worked frequently with Ornette Coleman, trombonist Clifford Thornton, who was later to play cornet on Murray's BYG recording, *Homage to Africa*, pianist Dave Burrell, Junie Booth on electric bass, and percussionist Art Lewis, who played everything from maracas and chimes to car-horn and washboard.

There was nothing new about using two drummers – Coltrane had done it some time before when he added Rashied Ali, to the Quartet, but when Murray made his decision, Art Lewis felt it was an honour to be chosen by such an important pioneer of the new music. 'He is very particular about the people he gets, especially in the percussion section,' he said. The two men started to work around New York, Lewis's essentially African devices highlighting Murray's floating, unchainable approach. As the new music becomes increasingly more percussion-oriented, Lewis visualises a new path for the drummer. 'If you notice, most drummers now play the cymbal basically. A lot of times you hear more cymbals than you do drums. I think that mostly the cymbals are going to be dropped to sort of like gongs and bells – that relationship. And I think the trap drummers are going to be playing on their drums what they played on their cymbals – in any music, in conventional music or the new music like you hear now.'

It sometimes seems when Murray plays that he is responding to the soloist (which is what the good drummer is supposed to do), but basically, he plays in such a way that either is free to go where they like. The overall effect, then, is the combination of their separate desires, but this can only be achieved by a drummer who is aware of the horn player's needs. His playing, and the freedom implicit in it, is not as simple as it appears. 'Even in freedom,' said Murray, 'there should be a certain amount of composition – if you're going out with the emphasis on being a professional musician. If you're just an amateur, you're trying to get yourself together, and so everything you do is understandable. But if you're working with major musicians, you're supposed to devote your time to existing as a sideman, albeit a constructive sideman.' The new direction for percussionists is one of controlled freedom, he maintained. '*Complete* freedom you could get from anyone who walks down the street. Give them twenty dollars and they'll probably do something pretty free!'

At one time, Murray felt that he was the judge where the young unknowns were concerned. To survive the obstacle course he built with his barrage of sound was one of New York's biggest challenges in the middle-sixties. He likened the position he held to Art Blakey's some years earlier. 'If you could get through with him, you could play with anyone. I have such a magnitude of strength about myself that I often destroy something that has set up on its own basis to be very way-out and creative. I've sent to Washington for musicians, given auditions, but I've seen them drop out because people usually expect the feeling of *drums*, and they aren't ready for what I do. I work for natural sounds rather than trying to sound like drums. Sometimes I try to sound like car motors or the continuous cracking of glass.

'Say a young artist is in town and he's played with about five young avant-garde drummers, and so he feels very substantial. But when it comes down to playing with me, he no longer hears himself because my knowledge of natural sound and music only tends to make me bring about twice as much as he creates within a second. So finally he is confronted with either complete physical exhaustion or exhaustion of creativity. When this is over, he realises that he is in a complete different state of being, confronted with not just the sound of drums but the sound of the crashing of cars and the upheaval of a volcano and the thunder of the skies. He never imagined himself being locked in a room with these kind of sounds being played off against him.'

Message to the Ancestors

Sunny Murray was away in Europe when Milford Graves arrived on the New York new music scene. Where Murray had established the drums in the frontline with a vengeance, by the time the line of succession reached Graves, the drummer was playing even less *for* the soloist and almost totally for himself. This is not to imply that he detracts from the music, for his contribution has been immense. He is equally impressive whether playing alone, in tandem with another percussionist or the pianist Don Pullen, with his own or Albert Ayler's group. The density of his work and its constantly changing directions on Ayler's Impulse album, *Love Cry*, for example, add immeasurably to the saxophonist's expansive concept.

Milford Graves was born in Jamaica, New York, in 1941. There was a drumkit in his house before he was born and by the age of three, he was playing on it. His earliest influences came from his uncle, who played North Carolina folk-music, and his maternal grandfather, who would sit down beside him and play the latest rhythm-and-blues tunes on his guitar. Like most Black musicians, he was exposed to plenty of rhythm-and-blues as a child, but he had a privileged introduction to the drums. Raleigh Sahumba, his boyhood friend, is a fine conga drummer who has played with Graves's various bands over the years, and it was his elder brother who first introduced the two boys to the congas. Graves was eight, Sahumba two years younger.

His interest in music and especially percussion, started there, and until the age of nineteen he studied African hand-drumming. He also devoted some time to the study of the Indian *tabla*, under Washantha Singh, a period he considers to have been highly significant in the development of his tonal concept. From 1959 to 1962, he led dance bands on Long Island and played all the big Latin gigs in New York. At one time he worked with Miriam Makeba, but he waited for the right moment before exposing his more creative side to the public. 'I was always aware, but I didn't like the conditions. I wanted to play with people who were involved in the music and didn't have too much of an economic thing in their minds.'

In 1963, two years after hearing Elvin Jones with John Coltrane for the first time, Graves ventured into the non-commercial music world. He was on the road in Boston when he met Giuseppi Logan,* who was studying there at the New England Conservatory. Logan, who comes from Norfolk, Virginia, and plays all the reed instruments, intrigued him and they started rehearsing together. Later, in New York, the bassist Don Moore invited Logan to a session that was being held at a loft owned by Mike Snow, a painter, sculptor and musician who played host to many of the musicians' activities in the 1960s. Graves decided to go along, too. The session turned out to be a rehearsal by a band known as the New York Art Quartet which comprised the drummer J. C. Moses, Moore on bass, trombonist Roswell Rudd, and John Tchicai, the alto saxophonist born in Denmark of Danish and Zaïrean parentage.

Moses, whose activities were sadly curtailed by the onset of a kidney dysfunction in 1970, was at the time one of the busiest freelance drummers in the city. While playing for pleasure with the NYAQ and Eric Dolphy, he earned his living on the road with Charles Lloyd and Rahsaan Roland Kirk. He and Moore had played together in Denmark with Archie Shepp, Tchicai and Don Cherry as the New York Contemporary Five, and Moses also worked in a group with Rudd and soprano saxophonist Steve Lacy. 'Milford was something of an up-and-becoming youngster,' he said. 'He had a funny little thing going on but Sunny Murray was my man. Sunny had so much *evolution* going on that if there was anybody to take anybody's place as far as the free music was concerned, it would have to be Sunny Murray.'

In the event, it was Graves who replaced Moses and Lewis

---

* Giuseppi Logan is no longer active in music but several musicians who rose to prominence in the late 'sixties have paid tribute to the depth of his influence. Don Pullen, the pianist who himself enjoyed a long association with Graves, was one of them. 'Giuseppi was like a teacher for me,' he told Giacomo Pellicciotti. 'My musical conception, my intellectual approach – all of that ripened through my association with him' ('Mingus Dynasty', *Jazz Magazine*, May–June 1975).

Worrell who took over from Don Moore, who has since married and left music. The NYAQ was responsible for the direction of a number of other musicians who heard their extensions of the ideas originally conceived by Ornette Coleman. 'Some people may say it's an ego thing right now,' said Graves, 'but I was the only drummer at that time playing in a certain free concept, using different rhythms in that way, and it kind of shook John and Roswell's thing up. They had their thing harmonically and melodically, and then the rhythm came in and changed the whole thing around.'

Tchicai confirmed this: 'This was a very pleasant surprise and more than that, because Graves simply baffled both Rudd and I in that we, at that time, hadn't heard anybody of the younger musicians in New York that had that same sense of rhythmic cohesion in polyrhythmics or the same sense of intensity or musicality.'[4] Groups were talking about playing loose, said Graves, but there were no drummers on hand to supply the looseness that they wanted. 'When we came together, we really clicked. John was hearing certain things and Roswell – he is really a perfect musician – was, too, but that rhythm thing laid down by a drummer was what they were looking for.'

Graves recorded two albums for ESP less than two months after appearing at the October Revolution in Jazz, one with the NYAQ and one with pianist Lowell Davidson and bassist Gary Peacock. During that event, which has become a landmark in the new music, he also played with Giuseppi Logan's group and pianist Paul Bley, and with these combinations notched up a couple more ESP appearances. Logan's was one of the label's first three releases and it immediately revealed a percussionist with an amazing technique. Graves moved around his drumset with astonishing speed, beating rapid two-handed tattoos on every surface. Each stroke was clearly defined so that there were no rolls in the conventional sense; the emphasis was on clarity. He used his cymbals in the way another drummer might use a gong or another drum. With the NYAQ, Graves's snare drum was tuned high as was the norm, but already his tom-toms were producing a deeper note than usual. By the end of the 'sixties, though, he had dispensed with the snare and his three tom-toms were tuned as loosely as is common in rock today. The resultant dampened sound contrasted strongly with the brighter, cutting precision customary to all the leading drummers until then. Now it is commonplace to see drums with a single head, but Graves was probably the first American drummer to remove all of his bottom heads because of their tendency to absorb sound. He later explained that he had removed all the additional encumbrances that might help destroy the 'bigger, richer' sound that was his preference.

Before he severed his ties with ESP in order to take control of his own production, Graves recorded five percussion tracks with another drummer, Sunny Morgan, who played regularly with the singer Leon Thomas until his tragic death in 1976. This remains just about the most brilliantly conceived and executed percussion album to date. Andrew Cyrille's *What About?* on BYG is a consummate performance, as is *Dialogue of the Drums* recorded by him and Graves for their own IPS label in 1974, but the ESP duets were certainly the most revolutionary at the time.

Graves approaches percussion from a broader than average perspective. His extensive study of both African and Indian drumming has obviously influenced him. He was one of the first Western musicians to play the *tabla* and the use of bells, gongs and shakers on the ESP album was, at the time, as much Indian-inspired as African. This recording took place, after all, at a time when the entire jazz and rock world was becoming immersed in a love affair with Indian music that began with John Coltrane's interest and use of certain Indian tonalities and lasted through the Beatles' fascination with Ravi Shankar until today. (For example, an Indian double-reed instrument, the *shenqi*, is often used by Clifford Thornton, Ornette Coleman and Dewey Redman play a version of it inaccurately referred to as the *musette*, but actually resembling a Tibetan oboe, and Miles Davis, circa 1974–75, employed the skills of an Indian *tabla* player, Badal Roy. It was, however, the multi-instrumentalist Yusef Lateef who was the first American to use Indian and other Eastern instruments. Ahmed Abdul-Malik, usually a bassist, performed on the Arabic *oud*, though unlike Lateef, whose name was adopted on accepting Islam, Abdul-Malik's father was from the Sudan.)

At the same time, Graves's use of Morgan in a subsidiary but contributing role heralded a whole new era of percussion. Coinciding with the growth of Black nationalism and the need felt by many players to express their African background by including supplementary percussion devices, hand-drums and so on, Graves's innovations were exemplary and well timed.

In 1966 he had bemoaned the fact that drummers had taken the drum too far from its African origins: 'There's an ethnic problem involved because of slavery and coming up through the New Orleans period. People completely lost their identity and so what drummers have been playing up to now has little to do with their African make-up. This has been a problem of all the musicians in America – they're playing with a Western vision.' Graves declared himself unable to understand how anyone of African heritage could reject the new music and predicted the time when it would be acceptable to the more traditional players. He was, of course, right. Later, any number of drum choirs were to spring up, among them the highly articulate M'Boom, an all-percussion co-operative started by Max Roach with Roy Brooks, Joe Chambers, Omar Clay, Richie 'Pablo' Landrum, Warren Smith and Freddie Waits.

With two albums recorded in concert at Yale University in 1966 and released later on their own SRP label, Graves and the pianist Don Pullen established yet another unbeatable combination. The duo's music was highly complex and the result of many hours spent playing together in private. 'There's a different rhythm of the self that a lot of people are not aware of, but when you condition and train yourself, it can come out at any time. Don Pullen and myself are like this, we motivate each other. But what we do calls for deep understanding of the instrument itself and years and years of just studying the possibilities of sound. The thing with jazz is that people just practise tunes! And in those tunes they know there's so many simple changes, but if you sit down and talk about *musician-ship* and just play *music*, all the scales you can conceive of, that's something different. People call this "way-out" music, but no – we're just not playing things that are that simplified.'

The essentially precise and exacting nature of his playing reflects Graves's own high personal standards. He lives his life at a rigorous ethical level that is comparatively rare in the music world. He has devoted a great deal of his time to intensive study of the possibilities of the drum as well as its history and the therapeutic value of music, and has played for the mentally retarded and held many lecture-demonstrations in schools and museums. At one time he worked with a youth programme in Brooklyn, later he turned his attention to laboratory work. 'I had the opportunity to make a lot of money in music but it would have been doing things that I didn't think I particularly wanted to do. I feel as though music has been controlled by people who have been using it as a kind of commercial, economic, tool, but I see something in music that goes beyond the ordinary things that people think about.' Above all, he is convinced that in order to play the music of the future, the drummer will have to study the instrument much more than he did in the past. 'When I say that, I mean that you can play on a drum-pad all day, you can put years in on drum-pads, but why put ninety-nine per cent on the drum-pad and only one per cent on the drumset? They're two different things. You have to determine between what you can play on the pavement and what you can play on the drums.'

Graves has been able to control the sound his drums produce. He believes that most drummers are over-occupied with the playing of rhythms and insufficiently with the actual sound. 'The drum itself is producing a lot of sound. It's a sound that they're not actually controlling, it's coming out by itself.' He considers it important for drummers to study the actual membrane, to try for different sounds or a different feeling by playing on every part of the skin and not merely the same area over and over again as drummers have usually done. In common with many of today's percussionists, he does not 'practise' as such; when he is alone, he *plays* with a constructive idea in mind until he reaches a point where he feels fulfilled. 'Sometimes I start playing and I'll take a look at the clock and maybe half-an-hour went by and I'll find I've energised my body to such a degree until I feel as though there's no need for me to continue. It's all according to your energy output. You reach a point where your body is so energised that physically you have to slow your metabolism down.'

The energy level of Graves's playing was almost captured for the first time on *Black Woman,* a record made under the leadership of the innovative guitarist Sonny Sharrock, but in the main it is only possible to give a mere indication of the impact of his live performance on record. As he has dispensed with the snare drum, the punctuations associated with Western drumming are played on one of two floor tom-toms. His bass drum, tied to his chair to stop it from moving, is in frequent use, and he habitually holds his sticks by the tip and uses them much as an African drummer would his beaters. Graves was using matched grip before it became fashionable, and he has another unique grip which enables him to hold two sticks and play on two surfaces virtually simultaneously. Sometimes he holds a huge mallet or maracas in the same hand as a regular drumstick, beating with this combination on the same surface or switching alternately from one beater to the other. He occasionally takes a small pair of tuned bongoes, places them in front of him on the skin of one tom-tom and hits them in that position. The result is a percussive maelstrom of multi-layered intensity.

Using a series of different grips brings about a psychological adjustment in the drummer's mind which automatically changes his overall approach to the music. 'A lot of drummers will play with the sticks always at one, two, or maybe three, heights from the skin. In other words their attack and the amount of pressure of actually hitting would vary but mostly the *actual* pressure on the skin would remain the same, the only difference being whether you let the stick rebound or let the stick hit the skin and you stop the vibrations. The Africans have their way of doing this, too, but the main thing is that they have a thorough understanding of the angle of attack.' (Interestingly, in 1974, a Ghanaian master drummer could be seen repeating the exact same lesson on a programme relayed over Ghana television.)

Most of Graves's playing these days is done in an educational context with a trio format. Hugh Glover, an associate of his since 1964, plays clarinet, bass-clarinet, alto saxophone, various flutes and percussion, and a succession of other reedmen including Arthur Doyle, Frank Lowe and Joe Rigby have filled a similar function in the group. From time to time he adds a conga drummer, Sahumba or Tony Wiles, and occasionally, trumpet or vibraharp.

The drummer rarely seeks out other musicians but there is no lack of applicants for a place at his side. To many young horn players, the open-ended format and vocalised style of playing he favours present the ideal opportunity for self-expression. He welcomes the fact that they have heard something attractive in his music, but then he finds himself analysing their motives. 'Is it a real honest feeling that they are digging on the music, or is it a feeling that they think they can exploit it to get *their* thing across?' Well qualified musicianship or obvious potential and the willingness to learn are the two alternative qualifications for admission to his hallowed circle, but in keeping with his declared standards, Graves is also concerned with the personality of those he allows to play with him. Some people could not care less about this as long as the music sounds right, but if a musician has certain hang-ups that are manifested in immature behaviour or that he can overcome only through heavy use of drugs or alcohol, Graves is sympathetic and tries to help. After a certain time, however, if the individual has shown no effort to adjust, he feels obliged to tell him that they can no longer play together.

Instead of spending several months in rehearsal to discover the player's potential, as he did formerly, Graves employs a kind of shock treatment now. 'I'll talk to a person maybe three times, or we'll get together twice, and I'll try to detect something then. And then the fourth time I'll give him what I call "on the job" training. I'll just put him right on the gig. I say, "Now get on the stage; I want to see you in front of the people and I want to see how you respond." And I'm constantly talking to players, in between sets and when the set is over. I'm constantly telling them, "You got to hold yourself down, don't try to project too hard."'

For newcomers to his group, Graves works out a certain amount of form and then guides them from the drums. Nothing is planned as to what will happen within that form, though. 'A lot of musicians today, they can't just begin it for themselves. The drums will be the starter with a lot of the things that we play, everybody is more or less getting their feeling from the drums.'

'Milford is talking about the saxophone being a drum itself,' said Frank Lowe, who benefited considerably from the time he spent with Hugh Glover as one half of a guttural, coarse-grained saxophone team. 'He says that it's all rhythm. We breathe in rhythm, we walk in rhythm and we get up in rhythm. All our things are rhythm whether we know it or not. Our time is based on the rhythm of the clock, and that concept became a little clearer to me with Milford.'

Multi-Directional Rhythms

In the spring of 1969, Graves and Andrew Cyrille played a musically rewarding concert together in Brooklyn. When it was decided to repeat the experience, Graves agreed immediately to Cyrille's suggestion that Rashied Ali be incorporated, too. This was unusual because, as he admitted, he is notoriously suspicious of the credentials of other percussionists. 'I do not like to play with a lot of drummers because it irritates me to play with someone who can't play *drums*. Every time I've seen Rashied, though, it was a different experience – the same thing with Andrew. In other words, it wasn't like an opposing force, like an ego thing or a challenge. With most drummers I meet, I get this kind of feeling that we're not coming together, that we're moving apart. It's competitive.'

The three men eventually got together for a series of concerts under the heading 'Dialogue of the Drums', but Ali himself, who had experienced his own personal upsets when he first began to work with Coltrane, confirmed that the ego problem is a common one amongst percussionists: 'It seems like drummers are actually natural leaders. With a good drummer there's no end to how far a band can excel. A band is only as good as its drummer – really. Saying that makes you think right away that "this drummer has ego", but I've heard it from so many people. The main idea of a group is the rhythm. If the front-line's not correct, then the rhythm can sometimes save the show. It can sweep up all the rough spots, smooth it right out and get it back in motion again, you dig?

'So now, as a consequence, every drummer that has gigs would have an *attitude* because he knows that he's keeping the band together. The drummers *know*, man, regardless of what's happening, and so they form these kind of attitudes like "tough guy" or "I'm the baddest motherfucker in the world", that kind of thing. They form that kind of attitude right away, and so when they get on the bandstand with another drummer, then it usually turns out to be a battle instead of any music being played. I mean, it's music being played, but they're fighting each other, more or less trying to cut each other up to see who *is* the baddest.'

Although Ali's vanity suffered when he had to share the stand with Coltrane's main man, Elvin Jones, the concept of using two drummers fostered initially through the 'fifties by Art Blakey, Max Roach, Charlie Persip, Art Taylor and Philly Joe Jones amongst others, was nothing new in his own experience. At home in

Philadelphia during the same period, he and his younger brother Muhammad played two drumsets in company with two bassists. Everything was done in strict time, trading fours and so on, but the idea was the elder Ali's. When he went to New York to stay in 1963, and worked with groups led by Bill Dixon and Paul Bley, he also put in some time with Sun Ra, whose music has always been highly percussion-oriented and who was using a second drummer at the time. The following year, he claims, Coltrane was influenced by listening to him and Sunny Murray playing together at the Dom on St Mark's Place with Albert Ayler. 'He really dug that sound, that beat. The whole drum thing turned him on to his new approach to music.'

Prior to this, Ali had been in and out of New York, playing and listening, sleeping rough in the summertime, and going back to Philadelphia when his money ran out. He heard the new direction the music was taking and struggled to find a way of playing that would fit. Each time he returned home, though, the local musicians would criticise him. 'They were still talking about playing what they had been playing. I was talking about, "Man, have you listened at Cecil Taylor?" and stuff like that.'

It was Coltrane who convinced him finally to leave Philadelphia. 'The last couple of years I was inactive because I had really stopped playing. I wasn't getting any more gigs and Trane said I had grown up, I had just outgrown Philly. I was starting to play free drums and I was just a leftist. The musicians, all the people, they just couldn't understand why I had changed to play the way I was playing.'

In 1965, Ali joined Coltrane's group and shortly after Elvin Jones left to join Duke Ellington. The saxophonist added another West Coast drummer, Ray Appleton, for about a year, and Frank Butler played a few engagements, but by the time the group went to Japan in 1966, Ali was the only drummer. Coltrane continued to add African percussion, congas and timbales from time to time, and Jack DeJohnette, J. C. Moses and Muhammad Ali also played with him for short spells, but it was the Philadelphian who was his final choice. Coltrane has stated that Ali's 'multi-directional rhythms' enabled him to play practically anything he wanted and remain secure in the knowledge that whatever the drummer was doing, they would be compatible. It was a compliment and a challenge that Ali continued to meet. The unique interplay that they established can be heard on *Interstellar Space*, a duo album issued after the saxophonist's death.

It is well known that when drummers are aware of factors outside the music, their arms and legs feel stiff and start aching. Ali is no exception to this but, he says, when he is really playing, he is aware of nothing other than the drum. 'I'm trying to get as many sounds as I can out of the instrument, and if I'm playing with somebody, then I just try to take them to heights that would really get the best out of them. Like I'm really *on their case.* Every time they make a move, I feel – if I could just do something to heighten it, make 'em really try different things and move in a different role! Like if a horn player's playing as high as he can play, I try to play something to make him play higher than that.

'I sure do know one thing, man, I sure be trying to get next to whoever I'm playing with. I'm trying to get right inside them, to just *think* with them with one mind. Sometimes I can get as close as playing what he plays before he plays it – I mean, not before, but when he comes out with it, I'm right on it and I might play it note for note. I try to leave so many things open by playing so open that the soloist can choose just about any direction he wants to take. Like, he can play very slow or if he wants to, play fast, or medium. I'm trying to play in a way that he can do all that. And sometimes we can get so close, man, until we can all sound like one person.'

Different Strokes for Different Folks

The question of fashion affects the world of percussion as much as any other field of endeavour. For this reason, the work of drummers who play more for effect than for the other musicians – Billy Cobham and Alphonze Mouzon, for example – is known to a considerably wider public than that of the other unique percussionists discussed in this chapter. Both men made the move from jazz to rock playing jazz polyrhythms over a rock pulse and bringing a new concern and technical quality to rock drumming. Amongst the other fine drummers playing today, Clifford Jarvis, Roger Blank, Joe Chambers, Andrew Cyrille, Art Lewis, James Black, Phillip Wilson, Beaver Harris, Norman Connors, Don Moye, Jerome Cooper, Thurman Barker, Alvin Fielder, Leonard Smith, Eric Gravatt, Lenny White, Steve McCall, Wilby Fletcher, Charles 'Bobo' Shaw Jr, Rashid Sinan, and the South African Louis Moholo, are all contributing something personal to the art of percussion.

Don Moye, who has played with the Art Ensemble of Chicago since 1970, has studied *tablas* and spent some time playing in conjunction with other drummers. To him, the ability to play specific rhythms is a matter of technique, but the actual feeling is dependent on the drummer rather than the drum. 'You could have a similar approach towards playing regular drums, towards conga drums – any style or type of drums – but it's the individual's approach that makes the difference. In order to master the *tabla* or any type of drums, I would have to spend a lot of time, but it's not that one type is any more difficult than any other.'

Billy Cobham, who has played with both Horace Silver and the Mahavishnu Orchestra, has a large enough audience to put his albums at the top of the charts. Unlike the archetypal rock drummer who uses limited dynamics despite the dazzling displays and the aura of 'cleverness' he projects, Cobham has concentrated on playing complicated patterns, but in doing so, he builds up such an unrelieved density of sound that he virtually negates the effectiveness of his polyrhythms. Nevertheless, singlehandedly he has brought the drummer into a prominence he has not enjoyed since the days when Gene Krupa held sway in the Benny Goodman

Orchestra. A British drummer suggested that his popularity was due to his exceptionally clean technique. In 1974, he was playing drums with shells made from recycled paper.

Alphonze Mouzon comes from Charleston, South Carolina, and has worked with McCoy Tyner, Weather Report and Larry Coryell's Eleventh House. He plays with his cymbals fixed at arm's length above his head and almost perpendicular to the ground. The visual effect is something like Krupa in the movie short *Shadow Rhapsody*. He reasons, that when the cymbals are kept away from the other drums, this prevents their vibrations being absorbed by the tom-toms. The flamboyant jump his arm must make in order to move from skin to cymbal looks pretty exhausting, and by 1974 his tom-tom set-up had grown to eight, necessitating a considerable amount of movement on his part. Aurally and visually, though, he is tight, and his flashy technique is attractive. Eventually, Mouzon's tom-toms encircled the stage.

In 1973 it was interesting to see two drummers, one of them Warren Benbow, working in tandem with Lynda and Sonny Sharrock's band. The influence of Sunny Murray was emphatic in their actual playing, yet both bowed to fashion by fixing their cymbals in the Mouzon style. In the end this fashion became ridiculous in some rock bands, drummers fixing their cymbals so high that they could barely be reached. What is more, by increasing the angle of suspension to the point where only the edge of the cymbal could be hit, any musical reason for such positioning was negated.

The Eternal Rhythm

The use of additional percussion as an assertion of Black identity effectively reverses the situation created when the slave owners exerted their control by banning the drum. Most bands today incorporate one or two hand drums, and the horn players themselves add frequently to the percussion picture with a variety of 'little instruments'. White musicians have adopted this percussion-centred concept, too, in rock as well as in jazz, so that it is rare to find any band today without at least a tambourine.*

The idea of participatory percussion has spread to the audience, too. When Osibisa, an 'Afro-rock' group composed of Africans and West Indians, returned from an American tour, they complained of the gratuitous tambourine-shaking and whistle-blowing at their concerts. People even take tambourines to discotheques. This may indeed be the electronic age in terms of the way the music is relayed, it is also the day of the drum.

Increasingly more and more African instruments have made their appearance in the music. Pharoah Sanders, for example, never records without using some African sound-device, usually the thumb-piano – *sansa*, *agidigbo*, *kalimba*, call it what you will. His 'Bailophone Dance' featured the *balafon*, or *bala*, to give its more ethnically correct name, the African xylophone. This instrument is amplified by resonating gourds suspended beneath its wooden slats. Holes in these gourds are sealed with mirlitons, generally the membrane from spiders' egg-cases, though they can be made of fish or snakeskin or bat's wing, and these vibrate sympathetically to give a distinctive sound. Graves, Murray and the bassist Malachi Favors are others who have recorded on the instrument.

The polyrhythmic effect of several drums played together can be very intense. Used properly, they build up compelling waves of sound behind the frontline action and actually lift it to another plane. Practically all musicians appreciate these effects now, but it

---

* Despite the superficial 'slickness' of Black vocal acts, the Copacabana did not swallow up all vestiges of African ritual. Take Labelle, for example, darlings of the New York gay set, who stand for bisexual ambiguity, 1950s nostalgia and 'camp'. They would appear to epitomise Western, i.e. white, taste and decadence, yet at their concerts, one singer shakes an African *cabassa* (gourd rattle) while another plays the tambourine. Their accompanying musicians set up a chant which the three women echo. To the cynics, such behaviour would seem to say more about fashion than any kind of Black consciousness, but to experience their act, it is hard to believe that Africa had ever been that far away.

was not always so. In the mid-sixties, the saxophone player Robin Kenyatta incorporated congas, bongoes and timbales with his group, the result of a year spent playing with the Latin band Pucho and the Latin Soul Brothers. 'At that time trap drummers didn't know how to approach it because they were so used to being free and playing by themselves,' he said. 'A lot of drummers hated to play with conga drums or timbales or whatever, but that establishes another groove right there, adds another thing to the music. Now most drummers accept it. They know how to play it, it's not a trap or a hindrance any more. They couldn't groove with it before, but it's just a matter of changing your swing. It still swings, but it's another kind of swing.'

* * *

When Milford Graves speaks of the saxophone as a drum, it could be said that his intentions are two-fold. First, he feels that the Black player is psychologically limited from the start by regarding the instrument as a European invention. As a result, his tendency is to consider its melodic possibilities – in the main – rather than exploring its actual *sound* and rhythm potential. Secondly, he is suggesting that any sound-machine played by a Black person automatically takes on a different meaning; in other words, whatever the actual origins of an instrument, in Black hands it becomes an African/American musical device.

The nationalist concept of Drum Culture can be applied when examining the historical past of the music as well as used to define contemporary specifics. It is not confined to a discussion of the actual instruments of percussion. Take, for example, one of the earliest techniques employed in playing the double-bass. This required the player to slap the fingerboard with the open palm of the right hand while the string to be played was grasped simultaneously. Alternatively, the string was pulled up away from the keyboard, its subsequent release causing it to hit the fingerboard and produce a forceful 'slap'. In New Orleans, 'slapping' was considered a 'hot' sound, equivalent to the highly vocalised tradition of 'growling' through the trumpet. It accentuated the *percussive* nature of the instrument, and Andrew Cyrille sees it as stemming from the essentially percussive plucking or strumming of the banjo – possibly the only imported African instrument to survive in America – and 'analogous in some ways to beating a vibrating membrane'.

Thus, slapping the double-bass could not only be likened to those sound-patterns allegedly nearest to the African roots of the music, it could be said to be a *reminiscence of the drum* itself. In practice, Sun Ra used Ronnie Boykins's bass as a drum when he built his music around its rhythmic pulse rather than its harmonic patterns. Also, in the absence of a 'drummer', Malachi Favors's bass played a major cohesive role in the Art Ensemble of Chicago's often deliberately arrhythmic explorations.

Then, whereas critics spoke of Earl Hines translating the trumpet style to the piano in the 1920s, it was the percussive possibilities of the instrument that became pronounced forty years later. To some ears Cecil Taylor's playing was grounded in Western concepts and techniques, but to others, his decidedly percussive attack was an extension of African tradition. Pianists in the 'seventies think of the keyboard as eighty-eight tuned drums.

The vibraphone itself, established in jazz by Lionel Hampton and Milt Jackson, has had a melodic function despite being, categorically, a percussion instrument like the xylophone. Later masters, Bobby Hutcherson and Walt Dickerson had favoured a harsher, more metallic tone than their predecessors, but the Philadelphian Khan Jamal, who had worked with Sunny Murray and Byard Lancaster, took percussion matters even further, often abandoning the instrument's 'prettier' characteristics to concentrate on the essentially rhythmic qualities of the instrument, itself descended via slavery and South America from the African *bala*.

The Chicago musicians, both in the AACM and Sun Ra's

Arkestra, were the first to clarify the possibilities of percussion for the non-drummer. There were plenty of accomplished drummers in the Association, yet the Art Ensemble, which had existed in one form or another since 1962, did not, in fact, have anyone regularly taking that role for eight years. Under Roscoe Mitchell's nominal leadership, the group's first drummer had been Alvin Fielder, followed by Leonard Smith, Phillip Wilson and, for one record, Robert Crowder, none of whom were members of the AACM. Wilson is one of the unsung heroes of the new music but his departure, a traumatic experience, apparently, for the others, coincided fortuitously with their growing feeling for group percussion. When no replacement could be found for him, Mitchell, and occasionally Jarman, took over whenever the regular drumset was required. The four principals' communal attitude is obvious from one of their French recordings, *People in Sorrow*, a contemporary symphony by Jarman, where almost an entire side is devoted to what is essentially a solemn examination of percussion sound-colours – *not* rhythms as such.

Joseph Jarman, though, was concerned with the political impact created by the ritualistic aspects of the Art Ensemble's performances, and naturally, the African drums he played took on a special significance in this context. There was, in a way, nothing new about a horn player banging on a cowbell or hitting a gong. Dizzy Gillespie had coaxed his sidemen into that role many years previously when he added the conga drummer Chano Pozo, a *lucumi* (Yoruba) cult drummer from Cuba, to his big band, and introduced the use of what became known as Afro-Cuban rhythms. Viewed from the essentially revolutionary perspective of the Art Ensemble, however, there were slightly different implications in their use of African percussion devices than when a Gillespie bandsman picked up a gourd and shook it. Jarman's face was painted and he was naked to the waist as he hit his carved African drums, after all. Gillespie had taken one deliberately radical step by turning to African rhythms for musical impetus, although to his sidemen the political implications of this were non-existent.* Jarman, however, had taken the situation further by making a revolutionary statement through his actual physical appearance.

There are any number of sociological conclusions to be drawn from the increased use of percussion in all areas of Afro-American music, as well as the change that has started to take place in the construction of the trap drum set itself. Andrew Cyrille surmises that the conventional drumset and its appendages evolved from 'the desire to play the reminiscent polyrhythms and tonalities of the African drum choirs', but that its shape and size was dictated by economic necessity. Although the point when the small tom-tom was actually attached to the bass drum has never been determined, Cyrille has also suggested the possibility of this occurring in the confined space occupied by the pit orchestras of the theatres in cities like New Orleans.

We have become so accustomed to the commercialised versions of those Black inventions which are available everywhere that the set of drums assembled from various sources is frequently regarded with disdain by the novice percussionist. When Sunny Murray recorded for Jihad, his cymbal set-up was self-designed – the ride cymbal hung from a wrought-iron structure while the hi-hat was anchored by a wire device between the two cymbals – and men like Ed Blackwell and Milford Graves have always taken great pride in constructing a set that is personal to them. Graves has also taught that the importance of the drum lies in the sound it produces rather than in its essentially Westernised appearance.

Just as Juma Sultan, leader of the Aboriginal Music Society, has studiously taken apart Western reed instruments in order to build them into something personal – something Afro-American, in

---

*This was confirmed by Charles Majeed Greenlee, a member of the 1949 Gillespie trombone section who has also worked with Archie Shepp. 'It was just a thing where you just did it, it didn't mean anything to us at that time. We only had maracas and claves, we were ignorant of all the African percussion devices and so on.'

fact – so many concerned percussionists are endeavouring to build drums that reflect their heritage a little more precisely than the mass-produced lines. To Art Lewis, Western drums are designed for their compactness, not for sound. Like Graves and Murray, he would like to alter these priorities. He has ideas for a new kind of drumset, but one of the first steps he envisages would be to change the actual beaters from sticks to mallets. By including every type of mallet from the very hardest to the softest, the widest possible variety of sounds could be achieved.

'Being a musician doesn't have much status here in America,' said Elvin Jones. 'I think you'd have more status if you're an auto-mobile mechanic or something like that. In Africa, though, the drum is part of and a very essential part of the culture, and so the people don't put it down. It's having some kind of status to be a drummer, not only in Africa but in other parts of the world.' The respect for the drummer is increasing in the West, though, as he himself stresses his importance as the spirit behind the music. 'You pick up the drum and you think of the Black man,' said Milford Graves, and so the evolving role of the percussionist clearly reflects the political changes taking place in the Black community. Whereas at one time the drum was forbidden, now it is dominant in every musical undertaking. The wheel has gone full circle.

Notes

1 Robert Levin, 'Sunny Murray: the Continuous Cracking of Glass', in Rivelli and Levin (eds), *The Black Giants,* New York and Cleveland, 1970.

2 ibid.

3 LeRoi Jones, 'Apple Cores No 6', *Down Beat* 1966; reprinted in *Black Music,* New York, 1968.

4 Notes to New York Art Quartet (Fontana 681 009 ZL).

10

A Family of Rhythms

Blackwell's music was the thing that led to the whole rock thing, to
the receptivity of rock where people could hear the *whole* feeling.
He just played like everybody is playing now, even though he
never played *obvious* music. Blackwell was always profound.

Alvin Batiste

'Blackwell is such an individualist. He don't allow anybody to tell
him anything about how the drums go because he *knows*.' Roger
Blank is one of Edward Blackwell's most devout admirers. He was
talking about the man who is identified as an integral part of the
Ornette Coleman Quartet and has been a hero and inspiration to
all the young drummers who find their way to New York.

Ray Charles's saxophonist Leroy Cooper confirmed his opinion.
He and Blackwell roomed together for a while when the drummer
played in a Charles small group. 'That was the time when Ray
Charles was telling all the drummers what to do. "Black" was
the only one he didn't tell. He'd say, "Lay out while I play a slow
one." Blackwell'd say, "Shit, man, I want to play my *drums!*" So he
played it his way and Ray loved it. He said, "Oooooh, *yes,* young
man! Go ahead and *play!*"'

'You look at the whole set of drums and you say to yourself,
what do they represent?' said Roger Blank. 'And actually they represent a family of rhythms, but very few drummers hook up to
that. Blackwell does and that's why I intuitively related to him.

240

He gets into these polyrhythms and that's what the drums are all about. Each drum represents a different tone and each drum establishes – or is supposed to establish – a different rhythm.'

Ed Blackwell could not by any stretch of the imagination be described as one of the world's most extrovert characters. You could be forgiven for passing him by in the street, too, dressed as he often is in a zippered windcheater, an old undershirt, and a flat woollen cap on his head. When he plays only his hands and feet seem to move. His eyes, if they are not closed, are hidden behind tinted glasses prevented from slipping down his nose by strips of adhesive tape wound around the earpieces. He keeps his head down and his lips drawn in; a picture of concentration. Coleman has only to breathe in a different way, it seems, for Blackwell to sense his change of direction.

Coleman himself said it when he wrote in the liner-notes for *This is Our Music*: 'Blackwell … has one of the most musical ears for playing rhythm of anyone I have heard. This man can play rhythm so close to the tempered notes that one seems to hear them take each other's place.'[1]

Blackwell's whole life is drums. When he's not actually sleeping he always seems to be playing music or preparing drum-exercises for his students or rebuilding some part of his drumset. And he is never without a pair of drumsticks – usually wrapped with adhesive tape for a better grip. I remember once sitting with him in an Indian restaurant in London's Queensway while the waiters looked on aghast as he carefully drew drum-patterns on the tablecloth with a felt-tipped pen. To Blackwell, the music always comes first.

'You take so much from yourself when you take time out and do something other than trying to perfect your art,' he once said. 'Like the Chinese say: if you neglect your art for one day it will neglect you for two days. I feel that says a lot. I've always thought about that whenever I'm sitting down not having any sticks in my hand: here's a time I could be sitting down limbering up my wrists and I'm just doing nothing. That's why I try to keep some sticks around me all the time. I never feel that you can ever practise too much. If I haven't played for quite a while and finally somebody hears me playing somewhere and says, "Oh, man, that sure is a gas!" I know myself that it's a drag, that it could have been much better if I hadn't been shucking.'

Blackwell's apartment, when he lived on New York's Lower East Side, was always full of musicians – often other drummers – who regard him as a kind of guru of the percussive arts. Roger Blank, who was once involved in collaborating on a book with him, said: 'Blackwell helped me so much in understanding what the cymbal beat was about, what that really means and how to articulate each individual drum; how important it is to tune your drums and relate to them individually and as a unit. You've got co-ordinated independence which demonstrates how important it is to get into a collective individuality, and that's what the four limbs are about. Blackwell is one of the very few drummers to do this.'

Blank described a concert where Alice Coltrane played with fifteen violins and saxophonists Pharoah Sanders and Archie Shepp. 'They were too loud and they weren't even rehearsed. They sounded terrible. Blackwell got up there and played with Alice and he played so softly you could hear the violins playing with her! That's a *drummer* – that can get his thing off *and* play soft and subtle.'

Blackwell – everyone, even his wife, calls him that – grew up in New Orleans. He met Ornette Coleman there in 1949, and four years later when their paths crossed again in Los Angeles, they started to play together. Blackwell always plays specific, clearly defined rhythms in a constant conversation with Coleman. It is a productive way of playing, but when they first met, he felt 'humbled' in the saxophonist's company.

'He was really showing me a new way for the drums to be played, the way I hadn't heard because I was one of the devotees of Max [Roach]. When I'd get together with Ornette, he showed me a different thing about the drums, about the sound and how they could be made to speak so you could play with more freedom.

242

Until I went to Africa, I didn't really get aware of what he was really talking about, but in Africa I got a really good picture – I mean a visual picture – of what he meant by freedom of the drums and how they should be played.

'We would get together and he would say, "OK – well, here, man, I want you to take these sticks and we'll see, we'll just swing." Well, when somebody tells you that, right away you get a mental block. You want to know what he means by "swing"! For a while I would get hung-up and he would say, "Well, just play, you know – whatever your idea about the swinging." So I would just start playing and then I would begin to realise what he was talking about because when he said "swing" he didn't really mean the old-type "swing", he used "swing" more or less as a term for playing free, for playing my own self.'

New Orleans's Booker T. Washington High School has produced several outstanding drummers, Earl Palmer, June Gardner and Blackwell among them. The eldest of Blackwell's brothers played piano. A sister sang and both of them tap-danced. The sister encouraged his interest in drums, and his family's positive reaction to a musical career contrasted with the experience of other musicians. As he himself notes: 'They think that maybe he should get something a little more concrete, more substantial, like working in the Post Office or driving a garbage truck! But I never was drug by that kind of thing.'

Alvin Fielder, studying pharmacy at Xavier University in New Orleans, wanted to continue with his percussion studies, too. He sought out Blackwell at the suggestion of Earl Palmer. He walked in on a session at Blackwell's house and discovered him sitting behind a huge bass drum flamboyantly painted in two shades of blue and silver. The set was old but as is Blackwell's custom, it was expertly tuned. He played a big ride cymbal, thicker than anything Fielder had ever seen. 'Most of the cymbals I had heard and played had a "splashy" type of effect. Blackwell was very clear. His cymbal actually sounded like a bell.'

The musicians were playing music from the repertoire of Parker, Davis and Roach, and Fielder 'sat there in awe, like in utter amazement. It was like this cat's playing all of the things that Max Roach is playing.' When the music finished, the young man asked Blackwell whether he could accept him as a student. 'I have all the time in the world,' was his characteristically humble reply, although it also denoted that in spite of his enormous talent, Blackwell could find little work.

In particular, Fielder was transfixed by Blackwell's technique. 'Being from Mississippi, this automatically made me what might be known as a disadvantaged student of the drums. You didn't have nobody in Mississippi cross-sticking – it was just all back-beat and shuffle drummers. Blackwell just influenced me so much and it made me really practise.' It was a result of studying with Blackwell and at his suggestion that Fielder started to transcribe the solos of Max Roach. He subsequently dealt with the work of Art Blakey, Kenny Clarke, Philly Joe Jones, Art Taylor and Roy Haynes. Fourteen years later, he completed a book about their drumming techniques, but it remains unpublished for reasons of his own. Should he decide to publish it, though, Al Fielder would dedicate it to Blackwell and arrange for him to receive all the royalties. Blackwell inspires that kind of response from the people who know him.

Ironically, in spite of his exceptional skill, he has seldom worked consistently. Even at the time Fielder met him, 'Everybody talked about him and said he was such a beautiful drummer, a fabulous drummer, but very few people used him. Blackwell would probably have stolen the show in most people's bands. He would have been a star player even though he wouldn't really try to be. His mannerisms and, of course, his coolness in playing, the way he was playing, was really *out there*.'

In 1951 Blackwell moved to Los Angeles, where he met Ornette Coleman. For three years they worked out daily, sharing a house until the saxophonist married, and apparently much of the groundwork for Coleman's first recordings was laid in those drab and penniless days.

Blackwell decided to return to New Orleans shortly before Coleman's long association with Don Cherry began, but his fortunes were to be inextricably linked with Coleman's. He was attracted by both the man and his music, 'because they were so close. I know that after we lived together for a while, I found that his personality is really such a peaceful thing. It rubbed off on me a lot because I was very wild in California! He was a big influence in channelling my way of playing to the way it is now. He knows that I can play more or less what he wants to hear on drums.'

Back in his hometown, Blackwell continued to play bebop with various small groups, among them the American Jazz Quintet which featured saxophonist Harold Battiste, clarinettist Alvin Batiste and pianist Ellis Marsalis. In the summer of 1957 he joined the Ray Charles band for a six-week tour and stayed till the end of the year. Texas-born Leroy Cooper credited Blackwell with establishing a new concept of 'funk' drumming during this period: 'He would do this thing where he'd play one thing for Ray and he'd play for the fellows, too. That was what started the whole thing off, the *tight* thing that they're doing these days. Blackwell started that.'

When Blackwell failed to return after a vacation, Charles called him constantly. 'Ray really liked the way I played but I didn't want to go back on the road, I wanted to play bebop. Any time anybody wanted to hear some modern jazz they would have to come to where we were playing.' One such group was Roy Montrell's, which also featured the late Nat Perrilliatt on tenor saxophone and Curtis Mitchell on bass. 'I used to listen to Blackwell a lot,' said James Black, who was later to take his place in this group. 'He's the cat that gave me the incentive to go on and practise.'

Earl Palmer was considered to be the King of the New Orleans drummers, but after he left for the West Coast, Charles 'Hungry' Williams presented the biggest challenge to Blackwell's supremacy despite the fact that the two worked in basically different fields.

Williams was the most 'in-demand' session drummer while Mac Rebennack (Dr John) remembers Blackwell as being 'too hip, too jazzy'[2] for what was needed in the studios. As a result it was Williams who subsequently played on all the sides made by Huey 'Piano' Smith, although Blackwell was working with the noted rhythm-and-blues pianist in the bars.* Around 1958, he participated in several rhythm-and-blues sessions and went into the studios with trumpeter Wallace Davenport and singer Blanche Thomas. He also recorded with Ellis Marsalis and the latter's mentor, Edward Frank. The same year Blackwell married his wife, Frances.

'Because of the fact that when I started playing I was playing rhythm-and-blues and you never get away from that r & b thing, I find it helps a lot,' he said in reference to his ability to think freely regardless of the idiom. 'A lot of musicians I hear that have never really listened at rhythm-and-blues, they've never really listened at any of the greats like Charlie Parker, either. You'd be surprised at the musicians now that's supposed to be stars that are not aware of Charlie Parker, man. I mean they've heard the name "Charlie Parker", but they really don't know who Charlie Parker is. And that takes a lot out of their music because they're losing quite a bit by not digging rhythm-and-blues because the blues is where it's at. Ornette, for example, has a tune that's called "When Will the Blues Leave?"'

James Rivers, a saxophonist who went on the road for the first time at the age of sixteen, claimed the other musicians accorded him respect when they discovered he was from New Orleans, but in the city, which is full of musicians, it often seems to be as common an occupation there as, say, motor mechanic. But for the musician who travels, there is a certain added respect from

---

* Despite what Rebennack said in a *Down Beat* interview, Blackwell did not try out for his band in New Orleans. As the drummer points out, the two American Federation of Musicians locals were still segregated in New Orleans at this time.

the birthright. 'They feel you're somebody, I guess,' said Blackwell. 'But myself, I had quite a number of what you might call "fans" in New Orleans.' In the late 'fifties, the audience was divided between those who wanted to hear Dixieland, for which the city is famous, and those who wanted to hear bebop, the new music of the day. The American Jazz Quintet were exponents of the latter. They worked regularly each weekend and had a large following – 'which was pretty hip because we were the only group that was playing the so-called "bebop". Until I had to leave New Orleans, I never had to think about playing anything other than what I wanted to play in order to survive – which was very hip.'

In 1959, Coleman had sent for Blackwell for his first recording session for the Contemporary label, but the drummer returned the ticket. 'I wasn't ready then, so he used Billy [Higgins] and then took him to New York.' The following year, the saxophonist recommended Blackwell to John Coltrane, who was then in the process of forming a new group. The drummer decided that the time was right for a move northwards, but in the meantime, Higgins had run into cabaret card difficulties in New York, and Blackwell arrived just in time to take his place with Coleman at the Five Spot. (This was in the days when a police record led to the denial of the permit necessary to work in a New York nightclub, a practice now, thankfully, abolished.)

The Quartet – Don Cherry, trumpet, and Charlie Haden, bass, were the other members – spent three months at the Five Spot, and the mixed reaction to their music is history. 'Whenever Ornette and I played together, people seemed to be able to hear what I was doing more than they did what Ornette was into. But I can't understand how they would differentiate so much as to prefer what I'm doing when I'm playing what *he's* playing!' Blackwell's words echoed Billy Higgins's comments on the same situation: 'People would say, "Man, I dig *you*, but I don't know what the hell *he's* doing." And Ornette would be playing his heart out.'

After the Five Spot engagement, the Coleman group went on

the road. On his return to New York, the drummer worked with Don Cherry and John Coltrane, making one record with them, *The Avant Garde*, in 1960. The following year he worked for a while with pianist Mal Waldron and bassist Richard Davis in the combo co-led by trumpeter Booker Little and Eric Dolphy. 'He reminded me a lot of Ornette in the way his music would go,' said Blackwell of Dolphy. 'Booker was the same way. He had the same personality that Ornette has; very humble and everything.'

Two barren years followed, with little or no work apart from the occasional coffeehouse or loft gig with Don Cherry, and a few record dates. In 1965, Blackwell started to work with pianist Randy Weston, who took him to Africa on a State Department tour the following year.

Although Charles Moffett replaced him in the Coleman group in 1961, Blackwell had always been the saxophonist's first choice and the drummer most indelibly associated with him. Billy Higgins replaced Moffett in 1967 when Blackwell was in Morocco with Randy Weston, but as soon as he returned, the job was his again.

The following year, the drummer again spent several months in Morocco with Weston and bassist Vishnu Wood, eventually taking his wife and three children with him, but after a while, Blackwell reported that he was tired of playing the same material. Weston, although a fine pianist and composer, stuck to a limited repertoire which could not compare with the constant diversity of Coleman's music. 'I never get tired of Ornette, that's the beautiful thing about playing with him. There's never a boring moment, man, every time we play. Even playing the same tunes, we never do it the same way. Usually when you're bored, it makes it like working. It shouldn't be work, it should be a pleasure. Playing with Ornette, that's what it is – a pleasure.'

Eventually, however, Weston could not secure sufficient work to keep the trio going so Wood and the Blackwells returned to New York. The drummer immediately rejoined Coleman and worked steadily with him until shortly before the failure of both his kidneys severely curtailed his playing career in 1973. His tragedy came at an ironic time. After years of scuffling he was working with a leader who was now able to command a sizeable sum of money for his concerts, and he had also been teaching for over two years at Wesleyan University in Middletown, Connecticut. The job came about through the good auspices of trumpeter/trombonist Clifford Thornton, who was Assistant Professor in African and African-American Music studies, and who has been responsible for arranging for several noted musicians to lecture there.

It was inevitable that Blackwell should take an active and remunerative role in the Black Studies programme because he has always been revered by those drummers who know the difference between technical brilliance and the need or desire for holding a conversation with the other musicians. Possibly if Coleman had worked as frequently as John Coltrane during the 1960s or if Blackwell had been less retiring, he would have been as well known as Elvin Jones. As it is, Alphonze Mouzon and Billy Cobham are the only drummers since Jones to capture the attention of the general public. Cobham, frighteningly competent but with little of Blackwell's love and understanding of the instrument, topped the jazz charts for several weeks in 1974 with his album *Spectrum*, recorded for a major label. At the same time, saxophonist Clifford Jordan was working hard to raise funds for the ailing drummer, with plans to issue an album he recorded several years ago on his own label and under Blackwell's name.

Initially the idea of catching a train to Connecticut every week and actually spending two days in the classroom was alien to Blackwell's day-to-day street existence. What's more, he had never considered the prospect of teaching. 'Maybe it's just a matter of being too humble or something, but I just never figured I was playing enough to teach anybody how to play. I figured that *I* should learn to play more first.' Nevertheless, soon the tattered notebook in which he was always laboriously drawing out exercises was replaced by a more academic-looking one, inscribed 'Only to be opened by drummers and important people', and proudly carried everywhere by him. In 1973 he was awarded a grant to write his own drum tutor, but the money had to be spent on medical expenses.

Roger Blank, Dennis Charles and Billy Higgins are three of the people who have continuously paid tribute to Blackwell's teaching, although Higgins's learning he said was acquired indirectly, through Coleman: 'Even later on, I heard a different style of playing rhythm and things that he got from Blackwell.' Art Lewis, who calls him 'one of the persons I admire most as a drummer', studied his exercises for strengthening the hands. Blackwell himself regarded these friendships as between peers. 'If they thought about it differently, maybe they didn't realise how much I was getting from them.'

Dennis Charles, heavily dependent on heroin in the early 'sixties and only moving when the rare call came from Cecil Taylor or Steve Lacy, has something to say that is highly revealing about the depth of Blackwell's dedication to his art. 'The first person who got me really into the music was Blackwell – and Billy Higgins, too. We were really tight at the time. They used to come around, even in Harlem where I'd be lying around, but after a while I noticed that whatever they were doing, it didn't interfere with their playing, with their music. That taught me a lesson from digging them, that they were still devoting a certain amount of time a day to their instrument. I wasn't. See, I would just flop out and not do it. And after a while they would start taking me out. Blackwell would say, "Get up, man, let's go," and take me to a record date, just to interest me in it.'

In contrast to the exchange of ideas that prevailed in New Orleans, Charles and Roger Blank are the only other drummers Blackwell has ever practised with regularly in New York. According to him, the majority tend to be in a 'star' bag and so it is hard to arouse their interest: 'Which is a drag because, you know, two heads are always better than one. You get a lot more accomplished that way, but some person thinks that maybe if he gets together with another drummer, maybe he'd steal his ideas or his technique or something. But I've never been of the opinion that I was that shallow whereby a cat could steal anything that I knew! I always figured that I had the talent or the ability to think of things – something new every day, in other words – and so I never had that feeling. But I've heard that some of the cats are very serious about that.'

An important influence on Blackwell's playing and on his life was the first of his three visits to Africa with Randy Weston. Unlike the other two which confined him to Morocco, the 1966 tour with a sextet took him to several countries, most of them in Black Africa as opposed to the Moslem North. In a country like Ghana where drums of different sizes are known as the 'mother', 'father', 'son' and 'daughter' in relation to their size and timbre, Blackwell found confirmation of his concept of the drumset as a 'family of rhythms'. The drummers he heard in Nigeria, Senegal, Gabon and so on fitted in with his love for musical freedom and his egalitarian notions about the functions of both the musician and the instrument itself:

'Usually they have a main drummer that has a whistle and he would blow the whistle as a signal for them to change the rhythm. They would be playing with these very strict rhythms but there would be so much freedom because each one would be doing a very simple rhythm yet the whole thing would be complex in its simplicity. And it was very hip. Like some cats would be playing maybe just a bunch of eighth-notes and somebody else would be playing maybe sixteenths, and another might be playing quarter-note triplets. In other words, not exactly those type of rhythms but that same, almost that same draw, really. And when you heard that overall thing, man, it'd make you tap your foot.'

At Wesleyan, Blackwell was planning to introduce pure African ideas into the course after he had instilled in the students the idea of the freedom that can be reached in drumming. 'To be able to play the things that I heard in Africa, the drummer has to really hear the drums as a singing instrument.' And Blackwell's own ability to make the drums sing is summed up by two duo albums made with Don Cherry for the French BYG label in Paris in October 1969. Entitled *Mu – First Part and Mu – Second Part*, they show just what the drums can do under the guidance of a sensitive artist.

Blackwell's unique sensitivity makes him, like Billy Higgins, the ideal drummer for any kind of group, yet because of his close association with Coleman, a lot of musicians seem to have felt he might impose restrictions on them. This hampered him financially during the period when Coleman increased his price yet worked very little. Apart from two weeks with Thelonious Monk, he received no calls at all for several months in 1972. 'Believe it or not, other musicians always approach me with a fixed thing in their minds whereby they feel that what I'm doing is not going to agree with what they're doing. And right away there's a clash. I guess they have the feeling, "He's got this way of playing with Ornette and I'm not going to play that way so it's going to be a clash," but really it's not a clash at all because there's no certain way to play. I've never had no certain way to play the drums, regardless of who I'm playing with.'

In spite of his genius, Blackwell has not been one of the lucky ones. Life for him has always been a struggle with poverty. While in no way excusing the negative state of affairs that prevails in the city where he made his home for so long, it is as a result of his impoverished condition, ironically, that he has been able to hone his skills. Roger Blank summed it up: 'A drummer can get sidetracked in this New York kind of thing, the style of life. The cats get away from something that requires a lot of time and a lot of effort to develop. If the job don't demand no more than you're putting into it and you're getting good money, you don't really try to get into it. Now someone like Blackwell, he don't work that much and so he got a lot of time to himself. And so he be thinking about his music, he'll be working on his stuff.'

And Blackwell, whatever his circumstances, is always working on some new idea. His notebook is added to daily, he carries a pair of rubber-tipped mallets in his pocket wherever he goes. The first time I interviewed him, he drummed on his thigh with those mallets for the length of our meeting. In September 1974, he moved with his family into one of the houses reserved for faculty members at Wesleyan. He continued teaching there and at the Creative Music Foundation in Woodstock, N.Y., although frequent spells on the dialysis machine made much active playing difficult. He has, however, recorded on several occasions and worked with Don Cherry and Karl Berger. In 1976 he travelled to Berlin with Berger to play a concert there. For a while he considered the possibility of a transplant; then changed his mind. 'Blackwell lives to play and he must play to live,' his wife has said. At the end of 1976, he returned briefly to New Orleans. He took his family with him and received a mayoral citation as an outstanding son of the city. He played with Ellis Marsalis and Alvin Batiste and was set for a return engagement at the New Orleans Heritage Festival. Ironically, the pressure that had forced him to leave the city sixteen years earlier seemed small compared to his personal tragedy.

Notes

1   *This is Our Music* by the Ornette Coleman Quartet (London LTZ-K 15228).
2   Quoted in John Broven, *Walking to New Orleans,* Bexhill-on-Sea, 1974.

PART FOUR

WOMAN'S ROLE

11

It Takes Two People to Confirm the Truth

As far as Black women are concerned, I think we're all waiting for some kind of exposition detailing the role and function of women in the music. And not only as musicians but as grandmothers, mothers, sisters, wives, managers, pillars of strength and encouragement – whatever! Women have been important to the preservation and furtherance of this culture. We know there have been many.[1]

Clifford Thornton

It was a cold spring morning when a determined young Black woman closed the door for the last time to the rugged basement apartment where she lived with her musician husband. With her four children and a handful of belongings, she made her way through the grimy streets of Manhattan's Lower East Side to the airport on the first leg of the journey to East Africa. 'Look,' Barbra said, explaining her move, 'I've been in New York for all these years and never got any further than East 4th Street. I have to be the strong one to reorganise my life because I feel I just can't stand to open the door one more time onto that street.'

Given those streets between Avenues A and D, violent and dangerous, littered with broken bottles and garbage, her decision was understandable. Had a Black woman made such a pronouncement a decade earlier, it would have been predictable. The traditional attitudes were explained by another woman, white herself but married for years to one of the great Black bass players: 'The Sister until very, very recently was unconcerned, unappreciative and deaf to jazz. She knew that a Black jazz musician would never make a dollar or get ahead or give her any concern or consideration as she always demanded of a Black husband. She is a matriarch, but her values are the Establishment values in this country: the fine home, the big car, the front.'

But this was in the 1970s, after Malcolm X, after Stokely Carmichael had informed women that their position in the movement should be 'prone', and after the Black woman's consciousness had been stirred to realise the importance – for the man's self-esteem – of rejecting the privileged role she is alleged to have enjoyed in white society by virtue of her sex. Although the evidence that she is equally exploited and frequently more so than the Black man has been clearly expounded,[2] the pressures on Black women to support the man, whether or not he is able to provide, are very strong. 'She has to step down off her pedestal and say, "He's a man, he's my man," even if sometimes he is not treated like one,'[3] said Fontella Bass. Eldridge Cleaver, discussing the status of women, referred to their 'pussy power'; later, the Black Panther Party modified that position slightly and disassociated themselves from such chauvinism, speaking of women as 'our other half'. 'We say that a Black woman must first be able to inspire her man, then she must be able to teach our children, and contribute to the social development of the [Black] nation,'[4] Imamu Baraka has written. Whatever the case, for Barbra to desert her struggling husband was not – politically, at least – the done thing.

Shirley Brown (not her real name) is a painter, but she has frequently taken an office job to support her husband, Raymond, when he could find no work as a drummer. Her view: 'I'm not saying that a lot of chicks out there in the Women's Liberation Movement are wrong, but I have to think of myself as a Black woman with a Black man who doesn't even have a job as good as they do. I mean I'd be a contradiction to myself standing out there saying "I want to be President of General Motors" when my man can't even get a job as a grease-monkey.'

Because of the peculiar nature of the music business and the need for the aspiring instrumentalist to be perpetually on call, Carmen Lowe, herself an artist, found it easier to be the partner subsidising their creative work with a day-job. 'If there's going to be a gig, Frank can't tell them, "Well, I get off at one o'clock in the afternoon, can we rehearse then?" Nine times out often, the things that he does do are spontaneous. He always has to be out there. Therefore, if you don't have anyone in your corner or some means of support, it's very difficult.' She stressed that the decision to do office-work was hers alone. 'It wasn't something that we sat down and discussed like, "Carmen, now you go to work and Frank'll play the music." No, this is how *I* feel. I'm sure that if he wanted to get a job as a dish-washer or a clerk he would, but it's the principle of the thing that means more to him – his music. Why should he have to be a dish-washer when he has qualifications and experience and ability to be a musician? I don't see why he should have to suffer.'

There is the suggestion that with the introduction of the extensive welfare programme in the United States, a number of musicians have been able to exist without a partner's help, but since jazz ceased to be the popular music of the day, the male musician without an established name has generally relied on his wife or 'old lady' for economic support. 'When you don't have to worry about money, it makes it much easier for you to get up in the morning and actually think *music*,' said Earl Cross in relation to a woman's support. 'I could pick up my instrument right now and blow a whole bunch of notes without thinking about it, but if I was to (be free to) think about it, I could *produce* something every trip.' Milford Graves is one of the exceptions – when he was running a medical laboratory he did so because he is interested equally in medicine and music – but there are those among the famous who would find themselves heavily in debt without their working wives. 'Most of the older musicians had a hard-working wife in the background that stuck with them,' said one such woman. 'It seems to me like most of them had white women because the Sister's just not going to put up with a man who's not going to bring home any money. A young man today, quite young in the music, told me that you could train a white woman the way you wanted her but you couldn't control a Sister. Today, though, the younger men seem to be into the thing where you should have a Black woman for political reasons.'

Indeed, with the onset of Black nationalism, several artists who had white wives left them and their children and set up home with a Black woman. The fact that one man, especially noted for his radical politics, seldom takes his wife anywhere drew this comment from the wife of one of his close associates: 'I don't know if he'd rather not have it well publicised that she's white. Maybe he feels she'll cramp his style.' At the same time, there was another man who left his Black wife and children at home in Chicago and moved to New York to live with a white woman who was better equipped to help support him until his music got off the ground. It was the realisation of the inequity of the situation in which he found himself, where the woman was the main breadwinner, that contributed to his eventual concern being more with the pursuit of money than fame.

But political considerations aside, the musician who puts his wife and family before the music has always tended to be rejected by the subculture. The group itself frequently takes the place of the conventional family, especially when there is little work to be had and the musicians come together often to play and develop a corporate philosophy. 'You establish the love and everything of a family, and then you can go inside and go to the depths of your inner self,' said Sirone, who experienced this playing almost daily with the Revolutionary Ensemble. In the case of one father who chose to stay home while his wife went to work, he found that taking care of the baby left him unable to attend rehearsals with the frequency demanded by the other members of the group with whom he played. 'I didn't really fit the form, the mould, that a member of that group should fit, or go along with their philosophy.

I did a lot of things that weren't good for the group, things like working in the daytime, having a family and taking certain gigs. They wanted to rehearse at the same time every day but actually they would have had to fit into *my* schedule. They didn't have to work because their ladies were taking care of them. All they had to do was music. Our love for the music should have cooled it out, but the personal thing is put on such a high level and I didn't think it was so important.'

The obvious suggestion is that this particular man was not up to the standard of his compadres, for everything points to the fact that had he been a real heavyweight, his personal life would not have been allowed to intrude and disturb the group's solidarity. After a replacement had been found for him, one of his erstwhile colleagues, commented: 'You see, being an artist, playing music, is a hell of a life. The sacrifices you have to make, like families and all that. It's not that you don't desire to have a family, but if it's about music, it's going to be music first and everything else will come from that. It's the understanding that a man has to have with his woman – you get crossed up between the love for her and the love for your instrument. So many cats go and get caught up in that bag and it's just one of so many traps. You're really like an outcast, you really *are* an outcast. The only thing you know is that the music must be played and you must keep yourself in shape to play it. All other activities of daily life are a waste.'

Another man, a drummer, summed up the general attitude: 'It would be a drag for some musicians if their woman – what they call their "first woman" – would split. But you must realise that the music is first and a woman is next. He's not going to give up the music for a woman, but he could give up the woman for the music.'

With such a punishing ideology driving the musician who may not even be able to find employment despite his dedication and the hours he puts into his music, it is not difficult to detect the root of the frustrations that may lead to him taking refuge in alcohol, narcotics or excessive sex. 'I imagine most cats feel kind of incomplete not being able to support their family,' suggested one man, and the great stress on *machismo* evident in the lifestyle of most musicians and manifested in heavy hanging-out rituals and self-conscious comradeship is an attempt to alleviate such insecurity. The way Ted Daniel sees it, the amount of ego-boosting required depends on the individual. 'If you have a problem, then you're going to be out there every day trying to get your masculinity thing together with the fellows. But you know, slapping fives and all that – that can really get a little bit much. After a while it just doesn't mean anything.'

Frank Lowe said: 'Someone who understands is like your backbone, like your spine. When you come in disgusted because you couldn't sit in with this cat or you blew this note and it didn't happen, you've got an outlet at home. You don't just hold it up in your skull for the next day and the next day and the day after; that'll take you to Bellevue.

'Maybe three months out of the year I want to spend chasing around with my kids or just being with my wife, and then maybe for three months I want to prepare and study hard to give a concert. But why should I have to be away from my wife? Black musicians are like nothing but gipsies, going around the country, living out of a suitcase. Being away from your family a lot of times, different cats can't stand it.'

Although there obviously are men who would prefer living alone, free from family ties, there is little doubt that for an equal number, a woman's support is of spiritual as well as economic significance. 'It's immensely so,' said one wife. 'I think we become their mothers. We're like their support, we're there for them to fall back on, to throw their garbage on – to throw their good feelings on, too.'

In the case of Albert Ayler, frustrated by the lack of appreciation for his music and convinced that his talent was being exploited, Mary Maria exerted a positive influence to stir his creative muse.

They shared a relationship that was both musical and personal. 'I would like to think that I was a force who continually inspired him on when at times he only wanted to meditate,' she said.

Ed Blackwell's marriage to his wife Frances, in 1958, was actually responsible for them each spending a few days in a New Orleans jail. He is Black, she is white, and they had broken the miscegenation laws which prevailed in Louisiana at that time. Their plight made the local headlines, yet they have stayed together. 'Women are very important to musicians,' said Blackwell. 'I think I would have survived without a woman, but I doubt whether I would have had the peace of mind after leaving the bandstand. As far as the music is concerned I would have survived, but then after, when you get home, you feel like it's always nice to have somebody nice to come home to.'

Sirone says: 'It takes two people to confirm the truth. One person has to be able to express and the other has to be able to sit and listen. But if you don't have somebody to talk to or someone to listen, it can be very nerve-racking.'

A number of musicians' wives are actually involved in their work through soliciting and arranging gigs for them, answering their mail, completing their tax returns, compiling publicity and aiding their applications for grants, as well as encouraging them to create even in their darkest moments, yet the idea of a wife or any woman being involved to the extent of following them on gigs or turning up at rehearsals is generally considered restricting. These are times when they want to relax in their all-male environment. Raymond Brown's wife is an exception to this rule. He says, 'I've been digging how my old lady will go to a gig with me and I ask her, "How'd it sound, baby?" and she'll say, "W-e-e-ll, you just wasn't too strong tonight." That kind of criticism is so vital. It gets back to that family thing again –you know, no man is an island. He's got to be with somebody else.'

Being a painter herself, Shirley Brown was no stranger to the impoverished life of the struggling artist. She moved with musicians 'because they seem to know what's really happening', and met Raymond when some artist and writer friends took her to the first loft she had seen where people were actually living. 'Raymond was rehearsing and we just started rapping and kind of hooked up from there. I knew all about the financial scene, but, being poor is a state of mind. You can make anything work if you want to. You can improvise on things. You pick things up, you fix 'em up, and you can have a hipper-looking place than somebody who spends, you know, twenty thousand dollars. So coming from a poor background and having to do that all my life, anyway, and being with the musicians, it was just a thing that I could go right into without any hesitation. I knew that the shit could work if you wanted it to work. There are a lot of people – even myself, sometimes – who think that if you've got an album out, you been on television a couple of times, and had interviews on the radio or something, that you're making a lot of money. But I found out that like, you know, you might have a lot of bread for a month, but the next month you're right down to where everybody else is. But nobody puts you down for that. It's common knowledge that a musician doesn't make a weekly salary. No matter how much you make for the month, the next month you could starve – if you choose to.'

Shirley Brown is in a more fortunate position than some musicians' wives; even with two children to care for she still finds time to draw and paint. Another woman, separated now from her husband, and equally talented with a paintbrush, was not so lucky. 'I always knew there couldn't be but one genius in the house and it was my thing to keep things quiet,' she said. 'I always felt he needed a lot of rest and a lot of protection from all the bloodsuckers and leeches that hung around him, people who couldn't play and would bug him.'

There is no doubt that being married to a musician is one of the most difficult roles for a woman to fulfil. She must be strong in order to cope with the lack of any regular income and the strange demands that the music puts on the man's priorities and time, yet not so aggressive as to question him or give too much unsolicited advice. The majority of musicians resent such 'interference', which is often given as one of the main reasons for marital break-ups. There are those women who have a romantic approach to the music – the 'one day he's going to be rich and famous' kind of attitude – but there are others whose influence is considered by the musicians' community to be destructive. These are the people who actively encourage a musician to give up playing and take a day-job in order to maintain a better standard of living. One man, recalling the fine drummers to be heard in his hometown during his youth, drew a sardonic cameo of the progress of one such player. 'He was out of the early Kenny Clarke thing and he should have left here years ago. But in time his wife stopped him – of course – from playing, and he just went down, down, down.' This luckless creature, as it turned out, is now holding down an excellent job as an aircraft builder, but the informant's attitude illustrates only too well the conflict that exists between art and personal relationships in the world of Black music.

His attitude is pretty general but not everyone would regard such female influence as negative. After almost twenty years on the road with a 'name' band, one saxophonist believed that for many musicians the road was a refuge from an unhappy domestic situation or the inability to find the right partner. Where he was concerned, the 'right woman' was the main reason for travelling musicians quitting the road. 'When a guy settles down, he'll let the lady take the blame for it. But she wasn't that powerful, he had eyes to do whatever she said, anyway!'

For some reason, the jazz world has tended to draw a high percentage of women who enjoy living vicariously. In the past, such women – usually they were white – tended to be dependent on the aura surrounding 'their' creative artist, but this is a situation that has changed along with the music. Carmen Lowe sees the change as part of the altered psychology that goes with the new music.

'Say in Bird's time, the women seemed to stay in the background because that was the psychology during that period. Most women weren't really into their own. They were more or less people to be shown – you know, "I have a woman", that type of thing; she's there when he needs her.'

'If I meet chicks like that, I don't even know what to tell them,' said Shirley Brown. 'You can't tell somebody to get a *hobby*. If you've got something that you've had all your life or that you've grown into, that's good because you're going to do it anyway, even if people are fighting you to stop it. But if somebody's just living for another person, that is bad, that is tragic. Once that person cancels or anything else happens, there's not much left for them. As far as I'm concerned, marriage is two people understanding and learning to live with each other and, if it happens, raising a family together. But each person has their own mind. And then again, I can't just go out with paint on my pants and hang around the Village when I have a family and food to take care of and all that stuff.'

The music life, lived at night in surroundings where others go to relax and socialise, has always attracted its share of men who saw it as providing an open ticket to a variety of sexual conquests. Certainly the male musician has more opportunities for meeting women than most men in other employment and more hope of exploiting those opportunities. An older trombonist, explaining how he no longer derived much pleasure from playing, referred to the fringe benefits, 'the novelty of the girls and everything when you're out there showing off', although the musician image is not always a recipe for instant success. When Earl Cross was in the Army, music played a minor part in his life. 'If you didn't have a job on an Army base making three or four hundred dollars a week, you wasn't into nothing. It was a drag, nobody really wanted to see you. I had a chick tell me once – she saw me and she decided to flirt with me – and all of a sudden I picked up my horn case and she said, "Oh, goddamn, he's got a horn case! I'm not going to fuck with him." So I just had to walk off, and I was embarrassed.'

A contemporary drummer likened dealing with an artist or a 'real musician' to dealing with a witchdoctor. 'I know a lot of musicians with a lot of women,' he said. 'You got to have a lot of wives because one doesn't satisfy. But it's not that they have a lot of women, it's just like a one-night scene. I couldn't say that sex is the main force [behind playing]. After it gets to the ultimate end state of music, you become the music, the music becomes you. So it has nothing to do with sex. The sex part of it comes when you're so much into the music and the music is so much a part of you, that you can project the feeling to someone. And usually it's a man up there doing it and it's a woman out there, and the woman feels that she must have this. The thing that he's projecting, it's coming from somewhere else but it comes through him and projects to the woman out there. She feels that the spirit is strong but she can't collect that thing where it's coming from. And so she has to collect the person it's coming through!'

The myth of the Black man's sexuality has often been traded on by the musician whose work brought him into contact with white women; he has used it for both economic and erotic profit. But just as women themselves have begun to realise their vulnerability through being regarded solely as sex-objects, so the Black man now recognises the double-edged exploitation he undergoes when sex is the only bargaining counter in the game of survival. 'It seems to me that the musicians have a problem, too,' said one woman. 'They're really objects – and as Black men are regarded as objects, too, I think they tend to play it out that way. The Black stud, you know, that's part of their history, and it's been a way of getting by for them and they haven't really given it up.'

The relationship between Black men and white women is, of course, a special one, likened by one woman who had lived in it to the consciousness-raising of the feminist revolution experience: 'The American white woman with the Black musician has rejected the white man's sense of values. She gets much more from the Black experience than from the white. Once your eyes are opened to the Black experience you can never close them. You see things from a Black point of view.' To the estranged wife of another man, though, there is a good deal of pain and frustration involved. 'I think I got a lot of his bad feeling for white people, and I think that he used me for that. I know I symbolised a lot of things to him like not me, *person,* but me – *white woman,* and one of the things that we talked about was well, maybe you should be with a Black woman, maybe that's what you're after.' When it comes to the woman – Black or white – who can no longer cope with the personal idiosyncrasies of the disturbed artist and, because of the situation of the Black artist in America, there are many who can be regarded as just that, she ends up inside, but never a part of, the jazz community. At best, said a woman who was forced to reject her paranoid husband for the sake of her own sanity, the white woman–Black musician relationship is one in which the woman is completely free to go as far as she is able. 'If she chickens out, as I had to, she is just a non-person so far as the Brothers are concerned. Oh, yes, they recognise her and love her, but to them, she only exists in relationship to "her" musician, not to herself.'

* * *

To an older-style player like trumpeter Cootie Williams, the music itself was directly connected with women. 'All great jazz musicians, every one of them, have had many loves and girls in their lives. People don't read about these things in books, but a girl *is* jazz music. They throw something into the mind to make you produce jazz.' In later times, though, musicians dwelt on other aspects of life and tended to analyse the situation a little differently.

Ornette Coleman, for example, has said that the musician's sex-life is disturbed and uses up a good deal of his energy. Lynda Sharrock, who sings with her guitarist husband, considers that the musician is forced into a peculiar position through the unusually varied sexual experiences available to him. 'The whole thing that goes with being a musician, like the kind of women for the kind of sexual experiences you might have, it's something that only a king might have. Musicians have a lot of things around them that are very unusual and this aura becomes a part of them. So they get to this point with the white ladies of having somebody with some money to help them, and it's just too complicated. The way they treat their women is just another example of how they don't respect them because they don't respect themselves. If you can't accept yourself, then you definitely can't accept a woman – of any race. But particularly a white woman if you're Black.'

It is in Europe, in particular, that American musicians have tended to capitalise on their 'stud' image. Very few of those new players who flooded into France at the end of the 'sixties seeking employment, publicity and exposure, could have made it without the sustenance and help of women. One of them described a typical day in the musician's life there. 'In Paris you just sit in the cafés all day and relax. Then the cats go down to the Chat [Le Chat Qui Pêche, now closed but then the musicians' favourite nightclub], hang out all night, then back to their women and back to the cafés. Anybody can survive there, all you have to do is work on it. I mean you can survive on the women, you know, the French woman will really keep you cool.

'This is something where the love for the music is so great, you're not even thinking about "Is this cool or not cool?" either morally, ethically or idealistically. I mean I like to be on my own – in a way – but you want to play so badly that you don't care how you survive. A meal today and place to stay is beautiful – so long as you can be playing and getting into your thing.'

His bluntness on the subject was unusual, but not everyone would agree with this means of survival. 'We do have several who go from lady to lady, but you have that in all walks of life,' said Ted Daniel. 'In Europe, that's somebody else's attitude as to how to do it. My direction is music and I really wouldn't like to get sidetracked into the pimp thing, you know, and I think that's what that borders on. Of course everybody likes to have someone – we have to acknowledge that – but to have somebody just to sustain you, I wouldn't endorse that. I wouldn't say that was a hip idea. I mean it's using someone and that's not good.'

Musicians, of course, have different ideas regarding the extent of their responsibility to their family. Sunny Murray, working in Europe with Albert Ayler in 1964, was forced to make his way home by troopship as a result of sending his wife what little money he had earned. Five years later he was living in Paris, doing fractionally better. Most of his colleagues were single, but as soon as the drummer had managed a couple of trips to the recording studio, he sent for his wife and two children and installed them in a poor but functional workingman's apartment. In common with other expatriates, his chances of work started to deteriorate after the novelty of his presence wore off, and he found himself in a difficult situation.

Contemporary Black music, in common with other styles and forms, has its 'groupies', women who collect musicians for their beds, but like the wives of the musicians involved in the new music, they tend to be more intelligent than their erstwhile counterparts. 'To me, most of the women who are living with the musicians dig the music,' said Jerome Cooper. 'That's where it's all stemming from, especially in jazz. Jazz musicians attract very intelligent women. When I was playing rock-and-roll, the women were kind of like ding-a-lings – to me, and that's with the whole rock scene, it's like on a ding-a-ling level. But in jazz and the new music – even more in the new music – they tend to attract very high-minded women.'

This would seem to confirm something a Californian saxophonist once told Sun Ra: 'He talked about the groups, the singing groups and the vocalists, and how you always have to be playing the same thing. He said it was "pussy-and-dick" music. He said he was tired of playing it and he needed to play something else. Basically, he said that that's what the musicians who are making the money are playing. It wasn't nothing about no *music*.'

Frank Lowe agreed. 'Now, when women come up to you, they have more of a "thank you for the music" type of thing going. If you get some vibes behind that, then it might be something that you want to follow up, but it's not like "hey, here's my phone-number". It's like somebody showing you that they appreciate what you're doing. You know, we've got a little more on our minds right now.'

And the attitude of wives themselves towards whatever women their man might meet when the set or the concert is over, is much freer than it once was. 'As far as the women that hang around with the musicians are concerned, I used to do it myself before I was married,' said Shirley Brown. 'And my whole thing wasn't, you know, being promiscuous. So any time I see chicks around, I can't be thinking that. They might really be digging the music. I can't be jumping up and paranoiac every time I see a bunch of chicks around. They can admire the man which is, you know, it's flattering to me.'

It is not uncommon for musicians' wives to be involved in the arts. The former wife of a musician who was often on the road with a name band was a dancer; she was well aware of the sexual freedom offered by this way of life. 'I felt that if I was going to marry somebody who was in that kind of profession where in a way they're on display, then I have to accept the fact that there's probably other women in his life. And if I'm the one who gets most of his time and attention, I'm the one he cares about. So it never really was a problem to me. If you have a husband that goes on the road for two and a half months in Europe, for you to sit home and imagine that there's not other women involved, I think that's just crazy.'

The Don Juans among musicians are generally explained away by men and women alike as caught up in following a stereotype. 'They just heard that that's the way they're supposed to be, and there are a lot of women available to them,' said Shirley Brown. 'But it's so much energy to be screwing all those chicks – I don't know how they can do it. And you know, cats that have to be screwing all the time, they're not supposed to be wrapped too tight! [Not very intelligent] That energy could be used in the head instead of coming out in your orgasm. Look at the Buddhist monks, wise men, they abstain so that they're really heavier up there. No, for God's sake give your mind a break.'

Ted Daniel agreed with her interpretation. 'It's more or less an ego thing with their peer group, but it can become destructive. If you're moving from woman to woman like that – this one in Harlem and another in Paris, and that's how it goes – you're not really building anything, you're just dissipating your energy. I think a lot of musicians should just check that out. I guess to an extent your background has something to do with it, but after a point it begins to be the individual who is responsible. If you say that you are a musician and this is what you want to do, this is your life's work, then this is where your energy goes.'

Art Lewis pointed out that the new music consumes more energy than some other forms. 'Sometimes you might play *to* women,' he said. 'You might see a certain woman in the audience and you do try to project to her. For a musician it's very beautiful to see a beautiful woman in the audience, it's very inspiring sometimes. It can be distracting, though, because you can't concentrate like you would like to. When I finish playing, I feel exhausted. I might feel like sex later on. When women come up to you, it's like, "OK, I did something for you, now you do something for me." And usually it's sex.'

The notion of excessive promiscuity in the musicians' camp is regarded by Carmen Lowe as part of the negative psychology inculcated in the artist. 'A lot of people think that's the way musicians are, just like they think the majority of musicians are dope addicts and everyone takes scag. It's the mentality that's been placed on the artist – not just musicians. But artists are like everyone else – they have families, they raise kids; they want big cars, they don't want cars; they want mansions, they don't want mansions.'

One New Year's Eve, Earl Cross was on the bandstand as midnight approached. He had just taken his trumpet from his lips to sing 'Auld Lang Syne' when a woman leapt up and embraced him. Someone took a photograph of this enthusiastic New Year's greeting, but when the trumpeter's wife saw it she became angry. 'I can understand the effect it would have on the woman if she has to stay at home and take care of the children and the man has cut out to do his things,' Cross sympathised. 'I remember once I went out on the road and came back with not a dime because the guy ran off with all the money. That really disillusioned her. I mean, she doesn't know what's going on, she wasn't there and you can't explain it. Really, though, it's one of the most enlightening things you could have – somebody who loves you and cares for you and all that stuff. And maybe, somebody that can go out and work so that you can play your music, because if you have to work a job and then come back and practise, it's different. If you can wake up – no matter what time it is – and pick up your instrument and go to practise without any hassles, it's altogether different. So that's why musicians try to get a lot of things established before they get a lady.

'But there are wonderful ladies in music – in life, period – who'll help them get their instrument fixed, or buy them an instrument or whatever, just for the pleasure of the music. But those kind of women are rare, they're not everyday things.'

Milford Graves is a strong believer in the traditional process of Yin and Yang or negative and positive, two opposing forces helping to equalise each other in order to work together. Based on this, his relationship with his wife is very important to him. 'I don't get into this thing about male supremacy or female supremacy, I really go beyond that. I think a male thinks a certain way, and I think my wife has looked at certain problems as a female would look at certain things. By having a relationship with a female where both can communicate and trust each other, it's been vital as far as I'm concerned. A lot of times I've made decisions – maybe at a time when I was angry – and if there was another male there, he'd be just as angry and we'd never get no place. But I notice a female would come in and cool it down or keep it quiet – or take it another place. That's very important.'

'As far as building something, a woman is important,' said Shirley Brown. 'Like a family, or a place to come and rest, have a good meal, sit down – a place to bring your friends or a place to play – that kind of warmth I think they should all have. I think they deserve it. I'm not saying that all of them have it, but they deserve it because of the situation here.

'When I got pregnant, everybody had to show their cards – right? Not everybody gets pregnant so you could go on for years supporting someone, but when I had to stop working, this was the ultimate proof of whether I was going to get put out or what was going to happen. And he took it right up from there. So like everything I knew about him, my sensitivity about his attitude towards me as a wife and a woman and a companion, he respected what I'd done for him and he appreciated it in that he would go out and hustle for me. Even nine-to-fives he's done. Not all musicians would do that because they haven't found women that would vibrate on that level. See, he's always worked. If it wasn't a music job, he was a plumber. He's a mover, he's an electrician – in case I can't go to work. But I knew the musicians all had something that's deeper than what I was doing as far as going to work every day and dealing with the Man and the system which is really a surface thing. It's light stuff when you really sit down and think about it. All it does is pay the bills that has to be paid, anyway. I respect the music and I respect the musicians. Music is the highest art form so, like, you've really got to get down with that.'

Raymond Brown's father was a trumpet player who worked at one time with a notable big band. Unlike his own father who was able to maintain his family by playing the saxophone, he gave up music because he felt he could not earn enough to support his family. He took a labouring job, an attitude that Raymond did not understand at the time. Now, however, he is very aware of the importance of the family. 'A big problem now in my ethnic group is that a lot of Brothers leave their families because they can't support them. My father is a perfect example of the other thing. We're men now and so I understand why he did what he did, but I know a lot of people – they've got families but they're someplace else. Consequently, that breaks up what they have left, and if anything's important, it's your historical past. A lot of people laugh at this, but your family ties are so important because that gives you a rock, that gives you a certain amount of strength. You can afford to be patient, you can take your time to build something.

'For myself, I've been bullshitting a lot, I've really been bullshitting. But thank God I've got a good woman. My woman's in my corner, we're working together, we're helping each other. She's a young painter, I'm a young musician, and all we want to do is stick together the best we can and raise ourselves.'

Notes

1   Correspondence with the author.
2   Maxine Williams, 'Why Women's Liberation is Important to Black Women', *The Militant*, 3 July 1970; reprinted in Maxine Williams and Pamela Newman, *Black Women's Liberation*, New York, 1970.
3   Interview with Pat Griffith in *Melody Maker*, date unknown.
4   Imamu Baraka, *Raise, Race, Rays, Raze*, New York, 1971, p. 148.

12

'You Sound Good – for a Woman!'

> There are enough men doing jazz! We must try to let more
> women into the music in order to have a balance. There are lots
> of women who play very well, but they can't be accepted in jazz,
> and it is equally true in other fields – musical or otherwise.[1]
>
> Rafael Garrett

In the summer of 1972 a poster from the women's movement was to be seen tacked to the wall in a male drummer's apartment. Things may not have been all they seemed, yet this was an indication of somewhat changing times within the world of creative Black music. The women's movement has analysed the sexism of Rock music content and practice; in the 'jazz' world the same standards, mores and attitudes prevail.

The dominant factor in most Black music is that the performer be aggressive – 'Blowing a masculine stick, avoiding the faggot's trick'[2] is how the poet Ted Joans sees the musician – and this attitude is expected to be carried over into his personal lifestyle. So, with a few exceptions, the jazz world has been very difficult for the woman instrumentalist to enter. It is true to say that women musicians have been actively discouraged by most of their male counterparts on a certain level. In the early days of the new music, for example, one of the younger saxophonists started rehearsing with a white female 'cellist. 'When the word got out that I was playing with a woman, the cats really came down on me,' he said.

'They said, "What the hell are you doing playing with a woman – and a white bitch at that?"' When they heard the actual music, though, several of the musicians changed their minds and actually wanted to play with her. 'We were all dressed up in weird clothes and she came on wearing a 1940s-type dress, high-heeled shoes, a pompadour hairstyle and lipstick, but she played the shit out of the 'cello,' he said. 'After that, some string players even asked for her address to take lessons from her.' Nevertheless, most women musicians who have the nerve to attempt to enter the hallowed male circle – Black or white – generally meet with a similar response.

In the case of Alice Coltrane, who was a musician before she met her husband, the saxophonist intentionally included her in his work. This gained her the respect of the other musicians who continued to work with her after Coltrane's death. Alice carried on with some of his ideas and some of her own, and her good standing with the Establishment, which allowed her to command respectable fees for live appearances, indirectly enabled other musicians to travel and live well when they worked with her. But for the majority of women musicians involved in a relationship with a male musician, it has been a very different story. For example, there was a Black drummer married to a white woman who also played drums. When he realised that she was getting more work than he was, he forced his wife to give up playing. In another case, a Black man, a bassist, insisted that his woman, a guitarist and singer, give up her music if they were going to get married. She refused and the relationship broke up.

Where women musicians were accepted in the past, they were generally expected to double in a 'maternal' role. Saxophonist Jimmy Lyons lived across the hallway from a woman who had a piano and held open house for such noted players as Bud Powell, Elmo Hope and Thelonious Monk. 'She was,' he observed, 'very beautiful, and I suspect all the musicians were in love with her.' And during the 'forties when the groundwork for bebop was being done, it was at Mary Lou Williams's apartment that Gillespie,

Parker, Monk and Powell gathered for appreciation, help and understanding. She was to be found nightly at Minton's, too, and was one of the few musicians of her generation to encourage the revolutionaries. In the case of trombonist/arranger Melba Liston, the pot was always on the stove and musicians even used her apartment as a mailing address.

Fontella Bass met her husband Lester Bowie when they both worked with Oliver Sain's blues band in St Louis. She has carved a separate career with recordings like the multi-million seller 'Rescue Me', but during the Art Ensemble of Chicago's two and a half years in Europe, the Bowies and their children lived in France as a family, and Fontella appeared and recorded with the trumpeter and his compadres doing *their* music rather than exercising any control over the end product. Other women vocalists who have made substantial contributions to contemporary activities in Chicago include Sherri Scott with Joseph Jarman and Rita Omolokun Worford with Kalaparusha.

It is as singers that women have traditionally secured their place in the jazz hierarchy. Lynda Sharrock offers more than her voice. She is responsible for the concept of much of the music she and her husband make together. Sonny Sharrock constantly acknowledges her growing influence, although their situation is not without its problems. He said: 'If the woman is going to invade the holy territory of the artist, she's in a *lot* of trouble. You know, it's hard enough for a cat to make it, but being a woman must be really ridiculous because I know that people refuse to give Lynda any recognition at all.

'I know that lots of the things I feel about music I've gained through her knowledge, what she's told me. There were a lot of things that I felt were true about making art, and Lynda came with a completely fresh approach because she had been denied all the learning and she had a different idea of what it should be. And so she taught me. But it's really weird – a lot of times when we're working, I get the feeling that a lot of the musicians refuse to recognise her as a part of the whole thing, as important as myself or anybody else that's in the band.'

More women – white and Black – are taking up instruments and really playing, but the prejudice against them continues. Whatever the extent of their talent, this discrimination is more pronounced in so-called jazz than in rock. No one paid much attention when Sly Stone, one of the most influential figures in contemporary Black rock, included two women instrumentalists – a trumpeter and organist – in the 1967 lineup of his Family Stone. Sonny Simmons, a saxophonist in the Ornette Coleman mould, brought his trumpeter wife Barbara Donald to New York, and a hefty percentage of the musicians turned their backs on her. This, despite the fact that she has been acknowledged as one of the more fluent performers on the instrument – 'She's great, she's fantastic,' was Earl Cross's opinion. In California where the couple make their home, Simmons says he is frequently offered gigs where he is unable to take his wife.

Another man, who prefers to travel the world with his wife, making music together, drew this begrudging comment concerning this relationship: 'The music's *all right*, but when is he going to settle down and make some *real* music?' The implication was that playing with *a* woman could not be considered a serious endeavour.

The creative woman's experience of being denied recognition because she is regarded as sex-object is in no way an exclusively white one. A Black woman who works with her husband – also Black – put it bluntly: 'With other musicians, all they want to do is fuck you. They figure they can't because I'm with him – plus I have the *audacity* to be up there on the stage – so they can't really deal with it and they have to put out some kind of negative comment.'

But this couple's case is unique. It is impossible for the other musicians to ignore them, but what they actually have to say to the woman herself depends on their attitude to the music. 'I know how to talk to them because I can understand a lot of things that men feel – especially musicians – because no matter how sick they are, they're still very interesting people and I dig them. So they'll say, "Oh, you sound good," or "Oh, you're really a showbusiness woman now," or something like that, but generally they feel that *he's* competing with them on a musical level and that I'm an extension of him. So, in order to get back at him, they'll say something to me.'

It is far from easy for a Black woman to be accepted in the new music, but because she has certain contemporary attitudes concerned with 'respect' on her side, her position is fractionally better than that of the white woman. Her participation in musical endeavours is not only a reflection of the changing role of women in Western society, it is directly connected with the growing acknowledgement by Black men of their failure to respect the contributions that have been made by the women in their lives. This omission results from their own lack of self-esteem, itself conditioned by various forms of enslavement and disenfranchisement. Popular singers, taking over the preacher's role, charted the changing attitudes within the Black community. 'All I'm asking for is a little respect when you come home,' implored Otis Redding (1965) and Aretha Franklin (1967). In 1971, the Staples Singers ordered, 'Respect Yourself'.

Monnette Sudler, a young Black woman who plays guitar, has been a member of Byard Lancaster's group for some time because the saxophonist feels that the rules of the past should be forgotten. He sees women as capable as men; all they need is sufficient motivation to play.

A number of the newer groups are starting to include women, usually singers, as an integral part of their unit. But still the challenge – rigorously applied to male and female newcomers alike, it must be admitted – persists. In the case of a Black woman conga drummer, arriving in New York and looking for other drummers to play with, the glove was thrown down by a group of stalwart young bloods from Bedford-Stuyvesant. She was led for miles through the decaying streets of the notorious Brooklyn ghetto without a word being spoken. On finally arriving at their destination, they simply told her, 'Play.' She had carried her congas for several miles on the subway and on foot but knew herself to be more than equal to the challenge. She proved her credentials by playing nonstop for over half-an-hour, judge and jury seated around her. The workout was sufficient for her to be accepted into their circle without question and treated with respect.

'Ten years ago I didn't even know a woman conga player,' said Carmen Lowe. 'I don't think she'd have been permitted to sit down and listen to the session, let alone play. Things are changing and I think for the best. Women have a lot to add to the music – not just the music, all the arts – as well as the men.'

A man who would agree with that viewpoint is Rafael Garrett. Always a pioneer, he now works in close collaboration with his young wife, Zuzaan Fasteau; they have recorded for ESP singing and playing a variety of instruments between them. Following in the footsteps of John Coltrane, there are a number of men who have gladly made room for women in their work; Albert Ayler with Mary Maria, for example. Nevertheless, Garrett's position is an unusual one. He considers that there are enough men playing jazz and that in order to establish an equilibrium and to more accurately reflect the ratio between the sexes, women should participate equally. He has worked with Alice Coltrane and Barbara Donald, and being possessed of a naturally egalitarian attitude, views sex in the same light as age and race, as similarly oppressive factors in the development and recognition of a musician. He said: 'People think women can only sing, dance and play legitimate music on certain instruments. No one will admit that they can play the saxophone strongly or the drums or the bass. In Chicago, I heard a woman bassist who could solo as strong as Richard Davis.'[3] (It is, of course, inevitable that women are still judged in comparison to men. 'You play like a man' was always the ultimate compliment a female musician could receive, fractionally better than the other painful cliché – 'You sound good – for a woman.')

Before meeting Albert Ayler, Mary Maria had never played the saxophone or considered the possibility of doing so. Ayler taught her the soprano and she played it in concert with him at Saint-Paul de Vence (though not on the tracks released on record). Rather than admit to the influence she had on him, she said, 'I would rather think that Albert influenced me in that he awakened in me a sleeping ambition.' In a previous era, the male musician would not have considered the possibility of teaching 'his' woman.

Several women have started learning an instrument expressly in order to participate and share in their husband's music. Moki Cherry is one, although her involvement in Don's music has existed on another level for some time: she specialises in sewing the creative hangings and backdrops he uses in concert, not to mention his expressionistic clothes. Carmen Lowe is another. She studies the Chinese stringed instrument, the *ching*, in addition to her adeptness with the needle. She has frequently derived inspiration for her visual creations from something played by her husband, whose albums have also been illustrated with her work. When Rashied Ali opened his studio to the public, he commissioned her to supply one of her unique wall-hangings. This combination of the visual with the music, incidentally, is prevalent in the work of many younger musicians. It grows out of the movement to cross-fertilise music with poetry, dance, theatre and the visual arts, not exclusive to Black music, but ideally suited to the ritualistic heritage of Afro-Americans. Sun Ra paved the way for this years back, and the Art Ensemble of Chicago have followed in this tradition.

Musicians have always revelled in cruel anecdotes, often with women as the butt of them. There is, for example, the one told about a female bassist called Donna Lee. Sitting in with Charlie Parker after a long lay-off from playing, her fingers blistered easily. She was told that the best way to raise callouses was to cut open the blisters and pour whisky in them, but no sooner had she followed this advice than the bass player flung his instrument at her and told her to finish the set. Then he and Parker sat in the audience and laughed while she struggled on for another thirty minutes with blood dripping from her fingers. When she finished, Parker pointed out that this was how to get callouses. 'So she made it,' was the narrator's laconic comment. 'This might also indicate why there are not too many girl musicians.'[4]

The story is probably apocryphal – other musicians remember Donna Lee, after whom Parker named one of his compositions, as a woman whose heart and home were always open to those on the road – but it sums up the way that most male musicians have tended to regard any woman who attempted to enter their camp. The improvement in the situation can be judged from another story, equally apocryphal in all probability, but told with relish by a young saxophone player not so long ago:

A Major Tenorman (it was said) was playing in a California nightclub when the stand was suddenly invaded by two women saxophonists. MTM is a giant, but the two newcomers were powerful, too. They all but blew him off the stage. His reply was to pack up his horn and leave. One of his long absences from the scene began then and there. Perhaps the story is a myth, possibly it is exaggerated – or maybe for MTM it was the straw that broke the camel's back. For women musicians, though, the mere fact that the tale is being repeated by one of the Young Turks is another step towards their liberation within the hitherto male-dominated art form.

Notes

1   Interview with Philippe Carles in *Jazz Magazine*, October/November 1973.
2   Ted Joans, 'The Black Jazz Smile', from *A Black Manifesto in Jazz Poetry and Prose*, London, 1971.
3   Carles, op. cit.
4   Robert George Reisner, *Bird – the Legend of Charlie Parker*, New York, 1962.

PART FIVE

THE CONSPIRACY AND SOME SOLUTIONS

13

Bill Dixon and the Jazz Composers Guild

I've been in the street but before I was there, I decided I wanted to
know something about the music itself. I didn't think like a lot of
guys out there 'don't study with anyone or it'll ruin your talent'. I
wasn't worried about the talent, I wanted to know about the *thing*.

Bill Dixon

One week early in October 1964, people like Archie Shepp,
Ornette Coleman and Cecil Taylor were amongst those leaning on
the railings outside the Cellar Café on New York's West Ninety-
Sixth Street, interested bystanders at a revolution that was taking
place within. It was a revolution that they were, in part, responsible for sparking off, for the October Revolution in Jazz, as it was
known, featured just about every new player in the city. The young
musicians were full of fire; trumpeter/composer Bill Dixon was
the man responsible for lighting the touch-paper.

The Cellar Café, a small room off Broadway, seated a minimal
sixty-five, but for the six nights of concerts the place was packed.
Dixon had maintained that there was an audience for the new
music, at that time still in its infancy, and the nightly turnout that
squeezed into the club and spilled out on the sidewalk confirmed
this. For most of the audience, this was their first chance to hear
people like Sun Ra, Milford Graves and Giuseppi Logan. Dixon
recorded his own portion, other musicians were less concerned
with posterity. However, a later concert, Four Days in December,

was taped, the participants including Shepp, Taylor, Graves, Paul Bley, Dixon with Rashied Ali on drums, and Sun Ra's Arkestra with Pharoah Sanders in the lineup. (All the music was recorded, but to date none of the tapes have been released.)

The Jazz Composers Guild, which was formed as a direct result of the success of the 'October Revolution', has been erroneously depicted as a collective. Like the Revolution itself, it was the brainchild of one man, Bill Dixon. According to pianist Carla Bley: 'People think it was something everyone was thinking of but, no, it was Bill's idea. It didn't work out because it was the wrong time in history.'

Dixon, who comes from Nantucket Island off the Massachusetts coast near Boston, is used to being ahead of his time. He was born in 1925, which makes him considerably older than the remainder – with the exception of Sun Ra – of the so-called avantgarde musicians. Prior to 1964 he had devoted himself to attempts to raise the status of the music and improve its image. In 1958 he formed the United Nations Jazz Society. He lectured frequently, conducted adult education classes and taught trumpet and composition privately. He has also painted and taught art history. In 1962 he went to Europe with a quartet he co-led with Archie Shepp and this, as it turned out, was to be the basis for the group known as the New York Contemporary Five, one of the landmarks in the new Black music.

After the impact of the October Revolution, Dixon discussed with Cecil Taylor the possibilities of forming an organisation that would protect the jazz musician/composer from the exploitation that had hitherto prevailed. 'You can't kill an organisation, but you can kill an individual,' said Dixon, who handpicked every member of the Jazz Composers Guild. Some, like Ornette Coleman, were invited to join but refused, others were not invited because Dixon was impatient to launch his brainchild and foresaw sufficient time for additional members to join in the future.

Dixon invited white musicians to join because he did not

consider the position of the white jazz musician to be much better than that of the Black. 'They are treated significantly better, but not much better – that's why they're in the Guild – than are Black musicians, and that is simply because they play jazz, which is looked on as something "primitive".'[1] Consequently, Roswell Rudd, Jon Winter, Mike Mantler, Burton Greene, and Paul and Carla Bley, who were married at the time, were the charter members of the Guild together with Sun Ra, Archie Shepp, John Tchicai, Cecil Taylor and Dixon himself. Primarily the Guild's plans were to withhold their labour and develop self-respect among the musicians. They planned to turn down work unless it was considered that accepting it would be advantageous to the Guild as a whole. The ball was set rolling with four concerts at Judson Hall in December 1964, two groups appearing at each concert. The Jazz Composers Guild Orchestra, under the leadership of Mantler and Carla Bley, was one of the groups and its lineup included Shepp, Graves and Paul Bley. The concerts continued on a weekly basis at the Contemporary Center, a triangular loft situated two floors above the Village Vanguard on Seventh Avenue.

Another plan was that contracts for nightclubs and concert work should be negotiated with the Guild rather than the individual musicians. The services of a sympathetic lawyer were retained and it was planned that the Guild would eventually be in a position to provide legal assistance for its members and other musicians as well as checking the record companies' books to ensure that royalties, where due, were being paid. The possibility of starting their own record label was also discussed, but at the time their organisation was insufficient for them to apply for a grant as a non-profit-making organisation.

The idea of the Guild was a good one, though as it turned out, it was inoperative amongst people who were used to surviving at near-subsistence level. Shortly after the Guild's formation, Archie Shepp commenced negotiations with Impulse for a recording contract without telling the other members. He excused himself by saying that everyone had to fend for themselves, but the Guild were furious. Shepp's action was the only possibility he could see with several children to support, but it was the first step in breaking down morale. Within a few months the regular Monday meetings had degenerated to the point where Sun Ra, who is something of a misogynist, was regaling the members with the old seamen's legend which says that taking a woman on a voyage will sink the ship. As a consequence, he maintained, it was bad luck for Carla Bley to be on board their particular vessel.

Finally Dixon himself quit the sinking ship, though the members continued to meet. Without their guiding light at the helm, however, they drifted apart. The Jazz Composers Guild was a brave venture, but given the state of the musicians' nation at the time, its failure was inevitable. It did, however, light the way for the organisations that were to follow six years later.

Notes

1   Robert Levin, 'The Jazz Composers Guild – An Assertion of Dignity', *Down Beat,* 6 May 1965.

14

Politics, the Media and Collectivism

> You know, it gets to be a drag when they're talking about
> that Iron Curtain that used to be around Russia. Shit, they
> moved that here and put it in front of the jazz musician.
>
> Hakim Jami

On 13 October 1970, one of Dick Cavett's guests on his ABC-TV
'chat' show was Trevor Howard. Cavett, who boasts an audience
of several millions, asked the British actor, 'What is it about New
York that has changed?' Howard's answer, that there was no longer
anywhere to go to hear jazz, was the signal for over two hundred
members of the audience to stand up and start blowing furiously
on wooden flutes and police whistles. The reply had been pure
coincidence; this onslaught was the third in a series of demonstra-
tions organised by the Jazz and People's Movement to draw attention to the way American television has ignored the music.

The J & PM first went into action two months prior to the
Cavett demonstration when sixty people led by Rahsaan Roland
Kirk interrupted CBS-TV's Merv Griffin Show in the same way.
They had gained admission quite legitimately by ticket, and took
everyone by surprise. Although the house band tried to drown out
the invaders on both occasions, they were no match for Kirk and
the powerful lungs of the J & PM. The taping was stopped as peti-
tions were passed out and signs displayed bearing slogans such as
'Stop the whitewash now, hire more Black artists on TV' and 'End

pollution of the eye and ear – we demand the termination of television's frozen music today!' The musicians taking part included the saxophonist Billy Harper, drummers Andrew Cyrille and Ron Jefferson, and the late Lee Morgan, the trumpeter. Between them they engaged network executives in discussion and explained the reasons for their protest to hastily assembled journalists and the outraged studio audience.

The immediate result of the pressure was a promise that jazz artists would be considered for the show. It was Lee Morgan, talking to a reporter, who summarised the demonstrators' creed: 'The airways belong to the public and we're here to dramatise that fact. Jazz is the only real American music, but how often do you see jazz musicians in front of the camera? And we're not talking about jazz musicians playing in the house band!'[1] (A token handful work in television, among them the trumpeters Clark Terry and Snooky Young.)

Five weeks later the J & PM struck again. Led by Rahsaan Roland Kirk, this time their target was NBC's Johnny Carson Show, where they blocked the doors and only allowed the taping to continue after a series of discussions between them and the network were promised. It was the attack on Cavett, however, that produced the most immediate results from the demands of the group whose stipulated goals included more jazz and Black musicians on television and other media, regular programming of shows that would educate the public about Black music, more Black musicians on daily and weekly network television, and more recognition of jazz musicians when they do appear as guests on television. The musicians secured a half-hour discussion and the following week Cecil Taylor, Freddie Hubbard, Harper, Cyrille, and Kirk's wife, Edith, appeared with Cavett and aired their grievances.

Cyrille said later, 'The general feeling I get from most of the people who co-ordinate these programmes is that anything that is called "art" is kind of subjective and personal in its appeal and may not be "tasteful" enough where the general public is concerned.

They don't want to have the music on many times because they don't want their ratings to go down.'

In spite of this, the discussion represented a triumph for the J & PM, who had been provoked into taking direct action only after repeated attempts by individual artists to secure bookings on television. Another outcome was a televised 'Dialogue of the Drums' between the three percussionists Cyrille, Milford Graves and Rashied Ali on NBC's 'Positively Black'.

The appearances arising from the demonstration culminated in an all-star group selected by Kirk playing on the Ed Sullivan Show. The doyen of the television personality cult, who only surrendered because he did not want his own show interrupted, provided history with an unforgettable quote. Asked by Kirk why he'd never had John Coltrane on the programme, the late lamented arbiter of public taste replied: 'Does John Coltrane have any records out?'

* * *

The move towards collective action started long before the inception of the Jazz and People's Movement with the AACM, founded in Chicago in 1965. The Jazz Composers Guild had been more of an elitist effort, but Collective Black Artists, another New York-based group, is a self-reliance programme headed by the business-like Reggie Workman, formerly a bassist in the Coltrane Quartet, and includes musicians involved in the new music as well as established artists like Rahsaan Roland Kirk. At one time CBA published their own newspaper, *Expansions*. All these groups grew out of an awareness that unless musicians attempted to control their own destinies, the music was doomed to an ever-diminishing audience in the face of economic pressures from the huge conglomerates that control the music industry.

The gap between the philosophies of musicians of different ages is not always easily closed, though there is more unity between the disparate groups than outsiders generally imagine. 'There were gaps before and there still are, really, in the different styles of music,' said Billy Harper. 'You could hardly get an older musician to respect the style that a younger musician might want to play, because the older musician knows more about music. Well, he's more *experienced*, but he doesn't necessarily know more about music. He's not so likely to trust what a younger musician is doing.'

Harper's commitment to the concept of collective musicianship is strong, because he feels it is the only way musicians will be able to change their situation – 'mainly Black musicians, that is, because they are the ones that really starve'. There must be a collective effort, he says, to raise the level of the music and improve its tarnished image. 'It's still a fact that so many musicians die early and that's terrible. The lifestyle itself, I suppose, would have something to do with that. If a musician gets so depressed that he can't express his music or can't get it out to be heard, then I suppose some of the older musicians, with the economic pressures that were there and that still are there, resorted to drugs sometimes, some to drink. And some were discouraged completely about trying to be into that thing, the groove of musicians who work and are noticed.'

Although he admitted that apart from appreciating its historic value, younger musicians often find difficulty in relating to an older style, Harper considers that it is left to some of them to be wiser than their predecessors. 'It's funny that it's the younger ones, but they'll seen a lot of musicians die for nothing and with nothing – and meaning nothing.'

Hakim Jami, the bass player, considers that aiming for a collective rather than an individual goal can help to save an artist from the kind of self-destruction that has been so prevalent in the music. 'It gives them some hope, some daylight, you understand? And that is what cats need – some hope, a chance.'

Lee Morgan, who was active in both the J & PM and CBA, was a brilliant trumpeter closely associated with the hard bop style and known to jazz listeners everywhere through his work with his own groups and Art Blakey's Jazz Messengers. He had joined the Dizzy

Gillespie big band as an eighteen-year-old prodigy and so, even after fifteen years in the music business, he was still a couple of years younger than people like Archie Shepp and Pharoah Sanders. When Shepp first arrived in Philadelphia, incidentally, it was the teenaged Morgan, already established in his hometown, who gave the saxophonist a helping hand. In common with the majority of contemporary Black musicians, Morgan felt that the word 'jazz' is frequently used to block the exposure given to the music. 'I think racism comes into this,' he said, and pointed out that the efforts of musicians' collectives are influenced by the idea of a deliberate conspiracy to inhibit the music's progress. 'We know *why* and we know the people in the media know *why*. So when they say you can't play this or you can't play that, we know this is hogwash because the public have very little to say about what they hear on the radio or what they see on TV ... so what we are trying to do is to try to direct our communication directly to the people, *our* people.'

LeRoi Jones's Black Arts group presented the new music in the streets of Harlem in 1963–65, attracting an audience of people who left their houses out of curiosity at first and stayed out of interest, but one of the first positive attempts to take jazz back into the Black community originally had less to do with collectivism and education than with advertising. The Jazzmobile, which started operations in 1964, and was the first of many mobile theatre projects, was instigated by the Harlem Community Council. It is just what its name implies – a bandstand set up on the back of a truck. It was originally sponsored by Coca-Cola and Ballantine beer and, for a nominal fee, musicians took their music each summer into Harlem, the Bronx, Brooklyn and other culturally deprived areas where many of the younger Blacks had never heard jazz before. By 1971, the Jazzmobile was receiving grants from the New York State Council on the Arts and other bodies, and in ten years it has progressed from a summer season of ten free concerts to a year-round programme which also presents public school lecture/concerts conducted by pianist Billy Taylor as well as a weekly workshop clinic for aspiring young musicians held at IS 201, a Harlem school.

Every Saturday, a staff of experienced musicians headed by the drummer David Bailey, now Executive Director of Jazzmobile but famous for his work with Gerry Mulligan, conduct a series of sessions at the Jazzmobile Workshop for students whose ages range from fifteen to fifty, with a syllabus that includes everything from instrumental basics to big band orchestration. Dizzy Gillespie lectures there whenever he is in town, and among the others are trumpeter Joe Newman, trombonist Curtis Fuller, saxophonists Jimmy Heath and Billy Mitchell, guitarist Ted Dunbar, bassist Richard Davis and drummers Freddie Waits and Albert 'Tootie' Heath. Lee Morgan was also a regular. The students, surrounded by the mandatory posters proclaiming the evils of narcotics, are impressively serious about their music.

Jazz Interactions started a similar programme in 1975 under the direction of Joe Newman. Both this and the Jazzmobile programme are concerned more with conventional values than avant-garde experiment, but they are oases in a desert of musical trivia. With the exception of the bookstores and centres that are the strongholds of Black Nationalism, recordings of the new music are unobtainable in Harlem, and rarely is anything at all representative of the *new* music broadcast. Radio Station WBLS, which calls itself 'the Black Experience in Sound', plays maybe one jazz record in two hundred, and then it is by an established record seller such as Donald Byrd or Eddie Harris. Even the selections of WRVR, a twenty-two-hour jazz station, are relatively middle-of-the-road.

Although the majority of Black songwriters pulled their heads out of the sand some time ago and took a political stance in their lyrics – 'We as a people are not interested in "baby, baby" songs anymore. There's more to life than that,'[2] says Stevie Wonder – the disc-jockeys continue to be rock-oriented and ignorant about jazz. 'You can't depend on someone else making sure your music gets across,' says Billy Harper. 'Musicians have to be concerned with it themselves.'

That there are few Black promoters for the new music helps to maintain the musical *status quo* in the ghetto, something many consider to be linked with politics and economic power. 'The point is to "keep the natives happy" by giving them some music they can dance to and be just concerned with *rhythm*,' said Harper. 'I think that if more of the contemporary Black music was played, people would probably think a little more, and that may be a little dangerous for some people politically. If people in Harlem – for example – are just dancing to the radio all day and just being gone on that, they're not going to worry about any of the problems.

'If we had realised a long time ago that it was necessary to do our own thing, then we should have been promoting it ourselves. But even when I started in music, I didn't want to do anything but create music. That's what I'm here for and that's what I was born for, but I have to be concerned with other things now. I'm still concerned with creating music but I'm also concerned about the direction of it and how it's handled. Before, the musicians depended on the promoter to take care of that.'

Harper is one of the musicians who recognise that there is an audience and a market for the new music that is not always accessible or catered to through conventional channels. 'There are always Blacks who know about the music but it's hard to get it to them. Some Black people do not realise the importance of this music … They're being brainwashed with all that stuff that's on the radio.

'Some of the musicians in contemporary Black music *say* on their horns that conditions are not right here – not verbally, but sometimes it comes through that the situation is not right. But there really is a total brainwash. I certainly don't think that Archie Shepp could play at the Apollo! The people who go there are programmed for a certain kind of music and that's all they can hear, that's all they can accept.'

To Billy Higgins, the drummer, it is the same story. 'If you keep telling somebody "This is what's happening", they really begin to believe it. It's like computers, they have us programmed whether we know it or not. You hear it in your sleep, you go to a club and after the set is over they turn the jukebox on … Young kids are talking about "Yeah, this is it!" They don't even know three notes. They get the bass and learn some blues and this is it …

'Take somebody slick as Miles Davis. They wired him up with all that electricity and shit only because that's what the media demanded. The sound – that was the "in" sound – but that's what stops you from having leaders and innovators, you understand? I feel sorry for the young kids now, they don't have nothing to look forward to. I asked a little kid on my block, I said, "What's your favourite instrument?" He said he wanted to play bass, but he doesn't even know what a bass-fiddle looks like. He's playing the Fender bass. I asked him about the upright bass and he didn't even know what it was. Every place you go, they're telling you 'bout "Soul music" or "rock-and-roll". But that shit is *old*. Black people been doing that shit for nine generations – just to stop from being bored. They used it as a tool to stop from going crazy.'

Don Pullen, the pianist who has reached his widest audience through his work with Charles Mingus, says: 'Everybody is not [just] a finger-popper and quite a few people dig the music. They have the records of many different artists, but when they go out, the tenor sax and organ groups are there and that's what they are presented. If you give them a chance to come to concerts, to see somebody they'd like to see, they go and get their tickets. But you have to do it yourself because not too many people want to take the chance; they don't think it will work.'[3]

* * *

In the past musicians practised a bar camaraderie but tended to be secretive about their work. They would keep news of their activities from each other so that there was no chance of losing a personal contact in the employment field. This 'gigging' mentality can be found today among musicians who lack the community spirit, but things are changing towards more collective thinking. Whenever Archie Shepp has a record date now, for example, he also drafts a number of stray musicians into the studio, some of whom are little-known, some of whom have fallen on hard times. Sometimes their contribution to the music is useful, often their part could just as easily have been played by a member of his regular band. The point is that the musician picks up a cheque for a session fee, though ultimately, the money comes out of the leader's pocket and not the record company's profits, as it is the leader who bears all the expenses on a recording date. A similar situation occurred in Paris in 1969 when BYG recorded all the Americans assembled en route to play at the Amougies Jazz and Pop festival held in Belgium. Sunny Murray, Clifford Thornton and others added hordes of other musicians to their sessions, and Shepp even included a couple of older musicians, temporarily domiciled in Paris, who – at the time – avowedly disliked most avant-garde music.

This is just one way in which the music world has been aligning itself with what Milford Graves calls 'socialism'. It is inspired by the recognition of the fact that in music, as in life, dividing the people weakens them and effectively lessens their contribution. This is not to imply that erstwhile bands were artistically weak, but there existed in jazz, and still does – to a degree – very much a 'star' versus 'sideman' syndrome. 'The ego thing, that's always been the problem with musicians,' said Billy Harper. 'There's always been the separation so that musicians – *and* other Blacks – have the thing about, "I'm the Greatest", "This is number one and that is number two." And that's silly. "You're number three so don't speak to me!" But what is this? Everybody here is trying to create music – you dig? And somebody's talking about "I had a hard time making it so you make it the way you can", the usual type of thing. And that's the way it was when I got to New York.'

The spirit of competition has always been strong in the music and is spurred on by such quaint ideas as polls in which readers and/or critics vote for their 'favourite performer'. The winners are often thereafter identified as being 'the best' on their instruments, an accolade that considerably helps their chances of employment in the subsequent months, especially in the recording field. It also leads to the possibility of the instrument companies asking them to endorse their products and being given a free instrument for doing so. There is also a system where critics award 'stars' to the records they review, their number depending on the alleged merit of the performance. To Archie Shepp, this reduces the artist to the status of a racehorse: 'I mean, did you ever see Rubinstein awarded stars for a performance? Bach wasn't no threat to Beethoven and they're both great – right? Nobody says who gets five stars. It's a way of treating Black culture which is discriminatory and divisive because it always creates competitiveness on the very jivest, lowest level.'*

Not everyone feels this way, of course. Noah Howard said: 'When you're a child, if you're good, your mother gives you a cookie. The artist is no exception. When he receives an award it makes him feel somebody out there appreciates what he's doing.'

Whether the competitiveness of the past hurt the music or was a necessary part of its history is debatable. As the musicians began to recognise the destructiveness of superimposed orders of merit, a number of groups adopted a co-operative policy. There had been co-operatives in the past – the Modern Jazz Quartet is an obvious example – but in the new music, one of the first was Music Inc., a quartet co-led originally by trumpeter Charles Tolliver and pianist Stanley Cowell. Others based in New York include Abdullah, the Melodic Art-tet, the Aboriginal Music Society, and

---

* It is, incidentally, not only Black musicians who feel this way. In the London *Sunday Times* in December 1973, the British writer John Berger explained his reason for giving fifty per cent of his Booker prize for Best Novel to the Black Panther Party: 'The whole emphasis on winners and losers is false and out of place in the context of literature.'

the Revolutionary Ensemble. In Chicago there are the many units from the AACM, among them the Third World, the Art Ensemble of Chicago, Air and the Light. St Louis' Black Artists Group had a membership of between twenty-five and thirty musicians at one time, as well as singers, poets, dancers and visual artists. BAG and the Human Arts Association nurtured groups like the Solidarity Unit and Children of the Sun. (Sadly, BAG exists now only on a spiritual level. Its members continue to work together and exchange ideas, but the demise of the group was hastened by the collapse of their funding programme, which coincided with the departure for Europe of their five leading members. Unlike the AACM, the younger members proved insufficiently mature to carry on the aims of BAG.)

Leroy Jenkins, violinist with the Revolutionary Ensemble, explained that co-operatives were often formed to dispose of the 'sideman' image. 'It takes a lot of the load off you. A leader has a lot of extra work and the other guys sit back and get all the benefits of his work. The leader also becomes a father complex and a lot of leaders just don't want to be a father.'

'We're opening up a lot of avenues for cats,' said Sirone, the group's bassist. 'I feel that if we can build up this rapport within ourselves to be wholly dependent on ourselves, then we really don't need anybody else. It's a simple matter – guys got to think first of all that the music is everything, and from the music, everything else happens.'

In the past, the average musician who sought to 'make it' would welcome personal publicity; now it is common for some groups to insist on being interviewed only as a unit. If they share responsibility for decisions about the music and where and how it should be presented, so they want to exercise some control over what appears in print. And some artists refuse to be interviewed at all.

A few have been so discouraged by their failure to find employment that, faced with the success gained by others apparently through personal publicity in the jazz press, they insist on payment in exchange for an interview. They are roundly condemned for this attitude by trumpeter/trombonist Clifford Thornton. To Thornton, these musicians are the same people who, when offered a job or a recording date, quote a price so high that the offer has to be withdrawn. 'I know some cats around here, they're always crying in their beer saying, "They never talk about me in the magazines," so there must be a great conspiracy; some mythological "they" is really at work to "block my shit" – right? But at the same time, when somebody comes along who is maybe in a position to shed some light on their situation – or is just curious about them – they will say, "Well, how much money you got in your pocket?" Like they are so *important* and so crucial to life's going on or to the sun rising tomorrow, that in order for you to approach them you've got to pay them! I mean, now isn't that ridiculous?

'[This type] doesn't understand that his enemy is not the person who is trying to write, because that's an important function in the sense that it communicates. His enemies might be the publisher, but he can't even relate to the writer as an artist. Nobody has talent but him, and nobody's important but him – these are strange attitudes. They have to be called counter-revolutionary because no change is going to be effected if we walk around with shit like that in our heads!'

Not everyone is confident that co-operatives are the answer to the problems facing the creative artist involved in Black music. Ted Daniel feels that their popularity depends on the economic situation of the members. 'If, for some reason, a whole lot of money gets poured into their colony, I think maybe the collective hit would disintegrate. Not necessarily, but I think people would tend to approach the music more or less as individuals. What did Blakey say? "The group that stays together plays together"? That's so true. We come and go so fast, man, especially in New York. You play with one group this time and next time the group hits there's fifteen other cats in the band! And you don't get a chance to establish a rapport and a really good band sound. You get good music, but take a band like 'Trane's – that was a unique sound. That was a band that had been established over a period of years.'

Lee Morgan and Billy Higgins came out of the 'star' syndrome – both were voted 'New Star' on their instruments in *Down Beat* – but through the doctrine of collectivism, their political attitudes were changed in varying degrees. Higgins outlined what he saw as the benefits of a co-operative: 'With a band that is not so much a *leader* band, but where you can get some cats that are cool enough so that everybody can make some money, each individual feels more like putting out. The Modern Jazz Quartet has been very beautiful for that, for the reason that everybody has been able to cash in on it. Those cats have got homes, they've been able to make a nice living plus play together. If there would be more of that I know that it would really be beautiful. I know I made records with this cat and that cat, and played with this cat and that cat – cats get famous and make money out of this and money out of that. You're a sideman and you don't get nothing. A lot of times you're not even given the recognition, but that's the way the business is and it really makes people go around feeling like they're "stars".'

To Hakim Jami it depends on the individual as to whether he would be satisfied with making a contribution to the music while remaining an 'unknown', though as he pointed out, there is strong economic pressure connected with recognition. 'I don't care if nobody don't know me as long as I'm comfortable in doing what I want to do. I'm straight once I reach that point. I'm not saying I've reached that now because, you dig, I'm living on a fifth-floor walk-up, but I guess when you think in terms of how much money you can demand, you got to have a certain amount of recognition because if you don't have it, people won't pay you any money to play. It's the "who are *you?*" scene. So it ain't so much the cat wanting *per se* recognition, but in terms of business it's sometimes a necessity to have a certain amount of publicity. It's a business – this is the whole thing that sometimes keeps the musicians held back. The businessmen are doing the thing so they can get the money, and a lot of the time they give the recognition to who they want to.'

Andrew Cyrille is proud of the fact that he has managed to make a living out of music alone. He recognises the need for a certain kind of personal organisation – 'I just try to keep my head levelled and my nose clean and walk the straight and narrow' – just as he recognises that it is necessary for Black musicians to think collectively about their own culture because whites will always, on the whole, identify with other whites.

He puts the blame at the doors of the Black community as a whole, not just the musicians. One solution Cyrille envisages would be for the community to encourage their 'artists-in-residence' to express their music and help provide the means whereby they can make an adequate living. 'It's still the case that Black people produce and white people package. We are more or less like a race of consumer employees. Now, because there seems to be a more concerted move towards education in this generation and the next, maybe cats will begin to think about business, to think about opening collective shops or producing records. It's the same thing with writers – we have writers but we don't have any Black publishing companies. And you don't even have Black people selling musical instruments, really.'

* * *

Traditionally, the musician has always waited for the phone to ring. He always knew that the audience was there, that was not the problem; it was the promoters who had to be convinced. It was a tiring system and eventually they started to realise that the only way they could control the situation was by organising their own activities. Max Roach and Randy Weston had had limited success with a musicians' organisation back in the 'fifties, but with the Jazz Composers Guild Bill Dixon had shown that it was possible for even the most anarchistic to come together and work for a mutual goal. During the 1960s, sessions held in lofts owned by musicians, painters and others were common. The audiences were small and very little money was involved, but the new music was being propagated. 'I know at that period everybody felt as though something new was forming,' said Milford Graves. 'It was like a revolution in the music and people felt, well, a lot of people won't understand what we're doing, voters won't help us or record companies – we're trying to get a listening audience.'

Gradually, too, the far-sighted musicians began hiring halls and putting on their own concerts. Judson (later Cami) Hall, across the street from Carnegie Hall, was a popular venue. Few musicians were in a position to turn down gigs, but by preference they had become less interested in working in clubs. 'Clubs have the atmosphere of a "gig"' – Sirone voiced an opinion shared by many. 'Not when Ornette plays a club nor when John played – you'd go there each night but each night was different. But six nights a week – that's slave trade. That's like putting some kind of helmet on your head and screwing it on as tight as you possibly can and saying, "Now, play beautiful music."'

In 1972, George Wein moved the Newport Jazz Festival to New York and received so much press coverage about the profit he was or was not making that one sometimes wondered where the actual creative artists came into the picture. 'The Newport Festival was supposed to be a medium for all the talent in New York, but some of them really were relics. The music was misrepresented, and it's insulting in a sense that they would decide what music to present and what to ignore.' Sam Rivers, tenor saxophonist, Professor in the African-American Music Department at Connecticut's Wesleyan University, late of the Cecil Taylor group and veteran of many other name bands – among them Miles Davis – was one of the prime movers in organising the counter-festival that ran concurrently with Wein's. 'The abundance of talent in New York as far as musicians are concerned is almost inexhaustible. To have the situation narrowed down to a few names is good for the businessman because in that way, the greater his control. And actually, those musicians who appeared at the Festival aren't all as good as the other musicians who aren't exposed.'

The main workhorses and catalysts for the first New York Musicians Festival were trumpeter James Dubois, Director of Studio We, a musicians' co-operative venture, and Juma Sultan, a conga drummer who once worked with Jimi Hendrix's Band of Gypsies, and is the driving force behind the Aboriginal Music Society, a band that originally used only non-Western and handmade instruments. Rivers was living in a loft near the Bowery and opened it as one of the Festival locations and gave it the name of Studio Rivbea. (Later Rivers received a grant from the New York State Council on the Arts which has enabled him to present concerts and workshops nightly at the loft.) The point of the counter-festival was not to compete with Wein on a commercial level, but to take advantage of the presence of visitors in town – many of them from overseas – and expose the music.

Nevertheless, the urgent need for even more concentrated collective action was made abundantly clear in 1974 when the young musicians, who had relied to a great degree on their continuing summertime employment in the New York parks, found themselves abruptly back in the streets. Displaying none of the magnanimity of the previous year, when he had provided a series of 'token 'concerts featuring the younger musicians, Wein managed to divert the financing of the Parks Department and the NY State Council on the Arts and apply it to his own programme. The difference was that at his *al fresco* concerts, only established artists were heard. For the most part, the formal Newport bill continued to groan under the weight of elderly performers and such 'jazz' artists as Diana Ross and Johnny Mathis.

It is hardly surprising that there has been a decline in the practice of playing together for the music's sake alone. There are some musicians who are always ready to play just for enjoyment, but for the majority, as they have seen their financial situation worsen in the face of the current economic crisis, they have also seen that of their commercially oriented counterparts improve. Understandably, their enthusiasm for the music is tempered with bitterness. In the loft days it was different; artists were concentrating on getting an idea across and not thinking of money. 'A lot of people stayed in with that particular movement in music and a lot have dropped out,' said Milford Graves. 'And the people that stayed in, they feel as though they have established themselves musically, that they have made their statements, and there's no more going out just for exposure. It's really survival now.'

The majority of musicians, though, are optimistic about the future in spite of the economic setbacks. Whatever the employment situation, said Andrew Cyrille, 'People are just going to be creative even if they have to get out on the streets like they used to do back in the washboard days. You just make the adjustment on how or where you are going to play.'

Notes

1 Reported in *Down Beat,* 15 October 1970.
2 Interview (untitled) with Chris Welch, in *Melody Maker,* 10 February 1973.
3 Interview by Bill Smith, 'Don Pullen', *Coda,* December 1970.

15

Recording – Getting the Music Out There

> There are some record companies in the States that have
> policies now of not recording any more Black musicians:
> 'Let's not record so many Black musicians, let's record
> somebody white who looks Black.' And that is really *out*.
>
> Billy Harper

Less than two years after the October Revolution of 1964, Milford
Graves and Don Pullen put out the first record on their own label.
Charles Mingus had done something similar in the 'fifties when
he joined forces with Miles Davis and Max Roach to issue their
product on Debut, but the company had been run more along
the lines of a commercial enterprise, while Sun Ra, recording on
Saturn as early as 1957, did not think in business terms and seldom
distributed his first pressings outside a close circle of friends and
the musicians' families. Graves and Pullen were the first musicians
to handle every facet of production themselves – transportation,
contracts, invoicing, and so on – establishing a precedent with
their appropriately named label, SRP (Self-Reliance Project).
(Mingus made another attempt in 1967 with a label available only
by mail order, but eventually sold the masters to an established
company.)

The covers of the original albums by the Pullen–Graves duo
in concert at Yale University were delicately hand-painted by the
drummer. While Graves was playing in Latin bands, Pullen often

occupied the piano chair in a combo led by alto saxophonist Charles Williams which worked the Long Island clubs and dances, and where, apparently, Cecil Taylor was a frequent visitor. Later they came together in a non-commercial setting, playing and recording with the multi-reedman Giuseppi Logan, and then as a duo. For *Nommo*, their second SRP release, Pullen contributed encouraging words in the liner-notes: 'Self-Reliance! The watchword of New musicians and artists determined to do for themselves. These musicians are now creating situations wherein those creative abilities, stagnant for so long because of repressive conditions, may now be fully realised.'[1]

By 1974 when Graves issued a third album, a series of percussion duets with Andrew Cyrille, many others had followed the lead set by him and Pullen. Whereas in the past the musician's main concerns were learning his instrument, maintaining an adequate standard on it and securing a gig, by the 1970s he had to familiarise himself with the whims of recording engineers, with sound-mixing, postal rates, packaging and the cost of vinyl. Unaccustomed as the artist had been to those considerations, whatever creative abilities that had remained undeveloped in the face of the shortsighted policies of the record companies were indeed starting to be more fully realised.

'It's not really about success, it's about owning your own product,' said Charles Tolliver, the trumpeter who has issued several albums on Strata-East, the label he co-founded in New York with pianist Stanley Cowell. 'We've been able to put out our own music knowing that we own it, and that any benefits that we reap from it will go back into making more music.'

In America, if a musician is to mean anything at all today, it is essential for him to have a record out. It is not for the sake of ego alone as some people seem to think, and as records by the new musicians still sell relatively poorly, it is not for the revenue. But it does give him some leverage with which to bargain, and it shows the rest of the world that he has reached a certain point in his career. Before the idea of self-help, this meant approaching record company executives or producers and asking for a date, often a humiliating process for the artist who knows he has something to offer yet whose 'product' means little or nothing to the company. Ted Daniel, who has taped his sextet in concert at Columbia University and released the music on his own Ujamaa label, recognised the problems facing the younger musician who wants to make his voice heard in this way.

'I feel that when you go to a record company and ask them, as an individual, "Would you record me?" you're putting yourself in a very vulnerable position. You don't have anything except for what you say you have. If you have a record company, a record, or a master tape, then that puts you in a completely different position from which to deal with someone.'

One of the main problems facing the musician in search of a contract (and precious few are available these days) is that the big companies, like the movie industry, are run by sales departments and lawyers who know little about art and care less. Even knowledgeable people in the companies are themselves restricted in what they can record and how far they can promote it; their own creative thinking is stifled by the demands of the sales department. Musicians have always had to take recording opportunities wherever and whenever they arose and, in recent years, this has been increasingly outside America. In France or Germany for example, although they would probably end up recording or selling an existing tape for a relatively small fee, at least the music would be heard outside their own immediate circle. As one man put it: 'If I had to wait here in this country to do something as good, I think that creative as (my) album was, I would never have done it. It would still be just inside me.'

In 1969, the French company BYG launched an unprecedented massive recording programme, taping scores of albums by Shepp, Murray, the Art Ensemble of Chicago, Grachan Moncur III, Clifford Thornton, Dave Burrell, Alan Silva, Frank Wright and others. Cecil Taylor was doing the round of the European festivals at the time, and two of his companions, Jimmy Lyons and Andrew Cyrille, were offered dates by the company. Cyrille seized the opportunity to record an amazing percussion album entitled *What About?* which features every imaginable aspect of the drumming art and was a veritable *tour de force*. Flushed with pride, Cyrille carried it back to the States and carted it round the major companies, relying on his creativity to be the incentive for the offer of a record date. He secured an audience with Columbia's John Hammond, millionaire brother-in-law of Benny Goodman and self-styled 'discoverer' of Billie Holiday and Count Basie, and placed *What About?* on the turntable. Hammond allowed it to revolve for a mere thirty seconds of its 46 minutes, 48 seconds' length before he lifted the arm and told Cyrille, 'The computer is not interested in creative drumming, it's interested in making money.' He also added that hardly any company in America would touch it with a ten-foot pole; yet, ironically, a couple of years later Columbia was all set to purchase the entire BYG catalogue, which would have included such allegedly non-commercial albums as Cyrille's. (The deal never went through because Columbia discovered at the last moment that not only did the older material being offered have a 'bootleg' origin, some of it was already their own copyright property!)

It is not only Black artists who have received this philistine treatment. Mike Mantler and Carla Bley, attempting to sell tapes of a concert by the Jazz Composers Orchestra, were told by the same producer: 'Don't be stupid – we're here to make money for the company. That shit's not going to sell.' Another producer refused to take any of their telephone calls, and Carla finally sent up a four-year-old boy carrying a sign saying 'Record Carla Bley!' in a desperate attempt to attract the company's attention.

There is little doubt that the record companies, while being prepared to subsidise classical music for prestige reasons, discriminate against Black and white artists who play jazz. For example,

Columbia once had a 'Young American Composers' series which they considered fell into the 'classical' category and was therefore justified; Ornette Coleman was signed to the same label yet they refused to put up the money for his symphonic work 'Skies of America', to be recorded by an American orchestra. Tired of waiting for the fulfilment of his project, Coleman decided to go to England to record the piece, in spite of the fact that Columbia actually have the New York Symphony Orchestra under contract. Coleman had to cross the Atlantic to save money for the company even though a new work was concerned, yet Columbia have no qualms about turning around and recording a Beethoven symphony for what must be the ninetieth time.

'The way I see it,' said Ted Daniel, 'the record companies had a choice in the early 'sixties. They could have gone in and developed the rock thing – which they did – or they could have developed the new music. And I think the new music was probably offensive to them, you know, the older people who were in established positions, and I think they more or less said, "Well, we'll just rock it up, we'll just go for the rock thing."'

The record companies have played an important part in the progress – or lack of it – of the music, as well as providing the sole means whereby it can be preserved for posterity. Art is still treated as 'product' by them if it is created by Black artists, yet it is still not promoted in the same way as other 'products' such as European music or rock. Jazz musicians are often recorded as a tax-deductible expense, yet even this is something that could be done more frequently. 'There really is a faction in America that would like to hold the music back,' declared Billy Harper. 'You know that if they can promote Tiny Tim, they can promote anything, but those who control it and who promote it, don't.'

There was, however, one company that at least gave the new music a chance to be heard. In 1965 the small independent ESP-Disk created a sensation with the release of three albums. Two of the artists, Byron Allen and Giuseppi Logan, were relatively obscure and remain so, the third was Albert Ayler. For six years from 1964 until he temporarily stopped recording, Bernard Stollman, a former New York lawyer, was to record just about every important musician in the avant-garde. His lists included Paul Bley, Ornette Coleman, Milford Graves, Henry Grimes, Noah Howard, Frank Wright, Sunny Murray, Sun Ra, Marion Brown, Marzette Watts, Burton Greene and the New York Art Quartet. Pharoah Sanders made his first date for ESP. It was Ayler who was indirectly responsible for the far-sightedness of the catalogue, for until Stollman heard him, he knew nothing about music, owned no record player – had never bought a record, in fact – and jazz was 'just a word'.

Stollman had worked on the Charlie Parker and Billie Holiday estates during the course of his legal career and, as a result, became Dizzy Gillespie's attorney. By word of mouth, other musicians became his clients, and it was one of them that led him to Harlem one cold Sunday afternoon. At the Baby Grand on 125th Street, the pianist was Elmo Hope and the bassist, according to Stollman, was Richard Davis (*he* says otherwise). Towards the end of the session, a small man with a black and white beard and wearing a leather suit jumped on stage with his saxophone and started to play. 'The cascades of sound were just magnificent,' recalled Stollman. 'The other musicians were awed, they just looked at him. Elmo Hope closed the lid of the piano and sat down in the audience to listen and "Davis" quietly laid his bass on its side and tiptoed off the stage. I knew that something very important was happening because of their reaction.'

Ayler played for twenty minutes for an audience of 'musicians' wives and sweethearts and a bemused bartender, polishing his glasses, trying very hard to, I guess, ignore the whole affair'. When Stollman was introduced to Ayler, he heard himself saying, 'I'm starting a record company – will you be my first artist?'

ESP's very first recording, *Spiritual Unity*, was made in a small mid-town studio that specialises in Latin 'demos'. Ayler arrived with two companions – 'A tall, very slender white American, very emaciated-looking, named Gary Peacock, and a large, corpulent jolly walrus who turned out to be Sunny Murray.' As soon as they started to play, the recording engineer fled the control room and did not return until the tape had almost run out. The engineer could not cope with the revolutionary sounds, but Stollman, unable to contain himself, broke into a dance. 'My God!' he exclaimed to Peacock's then wife Annette. 'What an auspicious beginning for a record label!' Two days later, he discovered that the tape had been made in monaural because the frightened engineer thought it was only intended for a demo.

Spiritual Unity was not released for a year because Stollman reasoned that the only way it would be known that ESP meant business was to launch it with a whole batch of albums. The way they were packaged was studiously funky. The label and liner-copy were in Esperanto as well as English, and the design on the reverse of *Spiritual Unity* revolved around what was loftily described as 'the symbol "Y" [which] predates recorded history and represents the rising spirit of man'. Of the three initial issues, Ayler's secured the most reaction. Criticism was confined to *Down Beat* and publications in Britain and France, and was mixed, but Stollman was exhilarated by the fact that 'his' artist had inspired 'such venom' in certain quarters.

During the six days of the October Revolution, Stollman was at the Cellar Café nightly. He heard Sun Ra there for the first time and invited all the participants to record. The albums were made under all sorts of conditions, in studios, at concerts, in people's living-rooms, but they shared one common factor – the course of events and presentation were dictated by the musicians themselves. Stollman had learnt his lesson when he suggested to Ayler that he record a single. 'He said hmm, perhaps something could be done, whereupon the group went into a two-minute song which taught me all I had to know about the subject – that I should damn well keep my hands to myself! He was deferential, he was respectful, but he communicated to me through that piece of music that I was really out of order. After that, I never asked a musician to cut anything short.' Unlike other companies, ESP will not release at a later date material rejected by the artist; Stollman makes a point of destroying such tapes. (The posthumous Ayler album *Prophecy* which ESP released in collaboration with the saxophonist's widow was prepared from tapes not originally recorded for the label.)

At first, the majority of the musicians were eager to record. When Coltrane played a New Year concert at the Village Gate, Frank Wright, whose parents were Mississippi sharecroppers and who had grown up in Cleveland with Ayler, sat in. Stollman approached him as he came off the stage and asked him if he would like to make an album. 'Would I? You bet I would!' was Wright's characteristic reply. But Stollman's popularity was short-lived.

Although he had planned a co-operative company with ESP financing what was essentially a co-production, none of the artists were actually paid other than a minute advance against royalties; and some did not even get this. They signed contracts to this effect but, naturally enough, they anticipated a speedy return in royalties. When this money was not rapidly forthcoming, there were a whole lot of angry musicians in New York. Once, when Sun Ra and his musicians were discussing the situation, someone ventured that there was no money involved in recording for ESP. Sun Ra's reply was: 'Well, he's the only one who records the music.' At the time, this was true, but as far as many of the new musicians were concerned, Bernard Stollman became simultaneously the most hated and most needed man in the recording industry.

It was inevitable that Stollman, with his shrewd knowledge of business practice, should become the whipping boy of frustrated musicians with an awareness of their talent. 'In a sense I could say he manipulated me because he was offering me something knowing that I didn't know what I was being offered,' said Noah Howard. 'But he gave me a contract when nobody else in America would have dreamed of doing so. He gave me a contract and I signed it – I *can* read. It wasn't what a musician should get for doing a record album but he didn't make any pretensions otherwise.'

There were some who refused to record for him, but they were few. As Sun Ra had perceptively noted, Stollman was the only person prepared to invest money in recording what was, in truth, an unknown quantity. And, for the jazz world at large, their introduction to Ayler, Graves, Sanders, Sun Ra and Murray came about through ESP, the label that, as part of its campaign to attract recognition, once pressed a record – Ayler's *Bells* – on one side of a piece of clear red plastic.

* * *

In contrast to the financial exigencies of the ESP operation and its grass-roots image, John Coltrane's recording career with ABC-Impulse was nothing short of amazing. In the five years up till his death, the saxophonist had a total of eighteen albums released on Impulse. From *Africa/Brass* to *Live at the Village Vanguard Again*, all were extravagantly packaged in a way that seemed to respectfully acknowledge his importance, all were recorded by the doyen of sound engineers, Rudy Van Gelder, and with the exception of the first named were all produced by Bob Thiele, who had been with the company for just one week when it was decided to record Coltrane 'live' at the Village Vanguard.

The saxophonist's relationship with Thiele was unique in two ways. First, they had an arrangement that whenever Coltrane wanted to record, Thiele would book studio time. This was despite the fact that his contract made no allowances for such freedom. Thiele would schedule the dates at night and 'face the music in the morning' when he presented the President with *a fait accompli*. In this way, Coltrane averaged four albums a year instead of the stipulated two, a process which has left Impulse with a substantial legacy of tapes they have been able to issue systematically since his death.

When Thiele left the company, he made copies of all the Coltrane tapes and gave them to his widow Alice. With her own studio facilities at her disposal, she has been able to listen carefully to all the material before deciding on what should be issued. *Cosmic Music* first appeared on Coltrane Records, the company formed by her, but more recent releases indicate that this venture has been partially swallowed up by Impulse again. Not all Alice Coltrane's decisions have met with the approval of the other musicians involved. Rashied Ali, on hearing the strings dubbed onto *Infinity*, where the bass of Charlie Haden was also added, said, 'It's like rewriting the Bible!'

The second unique aspect of the relationship between Coltrane and his producer was that whenever the saxophonist considered that a younger player was worthy of a hearing, he would approach Thiele and ask him to lend an ear. 'They'd call him [Coltrane] up twenty-four hours a day, crying to him on the phone about "somebody doing this – how come I can't do something like that?"' said Rashied Ali. 'And 'Trane was such a beautiful cat, he'd say, "Don't worry, man, I'll see what I can do." And he's got a lot of these cats a lot of these dates. They took 'em – and I'm going to tell you – they didn't make nothing. The record companies made all the money on them, man.'

It was through Coltrane's influence, though, that Albert Ayler, Marion Brown, Pharoah Sanders and Archie Shepp began their careers with Impulse. *Four for Trane*, the name of Shepp's first album for the label, expresses his feelings about the matter. Thiele, incidentally, was so excited during this particular late-night session that he telephoned Coltrane in the middle of it to urge him to hurry to the studio and listen to the tapes. The Master was in bed at the time, which explains his appearance on the cover photograph – wearing shoes, but no socks.

In spite of Thiele's initial raptures over working with Shepp, their good relationship did not continue. Thiele said of Coltrane, 'I honestly can't say if he was militant or if he hated me or didn't like me – the impression I had was the opposite, that he did enjoy working for me,' but he could not draw the same conclusions about Shepp and his militant stance. In spite of the tension that grew between them, several albums were made, but finally a point was reached where Thiele stopped a session three-quarters of the way through and told Shepp he could no longer work with him. 'I said, "You're under contract to the company, but they're going to have to get somebody else to work with you." I just couldn't make it, and that was strictly on the personal, social level. That was the problem, it wasn't about the music.

'The musicians feel that the record company stands for everything that's white and the producers are ripping off the Black musicians. They're always talking about how they would like to see the record companies owned by Black people, and one of my sarcastic remarks is, "Well, then, record for Motown," but the one Black company in the record business really doesn't record Black jazz music.'

Like Bernard Stollman, Bob Thiele became another target for the musicians' frustration and fury, though in his case he represented an even larger corporation in the shape of the massive American Broadcasting Corporation which controls ABC-Impulse. The unflattering reputation he earned is not confined to Black musicians, either. Charlie Haden fell out with him over the handling of the live recording of his *Liberation Music Orchestra*, a fine album which won awards in Europe and Japan and was instrumental in helping the bassist secure a Guggenheim fellowship for composition.

Thiele, who has been in the record industry for thirty years and had his own company for a while, presented his side of the story: 'The musician will meet you in a club or on the street and plead with you to record: "Gotta make records and you're the man to do it – you know my kind of music." So you lay it out in front, you say, "Look, I can't go for a lot of bread, I can pay you scale or a few bucks over scale – are you still interested?" And the guy says, "Man

– *anything*. Let's make the record." Usually, that artist is a new artist, someone that isn't that well-known. I do it because I believe in it, but after the record is made and it doesn't sell – because I don't have the resources to promote it and advertise it the way it possibly should be – then I become the villain again. The musician immediately turns round and says, "Well, this guy ripped me off. He's white – he took advantage of me." That's my side of it, yet I do understand how they figure it out.'

Until recently, the recording industry has expected the artist to leave all aspects of production and promotion to the company, but today performers in all sections of the music are more involved in doing their own mixing, editing and so forth. To Thiele's mind, the producer fulfils a particular function to which the artist is often oblivious. 'Sometimes the musician is into it *too* much to be objective. Coltrane, when I first started to work with him, was never satisfied with anything. He could spend all night recording one piece and slowly become more and more depressed. I think it's a producer's job to keep the spirits high. I think that one of the turning points in Coltrane's career was when I suggested the idea of doing the thing with Duke Ellington. I knew when the tape of "In a Sentimental Mood" ended that Duke was happy, but I knew that Coltrane wasn't. And I went out into the studio before he could say to Ellington, "Let's do it again." I said, "John, that was such a great performance," and I looked at Ellington and he said, "John, don't do it again. That's it." When Johnny Hodges heard it, he said it was the best reading of "In a Sentimental Mood" he had ever heard. Ellington told Coltrane, "When it happens it happens. Sometimes it could be ten takes, but when it *is* one, somehow you've got to recognise it."'

Thiele believes that given the money, it would theoretically be possible for a record company to promote an essentially non-commercial artist to the extent that he would be accepted by as wide an audience as that for, say, Freddie Hubbard, a jazz artist who achieves respectable record sales – providing that the artist in question has sufficient talent to come up with a continuing flow of good material. He stressed that the 'one-shot' artist with the single album has no hope of succeeding in the way that Sanders and Shepp have done. Even so, said Thiele, 'In many instances, the artist's notoriety develops more quickly than sales of his record. [This leads him to believe] that he's really greater than he is, and has more acceptance than he thinks he has.'

But the record companies are not prepared to put up the money to promote new Black music, they are only interested in records that stand to sell a million. This, combined with the racist system that apparently influences many decisions in the industry, has convinced many musicians that self-reliance projects are the best solution to the problem of achieving exposure. What is more, the musicians have never owned their own product – for example, they have until lately been compelled to use the recording company's publishing facilities for their compositions, although Coltrane, Shepp, Coleman and Sanders were amongst the first to form their own publishing companies. Even Thiele has said that one of the reasons why so few Black musicians are recording today is due, in part, to their distrust, 'their belief that the company is screwing them'.[2]

Such beliefs, engendered by the conditioning of four hundred years of slavery, are understandable but, dealing specifically with the record industry, they arise from actually proven instances of companies cheating the artist and from arrangements such as the one whereby the leader himself has always to pay all recording and production expenses – even when the company has its own studios he must pay to hire them – and all these charges are deducted from any possible profit the recording may earn in royalties. It is not uncommon for the artist, enquiring how his royalty statement stands, to be told that *he* owes money to the company because the album has not earned enough to pay back the advance he has received. The creative person finds these practices hard to relate to and so, he reasons now, why not go the whole way and do it yourself? 'I used to always scream about it,' said Rashied Ali. 'I'd say, "Why you do this, man, what's the point?" And they'd say, "I just want to get a record out." Some of the cats are still doing it, but I notice that it don't make them no money and they're no more known than me or other cats who haven't done that thing.'

With the leader paying for all production charges – studio hire, tapes, sidemen's fees, liner-notes, cover photographs, pressing, etc. – the company's expenditure is limited to the cost of promotion, administration and distribution. Until recently, sidemen were paid at a scale laid down by the union, the American Federation of Musicians. They are still rarely paid royalties, although a 'star' sideman can occasionally insist on a royalty payment. According to Rashied Ali, Coltrane was one of the people responsible for initiating this procedure. 'He said, like, "I want this cat to have ten per cent" or "I want that cat to have five per cent." Every six months or once a year I get a little money from Impulse, but 'Trane gave us a little more money than anybody else.' Doubtless this was because the saxophonist realised that his sidemen's contribution was worth far more than the minimum of 60 dollars paid for a three-hour session in 1965. Ten years later, scale had risen to a 95-dollar minimum, although some heavyweight sidemen can insist on more. (Richard Davis, for example, can earn double or 50% extra for any session when he feels it is necessary, but he is one of the most in-demand bassists in the music.)

In 1973 with the recording of Don Cherry's *Relativity Suite*, the Jazz Composers Orchestra Association arranged for each musician taking part to receive with the producers an equitable share (1.5%) of the total royalties. This system has been applied on subsequent occasions by the JCOA, which grew out of the Jazz Composers Guild and is partially funded by state and national grants. JCOA holds workshops conducted by composers like Cherry, Clifford Thornton, Roswell Rudd, Sam Rivers, Grachan Moncur III, Leroy Jenkins, Leo Smith and Dewey Redman which, in the cases of Cherry and Thornton, have actually been open rehearsals for their albums. JCOA has only held one actual concert, being unable to meet the expenses unless the work is to be recorded. The first of their own albums was of Mike Mantler's compositions, 'Preview' and 'Communications – Nos. 8, 9, 10 and 11', arranged by him and featuring soloists Cecil Taylor, Pharoah Sanders, Gato Barbieri, Don Cherry, Roswell Rudd and Larry Coryell, and the second was Carla Bley's opera, *Escalator Over the Hill*, whose production ran them deep into debt.

JCOA provide a distribution service, New Music Distribution Service, run at a financial loss, for most of the musicians' own labels, and has a reciprocal arrangement for distribution with individuals in Europe. In spite of these facilities, musicians continue to make their own tapes and sell them to any established company that can meet their price, but that such alternatives do exist, saves them from being forced into the exploitation/humiliation pattern that can confront the Black artist forced to deal with the established recording industry. This situation is best summed up by a story well known in the musicians' community: World Famous Jazz Musician is awarded a Gold Disc for exceeding a million record-sales on one of his albums. Famous Record Producer has this Gold Disc hanging on his office wall to show off to visitors, but WFJM is not aware of its existence because each time he visits the company, the producer takes down the Gold Disc and hides it away. One fateful day, however, WFJM turns up unexpectedly. Confusion reigns. 'Oh,' stammers FRP, 'I wanted this to be a surprise!'

It was, of course, always ever so in the industry. During Rex Stewart's lifetime, a writer asked another Famous Record Producer how many Fletcher Henderson records he had in his collection on which the former Ellington trumpet star played. 'As few as possible,' was the reply. Naturally, the writer sought an explanation from Stewart. 'Oh, he never did like me,' he said. 'He wanted me to be his nigger.'

Even back in the 'thirties, Rex Stewart was not prepared to fraternise with the white power structure representative in the way he demanded and enjoyed with other musicians. Stewart was an exceptional man in every way, but it has not always been possible for Black musicians to retain their pride in the cause of getting a record out. In the 'sixties, when Bill Dixon did some producing for Savoy, he was disgusted by some of the attitudes he came across. 'If I told you who the people were and how they kissed the white man's ass, you wouldn't believe it,' he said.

It has always been difficult for the Black musician to take a definite political stand, as Rex Stewart and the saxophonist Lucky Thompson discovered to their disadvantage. People talk politics in the office and on the assembly line and differences of opinion are tolerated, but in the music business, musicians are intimidated by their precarious position and the political wheeling and dealing involved in securing employment. When Lucky Thompson described the parasitic booking agents he was forced to deal with as 'vultures', none of the nightclubs would hire him. He was one of the leading saxophonists of the pre-Coltrane era, but because he spoke his mind, he had to go to Europe in order to work.

Milford Graves played with Albert Ayler at the 1967 Newport Festival and recorded with him, but he learned later from reliable sources that because of his political attitude, the saxophonist was told not to continue using him. 'When you come up and act like a man, I see you don't get that respect,' he said. 'I see that if people don't see they can manipulate you, then they have no use for you. I guess I wasn't *supposed* to be politically active, talking about musicians doing self-help programmes and recording themselves. I guess I was supposed to come up to the studio, shaking the A & R man's hand, shaking the President's hand and showing teeth like the real traditional thing.'

The desire to control one's own product has become very strong. Artists who, two or three years ago, would never have considered carrying a tape-machine on all their concerts are investing in recording equipment. Center of the World Productions, a publishing and production company formed by four musicians living in Paris – saxophonist Frank Wright, drummer Muhammad Ali, bassist Alan Silva and pianist Bobby Few – exists solely to tape their own music and license these tapes to other companies. Silva, who once headed a committee researching the record business for the Jazz Composers Guild, does most of the administration. He sees Center of the World's function as documentary rather than profit-making, an attitude which is psychologically mollifying in the face of the relatively small return they can expect for their product at the moment. The four musicians have little interest in forming a record company as such because of the amount of work involved, but they view taping all their five performances as a kind of invest-ment. Furthermore, they share the belief that 'live' recordings are more faithful to the emotional impact of their uncompromising brand of music. 'We feel the studio is not really our vehicle for work,' said Silva. 'We find that people in the room are constantly changing and this changes the character of the music.' Within a year, COTW could boast no less than five albums on the market: two by the Quartet, a Few trio, a Silva solo and an Ali/Wright duo.

It used to be thought unlikely that the musicians' own labels would be able to equal the distribution available to a major company, but since that potential has seldom been realised where any kind of creative Black music is concerned, there seemed to be nothing to lose. Strata-East, in fact, achieved major distribution for their product. By creating their own production and publishing companies, studying the legal aspects of publishing and copyright, building their own studios, and taking over every aspect of the recording process themselves, the musicians know that every penny profit is going to them. Publishing is an exceedingly important part of the recording operation, and the refusal of a label to sign an artist unless he agrees to use their affiliated publishing company has meant that label earning publishing royalties over and above their actual profits from the sale of records. For a long time few artists were aware of how to start their own publishing company. Now it is common for musicians to write their own liner-notes, shoot their own cover photographs and supply their own artwork. The records serve as an advertisement, and the system puts an end to the kind of humiliation an artist like Rashied Ali was once forced to experience.

The year was 1966 and *Coltrane Live at the Village Vanguard Again* had just appeared on Impulse. Rashied Ali, buoyant with satisfaction at his drumming on the album and his picture on the cover, made an appointment with a 'name' record producer. On arriving, he was told that the producer was out just as the man himself emerged simultaneously from his office. A confrontation ensued, which ended with the drummer being manhandled by two uniformed guards and the infuriated producer screaming, 'I'll see that you never get a record date, never, ever! I mean I'll see to it!' 'He said, "You might work as a sideman" – he couldn't help that because I was working with 'Trane at the time and there was nothing he could really do about that – "but I'll see *that you* don't do anything."'

And sure enough, when Art Blakey put forward his name to another company for a 'Drum Orgy' record at a roundtable conference planning the session, he was told: 'Uh-uh, that man has an attitude. You're going to have to use somebody else if you want to make this date with us.' To this date, Ali remains the only key Coltrane sideman who has never recorded with his own group for a major label. Pharoah Sanders, McCoy Tyner, Elvin Jones and Jimmy Garrison – not to mention Alice Coltrane – all have reaped the benefits of Coltrane's insistence that their talents be heard.

Ali started to record his own material and carried the tapes to various record companies. 'They were nutting on me – not because of the music but behind something else. There was a blackball thing going on down the line. Maybe they thought I was a "smart nigger" or something of that sense. I wasn't turned down flatly all the time, but it was like a prolonged kind of thing. It was like "now's not the time – unless you want to do something like this or that". Or they would say, "Oh, that's the stuff like Coltrane used to do, that's not what's happening any more! Everybody's into electronic music" – that was the trip they were running on me.'

After nearly ten years of being regarded as one of the leading percussionists in the music, Rashied Ali decided it was time he had a record out here. Two years previously, he would have been waiting for Impulse or Milestone to give him a call, but at the end of 1972 he walked downtown to City Hall and registered his own company. He called it Survival Records. Under the circumstances, the name was appropriate.

Notes

1   Notes for *Nommo* (SRP LP-290).
2   Interview with Bob Palmer, in *Coda*, June 1971.

16

Does the Music Have a Future?

We have to perform, this is our craft. We're not like a painter.
A painter can paint and have his pictures sell all over the world.
The performing artist is different, he must perform in order to
perfect his craft. The problems that musicians are having are based
upon society not accepting the whole craft of making music.

Alan Silva

'We're losing all our frontline players. I'm afraid that in five years' time we won't have any leaders left.' Sirone was bewailing the gap left in the musicians' street community by the men who have found sanctuary in the University. He sat in his apartment on East Thirteenth Street and shook his head sadly as he examined the shredded skin of his fingertips. Sirone had been playing so hard and so long that day that he had broken open the calluses that form on a bass player's fingers. At the time, he refused to use an amplified bridge pickup as most contemporary bassists do, preferring to retain as much as possible of the natural resonance of the wood of his instrument. So he had played too hard for too long and his ragged fingers were as painful as they looked, but at least he could reassure himself that he was doing what the jazz musician is supposed to do – playing music, not teaching.

Since the introduction of Black Studies, the American colleges have claimed a number of musicians as lecturers. The guaranteed income and the peaceful environment were very attractive to artists frustrated by the constant rejection of their wares, regardless of whether the academic life had been a part of their original plan. Bill Dixon was the first to turn his back on the uncertainty of the streets. His departure had nothing to do with the creation of Black Studies departments, for he was already known in academic circles as a teacher of art history, and when he added music, his campus was that of the elegant – and predominantly white – academy at Bennington, Vermont.

Cecil Taylor joined the music faculty as the University of Madison, Wisconsin, in 1970 but left under a cloud when he failed a considerable number of his first-year students. This did not prevent him from being immediately welcomed with open arms at Antioch in Yellow Springs, Ohio, where in a totally unprecedented situation, he was able to take the other members of his group with him as Artists-in-Residence for two academic years. For Jimmy Lyons, who once laboured in a Chicago copper-mill to support his family, this was the first chance he had ever had to relax. At the age of forty, he was able to start working on some music of his own. Andrew Cyrille, the adaptable percussionist who had always been able to play with anyone worthwhile, was no longer subjected to the tyranny of the telephone. For Taylor himself, who had lived for too long with the constant refusal of practising musicians to play his music, the professorship was a dream. Not only could he coach an enthusiastic bunch of students through his compositions with the benefit of unlimited rehearsals, but in the tradition of the 'legitimate' composer, he could limit the performance of these works to not more than, say, twice yearly. At the same time, he could continue to play concerts with his own group.

Yusef Lateef, Charles Mingus, Archie Shepp, Milford Graves, Art Davis, Max Roach, Andrew Hill, Clifford Thornton, Jackie McLean, David Baker, Donald Byrd, Nathan Davis and Ken McIntyre are amongst the other musicians who have held positions of varying permanence in American colleges and universities. In 1973, the Art Ensemble of Chicago visited Michigan State

University as Artists-in-Residence, but Taylor was the first to actually secure employment for his group in a longterm academic situation.

In the case of Clifford Thornton, who had had previous experience of teaching in the music school attached to LeRoi Jones's Black Arts Repertory Theater, once he was well established in the African-American Music Department at Wesleyan University in Connecticut, he used the authority of his position to improve the condition of the street musician. He made arrangements for Ed Blackwell, Jimmy Garrison, Sam Rivers and pianist Freddie Simmons to join the faculty as Visiting Artists alongside people like the Nigerian 'straight' composer Fela Sowande, and the Indian classical musician Ram Nayaran. For someone like Blackwell, who had never visualised teaching in the formal sense, the post was a challenge to which he proved more than equal. Despite the way he was revered in musical circles, though, it was necessary for an academic like Thornton to recommend him. The University powers-that-be left to their own devices would never have sought out an Ed Blackwell or a Jimmy Garrison, but through his insistence on their inclusion, Thornton demonstrated three ways that an inside ally can use the Establishment to ensure that the music actually has a future. One, by providing a decent salary for the practising musician; two, by raising his self-respect through the creation of a university role for him; three, by making his unique knowledge available to students who still know too little about their musical heritage. Furthermore, musicians who had initially been frightened at the prospect of facing a classroom of questioning students often found themselves appreciating their *own* music a little better when compelled to analyse it.

For the artist whose work is not commercially viable to find himself surrounded by respectful students would appear to be the ideal solution to the erstwhile struggle. For the first time, too, there is the lure of a decent salary, yet where some musicians are concerned, the flight to the university is the complete antithesis of what the creative artist is meant to do. Bill Dixon himself, who is totally cynical about the teaching qualifications of some of the musicians, is sure that most of them would prefer to continue being active in their traditional, if insecure, environment. 'Very few cats have realised that teaching is probably the most honourable profession there is because you're dealing with people's minds, but if you're not working first-class clubs or first-class festivals [they feel] you aren't doing the thing where you're being the most musicianly, that you aren't really an artist or musician.'

His cynicism stems from the time he organised a music programme for New York's University of the Streets. He successfully secured a grant of a quarter of a million dollars for the University, mainly through the merits of his own teaching programme, but when he invited other musicians to participate, they were suspicious of his intentions. 'I used to ask cats to come over and teach, but they'd want to party. They didn't want anything to do with it.'

While Sirone deplored the departure of so many first-rank players, Dixon disputed their right to be described as 'leaders'. 'I don't know if we have any leaders of any persuasion. We either consider a leader as someone the newspapers elect or someone we see ourselves before anyone determines that this person is a leader. This guy is talking about all the ones who have been named "stars" who are now being offered positions in places, but what these places are doing is dealing with the musicians who have gotten the most copy.'

Although Archie Shepp might appear to be one of the more obvious targets for such remarks, he himself considered that Black Studies or any Third World incursions into the University are essentially based on personalities, and as a result their credibility is bound to be in question. 'Anybody knows that in order to establish a department at a University, you have to deal with a school of thought. That's why you have a College of Music or a whole College of History or Social Sciences. But this way, it seems to me, they try to get an outstanding individual, perhaps LeRoi Jones, Ed

Bullins, Charles Mingus – or even Archie Shepp – and that seems to me like a thinly disguised form of tokenism.'

Like Bullins and Jones, Shepp has been active in the theatre, with his plays, *Junebug Graduates Tonight* and *The Communist*. In 1972, he taught a course in play writing at the University of Buffalo while holding the post of Consultant in Music. The following year he was lecturing at Amherst in Massachusetts. 'What it seems to me that everyone in this country is reluctant to do is to admit that people like John Coltrane or Charlie Parker or Lester Young are monoliths, that they are, in fact, gurus. They are schools in themselves and one day, in order for a youngster to really learn jazz in that kind of pedagogical way, he'd have to go through all the schools of thought. I mean he'd have to explore Sidney Bechet, he'd have to know Fletcher Henderson, Jimmy Lunceford – he'd have to know his entire history.'

Shepp's reference to Coltrane, Parker and Young as 'schools' was made in an abstract sense, yet he himself, like Coltrane in his lifetime, is a guru in actuality. Before he started teaching, his home was always full of young – and not-so-young – musicians, seeking his help and advice. They drew on his personal philosophy as much as his political analysis and his street training. Now, his wisdom and experience are not so readily accessible at grassroots level where they are needed.

On one occasion Shepp was faced with a roomful of students who were familiar with Pharoah Sanders's records but not with the masterworks of John Coltrane. He was momentarily taken aback when he realised that he was himself some four years older than Sanders and at this rate, his own contribution was well on the way to being overlooked. The gap between Shepp and his students could easily be resolved by academic application; not so easily filled was the gap he left in the musicians' community on moving from 27 Cooper Square. In his case, at least, Sirone was right.

The University is not the only place where the practising musician's skills and experience can be utilised. For some time now, people like Charles Tyler, the alto saxophonist who recorded for ESP on his own and with Albert Ayler, and the former Ornette Coleman sidemen Charles Moffett and Bobby Bradford, have been teaching in High Schools. There are any number of other community projects where the musician's specialised knowledge is valuable. Now that teaching is being done by Blacks versed in the new music and jealously aware of their heritage, young people are coming to look at Black music as something other than barroom entertainment. As recently as 1969, David Baker, director of the jazz programme at Indiana University, was stressing the need for Black teachers to be more concerned with their own music instead of being sidetracked by 'the notion [of getting] on with something respectable.'[1] At Indiana, he put this into practice with four courses that included jazz history, folklore, the contribution of Black 'legitimate' composers and the effect of Black musicians and composers on the music of cultures in other parts of America. Baker was himself a trombonist who worked with people like Dizzy Gillespie until a road accident broke his jaw. He switched to the 'cello and the classroom, but it is no coincidence that as in his own case, when the kind of teachers he spoke of began to emerge, many of them were recruited from the ranks of practising musicians. They knew the rigours of creating an art form in a nightclub far better than the middle-class teachers who had been the norm, and as a result, they are bound to make sure that credit is given where it is long overdue.

Andrew Cyrille, for example, who has lectured about the drum in a variety of teaching situations, will see to it that his own instrument will never again be taken for granted as it was when music was taught from a European perspective. It is up to the new teachers, too, to ensure that no one ever again refers to a group of instrumentalists as 'sixteen musicians and a drummer', or automatically hands the drumsticks to the one kid in the class who is slow to grasp music notation.

David Baker is dedicated to teaching the importance of

participation rather than stunning success. 'We want to get to the point where every Black cat won't have to be the cookingest dude going.' He quoted the actor Bill Cosby: 'Black artists want the opportunity even if it's to fail.'[2]

A young trumpet player, travelling in Greenville, Mississippi, was approached by an older musician who demanded his horn: 'Let me show you how to get that note down there, boy!' Frank Lowe, relating the story secondhand, pointed out that there is a full octave in the lower register of the trumpet that has been overlooked. 'It seems it's something that the older musicians did but at some point they stopped. They don't teach it in school, so how are they going to learn it?' It is obvious that there are many such skills that have vanished, but as the situation changes, it may well be that, as Shepp indirectly suggested, surviving crafts and techniques will become a part of the curriculum.

* * *

As the record companies have demonstrated their lack of interest in promoting the new Black music, and the media, including some sections of the so-called jazz press, have done their best to ignore it, the musicians themselves have begun to realise that if the music is to have a future, then they have to be more than artists. In all probability, then, this future lies in self-reliance programmes, and in individual and group activities sustained from outside by financial contributions in the form of grants. It is also dependent to a large extent on the support of the Black community. While it is true to say that the Harlems of the USA were not eager to jump up and embrace experimental music at first, the musicians and other community leaders have begun an educational plan at grassroots level with a heavy emphasis on cultural pride. The result is that a fair percentage of the people who might have been expected to turn their backs on the new music, preferring what the radio had to offer, are now eager to learn what is going on. A stroll through

Harlem or New York's Lower East Side will reveal walls and door-ways plastered with any number of handbills advertising activities in which the music plays a part, and it is no longer unusual to run across a 'name' musician with a bunch of students in tow. The Art Ensemble of Chicago claimed they missed the 'stimulation of the ghetto' during an extended sojourn in Europe, and indeed it is not a cliché to say that the inner-city areas are constantly throb-bing with sound. The concert hall still represents the ultimate goal for some, but there are many who would like to see the music nourish and itself, in turn, be nourished by, the Black community. Milford Graves has been one of the more successful when it comes to taking the new music into the community. This is because he adopts a sensible approach to the art form. For example, whenever he plays Uptown (Harlem), his childhood friend Sahumba brings along his conga-drums. 'I've seen so many musicians defeat them-selves when they go into the Black community to play. Number one, the music in the Black community is the foot-patting and snapping-the-fingers thing. And you must realise this. There are four things you can do: One, you can go into the community and compromise, play their thing. Number two, you can go in there and you can just go *out* on them. Number three, *don't* go in there! And number four, you can go in there, understand what it is, and kind of build up and bring them into a thing. Or you can realise what they dig and have that as an underlying statement, but don't have it so pronounced. It has to be well camouflaged, but if you start off like that, before they know it, they're into *your* thing!'

One of the first anti-poverty programmes in New York was the University of the Streets started on Avenue A in 1967 by a Puerto Rican group known as the Real Great Society. Later, when a radical change took place among the people who had thought themselves too hip and worldly to stand behind a desk, Andrew Hill, the pianist, took over the music programme started there by Bill Dixon. The nightclubs were closing down, too, and any oppor-tunity to earn a living could not be overlooked. Jimmy Lyons and

Jackie McLean were amongst those who worked with the narcotics rehabilitation programmes which included music classes as a positive way of re-channelling the energies of addicts, several of whom were musicians themselves. Lyons, whose employment by the Narcotics Addiction Control Commission at the Cooper Community Based Center came about, incidentally, through the auspices of McLean, found himself accorded as much respect or more respect as anyone involved with the programme. 'Addicts seem to have a deep respect for musicians. If they know you're a musician, they will never try to hurt you like they'd do to the ordinary person if they're uptight. I'd hear all their complaints. Being a musician, I guess they realise that it's not the first time I've come into contact with drug addicts; some of them even think that I use myself.'

At the same time, concerts were held in various prisons where the majority of inmates are Black. Archie Shepp played at Attica shortly after the tragic uprising and massacre there, and the following year, Andrew Hill and Art Lewis combined forces for a tour of the State's penal institutions.

The Black musician's position has been bettered by the interest in the Black community that has been shown by outside bodies. Whatever their motives, whether they act from guilt or fear or whether the situation has come about purely as a result of extensive Black lobbying, the music has at least taken on some status as art outside the relatively small world of musicians, critics and enthusiasts. Financial assistance in the form of grants is now available to individuals and organisations involved with so-called jazz. On an individual level, there are the Guggenheim Foundation's coveted Fellowships, which are worth around ten thousand dollars to a composer and have so far been awarded to Ornette Coleman, Charles Mingus, Charlie Haden and George Russell. Before jazz musicians were eligible for such awards – or discovered how to present their case in order to be considered – the only Black musicians who secured grants were those who played 'legitimate' European music. Some years previously, Cecil Taylor had named

Sunny Murray and Milford Graves as worthy candidates for the economic security offered by a grant. 'Can you imagine what that would do for the young cats, if they started doing that?' he asked A. B. Spellman. 'But Sunny Murray is an innovator, and he doesn't own his own set of drums. He doesn't have an instrument, I don't have an instrument.'³ In 1973, however, Taylor himself received a Guggenheim and put out two records on his own label.

It was in the shape of the National Endowment for the Arts that the United States Government finally decided it was time to support the country's only indigenous art form. Under their Jazz/Folk/Ethnic music programme, grants in the jazz field were inaugurated in 1970. The recipients included composers and arrangers writing new works or with works in progress, and amongst the first were Billy Harper, Lee Konitz, Grachan Moncur III, the JCOA and the late Kenny Dorham. Grants were also available to musicians who wanted to study or tour with professional jazz artists, and in another category, an award was made for a drummer to provide free instruction and tuition to underprivileged children in New York City. The National Endowment's grants are quite small, in the neighbourhood of one thousand dollars for composers, and like the others, are available only for composition or writing a method book. Ed Blackwell is an example of a recipient of money for the latter purpose.

In most cases, though, the onus is on the artist to produce a work for community consumption. 'Things have opened up,' said Earl Cross. 'If I get the right things together on paper, I can apply for a grant – supposedly to present something *to* the community. Whatever the community is, I have to present something to the *people*.' In the mid-seventies, nearly all the musicians were busily doing their best to get the right things together on paper.

In the past, grants had been available only to composers; instrumentalists did not consider for a moment that they qualified. The money has always been there, but even during the days of the Jazz Composers Guild the musicians remained in ignorance of their eligibility. Mike Mantler was actually one of the first to research the possibility of seeking finance from outside. He could see the advantages of being supported by individuals who did not treat the music as an investment and expect an immediate return in hard cash. Musicians who had always looked to the nightclubs as a means of survival started to realise that asking for grants was a frequently more expedient course than demanding an adequate wage from the evil club-owner. Initially, though, as far as Black artists were concerned, the mechanics of applying were totally foreign. Hakim Jami explained the predicament that has always afflicted the Black artist in his dealings with white society: 'Most cats have spent so much time learning to play the music that they didn't have time to go to business school. Now musicians have had an opportunity to do a little more studying. This gives us a little more power in dealing with people because we know what they're talking about, we know their language better. I think now we understand their language better than they do ours. We've still got a language-barrier problem – you know, speaking the King's English is not the way it is here. They might hear me say a certain thing, but the way it's being said might come out from like Avenue B or Twelfth Street – or Watts. It's a different language.'

David Baker has pointed out the inequity of the Black musician being accepted as a performer for years but not, until recently, as a composer. His reference was to composition in the legitimate sense, but with the newly acquired rationalisation of the improvising musician as composer and the understanding of what was actually meant by *curriculum vitae*, the musicians started to compile their achievements and stuff their lists into envelopes addressed wherever money was available. Even so, with millions of dollars being provided for activities arguably not as vital as Black music, it is hardly surprising that a number of people continue to feel, with Hakim Jami, that the establishment wants to recognise it but still does not want to give it that much credibility. They figure out a small amount of cats they can give help to and that makes it look like this is just one of the minor things happening. They say, "Oh, well, we'll just take a few of these guys who are *experimenting* and give 'em a little help.'" In other words, although the music is important enough to be publicised in every tourist brochure as America's only native art form, it is still not important enough to be subsidised to the same extent as ballet or opera.

* * *

Ajule Rutlin, poet, drummer and chairman of the Black Artists Group of St Louis, has written of the creative Black artist that they 'had to spend a majority of their time food-getting, hence the experiments and investigations were abandoned short of their goal, which was/is to find a way to re-establish the natural harmony of the Spiritual World which has been upset and polluted to the same degree as our physical world.'[4] He is not alone in this way of thinking. Many musicians who would like to be free to create and examine the spiritual and therapeutic effects of their music have been limited in how far they could go by the need to eat.

'It's money fucked the business up,' said Billy Higgins. 'Money and music have really got nothing in common. The whole reason behind music being played is like a spiritual healing type of thing. When you're paid to get up and play for so-and-so and so-and-so, well then you have to play a certain kind of music and it gets to be like vaudeville!'

Milford Graves holds workshops at his house where young musicians can not only examine the spiritual aspect of music but judge its effects on a scientific level. Graves considers that music can be used in a medical way to actually stimulate different parts of the body and even to heal, and to this end he has formed the Institute of Bio-Creative Intuitive Development in collaboration with his longtime associate Hugh Glover. They are engaged in researching the ways in which music can be used as a therapeutic means of assisting with physiological problems. At the same time Graves feels music may also have a place in agriculture. In many parts of Africa, after all, music is played to make the crops flourish.

To Graves, an individual with high moral principles, a musician is more than just someone who plays an instrument, he is in a unique position to understand life. 'Some people talk of freedom but they're playing what they *think* they should play. You can't go into freedom without conditioning yourself. If you've been living a certain way for twenty years and then all of a sudden you come out and say you want to be free, it doesn't work because you're fighting yourself. Really there's so much more involved internally that it's like being controlled by your subconscious self, deeper things of which you're not aware. When the musicians who can understand this type of freedom get together, we get a reward, but it's nothing you can analyse. It elevates you to maybe survive better in life.'

Since 1973, Graves has been teaching alongside Bill Dixon at Bennington College. There his most popular course deals with the Influence of Music. His students include people majoring in every subject from sculpture to medicine who come to hear him talk about the Medical Music of Asian and Indian Civilisations as well as the Application of African Body Rhythm. 'If you talk about "sounds" and "rhythms", you must understand *people*,' he said. 'If I talk about certain basic rhythmic developments, I'll talk about the heartbeat, and after I talk about the heartbeat, that automatically brings me into basic biology – circulation and things like that. And a discussion will go off from there about different kind of sicknesses and so on. People really begin to see that there's much more than just playing an instrument if you're a musician. So most people feel that they have been able to study their particular subject – whether it be architecture or sculpture – much *better* because their feelings, their whole rhythmic sense, has changed.'

Although Milford Graves's philosophy and teaching are admirable, not everyone has his strength of character. Generally speaking, economic survival has been the more immediate consideration, and for a number of musicians, regular commuting between Europe and America provided an answer. It was nothing new for American musicians to cross the Atlantic, there were plenty of expatriates living there, after all, and tours by 'name' groups had been going on for years, but the serious exodus started in 1969 when the news reached New York that BYG, the progressive French record company, were planning the Actuel Festival of Jazz, Rock and New Music. The bill was bursting with rock names, among them Frank Zappa, the Soft Machine and the Pink Floyd, but the word was out that if any of the avant-garde New Yorkers cared to pay their own way, there would be a place for them at the festival and, in all probability, a record date, also. For most of the musicians who could scrape the airfare together, there was nothing to lose.

New York was starting to foreclose on the new music that year, anyway. Noah Howard, the saxophonist, considered that it had been a good year for him, what with concerts at Town Hall and frequent gigs at Slug's, but he noticed an impending change. 'It was the height of the rock thing at the Fillmore East. I was living round the corner, and walking past there every night and seeing ten thousand kids standing outside, it was very depressing.' He had just met the tenor saxophonist Frank Wright, and they had decided to team up. Sunny Murray had already recorded for BYG in 1969 when he, Shepp, Grachan Moncur III, Clifford Thornton, bassists Alan Silva and Earl Freeman and others had played at the Pan-African Festival in Algiers and returned home by way of Paris. When Murray called Wright to say he was leaving for the Festival, Howard rounded up pianist Bobby Few and drummer Muhammad Ali, and joined Wright in the queue at the airlines.

The Festival was originally planned to take place at Les Halles in Paris, but the police were not exactly filled with brotherly love towards their youth so soon after the political events of 1968. They vetoed the city as the festival site altogether, and as it turned out the Actuel Festival actually took place in Belgium, inside a huge tent near the border town of Amougies. By all accounts, the listening conditions were pretty spartan, but the 75,000 who were drawn to the five days of concerts by the heavy rock names on the bill went home entranced by the music of people like Howard and Wright, Murray, Shepp, Steve Lacy, Joseph Jarman, Sirone, Ted Daniel, Earl Freeman, Ray Draper, Clifford Thornton, Grachan Moncur III, Dave Burrell, Leroy Jenkins, Don Cherry and so on. The Festival had been conceived courageously, if a trifle naively, but for several of the American musicians who took part, it represented the beginning of a new career. In spite of the chilly late October weather, there was plenty of enthusiasm for playing between the musicians. One jam set featured Frank Zappa sitting in with Shepp, Moncur and Freeman, as well as the veteran drummer Philly Joe Jones, and two phenomenal South Africans resident in England, bassist Johnny Dyani and drummer Louis Moholo.

Just as John Sinclair was to prove with the Ann Arbor Jazz and Blues Festivals that started two years later, the new music is totally acceptable to people who have never heard it before so long as it is not presented as 'jazz' (which implies something from an earlier generation) or treated as an esoteric refugee from the concert hall. Sinclair introduced Marion Brown and Leo Smith, the Art Ensemble of Chicago, Sanders, Shepp and Sun Ra to audiences who had come to hear Otis Rush and Muddy Waters; Frank Wright and Noah Howard tore the place up, although the people had gone to Amougies for Frank Zappa. When the musicians arrived in Paris, they were bombarded by photographers and journalists. 'It was a shock, but it was rewarding, too,' said Howard. 'In three days in Europe, I had gotten more publicity than I had in five years in New York.'

To the French youth, the Black musicians and their angry music represented the revolution taking place in America, and their arrival so soon after the Left Bank student revolts consolidated their heroic position. The French critics saw, as they have always done, political implications in everything the musicians did. They laid their own interpretations on the artists' actions and intent, often without the musicians themselves fully comprehending what they represented in the eyes of their host country. When Charlie Parker visited France in 1949, his outrageous lifestyle was seen as a living example of existentialism, and Jean-Paul Sartre, the leading prophet of this philosophy, expressed an interest in meeting him. Parker walked straight into a role that had almost been written for him; twenty years later, the Black expatriates were cast in another role by the French, that of nationalists and ghetto heroes.

When Clifford Thornton was refused entry to France because of his alleged political activity, his expulsion and the litigation that followed made his a *cause célèbre* in some sections of the French press, a minor version of the furore surrounding the trial of someone like Bobby Seale. In contrast to Britain or Germany, where the local musicians have developed their own national identity sufficiently for their devotees to be uninterested in the exploits of the Black originators, the French derived more from seeing a Black instrumentalist at work. The new expatriates did not reach quite the same level of acclaim as the New Orleans clarinettist Sidney Bechet, who was a national figure in France during his lifetime and was celebrated by the erection of a statue after his death, but in no time at all some of them started to attract the kind of following accorded to rock bands. As Robin Kenyatta put it: 'There's something else about seeing a Black face playing Black music rather than a white face playing Black music.'

There was no lack of work initially in France and in other parts for the newcomers, and BYG were as good as their word where recordings were concerned. In a matter of days they produced a phenomenal series of albums, even persuading Archie Shepp to break his Impulse contract in the proceedings. The money was still far from good, but most of the musicians leapt at the opportunity to publicise their music and also put some money by while they checked out their employment potential. As Noah Howard sardonically put it: 'The deal was better than ESP.'

Howard explained the attraction of a country where practically all he could say was 'Parlez-vous français?' He was playing in Rennes at la Maison de la Culture, when, for the first time in his career, he was made to feel like a concert artist. 'They had dinner for us, we had dressing-rooms – just little things like that. The sound system was incredible, and when we came off the stage after the concert, we were mobbed by young people and asked for autographs. It was just like they do here for movie stars, and I got a real freak-out thing from it.' For the first time, too, Howard and several others were able to make a living from their music. 'I didn't make a million dollars, but I paid the rent.'

Not all the people who played at Amougies had the good sense to use the experience for long-term rewards, but the wiser ones started to establish contacts, make up brochures detailing their achievements, and, temporarily at least, cancel on New York. The Art Ensemble of Chicago found themselves a house in the suburbs and moved there with a truckload of instruments, but most of the musicians retained Paris as their home-base. After all, the city had long had an expatriate Black American community which had included not only Sidney Bechet but writers James Baldwin and the late Richard Wright.

By 1975, French interest in her American visitors had waned. They no longer filled the political role that had been one of the reasons behind the enthusiasm with which they were espoused there. Alan Silva was one of the few that stayed behind. He explained: 'A lot of people came to the music for political reasons, for "fad-consciousness". They couldn't deal with the purity of what we were doing when they couldn't hang it on to something else, so now we only have people who really dig the music.

'The context in which the musicians play obviously came out of the struggle of the period, but politics have nothing to do with music. The music is pure when it comes from the artist; whatever connotations the culture puts on it, *they* have to deal with those problems. The musician is in advance of the culture, in advance of the emotions. He's the cat that will move the future people. He can make people think differently about what they hear, see or understand. He is like an encouragement to lift one's consciousness.'

It is obviously intriguing for artists like Silva to sift out the deadwood in their audiences. Nevertheless, it is difficult not to view the espousal of the Black Musician as Revolutionary Cult Hero as being a continuation of the idea of Black Artist as Minstrel. Politics may well have no place in art as seen from Silva's perspective, but as long as the Artist is considered in terms of fulfilling any role other than playing music to lift the senses, his or her creation is not being regarded as 'Art'.

Ironically, though, it was the lack of artistic discrimination that attracted most of the young Americans to Europe. Black expatriates of an earlier generation had often been motivated by the desire to escape racial discrimination, but the new musicians, arriving at another period in history, were not so lucky. 'People there do at least realise the fact that Black people are responsible for this kind of music and for its progress,' said Leroy Jenkins. 'You don't make much money there, that's for sure, but the acceptance is what makes it worth going for. It's just as hard, they're doing us up over there financially, too, but at least there's less artistic prejudice. Everywhere you're Black you're going to get that other certain feeling in white society, but in Europe they do at least realise the fact that we're good for *that*.'

The Frank Wright Quartet is the only band to survive intact away from home. Their history in the face of all obstacles is impressive. One night when Wright sat in with Coltrane, he told Rashied Ali that he needed a drummer. The next day he found Ali's brother, Muhammad, on his doorstep. Bobby Few, who had been playing with another heavy tenorman, Booker Ervin, joined the dynamic duo in 1970 and Alan Silva has been in and out of the group for some time. In 1971 they returned to New York for Christmas and a weekend of concerts. They soon realised that conditions in the musicians' community would not enable them to travel. As Silva said, 'I'd meet cats and ask them what they've been doing and they'd say, "Well, I worked up at the Library for 25 dollars ..." And I'd think, Damn, what can you project on that?'

In Europe the four men knew that they could expect to travel even if they were unable to earn the kind of money they felt their talents warranted. They weighed up the situation and headed back across the Atlantic.

* * *

Living in a society, surrounded by history, where culture plays a more important role than it does in the United States, Alan Silva experienced greater impetus for continuing to strive for perfection on his instrument. Despite the efforts of educators – including those involved in the community – there is still a vast gulf between the artist who aims for the summit and what the public will readily accept. Silva is just one of many schooled players puzzled by the readiness to embrace mediocrity as an acceptable standard on the part of those musicians involved in the so-called jazz/rock area. 'At one time, I thought to be a musician was the greatest thing a cat could be. It meant that you had to get *perfection*. These are the standards that I came from, and I come from the ghetto. My standard inside my culture was Charlie Parker – you had to respect what he did. And John Coltrane. I don't understand why people don't have the idea of being a perfect artist.

'One day the standards are up here, and then all of a sudden they're down there. The cat says, "Well, I don't have to do that," and so he plays the standard role instead of playing what the tradition has told him to do – to be a perfectionist. And due to the unwise connections between the youth of the land and the perfected artist, slowly but surely a wide gap has been forming.'

* * *

Money and the chance to play are the main reasons that musicians have left their familiar surroundings, but there are others. 'It's a "must" that any musicians would have to get out of this country,' said Sirone. 'If you don't, you could go on, live a lifetime and die, and never know that the music meant that much to someone else a thousand miles away from here.' Nevertheless, the musicians who have found a temporary answer to their financial plight in Europe and, increasingly now, in Japan, have had to live like gypsies in order to survive. The majority have broken their family ties in order to do so, but it is not a way of life that would suit everyone. Roger Blank is one of those men who preferred to stay home with the family; he is dedicated to increasing the audience for the new music on his own doorstep. With the Melodic Art-tet, a co-operative that comprises himself on drums, trumpeter Ahmed Abdullah, saxophonist Charles Brackeen and a bassist – initially Ronnie Boykins, like himself a former Sun Ra stalwart, later William Parker or Hakim Jami – Blank is endeavouring to break through some of the mystique that has surrounded the music and kept it a predominantly elitist pursuit. Musicians, he feels, are guilty of not bringing the music down to the people, although as community projects grow, it looks as though the situation he speaks of will be forced to change.

The Melodic Art-tet have put a lot of time into their music and it shows. To listen to they are one of the most satisfying of the younger bands playing in New York, and apparently that holds from the player's viewpoint, too. Blank is proud of the fact that they rehearse as frequently as musicians did in the days before the economic pinch became so acute. 'We seem to be working towards a common ecstasy now which is so important in the new music. All too often, brothers get together and just get out there and screech and holler and get off. But that's not right. It's just like going to bed with your woman and you get your thing off and she's laying there waiting on you. You can't do that.'

In spite of the setbacks entailed in being a creative musician, Blank is confident of his capacity to survive. 'I must endure, I *will* endure. I do a little work on the side, I've even had Welfare, but I'm not ashamed of that – it's all part of growing up. It was better than stealing or taking somebody off. I believe now that the Creator designates responsibility to certain people – a mason, a policeman, a musician, a politician – everybody's got their own function to keep this whole planet moving. And when a musician realises what his own function is, his responsibility to humanity, he can kind of take the ups and downs with a little more grace.

'I respect what the older musicians have done. I still maintain that in the beauty and glory of all these five or six people coming together on a bandstand, they still have to have a pulse. They still have to breathe and relate to that. Like in some parts of the so-called "new music", in a sense it's like a monkey throwing paint on the canvas. But it's an incubator. We have to be able to distinguish between what's got the pulse and what just palpitates.'

* * *

The question is, however, will there be future generations of musicians sufficiently interested to play this music if the financial returns remain small? There is little incentive for young players who have been drawn instead into the more lucrative rock field, yet the power of the new Black music is so strong that there are many who are willing to make sacrifices in order to play it.

One thing is certain, and that is that no matter how hard it becomes for musicians to earn a living, and even if, for some reason, the subsidies do not continue, there is no way that talent can be prevented from emerging. Ellis Marsalis is a contemporary of Ed Blackwell. He preferred to stay at home and support his family by teaching and playing the piano while Blackwell went on the road with Ornette Coleman, but he still has a good line in rhetoric. Coming from a city as blessed with talented musicians as New Orleans, he gets just a little tired of reading about the latest derivative 'boy wonder' to stand the music press on its ear. 'They talk about the Great White Hopes,' he snorted. 'Hell, we didn't have to *hope* for anything. We had too many people who were doing it!'

Where Milford Graves and others like him are concerned, neither the audience nor the money will determine their survival. 'I think that's been the failure of a lot of musicians. I've seen a lot of people go out with the desire to make records and to travel and get the admiration of the public, but when this desire is not fulfilled, they're really hung up. It's very hard to fill this without going through a lot of changes and I feel as though a lot of musicians weren't really prepared for this when they went out there. They were so busy taking their music and giving it out, out, out, that they really didn't know the *value* of the music. What we're doing is taking the music to benefit *ourselves*.'

To survive in the new music is a major achievement as can be seen on examining the number of artists who have sold out, dropped out or tragically fallen out. Recording and concert activity goes in fits starts and appears to be more impressive than it actually is, yet still the force continues. At the age of thirty-two, Hakim Jami was saying: 'You know, I'm in this thing where I feel like – wow, in ten years time they'll be calling me old-fashioned! Everything changes, though, and somebody has to change it. I mean I don't know what they're going to call it, but they're not going to call it "jazz" because cats don't want to hear that. If we don't do it, there's some cats behind us that is going to do it, but we're definitely implanting it in them now. Like I'm in my thirties and there's cats playing in their twenties … I even heard some kids playing, eleven and twelve years old, and they were *playing*. And so what's going to happen when they hit the scene, when they reach thirty? Man, they got some *other* ideas, so we can sit back and learn from them.'

* * *

When Wallace D. Muhammad succeeded his father, the late Elijah Muhammad, as leader of the Nation of Islam in 1975, he stunned Blacks and whites alike by his pronouncement that membership of the Nation would now be open to whites. Amiri Baraka, too, announced that he intended to forsake his separatist teaching based on African concepts and adopt a Maoist philosophy and political strategy. Both moves were indicative of the changes that were taking place within the Black community.

Whether such a *volte-face* was a reflection of improved circumstances is debatable. Successful purges conducted by the FBI and the CIA eliminated the threat of radical groups such as the Black Panthers, killing their members or putting them behind bars, and left the Black world ready for the Liberal takeover that plagues all revolutionary movements following the initial winning of some kind of position. Amongst musicians this Liberalism was reflected in decreased stress on the nationalistic content of the music and the partial relaxation of separatist structures. Thus, by the end of the 1970s, more white musicians were playing with blacks than had been permitted earlier in the decade.

Nevertheless, it came as a surprise in 1974 to find Milford Graves teaching at a white upper-middle-class academy such as Bennington. Where the drummer was concerned, though, the adoption of the separatist line was something that Blacks needed in order to establish an identity *within* themselves, *for* themselves. As socialist feminist historian Sheila Rowbotham has written: 'In order to create an alternative an oppressed group must at once shatter the self-reflecting world which encircles it and, at the same time, project its own image onto history. In order to discover its own identity as distinct from that of the oppressor it has to become visible to itself. All revolutionary movements create their own ways of seeing. But this is a result of great labour. People who are without names, who do not know themselves, who have no culture, experience a kind of paralysis of consciousness. The first step is to connect and learn to trust one another.'[5] Milford Graves felt that this was a step he had already made; now he and others like him could stand back and reassess the situation.

Graves received some criticism for his move from within the Black community, but as he views himself equally as educator and creative artist, he finds no conflict between educating and playing for people within his own community and doing the same thing outside it. Rather, he sees this progression on his part as a growth, a maturity. 'Some people make statements and say, "Well, as a Black musician, the white students are going to rip off all your stuff; they're going to steal all your knowledge." I say, "No, that's not true." I don't even worry about that. If they become more into it, more power to them. It's no different to me going to Carnegie or Cal Tech and studying Nuclear Physics and building an H-bomb or whatever it is. It should be that way; it should be open. It should be a challenge from all sources, especially for musicians.'

By the end of the 1970s, 'Jazz' was big business in New York again, but for only a handful of musicians. In no way was their improved situation indicative of conditions prevailing for Blacks elsewhere in the nation. Despite the advances in education and job opportunities, in 1980 Blacks were still at the foot of the table in terms of housing, education, health and incomes. The musicians are, as ever, hampered by economic conditions, frequently aimed at keeping them 'in their place'. So, when the recording scene started to pick up for some artists, all forms of funding were simultaneously cut back. By the end of the decade, most of the lofts that gave their name to an era of music had been forced to close. Despite such set-backs, the attitudes of the people, like the music itself, do not stand still. Marcuse said that no innovation designed to subvert the structure of post-Capitalistic society can escape the ability of that society to absorb every cultural threat; evidence proves him only partially right where African-American music is concerned. The daily struggle continues, with new forms and new ideas emerging daily. As Jerome Cooper said at the beginning, 'Black music is how *our* lives are, and how we are looking at, and relating to, the outside world.'

* * *

While it is true to say that the aims and philosophies of individual musicians differ, one common factor emerges from conversation. That is the almost overwhelming need to actually play. It is a need that is confusing to those with traditional, i.e. materialistic, principles.

A man who knows all the musicians – and most of the answers – sat deep in an armchair in a room on New York's Lower East Side, digging into a plate of fried chicken. 'This avant-garde – it got to the point where it became a religion,' he said. 'Cats never were that way about music before. It got to the point where their horn took the place of everything. It became their companion; it'd be all they'd want. They'd even sleep with their horn. Sometimes they let their children starve because the music *was* their religion.' Fat Bobby licked his fingers appreciatively, then shook his head. Where the man-in-the-street was concerned, the single-mindedness of the 'new' musicians was often puzzling.

It is precisely this music and the sociological/political ferment that nurtured it that keeps a man like Mustafa Abdul Rahim running between New York and his family in Cleveland, sleeping on floors and missing meals in order to be able to play. Once he earned an adequate living as a disc-jockey, now his energies are directed towards a higher plane. Playing the so-called 'new' music was something he felt he had been 'designed' for. 'The music took me to a higher level of consciousness,' he said, 'And that's the difference between it and "I love you, baby, let me do it to you."'

It is left to McCoy Tyner, essentially a spiritual man, to attempt to allay some of the confusion that surrounds this kind of dedication: 'The general public, I feel, are swayed by a lot of different things. They're persuaded by a lot of different elements around musicians without really understanding what music is supposed to mean. It's a personal thing, it has a lot of meaning to it. Music's not a plaything – it's *as serious as your life*.'

Notes

1   Interview by Mike Bourne, 'Defining Black Music', *Down Beat*, 18 September 1969.
2   ibid.
3   A. B. Spellman, *Four Lives in the Bebop Business*, New York, 1966.
4   Notes to *Ofamfa* by Children of the Sun (Universal Justice Records, University City, Missouri).
5   Sheila Rowbotham, *Woman's Consciousness, Man's World*, London, 1973.

Biographies

This listing does not claim to be comprehensive. Some omissions may seem surprising but space has limited the number of entries. For this reason, preference has been given to providing biographical information not available elsewhere.

AACM (Association for the Advancement of Creative Musicians). Founded in Chicago in 1965 by composer R. Abrams and others, a musical and spiritual co-operative dedicated to encouraging self-respect and increasing work opportunities for creative Black artists. Members incl. A. Braxton, L. Jenkins, A. Fielder, L. Smith, Kalaparusha, Robert Crowder, L. Bowie, J. Jarman, R. Mitchell, M. Favors, Jodie Christian.

ABDULLAH, Ahmed (Leroy Bland), *trumpet;* b. New York City, 10 May 1946. Played w. Calvin Massey, King Rubin and the Counts, the Master Brotherhood, Earl Coleman, Lynn Oliver, the Brotherhood of Sound. In 70s, working w. Melodic Art-tet; own group, Abdullah. Soloist, New York Dance-mobile. 1976 joined Sun Ra. Rec: S. Reid and M. Brotherhood.

ABRAMS, Richard 'Muhal', *piano, clarinet, saxophones, composer, arranger;* b. Chicago, Ill., 21 Sept 1930, d. New York City, 29 October 2017. Stud. piano Chicago Musical Coll at 17, pro. since 1948. Writing for King Fleming 1950. House pianist for visiting and local musicians incl. Miles Davis, Sonny Rollins, Gene Ammons, Johnny Griffin, Dexter Gordon, Art Farmer. 1955 formed MJT +3. Worked w. Eddie Harris, stud. and played w. D. R. Garrett. 1961 formed the Experimental Band w. Garrett which was to include practically all the new Chicago musicians. Created the AACM in 1965, became its President. Played with Woody Herman, Ruth Brown, Lambert, Hendricks & Ross. To Europe with own group 1973. Recs: Art Ensemble of Chicago, own.

ALI, Muhammad (Raymond Patterson), *drums;* b. Philadelphia, Pa., 23 December 1936. Played w. brother Rashied, F. Wright, with whom he moved to Europe 1969. Rec. w. Wright incl. duo album, Alan Shorter, D. Ayler, A. Ayler.

ALI, Rashied (Robert Patterson), *drums, congas, trumpet;* b. Philadelphia, Pa., 1 July 1933, d. New York City, 12 August 2009. Musical family, mother sang w. Jimmy Lunceford. Stud. Granoff School, worked w. Big Maybelle, Jimmy Smith, Jimmy Oliver, Tommy Coles, Orrin Marshall. First jazz gigs w. own group 1953. To NY 1963, met P. Sanders and immediately started working w. him and D. Cherry. Joined P. Bley w. Sanders, then w. B. Dixon, A. Shepp, Earl Hines, M. Brown, Sun Ra. Second percussionist w. J. Coltrane 1965 until his death, then joined A. Coltrane trio. Own groups since late '60s. Formed Survival Records 1972, opened own loft Ali's Alley/Studio 771973. Recs: J. Coltrane, Shepp, Bud Powell, A. Coltrane, J. L. Wilson, L. Jenkins, own.

ALLEN, Paul Byron, *alto sax;* b. Omaha, Nebraska, 9 December 1939. Began studying music 1948, infl. by Bartok, Ravel, Thelonious Monk. Rec. for ESP 1965, w. bassist Maceo Gilchrist, drummer Ted Robinson.

ALLEN, Marshall, *alto saxophone, flute, oboe, piccolo, drums;* b. Louisville, Kentucky, 25 May 1924. Clarinet, C-melody sax at school. Stud. National Conservatory of Music, Paris, played w. pianist Art Simmons. Toured Europe w. James Moody. On return to Chicago, met Sun Ra 1956, member of the Arkestra ever since.

ANDERSON, Fred Jr, *reeds;* b. Monroe, Louisiana, 22 March 1929, d. Chicago, 24 June 2010. Original AACM member. Formed Creative Jazz Ensemble 1965.

AYLER, Albert, *tenor saxophone;* b. Cleveland, Ohio, 13 July 1936, d. New York, 25 Nov 1970. Alto sax from age 7, various r&b groups incl. Lloyd Pearson's Counts of Rhythm and, in 1952, Little Walter Jacobs. Switched to tenor 1956 during Army service, settled in NY 1962. Rec. in Sweden and Denmark, met C. Taylor in Stockholm, played with him there and in NY. Formed trio with bassist Gary Peacock and drummer S. Murray, rec. for ESP. Toured Scandinavia w. them and D. Cherry. 1965 played NY Town Hall w. brother Donald, C. Tyler, Murray, bassist Lewis Worrell. Toured Europe 1966, 1970, recordings made on second visit released after his death.

AYLER, Donald, *trumpet;* b. Cleveland, Ohio, 5 Oct 1942, d. Northfield, Ohio, 21 October 2007. Stud. Cleveland Settlement and Cleveland Institute. Worked w. brother Albert, led own groups featuring C. Tyler, M. Ali, also P. Bley, Elvin Jones, J. Coltrane. Rec. w. A. Ayler on ESP and ABC-Impulse. Own album on Jihad unreleased. Inactive in music following brother's death, occasional sessions in Cleveland from 1975.

BAG (Black Artists Group). A musicians' collective founded in the late '60s in St Louis, Missouri, by drummer Charles Shaw and poet, percussionist, actor, theatre director Ajule Rutlin. Like AACM its goals were the elevation of self-respect among musicians and of an awareness for creative Black endeavour in the community. Now virtually defunct as an organisation, members included Joseph Bowie, Baikida Carroll, Marty Ehrlich, Julius Hemphill, Oliver Lake, Floyd LeFlore, Carol Marshall, James Marshall, J. D. Parran, Ajule Rutlin, Charles 'Bobo' Shaw, Luther Thomas, Abdallah Yakub.

BARBIERI, Leandro 'Gato', *tenor saxophone;* b. Rosario, Argentina, 28 November 1932, d. New York City, 2 April 2016. Musical family. Stud. clarinet, alto, composition. At 18 w. pianist Lalo Schifrin, switched to tenor. To Europe 1962, worked in Italy. Met D.. Cherry in Paris, their association lasted several years. Settled in NYC. Recs: Cherry, P. Sanders, S. Lacy, Dollar Brand, Jazz Composers Orchestra, own.

BARKER, Thurman, *drums;* b. 8 Jan 1948, Chicago, Illinois. Original member of AACM. Studied piano and percussion, worked and rec. w. J. Jarman, R. Abrams, Kalaparusha. Worked in pit-bands for musicals.

BERGER, Karl Heinz, *vibraphone;* b. Heidelberg, West Germany, 30 March 1935. Stud. piano, philosophy, musicology. Played at first Antibes jazz festival, switched to vibraphone 1961. Acc. American soloists in Germany, met E. Dolphy. 1964 played w. D. Cherry, S. Lacy in Paris, then moved to NYC w. Cherry. Formed Creative Music Foundation in Woodstock, NY, where teachers incl. percussionist E. Blackwell, saxophonist O. Lake.

BLACK, James, *drums;* b. New Orleans, Louisiana, 1 Feb 1940, d. 30 August 1988. Stud. music at Southern U., Baton Rouge, played in marching band. Infl. by parade drummers, E. Blackwell, June Gardner, Earl Palmer. First pro. job 1958 w. r&b band, replaced Blackwell w. Ellis Marsalis. To NY w. pianist Joe

Jones, on road w. Lionel Hampton. 1962 w. Cannonball Adderley, Yusef Lateef, Horace Silver. Returned to New Orleans, worked w. saxophonist James Rivers, Fats Domino, Professor Longhair. Recs: Adderley, Lateef, Marsalis, Lee Dorsey, Irma Thomas, The Meters.

BLACKWELL, Edward Joseph, *drums;* b. New Orleans, Louisiana, 10 October 1929, d. Hartford, Conn., 7 October 1992. infl. by street dancing, parade drummers, Paul Barbarin. First pro. job w. Plas Johnson, Roy Brown. Co-led American Jazz Quintet w. Ellis Marsalis. To Los Angeles 1951, met O. Coleman and played with him there. Returned to NO, played w. Earl King, Huey 'Piano' Smith, Edward Frank, Snookum Russell, on road w. Ray Charles 1957. To NYC 1960, joined Coleman at Five Spot. Worked w. J. Coltrane and Booker Little/E. Dolphy group, loft gigs w. D. Cherry and others, some recs incl. *The Avant Garde* w. Cherry and Coltrane. 1965 started working w. pianist Randy Weston, incl. 3 tours of Africa. Living in Morocco 1968. Briefly w. Thelonious Monk, A. Coltrane, rejoined O. Coleman until 1973. Since 1972 teaching in African-American music prog. at Wesleyan University, Connecticut, working w. Cherry and K. Berger. Recs: Coleman, Coltrane, Shepp, Berger, Clifford Jordan, Stanley Cowell, C. Brackeen, M. Brown, Cherry, incl. 2 part duo *Mu.*

BLANK, Roger, *drums;* b. New York City, 19 Dec 1938. Musical family, father played tpt w. Cootie Williams. Stud. w. Charlie Persip. House-drummer at Hotel Theresa, Harlem, early '60s. Met Sun Ra 1964, studied, played, rec. w. him. Lived at musicians' loft, sessions w. John Hicks, Charles Tolliver, O. Coleman, J. Coltrane, D. Cherry, D. Charles, Charles 'Majeed' Greenlee. Stud., collaborated on percussion book w. E. Blackwell. Worked w. Shepp, Sanders, Bill Barron, K. McIntyre, Walt Dickerson, Frank Foster, Tyrone Washington. Formed Melodic Art-tet. Recs: Shepp, Sanders, Dickerson, Sun Ra, L. Jenkins.

BLEY, Carla (Carla Borg), *piano, composer, arranger;* b. Oakland, Calif., 11 May 1938. Stud. piano. While selling cigarettes in NYC jazz club, became involved in creative music. Married pianist P. Bley, started writing for him and others incl. D. Ellis, Attila Zoller, Steve Kuhn, Gary Burton, Art Farmer, Jimmy Giuffre, C. Haden. Founder member of Jazz Composers Guild. Dec 1964 co-leader of Jazz Composers Orch at Judson Hall, NY, then to Europe w. quintet, 'Jazz Realities'. 1966 began personal and musical association w. M. Mantler, founding Jazz Composers Orchestra Association together. Recs: JCOA, D. Cherry, C. Thornton, G. Barbieri, R. Rudd, own *Escalator Over the Hill.*

BLEY, Paul, *piano;* b. Montreal, Canada, 10 November 1932, d. Stuart, Fl., 3 January 2016. Stud. violin, piano. Led own quartet 1945, playing Montreal nightclubs in the wake of Oscar Peterson. To NYC, stud. at Juilliard, played and rec. w. Charles Mingus, Art Blakey. To Calif., played w. Chet Baker, then formed trio w. bassist C. Haden, drummer Billy Higgins. Joined by D. Cherry and O. Coleman during engagement at the Hillcrest, Los Angeles. Worked w. George Russell, Jimmy Giuffre, D. Ellis. Became involved with the new music in NYC. Founder member Jazz Composers Guild. Numerous recs incl. ESP w. trumpeter D. Johnson, M. Allen, E. Gomez, M. Graves. 1970s working w. singer/pianist Annette Peacock.

BOWIE, Joseph, *trombone, conga drums, misc. instruments*; b. St Louis, Miss., 17 October 1953. Stud. piano, worked w. Paramounts, Lamontes and Oliver Sain. MD for Fontella Bass. Member of BAG, brother of trumpeter L. Bowie.

BOWIE, Lester, *trumpet, misc;* b. Frederick, Maryland, 11 October 1941, d. Brooklyn, NY, 8 November 1999. 1943 to Little Rock, settled in St Louis. Father professional musician. Started trumpet at 5, playing in religious meetings, school festivals at 10. Own band 1957, playing theatres, radio. Worked w. blues bands, stud. Lincoln U. Stayed in Texas, sessions w. saxophonists James Clay, David 'Fathead' Newman. Worked w. Little Milton, backing blues artists w. Oliver Sain. Married singer/pianist Fontella Bass. To Chicago, joined AACM. Became member of Art Ensemble of Chicago while continuing to work as Bass's M.D. To Europe with AEC, lived in France, made extensive tours. Recs: AEC, A. Shepp, S. Murray, J. Lyons, own.

BOYKINS, Ronnie, *bass;* b. Chicago, Ill., 17 December 1935, d. New York City, 20 April 1980. Stud. Du Sable High, and w. Ernie Shepard. Played w. Muddy Waters, Johnny Griffin, Jimmy Witherspoon; opened 'House of Culture', w. Sun Ra 1958–66 and rec. extensively w. the composer. Formed Free Jazz Society, own group w. F. LeFlore (tp), Frank Haynes (tnr), John Hicks (p). Played w. Sarah Vaughan, Rahsaan Roland Kirk, Mary Lou Williams, Melodic Art-tet. Recs: Sun Ra, A. Shepp, C. Tyler, J. L. Wilson, Elmo Hope.

BRACKEEN, Charles, *reeds;* b. Oklahoma, 13 March 1940. Piano and violin there and in Texas. To Calif. 1956, worked w. Dave Pike, Art Farmer, Joe Gordon, sessions w. D. Cherry, Billy Higgins, C. Haden. To NY 1966, played w. Cherry, D.

Moore, D. Izenzon, E. Blackwell, pianist wife Joanne. In 1970s w. F. Lowe, own group, Melodic Art-tet.

BRADFORD, Bobby Lee, *trumpet;* b. Cleveland, Mississippi, 19 July 1934. To Dallas 1946, began cornet 1949. At High School w. James Clay, Cedar Walton, David Newman. Sam Houston Coll 1952, playing in dance band w. Leo Wright. Worked around Dallas w. Buster Smith, John Hardee. To Los Angeles 1953, began playing w. O. Coleman. Also w. Wardell Gray, Gerald Wilson, Dolphy. Military Service and study, rejoined Coleman 1961–63 in NYC. In Los Angeles, co-led group with altoist John Carter. To Europe 1971, rec. w. John Stevens and Spontaneous Music Ensemble. Rec. w. Coleman NYC 1972, to Europe for extended stay, then teaching in Calif.

BRAXTON, Anthony, *reeds;* b. Chicago, Ill., 4 June 1945. 1959–63 at Chicago School of Music, then harmony, composition, philosophy. 1966 joined AACM, taught harmony. Company w. L. Smith, L. Jenkins, joined S. McCall In Paris with them for concerts and recordings. 1970 formed Circle w. pianist Chick Corea, bassist Dave Holland, drummer Barry Altschul. Performed solo and in duos, recorded frequently.

BRIMFIELD, William, *trumpet;* b. Chicago, Illinois, 8 April 1938, d. Chicago, Ill., 10 October 2012. Stud. piano, violin. 1957 stud. w. Fred Anderson. 1961 in Army, on discharge met R. Abrams. With Anderson, joined J. Jarman Sextet. Played w. George Hunter, Red Saunders, Lionel Hampton, Abrams big band, Edwin Daugherty's Third World. Member of AACM.

BROWN, Marion, *alto saxophone, percussion;* b. Atlanta, Georgia, 8 Sept 1935, d. Hollywood, Fl., 18 October 2010. Stud. sax, clarinet and oboe, then Music Education, Political Science, Economics, History at Clark College and Howard U. First job w. A. Shepp, member, Jazz Composers Guild. Rec. w. B. Dixon, J. Coltrane, played w. Sun Ra, then toured Europe, where he played and rec. w. German multi-instrumentalist Gunther Hampel and singer Jeanne Lee. On his return, became involved in education, formed duo with trumpeter L. Smith. Active in various faculties, playing in solo performance.

BURRELL, David 'Dave', *piano;* b. Middletown, Ohio, 10 Sept 1940. Stud. Berklee School of Music, Boston Conservatory, then U. of Hawaii. Moved to Cleveland, then NY, worked w. G. Logan, M. Brown, P. Sanders, S. Murray,

Shepp, S. Sharrock. 1969 at Pan-African Festival in Algiers. Recs: own, Shepp, Brown, Sanders, B. Harris.

CARROLL, Baikida, *trumpet, flugelhorn, composer, arranger*; b. St Louis, Missouri 15 January 1947. Member BAG. Studied USA and Germany. Directed the Third Infantry Division Ensemble, BAG Big Band. Played w. Little Milton, Oliver Sain, Julius Hemphill, Fontella Bass, Albert King, Sam and Dave, Oliver Nelson, Ron Carter, own groups. To Europe 1973 w. BAG musicians. Recs: own, Human Arts Ensemble.

CARTER, John, *alto saxophone;* b. Fort Worth, Texas, 24 September 1929, d. Inglewood, Calif., 31 March 1991. Sessions w. O. Coleman and C. Moffett late '40s in Fort Worth. BA in Music at Lincoln U, Missouri, MA at U of Colorado 1956. 1961 to Los Angeles to teach in school system, started working with B. Bradford and recorded together. Conducted symphony orchestra for Coleman at UCLA for 1967 concert.

CARTER, Kent, *bass;* b. Hanover, New Hampshire, 14 June 1939. Worked w. country & western bands, then w. pianist Lowell Davidson. Stud. Berklee School of Music, in houseband at Lennie's on the Turnpike, playing for Booker Ervin, Phil Woods, Lucky Thompson, Sonny Stitt, etc. 1964 w. Jazz Composers Orchestra. To Europe 1965 w. P. Bley. Continued studies in Boston, travelling frequently to Europe to play with S. Lacy. Also w. Steve Potts, A. Silva, Mal Waldron, B. Bradford, John Stevens, Trevor Watts's Amalgam.

CHAMBERS, Joe, *drums;* b. Philadelphia, Pa., 25 June 1942. Started playing 1951, professional since 1954. Played frequently in Philadelphia. Stud. composition and played w. Jimmy Giuffre, B. Hutcherson, James Brown, the Shirelles, E. Dolphy, Donald Byrd, Freddie Hubbard, Andrew Hill, Herbie Hancock, Charles Lloyd, A. Shepp, Joe Henderson. Rec. w. Shepp and M'Boom, all-percussion group.

CHARLES, Dennis 'Jazz', *drums, congas, percussion;* b. St Croix, Virgin Islands, 4 Dec 1933, d. New York City, 24 March 1998. Father played congas, guitar, banjo. Congas as child, to NYC 1945. Started drumming 1954, teaching himself by listening to records by Art Blakey and Roy Haynes. Played West Indian parties and dances w. calypso and mambo bands in Harlem in late '50s. Met C. Taylor at Connie's Inn, one of the few drummers to work with him. Rec. w. Taylor, S. Lacy. On stage for 3 mths in Taylor group w. A. Shepp on tenor in Jack Gelber play

The Connection. Played w. Gil Evans, Jimmy Giuffre, Wilbur Ware, Shepp and D. Cherry; rec. West Indian folk-tunes with brother Frank and Sonny Rollins.

CHERRY, Donald 'Don', *trumpet, flutes, percussion;* b. Oklahoma City, 18 November 1936, d. Malaga, Spain, 19 October 1995. To Los Angeles 1940, stud. tpt at college. 1951 working w. bassist Red Mitchell, saxophonists Wardell Gray, Dexter Gordon. Met O. Coleman, and made his first recordings, and worked w. him in NYC. In 1959 went together to School of Jazz in Lenox, Massachusetts. Worked w. Sonny Rollins, J. Coltrane. To Europe w. Shepp and New York Contemporary Five, then w. A. Ayler. Makes home in Sweden but plays w. Coleman, E. Blackwell, C. Haden, F. Lowe and others on his frequent visits to NYC. Recs: Coleman, Sanders, Ayler, Murray, Shepp, R. Rudd, George Russell, own.

CLARK, Charles E, *bass, 'cello;* b. Chicago, Illinois, 11 Mar 1945, d. Chicago, 15 April 1969. First stud. w. Wilbur Ware. Prof. in 1963, played w. R. Abrams's Experimental Band, many AACM groups, in particular J. Jarman's. Stud. w. David Bethe, Joseph Guastefeste, first bassist w. Chicago Symph. Scholarship member Chicago Civic Orch, the Symphony's official training orch. After he died of a cerebral haemorrhage, the orch. estab. an annual scholarship in his name to be given to a young, talented Black musician.

COLEMAN, Ornette, *alto saxophone, trumpet, violin;* b. Fort Worth, Texas, 9 March 1930, d. New York City, 11 June 2015. Started alto 1944, playing in school marching band w. cousin James Jordan, P. Lasha, C. Moffett. R&b in local bars, worked w. Thomas 'Red' Connors. On road w. minstrel show, stranded in New Orleans. With Pee Wee Crayton to Los Angeles. Worked at variety of jobs while studying theory, harmony. Started playing w. E. Blackwell, B. Bradford, later George Newman, Billy Higgins, D. Cherry, James Clay. Bassist Red Mitchell instrumental in securing him first rec. date, for Contemporary in 1958. Worked briefly w. P. Bley, formed nucleus of iconoclastic quartet (Cherry, Higgins, C. Haden). Stud. w. Cherry at School of Jazz, Lenox, Massachusetts. To NYC 1959, rec. w. quartet for Atlantic. Periods of inactivity, then formed trio 1964 w. D. Izenzon, C. Moffett. Worked in US and Europe, writing also for symphony orch., small string, woodwind ensembles. Added saxophonist D. Redman, own 12-year-old son Denardo. Rejoined by Haden, Blackwell. Periods of inactivity continued. Opened loft, Artist House, as centre for exhibitions, concerts 1971. Added electric gtr, bass, congas 1975.

COLTRANE, Alice/Turiya Aparna (Alice McLeod), *piano, organ, harp;* b. Detroit, Michigan, 27 Aug 1937, d. Los Angeles, Calif, 12 January 2007. Musical family, incl. bassist brother, Ernie Farrow. Stud. in Detroit, played in trio. To Europe 1960, infl. by Bud Powell. Worked w. vibraphonist Terry Gibbs. Met J. Coltrane 1963, married and had 3 children. 1966 replaced M. Tyner in Coltrane quartet, continuing husband's music after his death. Concerts leading R. Ali, P. Sanders, J. Garrison, later Ben Riley, V. Wood or Reggie Workman, F. Lowe. Rec. for Impulse and supervised programme of husband's unissued work. Also worked w. A. Shepp and O. Coleman, who was responsible for the transcription of music on *Universal Consciousness.* 1970 met Swami Satchidananda, converted to Hinduism, visiting shrines in India, Sri Lanka. Often works w. string ensembles incl. violinists L. Jenkins, John Blair; 'cellist Calo Scott.

COLTRANE, John William, *tenor saxophone, soprano saxophone;* b. Hamlet, N Carolina, 23 Sept 1926, d. Huntington, NY, 17 July 1967. Both parents musical. First instr. E♭ bugle. Stud. Granoff Studios, Ornstein Mus. Sch. in Philadelphia, played w. local trio 1945, then US Navy band in Hawaii. Worked w. Eddie 'Cleanhead' Vinson, Dizzy Gillespie big band, Johnny Hodges, Miles Davis, Thelonious Monk, Red Garland. Rejoined Davis 1957 during an especially formative period in the music. Formed own group, making first recs on soprano sax. Worked and rec. w. D. Cherry. By 1961, the innovative Coltrane quartet (M. Tyner, J. Garrison, E. Jones) was in existence, toured Europe w. addition of E. Dolphy. Started adding percussionists and others, incl. R. Ali. Eventually Tyner replaced by A. Coltrane, Jones by Ali, P. Sanders added, as music grew more experimental and open. Stopped all musical activity May 1967. Hospitalised on July 16, died the following day from primary hepatoma (cancer of the liver). At his request A. Ayler, O. Coleman played at funeral, attended by 1,000 people.

COOPER, Jerome D, *drums;* b. Chicago, Illinois, 14 Dec 1946, d. Brooklyn, NY, 6 May 2015. Stud. w. Oliver Coleman, Walter Dyett at Du Sable High, American Conservatory, Chicago, Loop College. Worked w. various leaders in Chicago incl. Tommy Hunt blues band. Lived and worked in Europe w. Art Ensemble of Chicago, A. Silva, F. Wright, N. Howard, S. Lacy, Sonny Grey; visited Gambia, Senegal, with organist Lou Bennett. Since 1970, member of the Revolutionary Ensemble w. L. Jenkins (violin), Sirone (bass). Active in New York, organising concerts in own loft 1976. Recs: Lacy, R. Kenyatta, Silva, C. Thornton, Revolutionary Ensemble.

CORYELL, Larry, *guitar;* b. Galveston, Texas, 2 April 1943, d. New York City, 19 February 2017. Began playing c & w, at 12. Stud. Washington U, dividing time betw. rock and jazz. Played w. Chico Hamilton, A. Shepp, involved in some of first jazz/rock experiments. Later w. the Free Spirits, vibraphonist Gary Burton. Soloist on M. Mantler's 1968 *Communications* album by Jazz Composers Orch. Led own group, the Eleventh House w. A. Mouzon on drums.

COURSIL, Jacques, *trumpet;* b. Paris, France, 1938. Started cornet at 16. To Senegal 1959 for 3 years, incl. 2 in Army. To NYC 1965, played with rock bands. Stud. w. pianist Jaki Byard, worked w. F. Wright, A. Jones, M. Ali, H. Grimes, Sun Ra, R. Ali, M. Brown, S. Murray. Recs: Murray, Wright, Burton Greene, own.

CROSS, Earl, *trumpet, flugelhorn;* b. St Louis, Missouri, 8 Dec 1933, d. 1987. Stud. music in high school. In Air Force, assoc. with pianists Freddie Redd, Boo Pleasants, saxophonist Frank Haynes, trumpeter Richard Williams. To music school in Calif., worked w. rock-and-roll bands in San Francisco and Oakland, incl. Larry Williams. Began association w. Monty Waters. Led own band, Bay Area Quintet in mid-60s, personnel incl. saxophonists Waters, D. Redman, trumpeters Norman Spiller, Alden Griggs, pianist Sonny Donaldson, bassist Benny Wilson, drummer A. Lewis. To NY 1967, worked w. Sun Ra, teaching and playing w. S. Murray in Woodstock. Worked w. N. Howard, A. Shepp, R. Kenyatta, S. Simmons/Barbara Donald, R. Ali, Monty Waters, own groups. Recs: Ali, Howard, C. Tyler.

CYRILLE, Andrew C, *drums;* b. Brooklyn, NY, 10 Nov 1939. Playing at St Peter Claver Church, Brooklyn, at 11; at 15 w. local trio. Hesitated betw. chemistry and music as career, worked w. Freddie Hubbard. Pro. debut w. pianist/singer Nellie Lutcher, then Mary Lou Williams. Accompanied dancers, played for TV commercial w. Jimmy Giuffre, rec w. Coleman Hawkins, bassist Ahmed Abdul-Malik, saxophonist Bill Barron and C Haden. Worked w. Illinois Jacquet, Junior Mance, G. Moncur III, Walt Dickerson, Howard McGhee, 1965 succeeded S. Murray w. C. Taylor. This assoc. lasted until 1975, incl. period as Artist-in-Residence at Antioch College, Ohio. Played all-percussion dates, *Dialogue of the Drums* with M. Graves and R. Ali, recorded with them, w. Taylor and M. Brown; own solo album for BYG (Paris). Teaching and leading own group Maono, 1976.

DANIEL, Ted, *trumpet;* b. Ossining, New York, 4 June 1943. Musical family, trumpet since 10. Teenage danceband gigs w. guitarist S. Sharrock. To Berklee, then 2 yrs Southern Illinois U. Army service in Vietnam, 1 yr Central State U. Back to NYC 1968, playing w. S. Murray. Rec. debut w. Sharrock. Has continued to play w. own groups, S. Rivers, A. Shepp, M. Graves, D. Burrell, G. Moncur III, N. Howard, D. Redman, A. Cyrille. Recs: Redman, Shepp, C. Thornton, Cyrille, own sextet and Richard.

DAVIS, Arthur D. 'Art', *bass;* b. Harrisburg, Pennsylvania, 5 Dec 1934, d. Long Beach, Calif., 29 July 2007. Stud. w. Anselme Fortier, through watching/listening to Oscar Pettiford, Manhattan Sch. of Mus. and Juilliard. Symphonic experience in Harrisburg and NYC, extensive employment in theatres, studios, singers and jazz groups. First pro. job w. Max Roach. Others incl. O. Coleman, *Dizzy* Gillespie, Art Blakey, Count Basie, Duke Ellington, Clark Terry–Bob Brookmeyer, Freddie Hubbard, Gene Ammons, Lee Morgan, Aretha Franklin. Pioneered second-bass concept w. J. Coltrane in early '60s, w. him (*Olé, Ascension, A Love Supreme*). Also worked and rec. w. Bo Little, Hassan Ibn Ali, Leo Wright, Abbey Lincoln, Al Grey–Billy Mitchell. Inactive in jazz since Coltrane's death, involved in teaching and theatres.

DAVIS, Charles, *baritone sax;* b. Goodman, Mississippi, 10 May 1933, d. New York City, 15 July 2016. Played w. Sun Ra in Chicago 1952; P. Patrick sold him first bari. Worked w. organist Jack MacDuff, singers Billie Holiday, Dinah Washington, trumpeter Kenny Dorham. Active in NYC 1961–65 w. J. Coltrane, J. Tchicai, Jazz Composers Guild. 1977 w. Clark Terry big band.

DICKERSON, Walt, *vibraphone;* b. Philadelphia, Pennsylvania, 16 April 1928, d. Willow Grove, Pa., 15 May 2008. Musical family. Grad. from Morgan State Coll, Baltimore, spent 2 yrs in Army before selling real estate in Calif. To NYC 1960, working and rec. w. Andrew Hill, H. Grimes, Sun Ra, A. Cyrille. Four albums under own name 1961–65. Inactive in music until mid-70s, rec. again w. sidemen Cyrille, Lisle Atkinson, Wilbur Ware.

DIXON, William Robert 'Bill', *trumpet, composer;* b. Nantucket Island, Massachusetts, 5 October 1925, d. North Bennington, Vt., 16 June 2010. Leading own band in NYC, met C. Taylor 1959. Worked together for a few months. Started to restrict himself to own comps. 1960, working intermittently w. A. Shepp. Formed New York Contemporary Five w. Shepp, J. Tchicai, D. Moore, J. C. Moses, D. Cherry later taking his place. Artistic director in charge of jazz catalogue for Savoy, gave opportunities to many younger artists. 1964 formed Jazz Composers

Guild. 1967, while teaching art history elsewhere, started music educ. at NY University of the Streets, first neighbourhood project of its kind. Fulltime teaching since 1968, at Madison, Wisconsin, then Bennington, Vermont, where student body performs his compositions. Engaged M. Graves, J. Garrison on faculty. Working on 20-record set documenting own work to present day, material for 4/5 books. To Paris 1976 for week of concerts. Recs: own septet, Shepp, Taylor.

DOLPHY, Eric Allan, *alto sax, flute, bass clarinet;* b. Los Angeles, California, 20 June 1928, d. Berlin, West Germany, 29 June 1964. Stud. clt. 1937, played w. local bands incl. drummer Roy Porter's. 1958 w. drummer Chico Hamilton, to NYC 1959 joined Charles Mingus. 1961 w. George Russell Sextet, J. Coltrane incl. European tour. To Europe 1964, worked and rec. w. local musicians before being taken ill. Died from uraemia. Recs: Hamilton, Mingus, John Lewis, Gil Evans, K. McIntyre, Russell, Coltrane, Max Roach, Oliver Nelson, Freddie Hubbard, Booker Little, O. Coleman's Double Quartet date *Free Jazz*.

DOYLE, Arthur, *tenor sax, bass-clarinet, flute;* b. Birmingham, Alabama, 26 June 1944, d. Alabama 25 January 2014. Playing music since 13. Attended Parker High School, Birmingham, Tennessee State U., Nashville, where stud. comp. w. Dr T. J. Anderson. Local engagements w. former Sun Ra trumpeter Walter Miller, trumpeter Louis Smith in Nashville. To NYC 1967 worked w. N. Howard, B. Dixon, D. Burrell, M. Graves. Recs: Howard, tapes (unreleased) w. Graves.

ELLIS, Donald Johnson, 'Don', *trumpet;* b. Los Angeles, Calif., 25 July 1934, d. Hollywood, Calif., 17 December 1978. In 1959, rec. w. composer George Russell and, under own name, w. P. Bley, G. Peacock. Formed big band at end of '60s, specialising in unusual time-signatures, d. 1978.

EWART, Douglas Randolph, *reeds, percussion, piccolo, bassoon;* b. Kingston, Jamaica, 13 Sept 1946. To Chicago June 1963, fundamental musical training w. AACM. Played w. The Cosmic Musicians, F. Anderson, R. Abrams big band, H. Threadgill. Duet concerts w. trombonist George Lewis. Craftsman, specialising in bamboo flutes and percussion devices.

FAVORS, Malachi, *bass, banjo, zither, balafon, percussion;* b. Lexington, Mississippi, 22 August 1927, d. Chicago, Ill., 30 January 2004. Father preacher. Started bass at 15, turned pro. on grad. from high school. Inspired by Wilbur Ware in Chicago. Sessions at the Beehive w. P. Patrick, Norman Simmons, etc. Worked w.

F. Hubbard, D. Gillespie, rec. w. pianist Andrew Hill. Founder member AACM, worked w. F. Anderson, R. Abrams, R. Mitchell, L. Bowie. To Europe w. Art Ensemble of Chicago, rec. extensively w. them, also J. Lyons, A. Shepp, Murray, Silva in Paris.

FEW, Robert 'Bobby', *piano;* b. Cleveland, Ohio, 21 Oct 1935. Acc. singer Brook Benton, worked w. saxophonists Jackie McLean, Booker Ervin, A. Ayler. Own trio in NY 1958. Began assoc. w. F. Wright 1956, to Europe w. him and N. Howard 1969. Rec. w. Ayler and Wright, also under own name for Center of the World Records, label owned by Few, Wright, M. Ali and A. Silva.

FIELDER, Alvin Jr, *percussion;* b. Meridian, Mississippi, 23 Nov 1935. Started playing 1948, local gigs 3 yrs later w. Duke Otis. To Xavier, New Orleans 1951 to stud. pharmacy, met Earl Palmer, E. Blackwell, stud. w. latter. Continued pharmacy at Texas Southern 1953, working w. Bobby Bland sidemen Pluma Davis, Joe Scott. Studio work for Duke Records backing gospel and blues artists, occasional live gigs w. Bland, 2 yrs at the Eldorado in Houston w. P. Davis, backing Big Joe Turner, Ivory Joe Hunter, Amos Milburn, etc. 1955 joined Eddie Vinson Sextet, 1957 to Chicago to continue studies, 2 yrs w. Sun Ra; worked w. R. Abrams, Kalaparusha. Founder member AACM, played w. L. Lashley/F. Anderson group, R. Mitchell Sextet. Returned to Miss. 1968 to take over family pharmacy. Secured grants to promote new music artists in Miss., e.g. Mitchell, J. Stubblefield, Favors, 1975 in NYC w. Kalaparusha, own group in New Orleans 1976.

FOLWELL, William Sheldon 'Bill', *bass*; b. Rochester, NY, 1939. Has divided time between music and drama, writing for plays and working in rock groups. Played w. M. Brown, S. Murray, S. Simmons, P. and C. Bley. Member of A. Ayler's 1966 group, rec. w. him and toured Europe.

FORTUNE, Cornelius 'Sonny', *saxophones, flute;* b. Philadelphia, Pennsylvania, 19 May 1939. Stud. Granoff Sch. of Mus., privately w. Roland Wiggins. Played w. Leon Thomas, Roy Brooks, worked and rec. w. Miles Davis, M. Tyner, Mongo Santamaria, Buddy Rich, Roy Ayers. Other recs. w. George Benson, Horace Arnold, Oliver Nelson and under own name.

FREEMAN, Earl, *bass, harp, flute;* b. Oakland, Calif., 11 March 1939. Piano as child. Stud. graphic design, took up bass. Played w. Sun Ra in Chicago at 19, w. saxophonist Frank Haynes on West Coast. Most professional exp. gained in

Europe 1969 w. Shepp, S. Murray, B. Greene, F. Wright, C. Thornton, A. Silva, K. Terroade, Ambrose Jackson, M. Brown, N. Howard. Visited Algeria w. Shepp, Cal Massey, Don Byas, S. McCall to make film. Recs: Thornton, Murray, Terroade, Silva Shepp, Howard.

GADDY, Christopher Leon Jr, *piano, marimba;* b. Chicago, Illinois, 8 April 1943; d. Chicago, 12 March 1968. Started piano age 7 at Holy Angel Church. 1952–60 American Conservatory of Music, also organ. Played for churches until age 18. 1961 became involved in R. Abrams's Experimental Band and later, the AASCM. Worked, rec. w. J. Jarman.

GARRETT, Donald Rafael, *bass, bass-clt, flutes, clarinet, percussion;* b. El Dorado, Arkansas, 28 February 1932, d. Champaign, Ill., 14 August 1969. Stud. Du Sable High, Chicago, where met Sun Ra, R. Abrams, Johnny Griffin, Rahsaan Roland Kirk, Eddie Harris, J. Gilmore. Started on clarinet, bass and sax by 1955. Co-founder w. Abrams of The Experimental Band, forerunner of AACM. Played w. Coltrane in Chicago late '50s. To San Francisco 1964, org. concerts, taught, made instruments. Rec w. A. Shepp during SF gig. 1965 played concerts w. Coltrane and rec. 3 albums; later w. A. Coltrane, S. Simmons/Barbara Donald. In Paris 1971 worked w. F. Wright, Jean-Luc Ponty, Oliver Johnson, N. Howard. Began musical/personal assoc. w. singer/multi-instrumentalist Zuzann Fasteau. Working together as the Sea Ensemble, rec. for ESP and travelled widely, incl. Zaïre, Senegal, Morocco, Yugoslavia, Haiti, India.

GARRISON, James Emory 'Jimmy', *bass;* b. Miami, Florida, 3 March 1934; d. New York City, 7 April 1976. To Philadelphia as child, stud. clarinet. To NYC 1958, playing bass w. Philly Joe Jones, Tony Scott, Kenny Dorham, Curtis Fuller, Benny Golson, Lennie Tristano, Bill Evans, O. Coleman. 1962–66 member of J. Coltrane quartet, participating in the definitive recordings. Formed trio w. pianist Hampton Hawes, then E. Jones. Played frequently w. A. Shepp, active in teaching. Recs. incl. Walter Bishop Jr, Jackie McLean, B. Dixon, E. Jones, A. Coltrane, Ted Curson, J. R. Monterose, Philly Joe Jones, Coleman.

GILMORE, John E., *tenor saxophone, drums;* b. Summit, Mississippi, 28 Sept 1931, d. Philadelphia, Pa., 20 August 1995. Stud. basics w. Chicago guitarist George Eskridge. Worked w. Earl Hines big band, since 1953 w. Sun Ra. Rehearsed frequently w. Miles Davis in late '50s, toured Europe w. Art Blakey, US w. Freddie Hubbard. Rec. w. Sun Ra and under own name.

GOMEZ, Edgar 'Eddie', *bass;* b. Santurce, Puerto Rico, 4 October 1944. Stud. Juilliard 1963, played w. drummer Rufus Jones and various Dixieland groups. Assoc w. P. Bley, M. Graves in early '60s, rec. for ESP under leadership of G. Logan (w. Graves/D. Pullen), and P. Bley (Graves, M. Allen, D Johnson). Since 1966 w. pianist Bill Evans. Rec. w. him, Jazz Composers Orch.

GRAVES, Milford Robert, *drums, percussion;* b. Jamaica, New York, 20 Aug 1941. Self-taught initially, playing at 3; was not taught formal sticking techniques till 17. Congas at 8, own perc. group at school, subsequently evolving into perc. work-shops. Stud. Indian hand-drumming w. musicologist Washantha Singh, other techniques w. George Stone in Boston. 1960–63 played for dancing in NYC, also w. singer Miriam Makeba. Worked w. the New York Art Quartet, G. Logan, P. Bley, A. Ayler, Lowell Davidson, S. Sharrock, Jazz Composers' Orchestra, D. Pullen. Since 1965 working closely with multi-reedman Hugh Glover, conducting research into the medical/psychological applications of music. Gave percussion performances in duo with A. Cyrille and trio w. him and R. Ali. Teaching at Ben-nington College, Vermont. Recs: own, Ayler, Bley, Logan, NYAQ.

GREENE, Burton, *piano;* b. Chicago, Ill., 14 June 1937. Founder member of Jazz Composers Guild. Played w. M. Brown, R. Ali, H. Grimes, acc. vocalist Patty Waters. Also plays synthesiser and 'prepared' piano. Rec. for ESP.BYG.

GRIMES, Henry Alonzo, *bass;* b. Philadelphia, Pennsylvania, 3 November 1935. Stud. violin, tuba; enrolled at Juilliard 1953. Acc. r & b saxophonists Arnett Cobb, Willis 'Gator-tail' Jackson. Worked w. Anita O'Day, Tony Scott, Gerry Mulligan, Sonny Rollins, then became involved with the New York avant-garde of mid-60s. Played and rec. w. clarinettist Perry Robinson, D. Cherry, A. Ayler, P. Sanders, B. Greene, A. Shepp, own trio. Worked regularly w. C. Taylor and rec. w. him, incl. 1965 Newport Festival.

HADEN, Charles Edward 'Charlie', *bass;* b. Shenandoah, Iowa, 6 August 1937, d. Los Angeles, Calif., 11 July 2014. Musical family, appeared daily on local country music radio programmes. Stud. music; to Los Angeles, playing w. local musicians. First jobs w. Hampton Hawes, Art Pepper, P. Bley. Also played w. Elmo Hope; 3 years w. Bley at Hillcrest Club, w. Billy Higgins on drums. O. Coleman, D. Cherry joined band briefly. To NYC w. Coleman as reg. member of group. Inac-tive for a period, then working w. Denny Zeitlin, Tony Scott. Rejoined Coleman

1966, worked w. him and Keith Jarrett. Recs: Coleman, Cherry, Jarrett, A. Shepp, G. Moncur III, own Liberation Music Orchestra.

HANNIBAL (Marvin Peterson), *trumpet;* b. Smithville, Texas, 11 November 1948. To NYC 1971. Worked w. Rahsaan Roland Kirk, P. Sanders, Roy Haynes, Richard Davis, Gil Evans. Leads own group. Recs Sanders, Haynes, Evans, G. Moncur, C. Thornton.

HARPER, Billy, *tenor saxophone;* b. Houston, Texas, 17 Jan 1943. Stud. N Texas State U, working prof. as saxophonist/singer simultaneously. Played w. r & b bands, also saxophonists James Clay, Fred Smith. To NYC 1966, working w. Gil Evans. 2 yrs w. Art Blakey, then E. Jones, Max Roach, Lee Morgan, Thad Jones–Mel Lewis Orchestra, own group. Recs: Gil Evans, own.

HARRIS, William Godvin 'Beaver', *drums;* b. Pittsburgh, Pennsylvania, 20 April 1936, d. New York City, 22 December 1991. Played clarinet, alto sax as teenager, involved in baseball, playing in all major Black leagues. Drums in service, encouraged by Max Roach. Worked w. Sonny Rollins, then to NYC to meet avant-garde musicians, incl. A. Shepp with whom has been assoc. since 1966. To Europe w. Ayler, played drums clinics w. Roach and Kenny Clarke. Worked w. Sonny Stitt, Dexter Gordon, Clifford Jordan, Joe Henderson, Clark Terry, Freddie Hubbard. Formed co-op group w. G. Moncur III, the 360 Degree Experience. 1970 played w. Shepp for LeRoi Jones's play *Slave Ship,* and 1973 for Aishah Rahman's *Lady Day: A Musical Tragedy.* Continued to work w. Shepp in '70s, also Thelonious Monk, Chet Baker and, on occasion, Dixieland groups. Recs: Moncur, Shepp, Charles Bell, M. Brown, R. Rudd, Ayler, S. Lacy, P. Sanders, G. Barbieri, JCOA, Sheila Jordan, own.

HEMPHILL, Julius, *alto sax, composer;* b. Fort Worth, Texas, 24 January 1938, d. New York City, 2 April 1995. Stud. clarinet w. J. Carter. US Army band '64, various Texas bands, Ike Turner. To St Louis '68, joined BAG. Stud. N. Texas State. Lincoln U. Group w. pianist John Hicks. Played w. A. Braxton in Chicago; performed Paris, Sweden 1973. Formed own record company, Mbari, 1972. Recs: Braxton, L. Bowie, Kool and the Gang, own.

HENDERSON, Errol (Earle Henderson), *bass, piano;* b. Dallas, Texas, 21 Oct 1941. Mother pianist, singer; father poet. Self-taught pianist, playing w. trumpeter Norman Howard in Cleveland 1961. Met A. Ayler on his return from Europe, played w. him and Howard. To NYC 1963, stud. bass. Played w. Ayler, C. Tyler, sessions w. O. Coleman. 1964 rec. *Witches and Devils* w. Ayler for Danish Debut. Ret. to Calif., stud. w. bassists Vic Malone, Richard Taylor. Occasional NYC gigs in 1970s w. C. Tyler, dance ensembles, poetry readings.

HOWARD, Noah, *alto saxophone;* b. New Orleans, Louisiana, 6 April 1943, d. France, 3 September 2010. Sang in choir as child. 1960 2 yrs in service, then to Calif. Met D. Johnson, B. Allen, S. Simmons, started stud. trumpet, sax. To NYC 1965, became part of new music movement. Rec. 2 albums for ESP, played w. B. Dixon, S. Murray, D. Ayler, own group. 1970 to Europe w. F. Wright, B. Few, M. Ali, worked and rec. together for over 1 yr. Divided time betw. NYC and Europe, involved with NY Musicians Festival 1972–74. Recs: Shepp, F. Wright, D. Ayler (unreleased), own.

HUNTER, Jerome, *bass, vocals, composer, songwriter;* b. Spartanburg, S. Carolina, 14 Jan 1942. Started on guitar, switched to bass 1954. Stud. w. John Lamb (Duke Ellington Orch); Dr W. O. Smith at Tennessee State; Carl Suggie, principal bassist Nashville Symph. Orch; Wendell Pritchett. Worked w. S. Sharrock, B. Lancaster, Grover Washington Jr, Dorothy Donegan, Johnny Hammond Smith, Philly Joe Jones, Roy Haynes, Ray Bryant. Recs: Lancaster, Marzette Watts, B. Lancaster/J. R. Mitchell.

HUTCHERSON, Robert 'Bobby', *vibraphone;* b. Los Angeles, Calif., 27 January 1941, d. Montara, Calif., 15 August 2016. Started on piano, vibes lessons from Dave Pike. To NYC, rec. *Out to Lunch* w. Jackie McLean, E. Dolphy. Newport Jazz Fest. w. A. Shepp 1965, joined saxophonist John Handy. 1967 worked w. saxophonist Harold Land. Recs: Shepp, Curtis Amy, Frank Butler, Ron Jefferson, Billy Mitchell–Al Grey, G. Moncur III, McLean, Dolphy, Dexter Gordon, Joe Henderson, Grant Green, Andrew Hill, Tony Williams, John Handy.

IZENZON, David, *bass;* b. Pittsburgh, Pennsylvania, 17 May 1932, d. New York City, 8 October 1979. Sang in local synagogue; began stud. bass 1956. Played w. B. Dixon, A. Shepp, P. Bley, Sonny Rollins. Member of O. Coleman trio 1962–66, later sharing bass role w. C. Haden. In 1970s working in psychiatric field, playing occasionally w. K. Berger. Recs. w. Shepp, Joseph Scianni, Dixon, Rollins, Coleman, d. 1979.

JACKSON, John Shenoy, *trumpet;* b. Hot Springs, Arkansas, 29 Oct 1923. Executive Sec. of AACM, prof. social worker, writer. Began mus. training at 40. Joined AACM 1966. Played w. AACM big band, M. R. Abrams, F. Anderson, Kalaparusha.

JAMAL, Khan (Warren Cheeseboro), *vibraharp, marimba;* b. Jacksonville, Florida, 23 July 1946. To Philadelphia as child, stud. Granoff Sch. of Mus., Combs Coll. To Europe w. Army for 2 yrs. In Philadelphia formed percussion-dominated Cosmic Forces Ensemble, Sounds of Liberation. Added saxophonist B. Lancaster for some concerts, recs. Worked w. S. Murray, Sun Ra, A. Shepp, D. Burrell, G. Moncur III, F. Lowe, N. Howard, Norman Connors, S. Rivers, Stanley Clarke, Gary Bartz, Calvin Hill, T. Daniel. Active in Black studies programme in Philadelphia. To Paris 1973 for concerts and recs.

JAMES, Stafford Louis, *bass, 'cello, composer;* b. Evanston, Illinois, 24 April 1946. Stud. violin from 7 to 11. Stud. bass in New Orleans w. Richard Payne, Chuck Badie, w. Rudolf Fahsbender at Chicago Conservatory, Julius Levine. Worked w. Monty Alexander, P. Sanders, Sun Ra, R. Ali, J. L. Wilson, Lonnie Liston Smith, A. Shepp, A. Coltrane. 1 yr w. vocalist Melba Moore. Also w. Danny Mixon, Bobby Timmons, Charles Sullivan, John Hicks, Roy Ayers, Gary Bartz, Art Blakey, Betty Carter, Dee Dee and Cecil Bridgewater, Al Haig, Chico Hamilton, Hannibal, Barry Harris. Recs: O. Lake, R. Kenyatta, Ali, Bartz, A. Cyrille, Ayler, own.

JAMI, Hakim, *bass, tuba, euphonium;* b. Detroit, Michigan, 13 Jan 1940. Educ. Cass Tech. high school, Teal Music Studios, stud. theory, orchestration, percussion; US Naval School of Mus, Washington, DC. TV, radio work as child, acting. Own group Detroit 1952–57, w. US Service bands 1957–61. Worked w. The Brothers, G. Logan, S. Rivers, Mae Arnette, Ali Yusef, Stony Nightingale. To NYC 1969, worked w. Roland Alexander, Kiane Zawadi, F. Hubbard, Don Byas, Duke Jordan, Philly Joe Jones, Kenny Barron, Cal Massey, Howard Johnson, Charles McGee, Dick Griffin, Frank Foster, Sun Ra, E. Jones, Ethno-Modes, own group, Manifestation. Recs. Shepp, T. Daniel, Cherry.

JARMAN, Joseph, *reeds, percussion;* b. Pine Bluff, Arkansas, 14 Sept 1937. To Chicago at early age. Stud. there, then travelled widely until 1961. Joined AACM, started playing with other members 1965, leading several large and small units. At times incorporated multi-media shows and on one occasion collab. w. John Cage. Recs: own group and Art Ensemble of Chicago w. whom lived in Paris 1969–70.

JARVIS, Clifford, *drums;* b. Boston, Massachusetts, 26 August 1941, d. London, England, 26 November 1999. Started on piano, guitar, playing drums at 10. Father, a musician, encouraged him. Stud. w. Alan Dawson and at Berklee. To NYC, worked w. Randy Weston, Barry Harris, Yusef Lateef. At 20, met Sun Ra rec. w. him 1965. Played regularly w. P. Sanders, Sun Ra, own group. Recs: Sanders, Sun Ra, A. Coltrane, Freddie Hubbard.

JENKINS, Leroy, *violin, composer;* b. Chicago, Illinois, 11 March 1932, d. New York City, 24 February 2007. Stud. violin from age 8, first in church, then w. Capt. Walter Dyett at Du Sable High. BA in music from Florida A&M U, Tallahassee, Florida. Taught string instruments in Mobile, Alabama, schools 1961–65. In Chicago, stud. w. Bruce Hayden, then taught in school system, after-hours prog, for Chi. Urban Poverty Corps. Joined AACM, worked and rec. w. A. Braxton, L. Smith. Toured Europe w. Creative Construction Company of Chicago, 1969 (Braxton, Smith, S. McCall). To NYC 1970, founded Revolutionary Ensemble w. J. Cooper (drums), Sirone (bass). Played w. O. Coleman, A. Coltrane, Rahsaan Roland Kirk, C. Taylor, A. Ayler, A. Shepp, Eddie Gale, Cal Massey, JCOA. Recs: Braxton, Rev. Ensemble, A. Silva, Shepp, R. Ali (duo).

JOHNSON, Dewey, *trumpet;* b. Philadelphia, Pennsylvania, 6 Nov 1939. Stud. trumpet at North East Public High School, Granoff Sch. of Mus. to NYC early '60s, worked w. P. Bley, Sun Ra, Gregg Bonds. Recs: Bley and J. Coltrane (*Ascension*), 1977 w. R. Ali, David Murray.

JOHNSON, Reginald Volney 'Reggie', *bass;* b. Owensboro, Kentucky, 13 December 1940. Trombone in college and military bands; started bass 1961. Worked w. A. Shepp, Rahsaan Roland Kirk, participated in the October Revolution concerts w. B. Dixon. Worked w. Sun Ra, Bill Barron, Art Blakey, Ted Curson. Rec. w. G. Logan, M. Brown, A. Shepp, Blakey, Booker Ervin, B. Hutcherson, Valdo Williams.

JONES, Arthur, *alto saxophone;* b. Cleveland, Ohio, 1940, d. New York City, 1998. Played w. rock-and-roll bands for 2 years before being introduced to the music of Dolphy and Coleman. Worked w. F. Wright, J. Coursil. In Paris 1969, rec. w. Coursil, B. Greene, A. Shepp.

JONES, Elvin Ray, *drums;* b. Pontiac, Michigan, 9 Sept 1927, d. Englewood, NJ, 18 May 2004. Self-taught, played in sch. band, Army band. Played in Detroit w. brother Thad, saxophonist Billy Mitchell. Worked w. Teddy Charles, Charles Mingus. To NYC 1956, worked w. Bud Powell, Pepper Adams/Donald Byrd, Tyree Glenn, Harry Edison. W. J. Coltrane 1961–65, left to join Duke Ellington. Formed trio w. J. Garrison, saxophonist Joe Farrell, continued to lead own groups, recording extensively.

JONES, Leonard, *bass, banjo, zither, guitar, percussion;* b. Chicago, Ill., 6 December 1943. Performed w. the AACM who have also played his comps. Worked w. Kalaparusha, J. Jarman, Paul Winter, R. Abrams and L. Smith in the duo, New Dalta Ahkri. Rec: Abrams.

KALAPARUSHA: see McINTYRE, Maurice.

KENYATTA, Robin (Prince Roland Haynes), *alto saxophone;* b. Moncks Corner, S. Carolina, 6 March 1942, d. Lausanne, Switzerland, 28 October 2004. Participated in 1964 October Revolution in NYC. Worked w. R. Rudd, K. Berger, Andrew Hill, S. Murray, A. Shepp, Sonny Stitt, Jazz Composers Guild. 1967 organised rehearsal band. Recs: JCOA, Valerie Capers, Stitt, Barry Miles, B. Dixon, Shepp, Hill.

LACY, Steve (Steven Norman Lackritz), *soprano sax;* b. New York City, 23 July 1934, d. Boston, Mass., 4 June 2004. Stud. w. Cecil Scott and others from 1952 played in Dixieland bands. Stud. at Schillinger Sch., Boston, Manhattan Sch. of Mus. 1956–57 working and studying w. C. Taylor, Gil Evans. Own band, co-leader w. R. Rudd, worked and rec. w. D. Cherry. 1965 started travelling, to France, Italy, Scandinavia, South America. Settled in Paris 1969, working in a variety of situations incl. solo, and w. wife, 'cellist Irene Aebi. Recs: Taylor, and under own name.

LAKE, Oliver, *saxophones, flutes, percussion;* b. Marianna, Arkansas, 14 Sept 1942. To St Louis at age 1. Sax in high sch., but did not stud. seriously until age 20. Worked in backup bands for r&b artists with trumpeter L. Bowie, drummer Phillip Wilson. Formed own group w. trumpeter F. LeFlore, drummer Leonard Smith. BA in music educ. from Lincoln U, Jefferson City, Mo., 1968, taught music in St Louis schools for 3 yrs. Founder member of BAG, co-ordinated exchange concerts with AACM and BAG. Stud. arranging, comp. w. Oliver Nelson, Ron

Carter. 2 yrs in France with other BAG members, stud. electronic music in Paris, played w. A. Braxton and others. To NYC 1974, rec. under own name and w. Braxton. Concerts w. L. Smith, L. Bowie, T. Daniel, etc.

LANCASTER, William Byard 'The Thunderbird', *saxophones, flute, bass-clarinet, percussion;* b. Philadelphia, Pennsylvania, 6 August 1942, d. Wyndmoor, Pa., 23 August 2012. Stud. Shaw U, Berklee Coll of Mus., Boston Conservatory. To school w. guitarist S. Sharrock, playing together w. pianist Dave Burrell, P. Sanders. Formed group w. J. Hunter (bass), Eric Gravatt (drums), working between NYC and Phila. for 2½ yrs. Began assoc. w. S. Murray 1965, appeared on his first rec. for ESP. Worked w. Sun Ra, Wilson Pickett, Herbie Mann, R. Ali, Inez & Charlie Foxx, M. Tyner, A. Silva, Milt Jackson, the Sounds of Liberation, the Management. Worked in Europe w. Murray, own groups. Recs: Murray, B. Dixon, B. Greene, Larry Young, Marzette Watts, own.

LASHA, Prince (W. B. Lawsha), *saxophones, flute, clarinet;* b. Forth Worth, Texas, 10 Sept 1929, d. Oakland, Calif., 12 December 2008. To school w. O. Coleman, played in church, high sch. marching band w. him and Coleman's cousin, James Jordan. Worked w. Buster Smith, Jimmy Liggins, locally w. Coleman, C. Moffett on trumpet. 1954 playing w. S. Simmons in Calif. NYC sessions and rec. w. Coltrane, Dolphy, own groups. To Europe 1965–66, rec. in London. In Calif., working w. Harold Land, B. Hutcherson, Moffett. Recs: Simmons, Dolphy, E. Jones/J. Garrison, Clifford Jordan, own.

LASHLEY, Lester Helmar, *trombone, bass, 'cello;* b. Chicago, Illinois, 23 Aug 1935. Self-taught, played in college orch., Army bands. Charter member AACM, played and rec. w. R. Mitchell, J. Jarman, in and around Chicago. Active in graphic arts, sculpture, leather and jewellery work.

LEFLORE, Floyd, *trumpet, percussion;* b. St Louis, Mississippi 1940, d. 2014. Self-taught musician, stud. St Louis Institute of Mus. Played w. Albert King, Little Milton, Rufus Thomas, Oliver Lake, Ronnie Boykins. Member of St Louis Black Artists Group, to Europe w. them, 1972 for concerts. Recs: BAG, Children of the Sun.

LEWIS, Arthur 'Art', 'Shaki', *drums, percussion;* b. New Orleans, Louisiana, 31 July 1936. To Calif., age 5, musical family. In San Francisco worked w. Harold Land, sessions w. Dexter Gordon, Bud Powell. Co-led big band w. saxophonist

Monty Waters. 2 yrs w. singer Jon Hendricks, to NYC w. him 1966. Played w. S. Murray, James Spaulding, Jackie McLean, N. Howard, E. Cross, J. L. Wilson, Andrew Hill. Acc. singer Novella Nelson and w. dance and theatre cos., trav. to Sierra Leone, Nigeria 1974. Recs: Murray, Hill, C. Thornton.

LOGAN, Giuseppi, *reeds;* b. Norfolk, Virginia, 22 May 1935. Self-taught on piano at 12, played drums in school bands, sang in church. Stud. New England Conservatory in Boston where he met M. Graves, and played w. Earl Bostic. To NYC 1964, played w. B. Dixon and in concert at Judson Hall w. Graves, pianist D. Pullen, bassist E. Gomez and strings. Played w. A. Shepp, P. Zanders, R. Rudd, Patty Waters. Recs: D. Burrell, Rudd, own.

LOWE, Frank, *tenor saxophone, flute;* b. Memphis, Tennessee, 24 June 1943, d. New York City, 19 September 2003. Stud. mus. in junior high school, sang in choir. Sax at 12. 1958 working for Stax Records, met many local musicians. Trav. betw. NYC and San Francisco, joined Sun Ra 1968. 1971 w. A. Coltrane, R. Ali. Worked w. own group, M. Graves, D. Cherry, Abdullah. Aboriginal Music Society. Recs: w. A. Coltrane, Ali, Cherry, own.

LYONS, James Leroy 'Jimmy', *alto saxophone;* b. Jersey City, New Jersey, 1 Dec 1931, d. New York City, 19 May 1986. Started playing at 15, befriended by pianists Elmo Hope, Thelonious Monk, Bud Powell, Kenny Drew. Met C. Taylor on return from Army service in Korea 1960, played together ever since, touring, teaching. Recs: Taylor, own.

McBEE, Cecil, *bass, composer;* b. Tulsa, Oklahoma, 19 May 1935. Clarinet in high school. Played duets w. sister, marching bands. Bass at 17, playing in local nightclubs. Stud. Central State, Wilberforce, Ohio, then 2 yrs in Army as cond. of military band at Fort Knox, Kentucky. To Detroit 1962, worked w. Paul Winter. To NYC 1964, worked and rec. w. G. Moncur, Jackie McLean, Wayne Shorter, Freddie Hubbard, Miles Davis, Charles Lloyd, Yusef Lateef, B. Hutcherson, P. Sanders, A. Coltrane, Charles Tolliver, Lonnie Liston Smith, Sonny Rollins, Michael White, own group.

McCALL, Steve, *drums, percussion;* b. Chicago, Ill., 30 September 1933, d. Chicago, 24 May 1989. Extensive local experience w. blues groups, show bands. Worked w. Gene Ammons, Dexter Gordon, Eddie Harris, Terri Thornton, Arthur Prysock. Co-founder AACM. Worked w. R. Abrams, J. Jarman. To Europe for extended stay, playing and rec. w. A. Braxton, L. Smith, L. Jenkins, Gunter Hampel, M. Brown, Lancaster, Air.

McINTYRE, Ken, *alto saxophone, flute;* b. Boston, Massachusetts, 7 September 1931, d. New York City, 13 July 2001. Stud. piano 1940–45, sax w. Andrew McGhee, Gigi Gryce, Charlie Mariano, 1954 Boston Conservatory. Taught at Brandeis U for 2 yrs. Met E. Dolphy 1960, rec. w. him, C. Taylor. Intermittent concert and rec. dates w. Taylor, own groups, concentrating on teaching.

McINTYRE, Maurice Benford/Kalaparusha Ahrah Difda, *tenor saxophone, clarinet;* b. Clarksville, Arkansas, 24 March 1936, d. New York City, 9 November 2013. Drums at 7; stud. Chicago Mus. Coll. Played and stud. w. J. Gilmore, Dave Young, Nicky Hill, Ken Chaney, R. Mitchell, Ollie Mabin. Joined R. Abrams's Experimental Band, BACM. Worked w. A. Braxton, percussionists W. Smith and Ajaramu (Gerald Donovan), guitarist J. B. Hutto, Little Milton, R. Abrams. Leader, The Light. Recs: Mitchell, Abrams, George Freeman, own.

MANTLER, Michael 'Mike', *trumpet, composer;* b. Vienna, Austria, 10 August 1943. Trumpet at 12, stud. Vienna Acad. of Mus. To USA 1962, worked w. pianist Lowell Davidson in Boston. To NYC 1964, worked w. C. Taylor, P. Bley. Founder member Jazz Composers Guild. W. C. Bley, formed Jazz Composers Orch., continued to be active together organising concerts, sessions for new musicians, record distrib. service, Recs: own, C. Bley.

MARSHALL, James, *saxophones, flutes, misc., composer;* b. St Louis, Missouri, 8 Jan 1943. Self-taught; active as musician, poet, painter, since childhood. Stud. and worked w. Ajule Rutlin, co-founder Black Artist Group, other BAG members since 1963. Played w. Alan Nichols Improvisational Theatre Co. Co-founder w. wife Carol, and Rutlin of Comm. for Universal Justice, Human Arts Assoc., Human Arts Ensemble, Universal Justice Records. Trav. to India, Nepal.

MITCHELL, J. R. (James R. Mitchell), *percussion, piano, composer, arranger, educator;* b. Philadelphia, Pennsylvania, 13 April 1937, d. New York City, 25 January 2004. At Germantown High Sen. w. A. Shepp, B. Lancaster, worked together at age 17. Also w. Lee Morgan, Jimmy McGriff, Reggie Workman. On road w. Red Prysock big band at 19. BA in perc. from Combs Coll. Stud. at Temple U., Boston Conservatory, Boston U, Berklee. Composition w. Jaki Byard, George Russell at New England Conservatory of Mus., grad. w. MA. MA in Urban Educ, taught in Philadelphia, Boston schools. Worked w. Al Grey-Billy Mitchell, Sonny Stitt, Betty Carter, Nina Simone, J. Byard, D. Redman, Lancaster. Leader J. R. Mitchell Universal Ensemble.

MITCHELL, Roscoe Edward Jr, *reeds, percussion;* b. Chicago, Illinois, 3 Aug 1940. Clarinet, baritone in high sch., alto in Army. To Europe w. Army band. Played w. Byron Austin, Scotty Holt, Jack DeJohnette. 1961 joined R. Abrams's Experimental Band, charter member AACM. Led own trio, and w. sextet rec. *Sound* in 1966, first rec. evidence of the new music's 'second wave'. Worked w. Art Ensemble of Chicago since 1965, incl. 2-yr stay in Europe.

MOFFETT, Charles, *trumpet, drums;* b. Fort Worth, Texas, 6 Sept 1929, d. New York City, 14 February 1997. Trumpet in high school band, nightclub work w. O. Coleman. Stud. percussion 1945. At 19 welterweight champ. of US navy's Pacific Fleet. BA in Mus. Ed., taught in Texas high schools for 8 yrs. To NYC 1961, joined Coleman, toured Europe w. him 1965, 1966, left 1967. Led own group, worked w. A. Shepp, MD for schools and youth orgs. Now active in mus. ed. in Calif. where leads band comp. of members of his family. Recs: Coleman, Shepp, own family.

MONCUR, Grachan Ill, *trombone, composer;* b. New York City, 3 June 1937. Father, Grachan II was bassist w. noted Harlem swing band, Savoy Sultans. Stud. Laurinburg Inst., N Carolina. Manhattan Sch. of Mus., Juilliard Sch. of Mus. In Newark as teenager worked w. Nat Phipps (Wayne Shorter also in band). On road w. Ray Charles 2½ yrs, then Art Farmer/Benny Golson Jazztet. Back w. Charles, then to Europe in onstage role w. James Baldwin's *Blues for Mr Charlie*. Worked w. own groups, Jackie McLean, Sonny Rollins. Co-leader 360 Degree Music Experience w. B. Harris. Toured and rec. w. A. Shepp, incl. Europe, Algiers 1969. Comps. rec. and perf. extensively, incl. *Echoes of Prayer* rec. w. JCOA.

MOORE, Don, *bass;* b. Philadelphia, Pa., 1937. Started on piano, bass in 1959. Toured Europe w. A. Shepp 1962. Member New York Contemporary Five. Worked w. Sonny Rollins, Jackie McLean, Frank Foster, Hank Mobley, Lee Morgan, Gil Evans, Thelonious Monk, E. Jones. Inactive in music. Recs: NYC5, B. Dixon/A. Shepp, E. Jones, J. Tchicai, Roland Kirk.

MOSES, J. C. (John Curtis Moses), *drums;* b. Pittsburgh, Pennsylvania, 18 Oct 1936, d. Pittsburgh, 1977. Self-taught. Started on congas, bongoes, playing w. drummer Paula Roberts. 1958–60 w. Walt Harper, then to NYC. Played w.

Dolphy, Shepp, Richard Davis, Cedar Walton, Herbie Hancock, Kenny Dorham, Clifford Jordan. To Europe 1963 w. New York Contemporary Five, worked w. New York Art Quartet. 1965–67 w. Roland Kirk. Freelanced 67–69, working w. J. Coltrane, Sonny Stitt, Walter Bishop Jr, Charles Lloyd, Chick Corea, Jackie McLean, Hubert Laws, Hal 'Cornbread' Singer, Mongo Santamaria, Willie Bebo, Nancy Wilson. To Europe for 18 mths, house-drummer at Jazzhus Montmartre, Copenhagen, playing with Ben Webster, Ted Curson, Dexter Gordon, B. Greene, Coleman Hawkins, Booker Ervin, Jimmy Woode, Red Mitchell, Tete Monteliou. Since 1970 active in music only spasmodically due to kidney dysfunction. Occasional gigs in Pittsburgh w. Nathan Davis, Eric Kloss. Recs: Dolphy, NYC5, Shepp, J. Tchicai, Marzette Watts, Kenny Dorham, S. Rivers, Andrew Hill, Gary Bertz, Bud Powell, Hancock. d. 1977.

MOUZON, Alphonse, *drums, percussion, vocals, composer;* b. Charleston, S. Carolina, 21 November 1948, d. Los Angeles, Calif., 25 December 2016. Drums at 12, pro. since 1962. To NYC at 17, worked w. Chubby Checker. Played and rec. v. Roy Ayers, M. Tyner, Weather Report, Eleventh House. Also rec. w. Stevie Wonder, Tim Hardin, Sonny Rollins, Doug Cam, own group.

MOYE, Don, *drums, percussion, vocals;* b. Rochester, NY, 23 May 1946. Stud. Wayne State U, Detroit, and w. trumpeter Charles Moore. Played w. Detroit Free Jazz, involved in the Artists' Workshop where met J. Jarman. To Europe and Morocco w. Detroit Free Jazz for 11 mths, played w. S. Lacy in Rome, met and joined Art Ensemble of Chicago in Paris.

MURRAY, James Marcellus Arthur 'Sunny', *drums;* b. Idabel, Oklahoma, 1937, d. Paris, France, 7 December 2017. Started drums at 9, self-taught, encouraged by stepbrother. Trombone, trumpet briefly; to NYC 1956, worked w. Henry 'Red' Allen, Willie 'The Lion' Smith, Jackie McLean, Rocky Boyd, Ted Curson. Met C. Taylor 1959, started playing together. To Europe w. him and J. Lyons 1963. Met A. Ayler and formed trio w. bassist G. Peacock, recording and playing in concert. Played w. O. Coleman, D. Cherry, J. Coltrane, R. Rudd, J. Tchicai, led own groups in NYC and Philadelphia, featuring many younger players prominent today. 1968 to France, then Pan-African Fest. in Algiers, playing w. A. Shepp, G. Thornton, G. Moncur III, A. Silva. Remained in Paris several mths, moved to Philadelphia where started musical relationship w. Philly Joe Jones and played w. own groups. Recs: Shepp, Taylor, Ayler, Burrell, Thornton, François Tusques, G. Hampel, own.

NEIDLINGER, Buell, *bass;* b. Westport, Connecticut, 2 March 1936. Stud. piano, trumpet, 'cello, bass. Led college band, went to Yale U, became disc-jockey, 1955 to NYC, played w. Vic Dickenson, Zoot Sims, Tony Scott, Coleman Hawkins, Tony Bennett. 1957 met C. Taylor, worked w. him incl. appearing on stage w. Jack Gelber play *The Connection,* 1961 rec. *NY R&B* for Candid Label w. Clark Terry, R. Rudd, A. Shepp, S. Lacy, Taylor, D. Charles. Worked w. Cherry, Jimmy Giuffre, joined Boston Symph. Orch. Active in symphonic world, brief periods w. own rock band and Frank Zappa.

PARKER, William, *bass;* b. New York City, 10 Jan 1952. Stud. w. Richard Davis, J. Garrison. Played w. C. Taylor, R. Ali, C. Tyler, Clifford Jordan, Melodic Art-tet. Rec. w. F Lowe.

PATRICK, Laurdine 'Pat', *saxophones, flute, bass, drums;* b. East Moline, Ill., 23 November 1929, d. Moline, Ill., 31 December 1991. Stud. piano, drums as child, trumpet lessons from father and Clark Terry. 1946, stud. sax, clarinet. At Du Sable High met J. Gilmore, Clifford Jordan, Richard Davis, Worked w. Muddy Waters, Lil Armstrong, Cootie Williams, Nat 'King' Cole, Cab Calloway, Earl Hines. Joined Sun Ra 1954. Later w. James Moody, Quincy Jones, Mongo Santamaria, Thelonious Monk, Duke Ellington. Recs: Sun Ra, J. Coltrane, G. Moncur III, C. Thornton.

PEACOCK, Gary, *bass;* b. Burley, Idaho, 12 May 1935. To Washington 1952, then Oregon, stud. piano, took up bass 1956 in Army; in Germany played w. local musicians, visiting Americans, 1958 to Calif.: in NYC 1962, played w. P. Bley, Jimmy Giuffre, A. Ayler, R. Rudd, S. Lacy, A. Shepp, Sonny Rollins, George Russell, D. Ells, Bill Evans. To Europe 1965 w. Ayler, Cherry, S. Murray, then briefly w. Miles Davis, P. Bley. Inactive in music until mid-70s, playing w. P. Bley and teaching. Recs: Bley, Ayler, Lasha, Bill Evans, Gil Evans, Anthony Williams, J. DeJohnette, others.

PHILLIPS, Barre, *bass;* b. San Francisco, Calif., 27 Oct 1934. Playing from 1948. Stud. at Berkeley, then in NYC w. Fred Zimmerman. Worked w. Don Heckman, Shepp, D. Ellis, Jimmy Giuffre, George Russell. To Europe w. Russell 1964, Giuffre 1965. Played w. NY Philharmonic, M. Brown and others. 1965 started working w. British saxophonist John Surman. Recs: Shepp, Attila Zoller, Bob James, Brown, Siegfried Kessler, Michel Portal, Surman, Dave Holland, own solo.

PULLEN, Don Gabriel, *organ, piano, composer, arranger;* b. Roanoke, Virginia, 25 Dec 1941, d. Los Angeles, Calif., 22 April 1995. Playing since age 10. Comp. and arr. for King, other record cos, led own organ group, w. Nina Simone, Art Blakey, saxophonist Charles Williams. Worked and rec. w. M. Graves in duo and w. G. Logan. Joined Charles Mingus 1972, worked in solo.

RAHIM, Mustafa Abdul (Donald Strickland), *bass-clarinet, tenor saxophone;* b. Birmingham, Alabama, 21 Sept 1943. Stud. piano age 9 at Cleveland Music School Settlement, stud. voice and performed in All-City Chorus. To school w. D. Ayler. Stud. bs-clt, tenor, gained assoc. degree in music. Worked w. A. Ayler, C. Tyler, Norman Connors, D. Ayler, own group. Worked as disc-jockey in Cleveland, session musician for recs., radio, TV. Recs: Prof. John Cox of the Cleveland Orch, Tyler, own.

REDMAN, Dewey, *tenor saxophone;* b. Fort Worth, Texas, 17 May 1931, d. Brooklyn, NY, 2 September 2006. Clarinet at 13; played in church and at Sam Houston College. In high school marching band w. O. Coleman, P. Lasha, another group w. C. Moffett, Richard Williams, Leo Wright. Stud. 1949–53 Austin, Texas, worked w. r&b groups, teaching. To Los Angeles 1960, played w. Joe Gordon, Jimmy Woods, Billy Higgins. 7 yrs in San Francisco, own jazz groups, gigs w. T-Bone Walker, the Five Royales, Pee Wee Crayton, Lowell Fulsom, Bay Area Quintet. Sessions w. E. Cross, D. Johnson, N Howard, Coleman. To NYC 1967, joined Coleman, worked and rec w. him, Keith Jarrett, C. Haden, JCOA, D. Cherry, own group.

REID, Robert 'Bob', *bass, tuba;* b. Birmingham, Alabama. Started on trumpet in Nashville, Tennessee, music educ at school, college, US Navy band. Worked w. Ray Charles, C. Taylor. To Europe early '70s, w. E Wright, S. Murray for 1½ yrs, also Memphis Slim, Willie Mabon, A. Shepp, S. Lacy, N. Howard, L. Bowie, O. Lake, Steve Potts, own group The Emergency Sound. Co-ord. sessions, teaching prog, at American Center, Paris. Comp. for opera, *Africa is Calling Me* 1974, Ret. to NYC 1976. Recs: Shepp, Howard, Wright/Howard, Murray/François Tusques, own.

REID, Steve, *drums;* b. New York City, 29 January 1944, d. New York City, 13 April 2010. Working w. C. Tyler at 21. 1965 grad. from Adelphi U, toured West Africa for 1 yr, played in Las Palmas, Ghana, Nigeria, Liberia, Sierra Leone, Senegal. With Sun Ra in NYC; then received 4-yr sentence as conscientious objector. Taught Black history course, music, to fellow inmates, paroled after 2 yrs. 1970 founded The Master Brotherhood w. saxophonist Joe Rigby. Worked w. Weldon Irvine, F. Lowe, Charles McPherson, Tyrone Washington, L. Bowie, Black Arthur Blythe, Cedar Walton, John Ore, Junie Booth, R. Boykins. Grants from National Endowment for the Arts to teach free drum clinic in NY ghettoes. Recs: Lowe, Tyler, Master Brotherhood.

RIGBY, Joseph 'Joe', *saxophones, flute, piccolo;* b. New York City, 3 September 1940. Stud. Juilliard, BA in Mus. Educ. from Richmond Coll, NYC. Taught music, and in nursery schools. Worked w. Latin bands, 360 Degree Music Experience, Norman Connors, Carlos Garnett, A. Cyrille, Ted Curson, Diane McIntyre Sounds & Motion Dance Co., M. Graves. Played and rec. w. S. Reid and the legendary Master Brotherhood.

RIVERS, Samuel Carthorne 'Sam', *saxophones, flute, composer, arranger;* b. El Reno, Oklahoma, 25 Sept 1923, d. Orlando, Florida, 26 December 2011. Musical family. Grandfather, minister and musician, pub. *A Collection of Revival Hymns and Plantation Melodies* in 1882. Father, a Fisk U grad., sang w. Fisk Jubilee Singers and Silverstone Quartet, mother acc. them on piano. Stud. violin and sang in church at 5. Stud. piano, switched to trombone at 11 in North Little Rock, Arkansas. Sax at 13, moved to Texas to continue studies. 3 yrs in Navy, first prof. gig in Vallejo w. Jimmy Witherspoon. 1947 to Boston Conservatory, played w. Jaki Byard, Quincy Jones, Gigi Gryce, K. McIntyre, Joe Gordon, Paul Gonsalves, Nat Pierce, Serge Chaloff, Alan Dawson. 1955–57 to Florida, writing for singers and dancers. Co-led band w. Don Wilkerson, acc. Billie Holiday on road. 1958 w. Herb Pomeroy big band in Boston, own quartet w. 13-year-old Tony Williams on drums. MD for band backing visiting artists Maxine Brown, Wilson Pickett, Jerry Butler, B.B. King, etc., then on road w. T-Bone Walker. Replaced George Coleman w. Miles Davis for 6 mths incl. visit to Japan, then to Calif., w. Andrew Hill. 6 yrs w. C. Taylor incl. period as Artist-in-Residence at Antioch Coll, Ohio, briefly w. M. Tyner. 1970 opened Studio Rivbea in NYC as centre for experimental music. Worked w. own groups, Harlem Ensemble, Winds of Manhattan. Composer-in-Residence for Harlem Opera Soc. Recs: Larry Young, T. Williams, B. Hutcherson/A. Hill. Bill Evans/George Russell, M. Davis, C. Taylor, Dave Holland, D. Pullen, own.

RUDD, Roswell Hopkins Jr, *trombone;* b. Sharon, Connecticut, 17 November 1935, d. Kerhonkson, NY, 21 December 2017. Parents musicians. Stud. voice,

French horn at coll., music at Yale U, 1954–58. To NYC, played w. Dixieland bands, S. Lacy. Formed NY Art Quartet w. J. Tchicai, played in Scandinavia 1965. Worked w. A. Shepp late '60s–'70s. Recs: C. Taylor, Shepp, JCOA, A. Ayler, NYAQ, Lacy, C. Haden's Liberation Music Orch., Barbieri, Kenyatta, own.

SANDERS, Farrell 'Pharoah', 'Little Rock', *tenor saxophone, flute, percussion;* b. North Little Rock, Arkansas, 13 October 1940. Piano lessons from grandfather, stud. drums, clarinet. Sax, flute at 16; played r&b locally, w. guitarist, sitting in w. visiting artists, e.g. Bobby 'Blue' Bland. To Oakland, Calif., 1959 on mus. scholarship. Played w. S. Simmons, Monty Waters, D. Redman, Ed Kelly, Robert Porter, Jane Getz, Marvin Patillo, Philly Joe Jones, Vi Redd. To NYC 1962, stud. w. Sun Ra. Played w. J. Coltrane until 1967, led own groups subsequently and played w. JCOA. Recs: O. Coleman, J. Coltrane, A. Coltrane, D. Cherry, JCOA, Gary Bartz, Leon Thomas, own.

SHARROCK, Lynda (Linda Chambers), *vocals;* b. Philadelphia, Pennsylvania, 2 April 1947. Singing folk music at 16, then jazz. Married guitarist S. Sharrock 1966, started singing 'free expression'. Moved to NYC, lessons from G. Logan. First prof. job w. P. Sanders, then working w. Sharrock, Herbie Mann. Recs: Sharrock, Mann, Joe Bonner.

SHARROCK, Warren Harding 'Sonny', *guitar;* b. Ossining, New York, 27 Aug 1940, d. Ossining, NY, 25 May 1994. Self-taught on guitar, stud. 1 yr at Berklee. Played bebop in Calif., to NYC 1965. Stud. w. Sun Ra, Worked w. Nigerian drummer Olatunji after introduction from P. Patrick. 1966 w. B. Lancaster, P. Sanders, D. Burrell, F. Wright, S. Murray. Travelled w. Herbie Mann. Own group w. wife Linda, Burrell, Sirone, T. Daniel, M. Graves. Recs: D. Cherry, Miles Davis, Sanders, Lancaster, Marzette Watts, H. Mann, own.

SHAW, Charles 'Bobo', *drums, percussion;* b. Pope, Mississippi, 5 Sept 1947, d. St Louis, Missouri, 16 January 2017. Stud. drums w. Joe Charles, Ben Thigpen Sr, Lijah Shaw, Charles Payne, Rich O'Donnell. Played trombone briefly, bass w. Frank Mokuss. Drums w. Oliver Sain, Julius Hemphill, Ike & Tina Turner, O. Lake, Roland Hanna, Ron Carter, E. Jones, Albert King, Reggie Workman, Art Blakey, St Louis Symphony Orch. Co-founded BAG, to Europe w. them for 1 yr. Played w. A. Braxton, S. Lacy, F. Wright, A. Silva, Michel Portal. Recs: BAG, Children of the Sun, Human Arts Ensemble, F. Lowe, own Red, Black & Green Solidarity Unit.

SHEPP, Archie, *tenor saxophone, soprano saxophone;* b. Fort Lauderdale, Florida, 24 May 1937. Started on clarinet, alto, in Philadelphia, played tenor w. r&b bands. Met Lee Morgan, Cal Massey, Jimmy Heath, J. Coltrane. Majored in theatre at Goddard Coll 1955–59; to NYC, played w. C. Taylor, incl. on-stage with Jack Gelber's *The Connection.* Co-led group w. B. Dixon, formed New York Contemporary Five with him, J. Tchicai, later D. Cherry. Started rec. frequently in late '60s featuring most of the young NY-based musicians, in particular G. Moncur III, B. Harris, D. Burrell, R. Rudd. Toured extensively in Europe in 1970s. Active in educ. as Prof. in W. E. B. Dubois Dept of African-American Music at Amherst, Massachusetts. Has also written plays, *The Communist, Junebug Graduates Tonight,* and, in collaboration w. Cal Massey, music for *Lady Day: A Musical Tragedy* by Aishah Rahman.

SILVA, Alan, *bass, 'cello;* b. Bermuda, 22 Jan 1939. To Brooklyn, NY, at 5, stud. piano, violin, drums. Stud. trumpet for 3 yrs w. Donald Byrd, then bass at NY Coll of Mus., w. NY Symphony players and Ollie Richardson. Played w. B. Greene, took part in the 1964 October Revolution, stud. w. B. Dixon, playing duets with him before he could read. Joined C. Taylor 1965–69, going to Europe w. him 1966. Played w. Sun Ra, A. Ayler, S. Murray, A. Shepp. In Paris 1969 formed the Celestial Communication Orch, the Celestial Strings. Since 1972 w. F. Wright Quartet, formed production co., Center of the World. Recs: Taylor, Wright, Shepp, own.

SIMMONS, Huey 'Sonny', *alto saxophone, English horn;* b. Sicily Island, Louisiana, 4 Aug 1933. Exposed as a child to voodoo ceremonies and African music. To Calif. at age 10, playing there and in Texas in early '60s. Played and rec. w. P. Lasha. To NYC 1963, briefly. Works w. wife, trumpeter Barbara Donald. Recs: Lasha, own.

SIRONE (Norris Jones), *bass, 'cello, trombone, composer;* b. Atlanta, Georgia, 28 Sept 1940, d. Berlin, Germany, 21 October 2009. Stud. w. Dr Raymond Carver, Ralph Mays, Alfred Wyatt, Dr Thomas Howard. Worked w. Sam Cooke, Jerry Butler, A. Ayler, C. Taylor, O. Coleman, J. Coltrane, A. Shepp, Sun Ra, P; Sanders, S. Murray, R. Ali, D. Cherry, B. Dixon, N. Howard, S. Sharrock, D. Burrell, R. Rudd, G. Barbieri, Jackie McLean. Since 1970 member of the Revolutionary Ensemble. Recs: Taylor, M. Brown, Sharrock, Burrell, Howard, Barbieri, Revolutionary Ensemble.

SMITH, Leo, *trumpet, percussion;* b. Leland, Mississippi, 18 Dec 1941. Stepfather blues performer, played piano, guitar, drums. French horn in high sch., trumpet in coll., played in local blues bands. To Chicago after service, stud. Sherwood Sch. of Mus. Introduced to AACM by R. Mitchell, played w. A. Braxton, L. Jenkins, S. McCall in Chicago and Europe. Worked in duo w. M. Brown, then in Europe w. bassist L. Jones in continuing concept, New Dalta Ahkri, started in Chi. w. Jones and H. Threadgill. Based in Connecticut, working on own music and teaching. Recs: R. Abrams, M. McIntyre, A. Braxton, M. Brown, L. Jenkins, New Dalta Ahkri.

SMITH, Warren, *drums, percussion;* b. Chicago, Ill, 14 May 1944. Musical family. Taught in schools, colleges, universities. Worked in NYC studios, w. Tony Williams's Lifetime, S. Rivers's Harlem Ensemble. Director of Composers Workshop Ensemble. Founder member of all-percussion unit, M'Boom, started by Max Roach.

STUBBLEFIELD, John, *saxophones, woodwind;* b. Little Rock, Arkansas, 4 Feb 1945, d. New York City, 4 July 2005. Played w. r&b bands while studying music, incl. the Drifters, Little Jr Parker, Jackie Wilson. In Chicago, joined AACM. Stud. w. R. Abrams, George Coleman, worked and rec. w. J. Jarman, A. Braxton, Maurice McIntyre, Abrams. To NYC 1971, played w. Mary Lou Williams, Charles Mingus, Thad Jones–Mel Lewis, Frank Foster, George Russell. To Europe w. Gil Evans, Dollar Brand. Recs: Miles Davis, M. Tyner, Roy Brooks, L. Bowie.

SUDLER, Monnette, *guitar, vocals;* b. Philadelphia, Pennsylvania, 5 June 1952. Mother singer, pianist; father gave her guitar lessons. Sang, played folk-songs, lessons in jazz guitar. Worked w. K. Jamal, B. Lancaster, S. Murray, Sounds of Liberation.

SULLIVAN, Charles, *trumpet, flugelhorn, piano;* b. New York City, 8 Nov 1944. Stud. Manhattan Sch. of Mus. Worked w. Lionel Hampton, Roy Haynes, Count Basie, Norman Connors, S. Fortune, own group. Recs: Carlos Garnett, Weldon Irvine, Fortune, own.

SULTAN, Juma, *bass, congas;* b. Monrovia, Calif., 13 April 1942. Stud. art at UCLA, worked as painter, sculptor, jewellery maker. Involved in folk-music as teenager, playing baritone sax, tuba, guitar, trumpet. Founded Aboriginal Music Society, ensemble devoted orig. to hand-made and non-Western instruments, played in Calif. w. S. Simmons. To NYC early '60s, worked w. Jimi Hendrix. Founded musicians' community centre, Studio We, w. trumpeter James Dubois. Active in org. NY Musicians Festivals. Worked w. N. Howard, S. Murray. Recs: Simmons, Howard.

SUN RA 'Le Sony'r Ra' (Herman Sonny Blount), *piano, organ, synthesiser, composer, arranger;* b. Birmingham, Alabama, 22 June 1914, d. Birmingham, Alabama, 30 May 1993. Stud. w. Prof. John Tuggle Whatley, Lula Randolph. To Chicago late '30s, worked w. Fletcher Henderson, Coleman Hawkins, Stuff Smith, wrote music for visiting artists at Club DeLisa. Rec. w. bassist Eugene Wright and his Dukes of Swing, led own trio. Built nucleus of larger ensemble w. saxophonists J. Gilmore, C. Davis, M. Allen, P. Patrick, James Scales, bassist R. Boykins. Started rec. w. them 1956. To NYC 1961, exercised as strong an influence over young players there as in Chicago. Played concerts and club-dates, travelled to Europe and Egypt, continued recording.

TAYLOR, Cecil Percival, *piano, composer;* b. Long Island City, NY, 25 March 1929. Started piano at 5, percussion w. member of NBC Symphony Orch. Infl. by Duke Ellington, Fats Waller records, the dance. Won 1st prize in amateur talent contest which earned him work with local band. The engagement was short-lived; he was only Black in band and nightclub owners refused to hire mixed ensembles. Stud. comp., harmony at NY Coll. of Mus., 4 yrs at New England Conservatory; stud. bebop w. saxophonist Andrew McGhee. Met Gigi Gryce, Serge Chaloff, Charlie Mariano, S. Rivers, Jaki Byard, Herb Pomeroy; became infl. by Bud Powell. To NYC, worked w. Hot Lips Page, Johnny Hodges, dancebands. 1953 formed quartet w. sax, vibes, drums, 1956 at Five Spot Café 1957 Newport Fest. First recs. w. bassist B. Neidlinger, drummer D. Charles, soprano saxophonist S. Lacy. Ted Curson, A. Ayler, A. Shepp, J. Coltrane, R. Rudd played w. Taylor, then he formed trio w. J. Lyons, S. Murray. Later groups incl. A. Cyrille, A. Silva, S. Rivers, H. Grimes, B. Dixon, Eddie Gale, Sirone.

TCHICAI, John, *alto saxophone;* b. Copenhagen, Denmark, 28 April 1936, d. Perpignan, France, 8 October 2012. Stud. violin, took up alto and clarinet. 3 yrs at Aarhus Acad. of Mus., then Acad. of Mus., Copenhagen. Playing w. local muscns, met Shepp, Bill Dixon at Helsinki Fest. Moved to NYC at their advice, played w. D. Cherry, formed New York Contemporary Five w. Shepp, Dixon, Don Moore, J. C. Moses. To Europe w. this group, Cherry replacing Dixon. In NYC worked w. R. Rudd, M. Graves, bassists Steve Swallow or E. Gomez as NY Art Quartet.

Joined Jazz Composers Guild, played w. C. Bley. Returned to Europe and participated in numerous sessions, rec. dates, etc. w. own groups, multi-instrumentalist Gunter Hampel. Cadentia Nova Dancia, and others.

TERROADE, Kenneth, *tenor saxophone, flute;* b. Jamaica, 1944. Started on flute. To London 1962, played in rock bands and continued studies. Worked w. British saxophonist John Surman, bassist Dave Holland and South Africans Chris McGregor, Ronnie Beer. In Paris 1968, worked and rec. w. S. Murray, Shepp, A. Silva, Claude Delcloo. Worked w. Ray Draper, McGregor's Brotherhood of Breath, own group in London. Ret. to Jamaica 1970.

THORNTON, Clifford, *trumpet, valve-trombone, shenai;* b. Philadelphia, Pennsylvania, 6 Sept 1936, d. Geneva, Switzerland 25 November 1989. Musical family (drummer J. C. Moses is a cousin). Started piano at 7, then trumpet. Stud. Temple U, Morgan State Coll, NY, and w. Donald Byrd. Worked w. Afro-Cuban, r&b bands. To Korea, Japan w. Army band. Met P. Sanders in San Francisco, worked w. him in NYC, also Ray Draper, Sun Ra, J. Tchicai, Marzette Watts, S. Murray. To Europe 1964. Worked w. A. Shepp in France, Algiers, NYC. Musical activity concentrates on writing, organising larger ensembles. Academically involved in NY. Sch, of Mus., LeRoi Jones's Black Arts Repertory Theatre School. Asst. Prof. in African and African-American Music Dept, Wesleyan U., Connecticut. Recs: own, Murray, Shepp. Died in Switzerland 1983.

THREADGILL, Henry Luther, *saxophones, woodwind;* b. Chicago, Illinois, 15 Feb 1944. Stud. Amer. Conserv. of Mus., Governor's State U. Played w. marching bands, theatre bands, Eugene Hunter, Richard Davis, Phil Cohran Heritage Ensemble, R. Abrams Sextet, own group Air. Active in educ. since 1963, as music instructor, choir director, etc. Member AACM. Trav. extensively. Recs. incl. tracks cut in Venezuela, Trinidad.

TYLER, Charles Lacy, *alto saxophone, baritone saxophone;* b. Cadiz, Kentucky, 20 July 1941, d. Toulon, France, 27 June 1992. Started on piano; clarinet in college. Grew up betw. Indiana, NYC, Cleveland where played w. A. Ayler. Involved with experimental music in NYC in early '60s, played w. Ayler's group 1965–66. Led own group, worked w. D. Ayler, Norman Connors. Teaching in Calif., ret. to NYC 1976, working w. own quartet, sextet, big band. Recs: Ayler, S. Reid, own.

TYNER, McCoy/Salaimon Saud, *piano, composer;* b. Philadelphia, Pa., 11 Dec 1938. Piano as child, stud. West Phila. Mus. Sch., Granoff Sch. Own septet at 15. W. Cal Massey at 17, met J. Coltrane. 1959 w. Benny Golson, then Jazztet for 6 mths. Joined Coltrane 1961, touring and rec. extensively. Led own groups since 1965, personnel incl. Sonny Fortune, Eric Gravatt, Azar Lawrence, Marvin Peterson, A. Mouzon, Gary Bartz.

WILSON, Joe Lee, *vocals, composer;* b. Bristow, Oklahoma, 22 Dec 1935, d. Brighton, England, 17 July 2011. Started pro. in Calif., then 3 yrs Mexico. To Canada, NYC, working in nightclubs. Worked and rec. w. A. Shepp, S. Murray, R. Ali; also sung w. M. Davis, S. Rollins, F. Hubbard, Lee Morgan, Jackie McLean, Roy Brooks, P. Sanders, Frank Foster, Roy Haynes, Milt Jackson, Collective Black Artists Ensemble. Proprietor Ladies' Fort, New York. Leads own group featuring saxophonist Monty Waters. Recs: Shepp, Mtume, Billy Gault, own.

WOOD, Vishnu (William C. Wood), *bass, oud, dil rhuba, tamboura, composer, educator;* b. North Wilkesboro, N. Carolina, 7 Nov 1937. Stud. harmony, piano, solfegg. at Detroit Inst, of Mus. Art; bass w. Gaston Brohan, John Matthews of Detroit Symph. Worked w. A. Coltrane, Max Roach, S. Rivers, A. Shepp, Terry Gibbs, Rahsaan Roland Kirk, P. Sanders, James Moody, w. dance troupes and in theatre. To Africa w. Randy Weston, incl. extended stay in Morocco. Directs Vishnu & the Safari East Concert Workshop Ensemble, playing instruments, mus. of various cultures. Director mus. prog. Hampshire Coll, Massachusetts. Recs: Weston, Shepp, A. Coltrane.

WORRELL, Lewis James, *bass;* b. Charlotte, N. Carolina, 7 November 1934. Tuba at 11, bass at 17. Member National Youth Orch., John Lewis's Orchestra USA, New York Art Quartet. Worked w. Bud Powell, A. Shepp, S. Lacy, Sun Ra, C. Taylor, A. Ayler. Recs: NYAQ, Shepp.

WRIGHT, Frank, *tenor saxophone, bass;* b. Grenada, Mississippi, 9 July 1935, d. Wuppertal, Germany, 17 May 1990. Grew up in Memphis and Cleveland, where played bass w. local band leader Little Chickadee, and backed r&b artists incl. Rosco Gordon, Bobby 'Blue' Bland, B.B. King. Switched to tenor saxophone following infl. of A. Ayler, moved to NYC, rec. w. H. Grimes (1965), J. Coursil, A. Jones (1967). Played w. Ayler, Larry Young, S. Murray, briefly w. C. Taylor, J. Coltrane. To Europe 1969 w. N. Howard, B. Few, M. Ali. Based in Paris. Howard eventually replaced by A. Silva. Recs. incl. duo w. Ali *Adieu Little Man,* rec. for own Center of the World productions.

Additional Biographies

ALTSCHUL, Barry, *drums;* b. New York City, 6 January 1943. Stud. w. Charlie Persip, Sam Ulano, Lee Konitz. W. Paul Bley trio, Jazz Composer's Guild Orch. Carmell Jones, Leo Wright, Sonny Criss, Hampton Hawes, Tony Scott. 1971 formed Circle w. Chick Corea, Braxton, Dave Holland. Worked since w. Braxton, S. Rivers, K. Berger, G. Barbieri, A. Hill, R. Rudd, G. Peacock, R. Kenyatta. Recs: Buddy Guy, A. Silva, Peter Warren, Dave Liebman, own.

BLUIETT, Hamiet, *saxophones;* b. Lovejoy, Illinois, 16 September 1940. Stud. w. choir director aunt, started on clarinet, later flute, baritone sax, bass-clt. Served in Marines, joined BAG in St Louis. To NY, played w. Sam Rivers, Tito Puente, Leon Thomas, Howard McGhee, Cal Massey, Mingus, Clark Terry, Thad Jones–Mel Lewis, Dollar Brand, Beaver Harris. 1977 baritone sax. w. World Saxophone Quartet (Hemphill, D. Murray, Lake).

BLYTHE, Arthur 'Black Arthur', *alto, soprano saxophones;* b. Los Angeles, 5 July 1940, d. Lancaster, Calif., 27 March 2017. Stud. w. David Jackson, Kirk Bradford (ex-Jimmy Lunceford). Played w. Horace Tapscott, Owen Marshall, Stanley Crouch. To NY 1974, w. Leon Thomas, Ted Daniel, J. Hemphill, Chico Hamilton, L. Bowie. Own group feat. Guitarist 'Blood' Ulmer. Recs: own, Ulmer.

FREEMAN, Earl Lavon Jr 'Chico', *saxophones;* b. Chicago, Ill., 17 July 1949. Son of legendary saxophonist Von Freeman. Played w. r&b groups, Chi-lites, Junior Wells. Stud. North Western U., R. Abrams. Joined AACM, played w. E. Jones, C. McBee, J. Jarman, Abrams, Sun Ra, O. Lake, Mingus, C. Tyler, Braxton.

HOPKINS, Frederick J. 'Fred', *bass;* b. Chicago, Ill., 10 October 1947, d. Chicago, 7 January 1999. Stud. w. Walter Dyett at Du Sable High Sch., Joseph Guastafeste. Played w. Kalaparusha, Reflection (Threadgill, McCall), Jarman, M. Brown, / AACM. To NYC 1975, w. D. Redman, Air (formerly Reflection). Recs: Abrams, James Moody, Kalaparusha, Brown, Lake, D. Murray, Bluiett, Pullen, Braxton, Marcello Melis.

JACKSON, Ronald Shannon, *drums, percussion, flute, piano;* b. Fort Worth, Texas, 12 Jan 1940, d. Fort Worth, 19 October 2013. Piano at 5, clarinet and drums in school marching band. Sung in choir, formed school dance band. 1958 to Lincoln U., Jefferson City, Mo. school band incl. Hemphill, L. Bowie, Oliver Nelson, bassist Bill Davis, pianist John Hicks. Studies cont. at various colleges. First pro job at 15 w. James Clay and the Red Tops. To NYC 1966, worked w. Ayler, Tyler, Mingus, B. Carter, J. McLean, R. Bryant, S. Turrentine, J. Henderson, K. Dorham, Joe Williams, C. Lloyd, F. Foster, Tyner, Coleman, Taylor, 'Blood' Ulmer. Recs: Taylor, Coleman, Tyler, Weldon Irvine, Bryant, Teruo Nakamura, own group the Decoding Society.

LEE, Jeanne, *singer;* b. New York, 29 January 1939, d. Tijuana, Mexico, 25 October 2000. Early 'sixties duo w. pianist Ran Blake, 1968 commenced long assoc. W. Gunter Hampel. Recs: Blake, Hampel, M. Brown, A. Shepp, S. Murray, C. Bley, J. DeJohnette, Braxton, Bob Moses, F. Lowe, R.R. Kirk, A. Cyrille, own.

LEWIS, George, *trombone;* b. Chicago, 14 July 1952. Started on trombone 1961, reproducing Lester Young solos. Joined AACM 1971, stud. w. Abrams, played w. D. Ewart. Philosophy at Yale, worked w. Fred Anderson, Abrams big band, Basie. Trios and duo w. Braxton, own group w. Ewart, electronics exponent Richard Tietelbaum. Recs: R. Mitchell, Braxton, Altschul, Heiner Stadler, M. Melis, Gerry Hemingway, own.

MURRAY, David, *tenor saxophone;* b. Berkeley, Calif., 19 February 1955. Father guitarist, mother pianist in Sanctified Church where he started playing. At 12, formed own r&b group. Met trumpeter B. Bradford and Arthur Blythe, worked w. trumpeter Butch Morris. To NYC 1975, worked w. own group, S. Murray, duo w. Stanley Crouch, solo. Member World Saxophone Quartet (Lake, Hemphill, Bluiett), travelled often to Europe, recorded extensively under own name.

MYERS, Amina Claudine, *piano, organ, vocals;* b. Blackwell, Arkansas, 21 March 1942. Playing, singing at 4, formal training at 7. Formed children's gospel group in Dallas, Texas, began extensive career as choir, director, church pianist that continued during stud. at Philander-Smith College, Little Rock, Ark. Formed gospel groups, played jazz and rock while continuing church activities and study. Taught in Chicago Public Schools, played weekends with the Vanguard Ensemble led by drummer Ajaramu (Gerald Donovan). Joined AACM, worked w. Sonny Stitt, Gene Ammons. 1976 to NYC, worked w. L. Bowie, L. Jenkins, own groups.

To Europe. Recs: gospel groups, Little Milton, Fontella Bass, Bowie, Abrams, Kalaparusha, Threadgill, own.

NEWTON, James, *flute;* b. Los Angeles, Calif., 1 May 1953. Stud. UCLA, playing in symph. orch. there. Played and rec. w. Stanley Crouch, D. Murray, S. Rivers, Anthony Davis.

WILSON, Phillip Sanford, *drums;* b. St Louis, Missouri, 8 September 1941, d. New York City, 25 March 1992. Stud. violin, drums, met L. Bowie at college. Pro. at 16, played w. organists Don James, Sam Lazar; Jackie Wilson, Solomon Burke, J. Hemphill, David Sanborn. 1965 to Chicago, joined AACM. Worked w. R. Mitchell Art Ensemble, Paul Butterfield. To NYC 1972, worked w. Braxton, Chico Hamilton. Recs: Hemphill, Bowie, AEC, Butterfield, Lazar, D. Murray, Bluiett, Lowe.

YANCY, Youseff, *trumpet, theremin, electro-acoustical percussion, composer;* b. New Orleans, 19 February 1937, raised in Kansas City, Missouri. Stud. w. Charlie Parker's teacher, Leo H. Davis, later at K.C. Conservatory, in Norfolk, Virginia, New York and Morocco. Worked in K.C. w. Jay McShann, T-Bone Walker, Jimmy Witherspoon, Eddie Jefferson, Big Maybelle, etc. Extensive roadwork w. Eddie Vinson, Fats Dennis, Chuck Jackson, Cab Calloway, Ink Spots, partic. James Brown. MD for Dave Wiles, Little Willie John. To NYC worked w. Sun Ra, Shepp, Rivers, S. Murray, N. Howard, T. Daniel, Collective Black Artists, B. Lancaster, Garrett List, Ronald Shannon Jackson.

Bibliography

Wherever possible, both British and American editions are given.

General Background

Baraka, Imamu Amiri, *Raise, Race, Rays, Raze.* New York, Random House, 1971.

Brown, H. Rap, *Die, Nigger, Die!* New York, Dial Press, 1961; London, Allison & Busby, 1970.

Cleaver, Eldridge, *Soul on Ice.* New York, Dell, 1968; London, Jonathan Cape, 1969.

Cleaver, Eldridge, *Post-Prison Writing and Speeches.* New York, Random House, 1969; London, Jonathan Cape, 1969.

Dillard, J. L., *Black English – Its History and Usage in the United States.* New York, Random House, 1972.

Essien-Udom, E. U., *Black Nationalism: The Rise of the Black Muslims in the U.S.A.* Chicago, University of Chicago Press, 1962; London, Pelican 1966.

Fanon, Frantz, *Black Skin, White Masks.* New York, Grove Press, 1967; London, MacGibbon & Kee, 1968.

Fanon, Frantz, *The Wretched of the Earth.* New York, Grove Press, 1964; London, MacGibbon & Kee, 1965, Penguin, 1967.

Herskovits, Melville J., *The Myth of the Negro Past.* Boston, Beacon Press, 1958.

Jackson, George, *Soledad Brother.* London, Cape and Penguin, 1971.

Jackson, George, *Blood in My Eye.* London, Jonathan Cape, 1972.

Joans, Ted, *A Black Manifesto in Jazz Poetry and Prose.* London, Calder and Boyars, 1971.

Keating, Edward M., *Free Huey!* New York, Dell, 1970.

Lester, Julius, *Look Out, Whitey! Black Power's Gon' Get Your Mama.* New York, Dial Press, 1968; London, Allison & Busby, 1970.

Malcolm X, *The Autobiography of Malcolm X* (with Alex Haley). New York, Grove Press, 1962; London, Penguin, 1970.

Malcolm X, *By Any Means Necessary.* New York, Pathfinder Press, 1970.

Newton, Huey P., *Revolutionary Suicide.* New York, London, Wildwood House, 1973.

New York 21 (Collective Autobiography), *Look for Me in the Whirlwind.* New York, Random House, 1971.

Rowbotham, Sheila, *Woman's Consciousness, Man's World.* London, Pelican, 1973.

Seale, Bobby, *Seize the Time.* New York, 1970; London, Hutchinson, 1970.

Williams, Maxine, and Newman, Pamela, *Black Women's Liberation.* New York, Pathfinder Press, 1970.

Music

Baraka, Imamu; Neal, Larry and Spellman, A. B. (eds), *The Cricket.* Newark, Jihad Productions, 1969.

Bebey, Francis, *African Music – A People's Art.* New York and Westport, Lawrence Hill, 1975; London, George Harrap, 1975.

Berendt, Joachim-Ernst, *The Jazz Book.* New York and Westport, Lawrence Hill, 1975; London, Paladin, 1976.

Broven, John, *Walking to New Orleans.* Bexhill-on-Sea, Blues Unlimited, 1974.

Brown, Marion (ed.), *Afternoon of a Georgia Faun.* Marion Brown/NIA Music, 1973.

Carles, Philippe and Comolli, Jean-Louis, *Free Jazz/Black Power.* Paris, Editions Champ Libre, 1971.

Davis, Brian, *John Coltrane Discography.* London, Brian Davis and Ray Smith, 1976.

Fahey, John, *Charley Patton.* London, Studio Vista, 1970.

Feather, Leonard, *Encyclopaedia of Jazz in the Seventies.* New York, Horizon Press, 1976.

Garland, Phyl, *The Sound of Soul.* Chicago, Henry Regnery Co., 1969.

Goldberg, Joe, *Jazz Masters of the Fifties.* New York, Macmillan, 1965; London, Collier-Macmillan, 1965.

Harrison, Max (ed.), *Modern Jazz 1945–70 – The Essential Records.* London, Aquarius Books, 1975.

Hentoff, Nat, *The Jazz Life.* New York, Dial Press, 1961; London, Peter Davies, 1962.

Hentoff, Nat and Shapiro, Nat (eds), *Hear Me Talkin' to Ya.* New York, Rinehart, 1955; London, Peter Davies, 1955, Penguin, 1962.

Jones, LeRoi, *Blues People.* New York, William Morrow, 1963; London, MacGibbon & Kee, 1965.

Jones, LeRoi, *Black Music.* New York, William Morrow, 1967; London, MacGibbon & Kee, 1969.

Keil, Charles, *Urban Blues.* Chicago, Chicago University Press, 1966.

Kofsky, Frank, *Black Nationalism and the Revolution in Music.* New York, Pathfinder Press, 1970.

McRae, Barry, *The Jazz Cataclysm.* London, Dent, 1967; New York, A. S. Barnes, 1967.

Newton, Francis, *The Jazz Scene.* London, MacGibbon & Kee, 1959, Penguin, 1961; New York, Monthly Review Press, 1960, Da Capo Press, 1975.

Nketia, J. H. Kwabena, *The Music of Africa.* London, Victor Gollancz, 1975.

Raben, Erik, *A Discography of Free Jazz.* Copenhagen, Karl Emil Knudsen, 1969.

Reisner, Robert George, *Bird – The Legend of Charlie Parker.* New York, The Citadel Press, 1962; London, Quartet Books, 1974.

Rivelli, Pauline and Levin, Robert (eds), *The Black Giants.* New York and Cleveland, the World Publishing Co., 1970.

Roberts, John Storm, *Black Music of Two Worlds.* London, Allen Lane, 1973.

Sidran, Ben, *Black Talk.* New York, Holt, Rinehart & Winston, 1971.

Simosko, Vladimir and Tepperman, Barry, *Eric Dolphy – A Musical Biography and Discography.* Washington, Smithsonian Institution Press, 1974.

Simpkins, Cuthbert O., *Coltrane: a biography.* New York, Herndon House, 1975.

Sinclair, John and Levin, Robert, *Music and Politics.* New York and Cleveland, The World Publishing Co., 1971.

Smith, Leo, *notes (8 pieces) Source a new world music: creative music.* Connecticut, Leo Smith, 1973.

Spellman, A. B., *Four Lives in the Bebop Business* (subsequently entitled *Black Music: Four Lives*). New York, Pantheon, 1966; London, MacGibbon & Kee, 1967.

Thomas, J. C, *Chasin' The Trane – The Music and Mystique of John Coltrane.* New York, Doubleday, 1975; London, Elm Tree Books, 1976.

Walton, Ortiz M., *Music: Black, White and Blue.* New York, William Morrow, 1972.

Wilmer, Valerie, *Jazz People.* London, Allison & Busby, 1970; New York, Bobbs-Merrill, 1971.

Reference has also been made to the following music periodicals: *Black Music* (London), *Blues Unlimited* (London), *Coda* (Toronto), *Down Beat* and *Down*

Beat Yearbook (Chicago), *Jazz Forum* (Warsaw), *Jazz Hot* (Paris), *Jazz Journal* (London), *Jazz Magazine* (Paris), *Living Blues* (Chicago), *Melody Maker* (London), *New Musical Express* (London), *Sun Dance Magazine* (Chicago), and to the now defunct British publications, *Into Jazz, Jazz Monthly, Jazz & Blues* and *Jazz News*. Non-musical papers such as *Village Voice* (New York), *Chroniques de l'Art Vivant* (Paris), *The Black Panther* (Oakland), *The Black Scholar* (New York), *Black World* (Chicago), *Liberator* (New York), and *Muhammad Speaks* (Chicago), later entitled *Bilalian News,* have also been consulted from time to time.

Acknowledgements

The idea for this book really started when I picked up a volume entitled *The New Music* in New York's famous Eighth Street Bookstore and, instead of reading about Cecil Taylor and Sun Ra, found myself into a treatise on Cage and Stockhausen. I discussed the possibility of attempting to right the balance with Chris Albertson, who provoked my thoughts on the matter and, later, my action.

Many people have helped in bringing this book into being. My ideas and attitudes have developed out of many hours of conversation as well as my own experiences. My gratitude to the musicians for their music as well as the insights they have contributed cannot be measured. Most of the following people were interviewed directly in connection with this project, although in some cases I have utilised information acquired in the course of preparing a newspaper or magazine article. The musicians come from diverse worlds, but all have given willingly of their time: Rashied Ali, Donald Ayler, Alvin Batiste, James Black, Edward Blackwell, Roger Blank, Carla Bley, Lester Bowie, Anthony Braxton, Marion Brown, Frank Butler, Dennis Charles, Don Cherry, James Clay, Frank Clayton, Ornette Coleman, Jerome Cooper, Leroy Cooper, Pee Wee Crayton, Earl Cross, Andrew Cyrille, Ted Daniel, Art Davis, Richard Davis, Bill Dixon, Malachi Favors, Earl Freeman, Alvin Fielder Jr, Rafael Garrett, Milford Graves, Charlie Haden, Chico Hamilton, Billy Harper, Beaver Harris, Billy Higgins, Andrew Hill, Red Holloway, Noah Howard, Hakim Jami, Nancy Janoson, Joseph Jarman, Keith Jarrett, Clifford Jarvis, Leroy Jenkins, Plas Johnson, Elvin Jones, Robin Kenyatta, Steve Lacy, Oliver Lake, Byard Lancaster, Prince Lasha, Art Lewis, Giuseppi Logan, Frank Lowe, Jimmy Lyons, Mike Mantler, Ellis Marsalis, Roscoe Mitchell, Grachan Moncur III, Don Moye, Sunny Murray, Charles McGee, Mary Maria Parks, Lloyd Pearson, Barre Phillips, Sun Ra, Mustafa Abdul Rahim, Dewey Redman, Bob Reid, Sam Rivers, Jane Robertson, Roswell Rudd, Lynda Sharrock, Sonny Sharrock, Archie Shepp, Alan Silva, Sirone, Leo Smith, Cecil Taylor, Clifford Thornton, Charles Tolliver, Charles Tyler, McCoy Tyner, Chris White and Frank Wright. The quotation from Pat Patrick at the beginning of the book comes from an interview with Tam Fiofori in *Melody Maker* (London), 10 March

1971. I would also like to acknowledge interviews given to me before their deaths by Albert Ayler, Call Cobbs Jr, John Coltrane, Eric Dolphy, Jimmy Garrison and Lee Morgan.

Facts have been checked and double-checked with other interested individuals. They, and others who have contributed various items of information, include John Broven, John Chilton, Martin Davidson, Charles Majeed Greenlee, Bill Greensmith, Errol Henderson, John Shenoy Jackson (AACM), Khan Jamal, Carol Marshall (BAG), Barry McRae, Bob Palmer, Evan Parker, Bernard Stollman, Bob Thiele, Helen Ware, Trevor Watts, Mary Lou Webb, Jane Welch, Roberta Garrison, Mike Hames and the late J. C. Moses.

I am indebted to John Stevens for several of the insights that helped in writing the section on drums, and to Terri Quaye for continuing discussion on this and other matters. Max Harrison and Victor Schonfield confirmed and corrected some of my musical suppositions; the latter, with Michael Schlesinger, provoking some rewarding aural research.

I am grateful to Richard Williams, who shared with me a belief, nurtured in our teens, that the stories of the lesser-known musicians were as interesting as those of the stars, and who, with a breadth of vision unique in Britain, encouraged my interviews with the less-publicised instrumentalists during his days as assistant editor of *Melody Maker*. There is little here in the form in which it originally appeared in that newspaper, but I am grateful to Ray Coleman, the editor, for permission to reprint extracts from the resulting features.

For the same permission I thank John Norris and Bill Smith of *Cod* (Toronto), Kiyoshi Koyama of *Swing Journal* (Tokyo), and Philippe Carle of *Jazz Magazine* (Paris), who also generously allowed me to plunder the biographical section of the book he wrote with Jean-Louis Comolli, *Free Jazz/Black Power*. In the event space precluded the use of the excellent translation provided by Connie Garbutt Ostmann in its entirety, but my thanks to her nonetheless. Also to my neighbour, Sandra Stimpson, who specialises in rapid translations from the French while cooking or changing nappies, and Bayo Martins and Joe Ola Ogidan, who have provided information on Yoruba language and culture from time to time.

Halina and Mikolaj Trezciak-Seginer and Elizabeth Spiro have, at different times, given me a quiet space to write away from the tyranny of the telephone; Lyn Allison, Cathy Bearfield, Chris Goodey and Angela Phillips read parts of the manuscript and made useful suggestions, and John 'Hoppy' Hopkins and Elisabeth van der Mei introduced me to the new music and the innovators in New York in the 'sixties. All have helped to make this book a reality, no less the people who helped sustain me while I researched in New York: Chris Albertson, Bob

Amussen, Ed and Frances Blackwell, Carol and Roger Blank, Edgar and Barbara Blakeney, Jill Christopher, Ornette Coleman, Art and Aura Lewis, Barbara Malone, Leslie Moëd, Kunle Mwanga, Lynda and Sonny Sharrock, Jean and Earl Warren, Helen Ware, Jane Welch, Joe Lee Wilson and Abdul Razaq Yunusa. My thanks also to Fatima and Mustafa Abdul Rahim for the hospitality in Cleveland and to Edward and Myrtle Ayler for their patience.

James Marshall, saxophonist with the Human Arts Ensemble of St Louis, whose letter sparked my flagging faith and reminded me of the respect all great musicians have for their predecessors, had a lot to do with the completion of this book. So also did my publishers, Clive Allison and Margaret Busby. To all of them and to the women who share the musicians' lives, my thanks for their belief in the truth.

Val Wilmer
London

Index of Names